ADVANCED JAVA

[Concepts and Implementation]

Anuradha A. Puntambekar

M.E. (Computer)

Formerly Assistant Professor in

P.E.S. Modern College of Engineering,

Pune

®TECHNICAL® PUBLICATIONS

SINCE 1993

An Up-Thrust for Knowledge

ADVANCED JAVA

First Edition : December 2020

Published by :

TECHNICAL PUBLICATIONS
SINCE 1993 An Up-Thrust for Knowledge

Amit Residency, Office No.1, 412, Shaniwar Peth, Pune - 411030, M.S. INDIA
Ph.: +91-020-24495496/97, Email : sales@technicalpublications.org
Website : www.technicalpublications.org

ISBN 978-93-332-2385-0

9789333223850

PREFACE

The importance of **Advanced Java** is well known in computer engineering fields. Overwhelming response to my books on various subjects inspired me to write this book. The book is structured to cover the key aspects of the subject **Advanced Java.**

The book uses plain, lucid language to explain fundamentals of this subject. The book provides logical method of explaining various complicated concepts and stepwise methods to explain the important topics. Each chapter is well supported with necessary illustrations, practical examples and solved problems. All chapters in this book are arranged in a proper sequence that permits each topic to build upon earlier studies. All care has been taken to make students comfortable in understanding the basic concepts of this subject.

Representative questions have been added at the end of each section to help the students in picking important points from that section.

The book not only covers the entire scope of the subject but explains the philosophy of the subject. This makes the understanding of this subject more clear and makes it more interesting. The book will be very useful not only to the students but also to the subject teachers. The students have to omit nothing and possibly have to cover nothing more.

I wish to express my profound thanks to all those who helped in making this book a reality. Much needed moral support and encouragement is provided on numerous occasions by my whole family. I wish to thank the **Publisher** and the entire team of **Technical Publications** who have taken immense pain to get this book in time with quality printing.

Any suggestion for the improvement of the book will be acknowledged and well appreciated.

Author
A. A. Puntambekar

Dedicated to God.

SYLLABUS

1 Java Networking

Network Basics and Socket overview, TCP/IP client sockets, URL, TCP/IP server sockets, Datagrams, java.net package Socket, ServerSocket, InetAddress, URL, URLConnection. **(Chapter - 1)**

2 JDBC Programming

The JDBC Connectivity Model, Database Programming : Connecting to the Database, Creating a SQL Query, Getting the Results, Updating Database Data, Error Checking and the SQLException Class, The SQLWarning Class, The Statement Interface, PreparedStatement, CallableStatement The ResultSet Interface, Updatable Result Sets, JDBC Types, Executing SQL Queries, ResultSetMetaData, Executing SQL Updates, Transaction Management. **(Chapter - 2)**

3 Servlet API and Overview

Servlet Model : Overview of Servlet, Servlet Life Cycle, HTTP Methods Structure and Deployment descriptor

ServletContext and ServletConfig interface, Attributes in Servelt, Request Dispacher interface The Filter API: Filter, FilterChain, Filter Config

Cookies and Session Management : Understanding state and session, Understanding Session Timeout and Session Tracking, URL Rewriting **(Chapter - 3)**

4 Java Server Pages

JSP Overview : The Problem with Servlets, Life Cycle of JSP Page, JSP Processing, JSP Application Design with MVC, Setting Up the JSP Environment

JSP Directives, JSP Action, JSP Implicit Objects

JSP Form Processing, JSP Session and Cookies Handling, JSP Session Tracking

JSP Database Access, JSP Standard Tag Libraries, JSP Custom Tag, JSP Expression Language, JSP Exception Handling, JSP XML Processing. **(Chapter - 4)**

5 Java Server Faces2.0

Introduction to JSF, JSF request processing Life cycle, JSF Expression Language, JSF Standard Component, JSF Facelets Tag, JSF Convertor Tag, JSF Validation Tag, JSF Event Handling and Database Access, JSF Libraries: PrimeFaces **(Chapter - 5)**

6 Hibernate 4.0

Overview of Hibernate, Hibernate Architecture, Hibernate Mapping Types, Hibernate O/R Mapping, Hibernate Annotation, Hibernate Query Language **(Chapter - 6)**

7 Java Web Frameworks : Spring MVC

Overview of Spring, Spring Architecture, bean life cycle, XML Configuration on Spring, Aspect – oriented Spring, Managing Database, Managing Transaction. **(Chapter - 7)**

TABLE OF CONTENTS

Chapter - 1 Java Networking (1 - 1) to (1 - 46)

1.1 Network Basics ....1 - 2

1.1.1 IP Address....1 - 4

1.1.2 Domain Name Service....1 - 5

1.2 Socket Overview ....1 - 7

1.3 TCP/IP Client Sockets ....1 - 8

1.4 TCP/IP Server Sockets ....1 - 10

1.4.1 TCP Socket Programming (Client-Server Programs) ....1 - 10

1.5 Datagrams....1 - 24

1.5.1 UDP Socket Programming (Client-Server Programs)....1 - 25

1.6 Java .net Package....1 - 31

1.7 ServerSocket....1 - 32

1.8 InetAddress ....1 - 33

1.8.1 Methods for Types of IP Addresses ....1 - 39

1.9 URL....1 - 40

1.9.1 URL Formats ....1 - 41

1.9.2 URL Paths....1 - 41

1.9.3 URL Class ....1 - 42

1.10 URLConnection....1 - 43

Chapter - 2 JDBC Programming (2 - 1) to (2 - 34)

2.1 The JDBC Connectivity Model....2 - 2

2.1.1 How JDBC Works ? ....2 - 2

2.1.2 JDBC Architecture....2 - 2

2.2 The Java.sql Package....2 - 3

2.3 Database Programming ....2 - 4

2.3.1 Connecting to Database ....2 - 5

2.4 Creating a SQL Query ....2 - 9
2.5 Getting the Results ....2 - 10
2.6 Updating Database Data ....2 - 12
2.7 Error Checking and SQLException Class ....2 - 15
2.8 The SQLWarning Class ....2 - 17
2.9 The Statement Interface ....2 - 17
2.9.1 Prepared Statement ....2 - 18
2.9.2 Callable Statement ....2 - 20
2.10 The ResultSet Interface ....2 - 24
2.10.1 Navigating Methods ....2 - 25
2.10.2 Reading the Result using ResultSet ....2 - 25
2.10.3 Updating ResultSets ....2 - 26
2.11 JDBC Types ....2 - 26
2.12 Executing SQL Queries ....2 - 29
2.13 ResultSetMetaData ....2 - 29
2.14 Executing SQL Updates ....2 - 31
2.15 Difference between executeQuery(), executeUpdate() and execute() ....2 - 31
2.16 Transaction Management ....2 - 31

Chapter - 3 Servlet API and Overview (3 - 1) to (3 - 46)

3.1 Overview of Servlet ....3 - 2
3.2 Deployment of Servlet ....3 - 4
3.3 Architecture of Servlet ....3 - 4
3.3.1 How to Execute Servlet ? ....3 - 5
3.4 Servlet Life Cycle ....3 - 8
3.5 HTTP Methods Structure ....3 - 10
3.5.1 Interface ....3 - 10
3.5.2 Classes ....3 - 12
3.6 Deployment Descriptor ....3 - 14
3.7 ServletContext and ServletConfig Interface ....3 - 21

3.7.1 Interfaces . . . . 3 - 21
3.7.2 Classes . . . . 3 - 23
3.8 Attributes in Servlet . . . . 3 - 24
3.9 Request Dispatcher Interface . . . . 3 - 27
3.10 The Filter API . . . . 3 - 30
3.10.1 Filter . . . . 3 - 31
3.10.2 FilterChain Interface . . . . 3 - 31
3.10.3 FilterConfig . . . . 3 - 31
3.10.4 Uses of Filte . . . . 3 - 34
3.11 Cookies and Session Management . . . . 3 - 34
3.11.1 Understanding State and Session . . . . 3 - 34
3.11.2 Session Tracking . . . . 3 - 35
3.11.3 Understanding Session Timeout . . . . 3 - 38
3.11.4 URL Rewriting . . . . 3 - 39
3.11.5 Cookies . . . . 3 - 42

Chapter - 4 Java Server Pages (4 - 1) to (4 - 88)

4.1 JSP Overview . . . . 4 - 2
4.1.1 Advantages of Java Server Pages(JSP) . . . . 4 - 2
4.2 Problems with Servlets . . . . 4 - 2
4.2.1 Comparison between JSP and Servlet . . . . 4 - 3
4.3 Life Cycle of JSP Page . . . . 4 - 3
4.4 Anatomy of JSP Page . . . . 4 - 4
4.5 JSP Application Design with MVC . . . . 4 - 5
4.6 Setting up JSP Environment . . . . 4 - 6
4.7 Declarations . . . . 4 - 9
4.8 JSP Directives . . . . 4 - 11
4.9 Code Snippets . . . . 4 - 13
4.10 JSP Action . . . . 4 - 15
4.10.1 Standard Action . . . . 4 - 15

4.11 JSP Implicit Objects....4 - 20
4.12 JSP Form Processing....4 - 21
4.13 JSP Cookies Handling....4 - 25
4.14 JSP Session Tracking....4 - 32
4.15 JSP Database Access....4 - 34
4.15.1 Use of Prepared Statement....4 - 45
4.15.2 ResultSetMetaData....4 - 49
4.15.3 More Examples on Database Connectivity....4 - 51
4.16 JSP Standard Tag Libraries....4 - 57
4.16.1 Core Tag Library....4 - 59
4.16.2 Function Tag Library....4 - 69
4.16.3 SQL Tag Library....4 - 73
4.17 JSP Custom Tag....4 - 76
4.17.1 Tag Extensions API....4 - 76
4.17.2 Tag Handlers....4 - 76
4.18 JSP Expression Language....4 - 82
4.19 JSP Exception Handling....4 - 83
4.20 JSP XML Processing....4 - 85

Chapter - 5 Java Server Faces 2.0 (5 - 1) to (5 - 46)

5.1 Introduction to JSF....5 - 2
5.1.1 JSF Versions....5 - 2
5.1.2 Advantages and Disadvantages....5 - 2
5.1.3 User Interface Component Model....5 - 3
5.2 JSF Architecture....5 - 3
5.3 Writing First JSF Program....5 - 4
5.4 JSF Page Structure....5 - 8
5.5 JSF Request Processing Life Cycle....5 - 8
5.6 Form Handling....5 - 10

5.7 Managed Bean .... 5 - 11
5.8 JSF Expression Language .... 5 - 17
5.9 JSF Standard Component .... 5 - 21
5.10 JSF Facelets Tag .... 5 - 24
5.11 JSF Convertor Tag .... 5 - 29
5.12 JSF Validation Tag .... 5 - 34
5.13 JSF Event Handling .... 5 - 38
5.14 Database Access .... 5 - 40
5.15 JSF Libraries : PrimeFaces .... 5 - 45

Chapter - 6 Hibernate 4.0 (6 - 1) to (6 - 26)

6.1 Overview of Hibernate .... 6 - 2
6.2 Hibernate Architecture .... 6 - 2
6.3 Hibernate Mapping Types .... 6 - 4
6.4 Hibernate O/R Mapping .... 6 - 4
6.5 Hibernate Annotation .... 6 - 16
6.6 Hibernate Query Language (HQL) .... 6 - 22

Chapter - 7 Java Web Frameworks : Spring MVC (7 - 1) to (7 - 36)

7.1 Overview of Spring .... 7 - 2
7.1.1 Spring MVC Framework. . . . . 7 - 2
7.2 Spring Architecture .... 7 - 4
7.3 Creating First Application with Spring .... 7 - 6
7.4 The IoC Container .... 7 - 9
7.5 Bean Lifecycle .... 7 - 11
7.6 XML Configuration on Spring .... 7 - 14
7.7 Aspect-Oriented Spring .... 7 - 14
7.8 Managing Database .... 7 - 27
7.9 Managing Transaction .... 7 - 35

Solved GTU Question Papers **(S - 1) to (S - 24)**

Summer - 2016 .... (S - 1) to (S - 4)

Winter - 2016 .... (S - 5) to (S - 9)

Summer - 2017 .... (S - 10) to (S - 24)

(Q - 1) to (Q - 48)

Short Questions and Answers .... (Q - 1) to (Q - 18)

Winter - 2017 .... (Q - 19) to (Q - 29)

Summer - 2018 .... (Q - 30) to (Q - 36)

Winter - 2018 .... (Q - 37) to (Q - 40)

Summer - 2019 .... (Q - 41) to (Q - 48)

1 Java Networking

Syllabus

Network Basics and Socket overview, TCP/IP client sockets, URL, TCP/IP server sockets, Datagrams, java.net package Socket, ServerSocket, InetAddress, URL, URLConnection.

Contents

1.1 Network Basics

1.2 Socket Overview

1.3 TCP/IP Client Sockets

1.4 TCP/IP Server Sockets . . . . ***Winter-11, 14, Summer-16,*** · *Marks 7*

1.5 Datagrams . . . . ***Summer-14, Winter-14,*** · · · · *Marks 7*

1.6 Java .net Package

1.7 ServerSocket . . . . ***Summer-14,*** · · · · · · · · · · · · · *Marks 7*

1.8 InetAddress . . . . ***Winter-11, 12,*** · · · · · · · · · · · *Marks 7*

1.9 URL . . . . ***Summer-13,*** · · · · · · · · · · · · · *Marks 4*

1.10 URLConnection . . . . ***Winter-13,*** · · · · · · · · · · · · · · *Marks 7*

1.1 Network Basics

The important protocol in network communication is Transmission Control Protocol/Internet Protocol (TCP/IP). The purpose of any protocol is to establish the set of rules to perform specific activity related to network communication.

The TCP/IP stack is a four layered model. The TCP/IP stack along with the corresponding protocols is as shown by following Fig. 1.1.1.

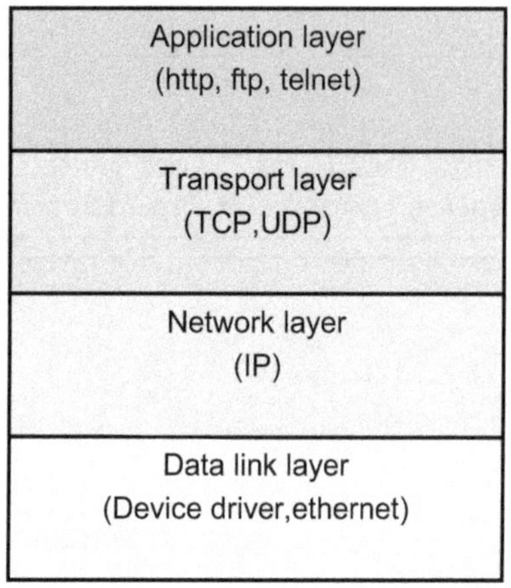

Fig. 1.1.1 TCP/IP stack with the protocols at each layer

Internet Protocol(IP)

- Internet protocol is a major protocol in the TCP/IP suit.
- It is a **connectionless**, **unreliable** protocol which supports the transfer of data in the form of **packets**.
- This is called connectionless protocol because it does not exchange any **control information** before transmitting any data. The data is just sent to the destination with a hope that it will reach at appropriate place.
- IP is known as an unreliable protocol because it does not have the provision of retransmitting the lost packets or detect the corrupted data.
- The **addressing scheme** used in IP is by means of **IP addresses**(we will discuss it in section 1.1.1). An IP address is a 32-bit unique number. IP addresses are generally written as four numbers, between 0 and 255, separated by period. Using the IP address defined in IP packet header, the IP packets can be routed to its destination.

Transmission Control Protocol (TCP)

- Transmission control protocol is a **connection-oriented**, **reliable** protocol which supports the transfer of data in continuous **streams**.
- This is called connection-oriented protocol because **control information** is sent before transmitting any data. This process is sometimes called as **handshaking**.

- This is a reliable protocol because any data which when gets lost or corrupted, the TCP has a provision to retransmit it. Because of these characteristics, TCP is used by most Internet applications. However, TCP requires a lot of overhead while coding it.
- The **addressing scheme** used in TCP is by means of **ports**. On separate ports the communication can be established concurrently by the system. During this communication, the server waits for the client to get connected to a specific port for establishing communication. This type of communication is called as **socket** programming.
- There are some ports which are reserved for specific service. These ports are called as **reserved ports**. Various port numbers specifying their services are given in the following table -

Port number	Service
21	FTP
23	Telnet
25	SMTP
80	HTTP
110	POP3

- User level processes or services generally use port numbers **>=1024**.

Following Fig. 1.1.2 shows the role of TCP/UDP and IP in TCP stack

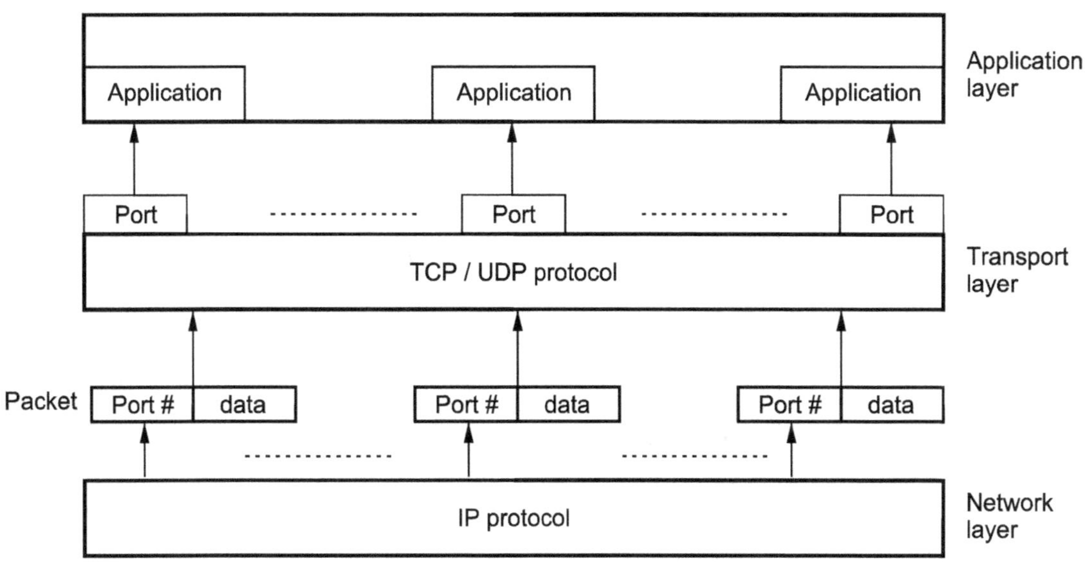

Fig. 1.1.2 Role of TCP, IP, UDP

User Datagram Protocol (UDP)

- The User Datagram Protocol(UDP) is a low-overhead protocol which can be used as an alternative to TCP protocol.
- The UDP is a **connectionless, unreliable** protocol in which the data is passed in the form of **datagrams**.
- This is called connectionless protocol because it does not exchange any **control information** before transmitting any data. The data is just sent to the destination with a hope that it will reach at appropriate place.
- UDP is known as an unreliable protocol because it does not have the provision of retransmitting the lost datagram or detect the corrupted data.
- The addressing scheme used UDP is by means of **ports**. On separate ports the communication can be established concurrently by the system. UDP ports are distinct from the TCP port.

1.1.1 IP Address

Each host on a TCP/IP network is assigned a unique 32-bit logical address that is divided into two main parts : the **network number** and the **host number**. This address is called IP address. The IP address is grouped four into 8-bits separated by dots. Each bit in the octet has binary weight.

2^7	2^6	2^5	2^4	2^3	2^2	2^1	2^0
↑	↑	↑	↑	↑	↑	↑	↑
128	64	32	16	8	4	2	1

As we know the IP address is divided in two categories network number and host number.

Network number	Host number

There are 5 classes based on two categories viz. A, B, C, D and E.

IP address class	Format	Range	Purpose
Class A	N.H.H.H	1 to 126	Very few large organizations use this class addressing.
Class B	N.N.H.H	128 to 191	Medium size organizations use this addressing.
Class C	N.N.N.H	192 to 223	Relatively small organizations use this class.
Class D	–	224 to 239	This class address is used for multicast groups.
Class E	–	240 to 254	This class addressing is reserved for experimental purpose.

Here N stands for network number and H stands for host number. For instance in class C first three octets are reserved for network address and last 8-bits denote host address.

IP address is assigned to the devices participating in computer network. The IP protocol makes use of this address for communication between two computers. Using IP address particular node can be identified in the network.

1.1.2 Domain Name Service

It is very difficult to remember numerical information but it is simple to remember the textual information. Consider that we want to access Priyanka's PC, then accessing it using the IP address **www.192.168.0.101** is definitely not comfortable, rather if we have the address **www.priyanka@technical.com** then accessing and remembering Priyanka's PC address is very simple. The names which are used to identify computer within a network are called **domain names**. Thus domain name is the name given to a network for human reference.

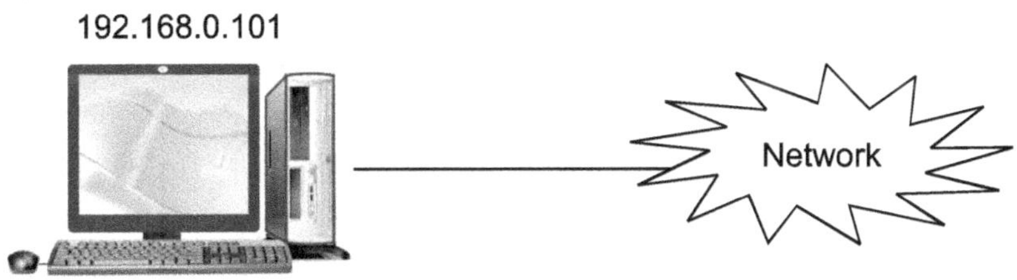

Hence in DNS, instead of using the IP address name of the Computer is used to access it. But two names can be the same. Hence to uniquely identify your computer the name must be referred using **DNS hierarchy**. Before understanding this hierarchy let us list out some commonly used domain names -

Domain names	Purpose
com	Commercial organizations
gov	Government organizations
edu	Educational institutes/organizations
int	International organizations
net	Network group
org	Non profit organizations
mil	Military group/organizations
in	Sub domain name used to refer India
uk	Sub domain name used to refer United Kingdom
jp	Sub domain name used to refer Japan

Fig. 1.1.3 Communication using domain names

The **domain name space** is used to locate the computer uniquely. The internet logically arranges the domain names in an hierarchical form. There are some top level DNS such as com, org, edu, mil, net, uk, in and so on. Then each domain name is further divided into sub-domains then sub-sub-domains and so on.

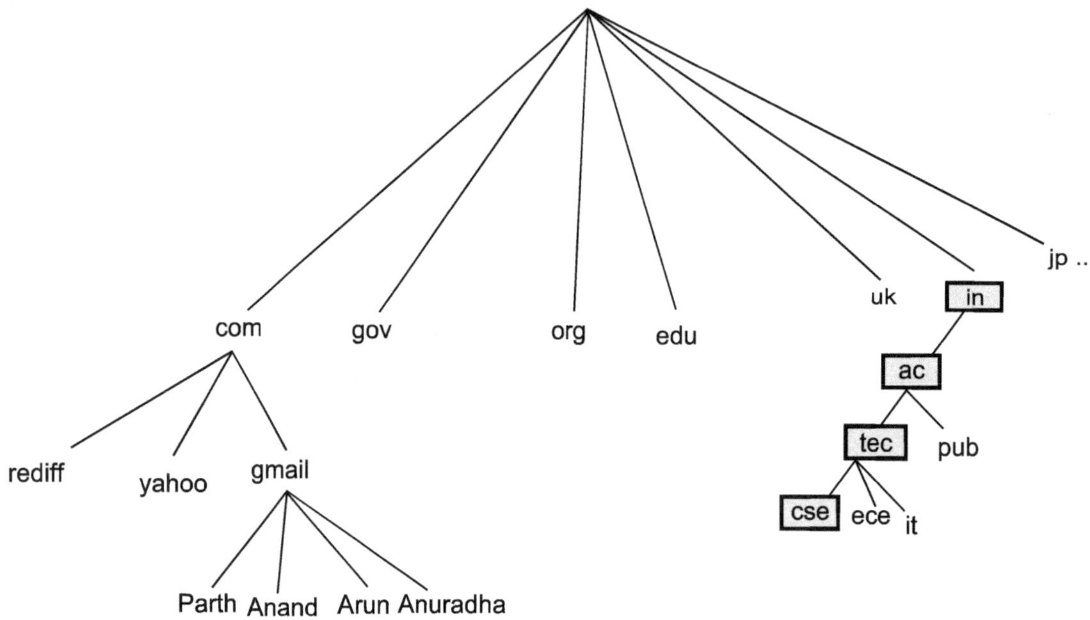

Fig. 1.1.4 Domain name space

For example the complete path for **http://www.cse.tec.ac.in** can be uniquely traced out with the help of domain name space.

Working of DNS

There are two tasks that can be carried out by DNS servers -

1. Accepting and then requesting the programs to convert domain names to IP addresses.
2. Accepting and then requesting the other DNS servers to convert domain names to IP addresses.

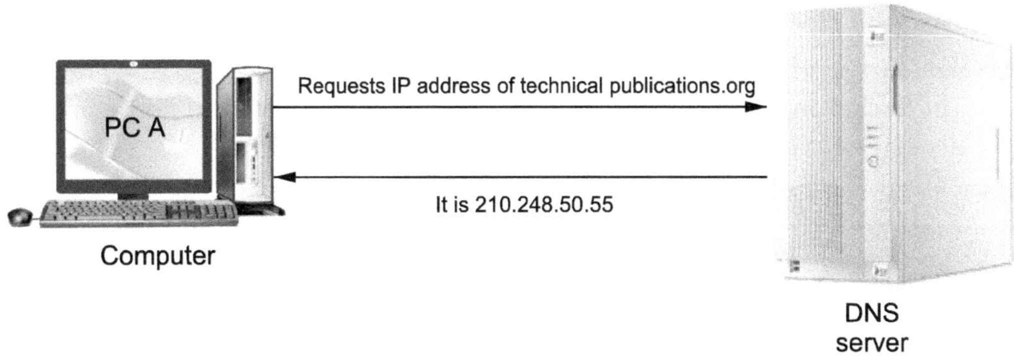

Fig. 1.1.5 Working of DNS

Suppose PC A is interested in knowing the IP address of **technicalpublications.org** then it contacts nearest DNS server. This DNS server maintains huge **database of domain names**. The entry domain name technicalpublications.org is searched within this database and if the IP address for corresponding name is found then the IP address is returned PC A. If the domain name requested by you is not there in the DNS server then name of another DNS server is suggested. If the request is made for some invalid domain name then the error message is returned.

1.2 Socket Overview

- Socket is the most commonly used term in network programing. Socket provides the way by which the computers can communicate using **connection oriented** or **connection less communication**.
- A socket is basically an **endpoint** of a two-way communication link between two programs running on the network. Typically these programs are Server program and Client program.
- Thus socket is OS-controlled interface into which the applications can send or receive messages to and fro from another application.
- A socket is bound to a port number so that the TCP/UDP from transport layer can identify the corresponding application at destination.
- The **java.net.Socket** class represents the socket.
- Two key classes are used to create the socket.

  i) ServerSocket

  ii) Socket
- A server program creates a specific type of socket that is used to listen for client requests (server socket), In the case of a connection request, the program creates a new socket through which it will exchange data with the client using input and output streams.

- The **ServerSocket** can be created with the help of Port number. For example

```
ServerSocket server_socket=new Socket(1234);
```

- The **Socket** object can be created with the help of hostname and port number. The general syntax of socket instantiation is

```
Socket client= new Socket(serverName, portNumber);
```

For example

```
Socket client_socket=new Socket("myserver",1234);
```

The **ServerSocket** listens the client using the **accept** method. For example

```
Socket Listen_socket=server_socket.accept();
```

There are two types of sockets -

i) **TCP Sockets :** These are denoted by **streams**

ii) **UDP Sockets :** These are denoted by **datagrams**

1.3 TCP/IP Client Sockets

- Transmission Control Protocol(TCP) is a connection-oriented, reliable protocol which supports the transfer of data in continuous streams.
- The addressing scheme used in TCP is makes use of **ports**. On separate ports the communication can be established concurrently by the system. During this communication, the server waits for the client to get connected to a specific port for establishing communication. This type of communication is called as **socket programming.**
- There are some ports which are reserved for specific service. These ports are called as reserved ports. Various port numbers specifying their services are given in the following table

Port number	Service
21	FTP
23	Telnet
25	SMTP
80	HTTP
110	POP3

- **User level processes** or services generally use port numbers **>=1024.**
- A socket is bound to a port number so that the TCP/UDP from transport layer can identify the corresponding application at destination.

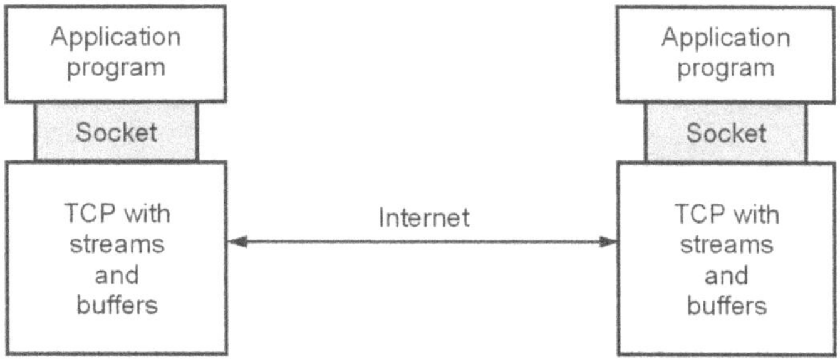

- Server is a device which has resources and from which the services can be obtained. For example : there are various types of servers such as web server which is for storing the web pages, there are print servers for managing the printer services or there are database servers which store the databases.
- Client is a device which wants to get service from particular server.
- First of all server starts and gets ready to receive the client connections. The server-client communications occurs in following steps

Sr. No.	Client	Server
1.	Creates TCP socket.	Creates TCP Socket
2.	Client initiates the communication. i) Communicate.	Creates another socket for listening client. i) Accept message from client and repeatedly communicate.
3.	Close the connection	Close the connection.

These steps can be illustrated by following figure -

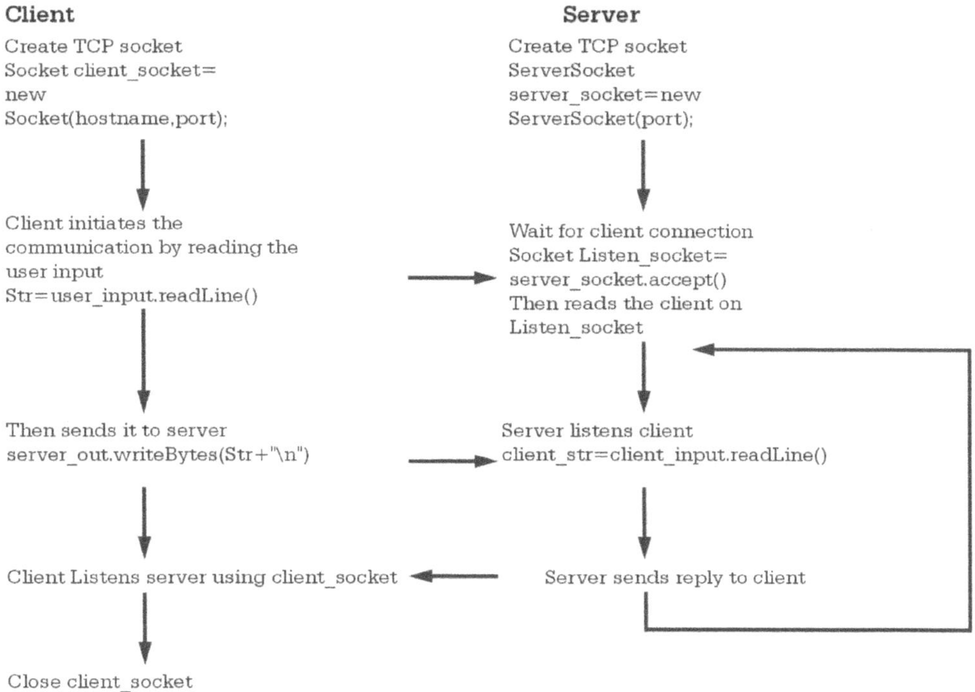

- There are two constructors used to create **client socket** -

Constructor	Meaning
Socket(String *hostName*, int *port*)	Creates a socket connecting the local host to the named host and port.
Socket(InetAddress *ipAddress*, int *port*)	Creates a socket using a pre-existing **InetAddress** object and a port.

- The methods used for examining the socket are -

InetAddress getInetAddress( )	Returns the **InetAddress** associated with the **Socket** object.
int getPort( )	Returns the remote port to which this **Socket** object is connected.
int getLocalPort( )	Returns the local port to which this

1.4 TCP/IP Server Sockets

GTU : Winter-11, 14, Summer-16, Marks 7

The **ServerSocket** class is used to create servers that listen to its clients. When **ServerSocket** is created, it will register itself with the system so that clients can connect to it. This class throws exception **IOException.**

The various ways by which **ServerSocket** can be created is as follows -

```
ServerSocket(int port)
ServerSocket(int port, int maxQueue)
ServerSocket(int port, int maxQueue, InetAddress localAddress)
```

Using the accept() method, the server initiates the communication with the client.

Following is a simple client server chat application that illustrates the client server communication using the TCP/IP.

1.4.1 TCP Socket Programming (Client-Server Programs)

Let us see the simple socket program in which the client sends the string to the server.

Java Program

```
/*
**************************************************************************
                              Server Program
**************************************************************************
*/
import java.io.*;
import java.net.*;
class Server
{
```

```
    public static void main(String args[]) throws Exception
{
 ServerSocket server_socket=new ServerSocket(1234);
 while(true)
 {
  Socket Listen_socket=server_socket.accept();
  BufferedReader client_input=new BufferedReader(new
  InputStreamReader(Listen_socket.getInputStream()));
  String client_str;
  client_str=client_input.readLine();
  System.out.println(client_str);
 }
 }
}
/*
*******************************************************************************
                              Client Program
*******************************************************************************
*/
import java.io.*;
import java.net.*;
class Client
{
public static void main(String args[]) throws Exception
{

 Socket client_socket=new Socket("aap",1234);
 BufferedReader user_input = new BufferedReader(new
  InputStreamReader(System.in));
 DataOutputStream server_out=new
 DataOutputStream(client_socket.getOutputStream());
 String Str;
 Str=user_input.readLine();
 server_out.writeBytes(Str+"\n");
 client_socket.close();
}
}
```

These two programs can be run on separate command-prompt windows so that we can see the client-server communication getting established. Note that the **server program must be running before starting the client**. Here is an illustrative output

Output

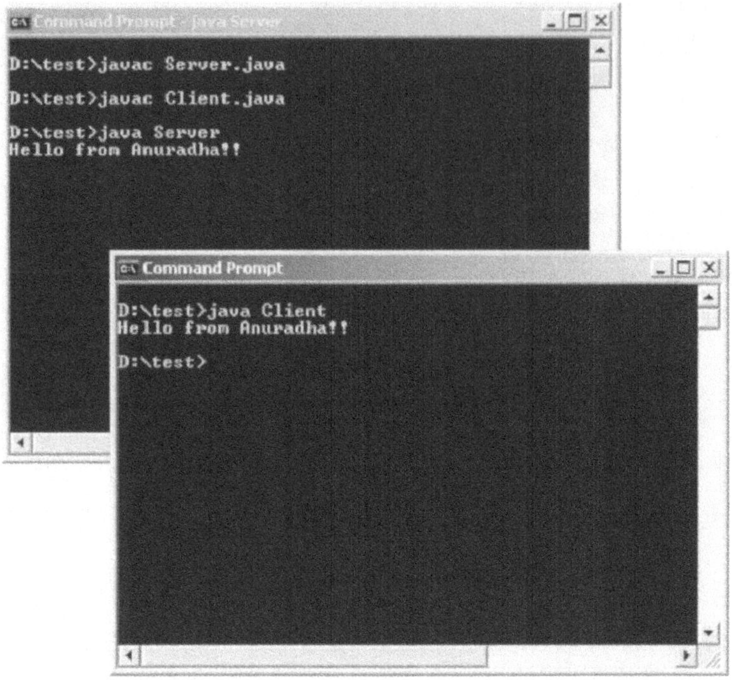

Explanation

In the server program first two lines are

```
import java.io.*;
import java.net.*;
```

The **java.io package** is required to support I/O operations. And for socket programming **java.net package** is required because it contains the class **Socket** which is required in our program. **Socket** class creates a stream socket and connects it to a specific port at a specific IP address/hostname. Hence in the main() we have written

```
ServerSocket server_socket=new ServerSocket(1234);
```

Here *aap* is a host name of the machine on which the server is running and *1234* is the port number. That means the server creates a socket *server_socket* for establishing the connection with the client.

The server creates another separate socket for listening to the client

```
Socket Listen_socket=server_socket.accept();
```

Thus only on Listen_socket server can listen to the client. Then comes

```
BufferedReader client_input=new
BufferedReader(newInputStreamReader(Listen_socket.getInputStream()));
```

The *BufferedReader* is for creating the object *client_input*. We have used **getInputStream()** method which returns an input stream from the other side of the socket. The *InputStreamReader* takes **getInputStream()** as a parameter.

Then in the string *client_str* the client message can be collected by a using a method *readLine()* as follows

```
String client_str;
client_str=client_input.readLine();
```

Then the message obtained from client is printed on the console using following code

```
System.out.println(client_str);
```

Now let us discuss the client program. In client program we have to create a socket for client as follows

```
Socket client_socket=new Socket("aap",1234);
```

When the client runs something must be typed on the console and that message will be sent to the server. Using *System.in* we can get the input written on the console. Hence to get the message typed by the user following declaration must be made

```
BufferedReader user_input = new BufferedReader(new
    InputStreamReader(System.in));
```

The **BufferedReader** object is created to read the input from keyboard.

The **InputStreamReader** is for reading the stream input. We have send ***System.in*** as a parameter to **InputStreamReader**. Then an output stream has to be created on which the data can be sent to the server. Hence we declare *server_out* as an output stream.

```
DataOutputStream server_out=new
DataOutputStream(client_socket.getOutputStream());
```

The method getOutputStream() returns an output stream to the other side the socket. Then using readLine() function we can read the message written on the console.

```
Str=user_input.readLine();
```

The client then sends this message (collected in string Str) to the server using **writeBytes()** method as follows

```
server_out.writeBytes(Str+"\n");
```

Finally the client closes its connection by

```
client_socket.close();
```

Last but not the least, we have to throw some Exception to handle the unknown host or connection not getting established situation. Hence the **main()** method throws a general exception **Exception**. Let us now see another program in which client sends some message to the server and server sends the acknowledgement to the client.

Java Program

```
/*******************************************************************
        Server Program which sends acknowledgement to the client
*******************************************************************/
import java.io.*;
import java.lang.*;
import java.net.*;
class S
```

```
{
 public static void main(String args[]) throws Exception
{
 String str3;
 String str4;
 ServerSocket s2=new ServerSocket(1234);
while(true)
{
 Socket s3=s2.accept();
BufferedReader in_client=new BufferedReader(new
InputStreamReader(s3.getInputStream()));
 DataOutputStream out_client=new  DataOutputStream(s3.getOutputStream());
 str3=in_client.readLine();
 str4=str3+"—>Received"+'\n';
 out_client.writeBytes(str4);
 }
}
}
```

Input stream is created to send the acknowledgement to the client.

Using **writeBytes** method the acknowledgement is sent to client.

```
/*****************************************************************
                    Client Program
*****************************************************************/
import java.io.*;
import java.net.*;
class C
{
public static void main(String args[]) throws Exception
{
  String Str;
  String Str1;
  BufferedReader input_user = new BufferedReader(new
    InputStreamReader(System.in));
  Socket s1=new Socket("aap",1234);
 DataOutputStream out_server=new
 DataOutputStream(s1.getOutputStream());
 BufferedReader in_server=new BufferedReader(new
 InputStreamReader(s1.getInputStream()));
 Str=input_user.readLine();
 out_server.writeBytes(Str+"\n");
 Str1=in_server.readLine();
 System.out.println("From server:  "+ Str1);
 s1.close();
}
}
```

Client reading the acknowledgement from the server and printing it on its console

Output

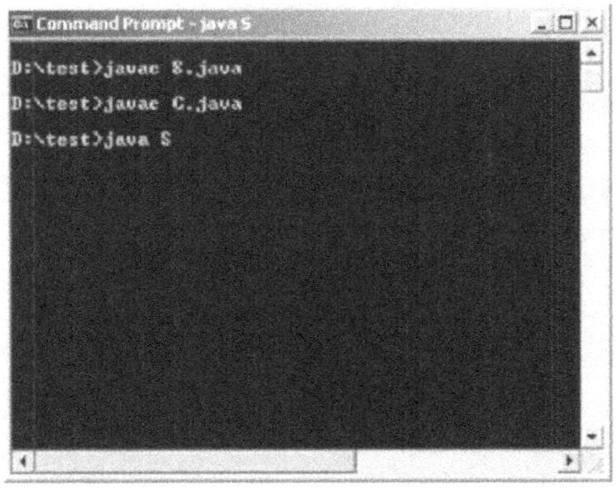

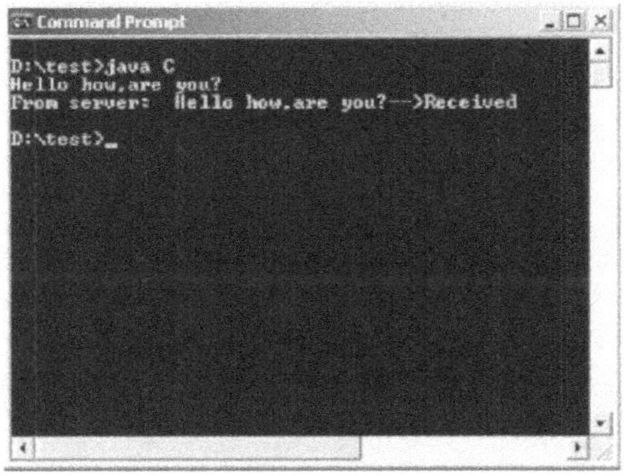

Here is one more interesting program in which client and server both communicate by sending and receiving message to each other just like a chat application.

Java Program

```
/**********************************************************************
                              Server Program
**********************************************************************/
import java.io.*;
import java.net.*;
class S2
{
 public static void main(String args[]) throws Exception
 {
  System.out.println("Server started...wait");
   try
  {
   ServerSocket server_socket=new ServerSocket(1234);
   while(true)
   {
    Socket Listen_socket=server_socket.accept();
    BufferedReader client_input=new BufferedReader(new
    InputStreamReader(Listen_socket.getInputStream()));
    BufferedReader server_input=new BufferedReader(new
```

```
   InputStreamReader(System.in));
   DataOutputStream client_out=new
   DataOutputStream(Listen_socket.getOutputStream());
   String client_str,server_str;
   server_str=server_input.readLine();
   client_out.writeBytes(server_str+"\n");
   client_str=client_input.readLine();
   System.out.println(client_str);
  }//end of while loop
 }//end of try block
 catch(Exception e)//catch block immediately starts
 {
 //caught exception is displayed using getMessage()
   System.out.println("Error: "+e.getMessage());
  }//catch ends
 }//end of main
}//end of server class S2
/****************************************************************
                          Client Program
****************************************************************/
import java.io.*;
import java.net.*;
class C2
{
 public static void main(String args[]) throws Exception
 {
  System.out.println("Enter something to start communication....");
  try
  {
   while(true)
   {
    Socket s1=new Socket("aap",1234);
    BufferedReader user_input = new BufferedReader(new
    InputStreamReader(System.in));
    BufferedReader server_input=new BufferedReader(new
    InputStreamReader(s1.getInputStream()));
    DataOutputStream server_out=new
    DataOutputStream(s1.getOutputStream());
    String Str,Str1;
    Str=user_input.readLine();
    server_out.writeBytes(Str+"\n");
    Str1=server_input.readLine();
    System.out.print(Str1);
    s1.close();
   }//end of while loop
  } //end for try block
```

```
catch(Exception e)//catch block starts immediately
 {
   System.out.println("Error: "+e.getMessage());
  }//end of catch
 }//end of main
}//end of client class C2
```

Output

```
D:\test>javac S2.java
D:\test>javac C2.java
D:\test>java S2
Server started...wait
```

Then start the client using

```
D:\test>java C2
Enter something to start communication....
Hello,I am Anuradha
```

Then at the server console type some message

```
Hello,I am Anuradha
```

Server can now send some message to client

```
Hello I am Anand
```

This message can be received at the client console

```
Hello I am Anand
```

Thus the communication can be continued as long as we want!

Do not forget to note that we have used **try...catch** block in our program in order to handle exception in some smoother manner. It's a good habit to catch the exception in this way.

Example 1.4.1 : *Write a client program to send any string from its standard input to the server program. The server program reads the string, finds number of characters and digits and sends it back to client program. Use connection-oriented or connection-less communication.* **GTU :Winter-11, Marks 7**

Solution : Following application makes use of **connection oriented socket programming**.

Step 1 : We will write a client program which accepts some string containing alphanumeric string. This string is then sent to the server. The program is as follows -

```
/*****************************************************************
              Client Program
*****************************************************************/
import java.io.*;
import java.net.*;
class Client
{
public static void main(String args[]) throws Exception
{
      String Str=" ";
      String Str1;
      String Str2;
```

```
      Socket s1=new Socket("127.0.0.1",1234);
      try
      {
      System.out.println("Enter Some string...");
      while(true)
      {
       BufferedReader input_user = new BufferedReader(new
InputStreamReader(System.in));
       DataOutputStream out_server=new DataOutputStream(s1.getOutputStream());
       BufferedReader in_server=new BufferedReader(new
InputStreamReader(s1.getInputStream()));
       Str=input_user.readLine();
       out_server.writeBytes(Str+"\n");
       Str1=in_server.readLine(); //obtaining the from server
       Str2=in_server.readLine(); //obtaining the from server
       //displaying this count on client console
       System.out.println("Number of digits is "+Str1);
       System.out.println("Number of characters is "+Str2);
       s1.close();
      }//end of while
     }catch(Exception e){System.out.println(e.getMessage());}
 }
}
```

Step 2 : Now we will write down some server program which will accept the string from the client and count the total number of characters and digits into it. These counts will be then returned to the client. The Client program will display these counts. The server program is follows -

```
/*************************************************************
            Server Program
*************************************************************/
import java.io.*;
import java.lang.*;
import java.net.*;
class Server
{
 public static void main(String args[]) throws Exception
 {
  ServerSocket s2=new ServerSocket(1234);
  String text=" ";
  int counts=0;
  int charcounts=0;
  System.out.println("\t\tServer started.....");
  while(true)
  {
   Socket s3=s2.accept();
```

```
  BufferedReader in_client=new BufferedReader(new
InputStreamReader(s3.getInputStream()));
  DataOutputStream out_client=new DataOutputStream(s3.getOutputStream());
  text=in_client.readLine();//getting data from client
  System.out.println("Receiving data...");
  for(int i=0;i<text.length();i++)
  {
    if((text.charAt(i)>='0')&&(text.charAt(i)<='9'))
     counts++;
  }//end of for
  out_client.writeBytes(counts+"\n");//sending number of digits to client
  charcounts=text.length()-counts;
  out_client.writeBytes(charcounts+"\n");//sending number of characters to client
  System.out.println("Data is sent...");
 }//end of while
 }//end of main
}//end of class
```

Step 3 : Now open two command prompt windows to get the output. First execute the server program and then the client program. The output is as follows -

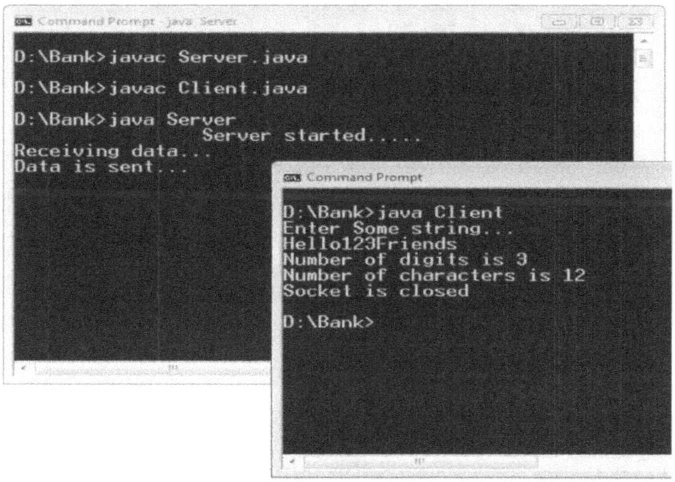

Example 1.4.2 : *Write a client server program using TCP where client sends two numbers and server responds with sum of them.* **GTU : Winter-14, Marks 7**

Solution : Step 1 : Create a client program which takes the two numbers from the user and send it to the server for calculating their sum. When client receives this sum from the server, it displays that sum on the console.

```
/*******************************************************************
 Client Program For sum of Two Numbers
 *******************************************************************/
import java.io.*;
import java.net.*;
```

```
class Client
{
  public static void main(String args[]) throws Exception
  {
    String Str=" ";
    String Str1;
    Socket s1=new Socket("127.0.0.1",1234);
    try
    {
      System.out.println("\tProgram for Addition of Two Numbers using TCP...");
      while(true)
      {
        BufferedReader input_user = new BufferedReader(new
InputStreamReader(System.in));
        DataOutputStream out_server=new DataOutputStream(s1.getOutputStream());
        BufferedReader in_server=new BufferedReader(new
InputStreamReader(s1.getInputStream()));
        for(int i=1;i<=2;i++)
        {
          System.out.println("Enter number(put#at the end)");
          Str=Str+input_user.readLine();
        }
        out_server.writeBytes(Str+"\n");
        Str1=in_server.readLine(); //obtaining the sum from server
         //displaying this sum on client console
        System.out.println("The sum is: "+Str1);
        s1.close();
      }
    }catch(Exception e){System.out.println(e.getMessage()); }

  }
}
```

Step 2 : Now we will create a server program that receives two numbers from the client and calculate its sum. Then this server sends this sum to the client for display.

```
/*****************************************************************
 Server Program for calculating sum of two numbers
 *****************************************************************/
import java.io.*;
import java.lang.*;
import java.net.*;
class Server
{
  public static void main(String args[]) throws Exception
  {
    ServerSocket s2=new ServerSocket(1234);
    String[] temp;
```

```
        String str3=" ";
        String del="#";
        System.out.println("\t\tServer started.....");
        while(true)
        {
          Socket s3=s2.accept();
          BufferedReader in_client=new BufferedReader(new
InputStreamReader(s3.getInputStream()));
          DataOutputStream out_client=new DataOutputStream(s3.getOutputStream());
          str3=in_client.readLine();//getting data from client
          temp=str3.split(del);//separating out # character and storing the data in temp
//arrray
          System.out.println("Receiving data...");
          for(int i=0;i<temp.length;i++)
            System.out.println("Number: "+(i+1)+" is "+temp[i]);//displaying received data
          System.out.println("\tNow calculating sum and sending it to client");
          double sum=0.0;
          for(int i=0;i<temp.length;i++)
          {
            float num=Float.parseFloat(temp[i]);
            sum=sum+num;
          }
            String str4=sum+"\n";
            out_client.writeBytes(str4);//sending commission data to client

        }
    }
}
```

Step 3 : Firstly, open one command prompt window and start the server by running the program in Step 2. Then open another command prompt window and then run the client program. The output is as shown below -

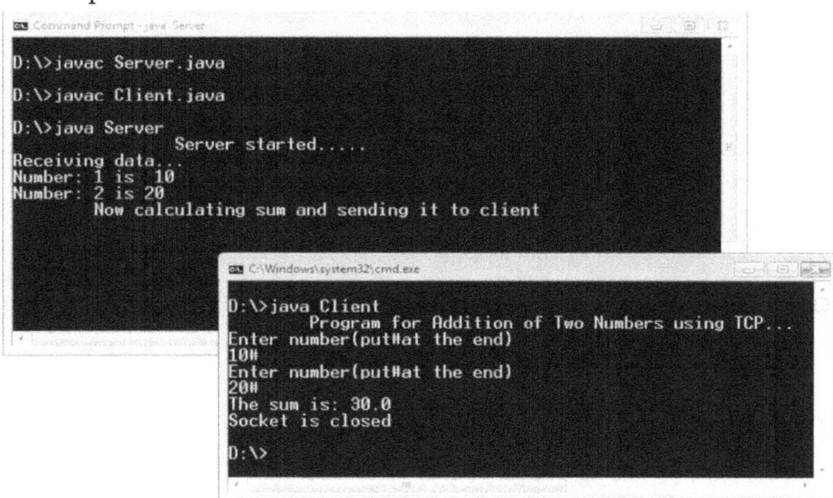

Example 1.4.3 : *Write a client - server program using TCP or UDP where the client sends 10 numbers and server responds with the numbers in sorted order.* **GTU : Summer-16, Marks 7**

Solution : **Step 1 :** Create a client program that reads the 10 numbers from keyboard

Client.java

```
import java.io.*;
import java.net.*;
class Client
{
  public static void main(String args[]) throws Exception
  {
    String Str="";
    String Str1;
    Socket s1=new Socket("127.0.0.1",1234);
    try
    {
      System.out.println("\tProgram for Sorting Numbers using TCP...");
      while(true)
      {
BufferedReader input_user = new BufferedReader(new InputStreamReader(System.in));
DataOutputStream out_server=new DataOutputStream(s1.getOutputStream());
BufferedReader in_server=new BufferedReader(new
InputStreamReader(s1.getInputStream()));
        for(int i=1;i<=10;i++)
        {
          System.out.println("Enter number(put#at the end)");
          Str=Str+input_user.readLine();
        }
        out_server.writeBytes(Str+"\n");
        s1.close();
      }
    }catch(Exception e){System.out.println(e.getMessage()); }

  }
}
```

Step 2 : Create a server program, that sorts the numbers obtained from the client. This program also displays the sorted numbers on console

Server.java

```
import java.io.*;
import java.lang.*;
import java.net.*;
class Server
{
    public static void main(String args[]) throws Exception
    {
        ServerSocket s2=new ServerSocket(1234);
```

```
        String[] temp;
        int a[],i,n,swap;
        String str3="";
        String del="#";
        a=new int[10];
        System.out.println("\t\tServer started.....");
        while(true)
        {
            Socket s3=s2.accept();
                                    BufferedReader in_client=new BufferedReader(new

    InputStreamReader(s3.getInputStream()));
                                    DataOutputStream out_client=new
                                    DataOutputStream(s3.getOutputStream());
                                    str3=in_client.readLine();//getting data from client
                                    temp=str3.split(del);//separating out # character and
storing the data in
                                    temp //arrray
            System.out.println("Receiving data...");
            for(i=0;i<temp.length;i++)
                                            System.out.println("Number: "+(i+1)+" is
"+temp[i]);//displaying
                                            received data
            System.out.println("\tNow Sorting the Numbers...");
            for(i=0;i<temp.length;i++)
            {
                a[i]=Integer.parseInt(temp[i]);

            }
            n=10;//total number of elements in array
            System.out.println("Before Sorting...");
            for(i=0;i<n;i++)
                System.out.print(" "+a[i]);//displaying received data
            for (int j = 0; j < ( n - 1 ); j++)
            {
                for (int k = 0; k < n - j - 1; k++)
                {
                    if (a[k] > a[k+1])
                    {
                        swap=a[k];
                        a[k]=a[k+1];
                        a[k+1]=swap;
                    }
                }
            }
                                    System.out.println("\nAfter Sorting...");
```

```
			for(i=0;i<n;i++)
				System.out.print(" "+a[i]);//displaying received data
		}
	}
}
```

Output

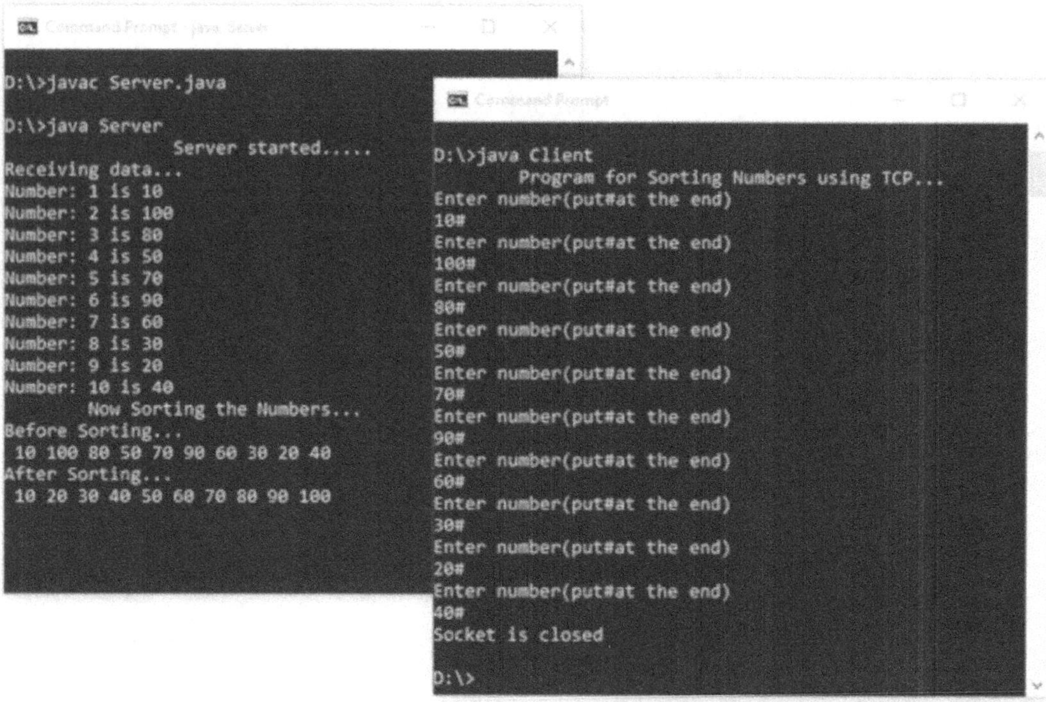

1.5 Datagrams

GTU : Summer-14, Winter-14, Marks 7

A *datagram* is an independent, self-contained message sent over the network whose arrival, arrival time and content are not guaranteed.

It is a basic transfer unit associated with a packet-switched network. The applications that communicate via datagrams send and receive completely independent packets of information.

The java.net package contains three classes to help you write Java programs that use datagrams to send and receive packets over the network : **DatagramSocket, DatagramPacket,** and **MulticastSocket**.

An application can send and receive **DatagramPackets** through a **DatagramSocket**. In addition, **DatagramPackets** can be broadcast to multiple recipients all listening to a MulticastSocket.

1.5.1 UDP Socket Programming (Client-Server Programs)

From the **java.net** package for handling the UDP sockets mainly we use two classes : **DatagramSocket** constructor is used to create the UDP socket. Remember that when we want to transmit or receive any data it must be encapsulated in the packets. Hence **DatagramPacket** is used to create the packet for the data. To retrieve data from the packet **getData()** method is used. Following are a Java programs for client and server. The client sends some message to the server and server displays the received message on its console.

Java Program

```
/*
*************************************************************************
                         UDP Client Program
*************************************************************************
*/
import java.io.*;
import java.net.*;
class UDPClient
{
 public static void main(String args[]) throws Exception
 {
   BufferedReader user_input=new BufferedReader(new
   InputStreamReader(System.in));
   //creating the client socket
   DatagramSocket client_socket=new DatagramSocket();
   //getting the IP address of host "aap"
   InetAddress IP_add=InetAddress.getByName("aap");
   //creating the buffer for sending the data
   byte out_data[]=new byte[1024];
   //reading the input through keyboard
   String str=user_input.readLine();
   out_data=str.getBytes();
   //creating the datagram packet in which data is
   //encapsulated
   DatagramPacket Packet1=new
   DatagramPacket(out_data,out_data.length,IP_add,1234);
   //sending the packet to the server
   client_socket.send(Packet1);
   //closing the client's connection
   client_socket.close();
 }
}
/*
*************************************************************************
                         UDP Server Program
*************************************************************************
```

```
*/
import java.io.*;
import java.net.*;
class UDPServer
{
 public static void main(String args[]) throws Exception
 {
  //creating the socket for server
  DatagramSocket server_socket=new DatagramSocket(1234);
  //array which reserves the input data getting from
  //client
  byte in_data[]=new byte[1024];
  while(true)
  {
    //creating the datagram packet
    DatagramPacket Packet2=new
    DatagramPacket(in_data,in_data.length);
     //the data from the client is received in the packet
    server_socket.receive(Packet2);
    String str=new String(Packet2.getData());
    //printing the received data on the console of server
    System.out.println(str);
  }
 }
}
```

Output

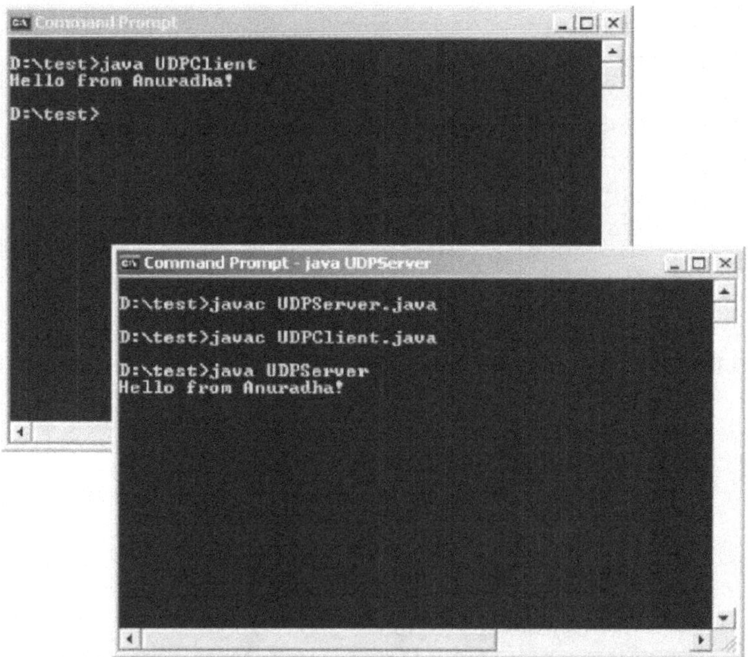

Here are some useful methods for UDP socket programming

Method	Description
InetAddress getByName(String *hostname*)	This method returns the IP address when the *hostname* is given
InetAddress getAddress()	This method returns the IP address
int getPort()	It returns the port number
Byte [ ]getData()	It returns the data containing in the datagram. This is stored in the array of bytes.
int getLength()	Returns the length of data obtained by getData method.

Here is one more program in which UDP client sends some message to the server and server sends some another message to the client.

Java Program

```
/*
*****************************************************************
                    UDP Client Program
*****************************************************************
*/
import java.io.*;
import java.net.*;
class UDPClient
{
public static void main(String args[]) throws Exception
{
 BufferedReader user_input=new BufferedReader(new
 InputStreamReader(System.in));
 //creating the client socket
 DatagramSocket client_socket=new DatagramSocket();
 //getting the IP address of host "aap"
 InetAddress IP_add=InetAddress.getByName("aap");
 //creating the buffer for sending the data
 byte out_data[]=new byte[1024];
 byte in_data[]=new byte[1024];
 //reading the input through keyboard

 String str=user_input.readLine();
 out_data=str.getBytes();
 //creating the datagram packet in which data is
 //encapsulated
 DatagramPacket Packet1=new
 DatagramPacket(out_data,out_data.length,IP_add,1234);
 //sending the packet to the server
 client_socket.send(Packet1);
```

Sending the data stored in array **out_data** to the server in **Packet1**

```
    DatagramPacket Packet4=new
 DatagramPacket(in_data,in_data.length);
 //the data from the server is received in the packet
 client_socket.receive(Packet4);
 String receive_str=new String(Packet4.getData());
 //printing the received data on the console of client
 System.out.println(receive_str);
 //closing the client's connection
 client_socket.close();
 }
}
```

Receiving the data stored in array **in_data** from the server in **Packet4**

```
/*
*****************************************************************************
                         UDP Server Program
*****************************************************************************
*/
import java.io.*;
import java.net.*;
class UDPServer
{
public static void main(String args[]) throws Exception
{
//creating the socket for server
DatagramSocket server_socket=new DatagramSocket(1234);
BufferedReader server_input=new BufferedReader(new InputStreamReader(System.in));
InetAddress IP_add=InetAddress.getByName("aap");
//array which reserves the input data getting from client
byte in_data[]=new byte[1024];
byte out_data[]=new byte[1024];
while(true)
{
//creating the datagram packet
DatagramPacket Packet2=new
DatagramPacket(in_data,in_data.length);
//the data from the client is received in the packet
server_socket.receive(Packet2);
String str=new String(Packet2.getData());
//printing the received data on the console of server
System.out.println(str);
```

Receiving the data stored in array **in_data** from the client in **Packet2**

```
InetAddress IP_add1=Packet2.getAddress();
int port=Packet2.getPort();
String send_str=server_input.readLine();
out_data=send_str.getBytes();
DatagramPacket Packet3=new
DatagramPacket(out_data,out_data.length,IP_add1,port);
//sending the packet to the client
server_socket.send(Packet3);
}
```

Sending the data stored in array **out_data** to the client in **Packet3**

```
}
}
```

Output

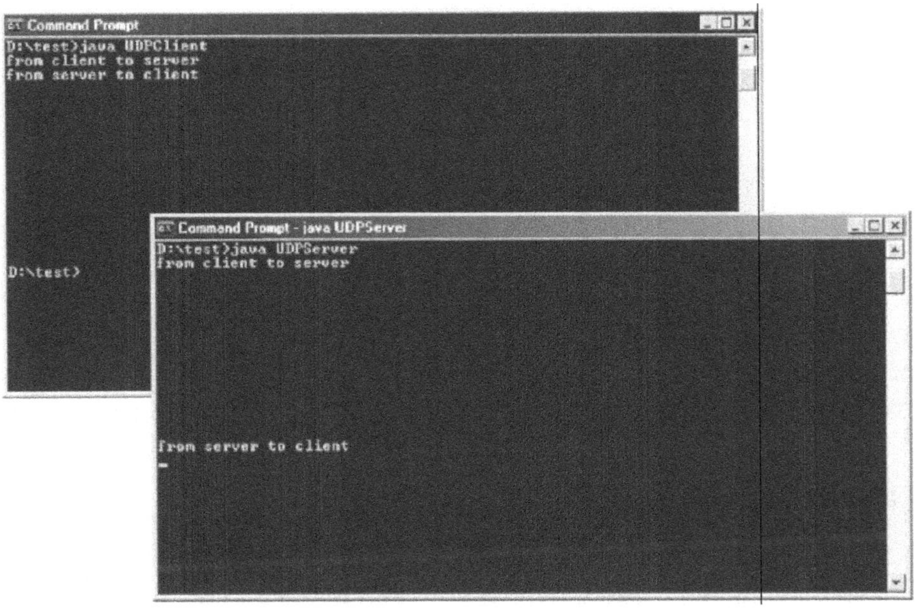

Example 1.5.1 : *Write an UDP client and server program to do the following :*
Client send any string and server respond with its capital string.

GTU : Winter-14, Marks 7

Solution :

```
/*
****************************************************
UDP Client Program[UDPClient.java]
*****************************************************
*/
import java.io.*;
import java.net.*;
class UDPClient
{
 public static void main(String args[]) throws Exception
 {
   BufferedReader user_input=new BufferedReader(new
   InputStreamReader(System.in));
   //creating the client socket
   DatagramSocket client_socket=new DatagramSocket();
   //getting the IP address of host "aap"
   InetAddress IP_add=InetAddress.getByName("localhost");
   //creating the buffer for sending the data
   byte out_data[]=new byte[1024];
```

```
    //reading the input through keyboard
    String str=user_input.readLine();
    out_data=str.getBytes();
    //creating the datagram packet in which data is
    //encapsulated
    DatagramPacket Packet1=new
    DatagramPacket(out_data,out_data.length,IP_add,1234);
    //sending the packet to the server
    client_socket.send(Packet1);
    //closing the client's connection
    client_socket.close();
 }
}
/*
*****************************************************
UDP Server Program[UDPServer.java]
*****************************************************
*/
import java.io.*;
import java.net.*;
class UDPServer
{
 public static void main(String args[]) throws Exception
 {
  //creating the socket for server
  DatagramSocket server_socket=new DatagramSocket(1234);
  //array which reserves the input data getting from
  //client
  byte in_data[]=new byte[1024];
  while(true)
  {
    //creating the datagram packet
    DatagramPacket Packet2=new
    DatagramPacket(in_data,in_data.length);
     //the data from the client is received in the packet
    server_socket.receive(Packet2);
    String str=new String(Packet2.getData());
    //printing the received data on the console of server

    System.out.println(str.toUpperCase());
  }
 }
}
```

Review Question

1. *What is Datagram socket ? Explain it with example.* **GTU : Summer-14, Marks 7**

1.6 Java .net Package

Purpose : This package is for providing the useful classes and interfaces for networking applications which are used in sockets and URL.

Interfaces :

Name	Description	Some methods
ContentHandlerFactory	This interface is for defining the factory for content handlers.	*createContentHandler(string MIME_type)*- creates ContentHandler.
SocketImplFactory	This interface is for defining the factory for implementing the sockets.	*createSocketImpl()*- creates a new instance for implementing socket.
URLStreamHandlerFactory	For implementing URL stream protocol handlers the factory can be defined by this interface.	*createURLStreamHandler(String p)*- For specific protocol 'p' a new URLStreamHandler instance can be created by this method.

Classes :

Name	Description
ContentHandler	This class is a superclass of all the classes that read the data from a class URLConnection.It also builds the appropriate local object based on MIME types.
DatagramSocket	This class represents the Datagram Socket(UDP socket)
DatagramPacket	This class represents the Datagram Packet(UDP packets for containing data)
InetAddress	This class represents the IP address.
InetSocketAddress	The IP socket address is a combination of IP address and port number. To implement such IP socket address this class is used.
ServerSocket	For implementing serverside sockets this class is useful.
Socket	For implementing client side sockets this class is useful.
SocketAddress	This class helps to represent the socket address without specification of protocol.

URL	This class is for creating a reference of Uniform Resource Locator which pointes to WWW.
URI	This class provides the object of Uniform Resource Identifier.
URLConnection	For establishing a communication between application program and URL this class is used.

Exceptions :

Name	Description
UnknownHostException	If the IP address of corresponding Host could not be located then this kind of error is indicated.
MalformedURLException	This exception is for indicating the bad URL.
BindException	If a failure occurs while binding socket to local address or port then this exception must be thrown.
ConnectException	If connection between socket and remote address and port could not get established then this exception must be thrown.
ProtocolException	This exception is for raising error in underlying protocol.
SocketException	This exception is for raising error in socket communication.

1.7 ServerSocket

GTU : Summer-14, Marks 7

The class **ServerSocket** in Java implements server sockets.

The **ServerSocket** class is used to create servers that listen to its clients. When **ServerSocket** is created, it will register itself with the system so that clients can connect to it. This socket after getting registered waits for requests to come in over the network. This class throws exception **IOException**.

The various ways by which **ServerSocket** can be created is as follows -

```
ServerSocket(int port)
ServerSocket(int port, int maxQueue)
ServerSocket(int port, int maxQueue, InetAddress localAddress)
```

Review Question

1. *What is ServerSocket ? How it works in Java ? Explain with the help of example*

GTU : Summer-14, Marks 7

1.8 InetAddress

GTU : Winter-11, 12, Summer-16, Marks 7

- The InetAddress class from **java.net** package represents the IP addresses. It works with either **host name** or **numerical IP address** of corresponding host.
- **InetAddress** class offers many useful methods for handling IP addresses and host names.
- We will now discuss the three important **methods** from InetAddress class and those are
  - getLocalHost
  - getByName
  - getAllByName

Following program illustrates the use of **getLocalHost()** method -

Java Program

```
/*************************************************************************************
This program make use of the method getLocalHost()
method for finding the IP address of local host machine.
*************************************************************************************/
import java.net.*;
class InetAdd1
{
    public static void main(String args[]) throws UnknownHostException
    {
        InetAddress local_add=InetAddress.getLocalHost();
        System.out.println("Local Host is: "+local_add);
    }
}
```

Output

```
D:\test>javac InetAdd1.java

D:\test>java InetAdd1
Local Host is: aap/192.168.0.166
```

Program Explanation :

When you run the above program you get the IP address of the local machine on which you are running your program along with the host name. In above case, *aap* is the name my machine on which I am running this program and 192.168.0.166 is my machine's IP address. Note that while running this program your machine should be in network. If it is not in the networking (i.e. standalone machine) then you will get the output in the following manner

```
D:\test>javac InetAdd1.java
D:\test>java InetAdd1
Local Host is: aap/127.0.0.1
```

Here 127.0.0.1 is a reserved IP address corresponding to the host computer which is also known as loop-back address. 127.0.0.1 is used whenever program needs to access a network running on the local computer itself.

One more important thing about the above Java program and that is definition of main function. It should be

```
public static void main(String args[]) throws UnknownHostException
```

That means, it is a must to throw an exception for Unknown host in order to handle unknown host situation. Hence precisely UnknownHostException should be thrown.

Our programs which makes use of the methods in InetAddress class must have following statement at the beginning -

```
Import java.net.*
```

Remember that it is java.net package only which deals with InetAddress class functionalities. Let us have fun with another java program.

Java Program

```
/*******************************************************************************
This program shows the use of the method getByName
for getting the IP address for the corresponding host name
*******************************************************************************/
import java.net.*;
class InetAdd2
{
 public static void main(String args[]) throws UnknownHostException
 {
  InetAddress addr =InetAddress.getLocalHost();
  System.out.println(addr);
  Address=InetAddress.getByName("vtubooks.com");
  System.out.println(addr);
 }
}
```

Output

```
D:\test>java InetAdd2
aap/192.168.0.166
vtubooks.com/202.137.237.142
```

While running the above program if your computer is not connected to internet then it will generate following output [In fact here is the real use of throwing an exception]

Output

```
D:\test>javac InetAdd2.java

D:\test>java InetAdd2
```

```
aap/127.0.0.1

Exception in thread "main" java.net.UnknownHostException: vtubooks.com
at java.net.Inet4AddressImpl.lookupAllHostAddr(Native Method)
at java.net.InetAddress$1.lookupAllHostAddr(Unknown Source)
at java.net.InetAddress.getAddressFromNameService(Unknown Source)
at java.net.InetAddress.getAllByName0(Unknown Source)
at java.net.InetAddress.getAllByName(Unknown Source)
at java.net.InetAddress.getAllByName(Unknown Source)
at java.net.InetAddress.getByName(Unknown Source)
at InetAdd2.main(InetAdd2.java:8)
```

To avoid such dirty output we can slightly modify the above program as follows -

Java Program

```
/**************************************************************************************
This program shows the use of the method getByName
for getting the IP address for the corresponding host name
**************************************************************************************/
import java.net.*;
class InetAdd2
{
 public static void main(String args[]) throws UnknownHostException
 {
  try
  {
   InetAddress addr=InetAddress.getLocalHost();
   System.out.println(addr);
   Address=InetAddress.getByName("vtubooks.com");
   System.out.println(addr);
  }
  catch(UnknownHostException e)
  {
   System.out.println(e);
  }
 }
}
```

Output

```
D:\test>javac InetAdd2.java

D:\test>java InetAdd2
aap/127.0.0.1
java.net.UnknownHostException: vtubooks.com
```

Now, let us discuss the function **getAllByName()**. This function is used to find the several machines that are associated with single several IP addresses. There are some cases in which single domain name may be associated with several machines. Here is an illustration

Java Program

```
/*****************************************************************************
This program shows the use of the method getAllByName
for getting all the IP addresses related to the same host name
*****************************************************************************/
import java.net.*;
class InetAdd3
{
 public static void main(String args[]) throws UnknownHostException
 {
     InetAddress[]
     addr=InetAddress.getAllByName("www.microsoft.com");
   for(int i=0;i<addr.length;i++)
   System.out.println(addr[i]);
 }
}
```

Output

```
D:\test>javac InetAdd3.java

D:\test>java InetAdd3
www.microsoft.com/207.46.19.254
www.microsoft.com/207.46.192.254
www.microsoft.com/207.46.193.254
www.microsoft.com/207.46.19.190
```

We can obtain the host name from the IP address as well. In the following program the IP address 192.168.0.166 is given as a string to the method getByName. And then using getHostName method we can obtain the host name of corresponding machine.

Java Program

```
/*
This program shows the use of IP address from which
the host name can be obtained

*/
import java.net.*;
class InetAdd4
{
 public static void main(String args[]) throws UnknownHostException
 {
   InetAddress
       addr=InetAddress.getByName("192.168.0.166");
     System.out.println(addr.getHostName());
 }
```

```
}
```

Output

```
D:\test>javac InetAdd4.java

D:\test>java InetAdd4
aap
```

Example 1.8.1 : *Write a java program to find an IP address of the machine on which the program runs.* **GTU : Winter-11, Marks 7**

Solution : The program for finding the IP address of the machine on which following program runs is as follows -

```
import java.util.*;
import java.lang.*;
import java.net.*;
public class GetHostIP
{
 public static void main(String args[])
 {
  try
  {
   InetAddress in=InetAddress.getLocalHost();
   System.out.println("IP of my system is := "+in.getHostAddress());
  }
  catch (Exception e)
  {
   System.out.println("Exception caught ="+e.getMessage());
  }
 }
}
```

Example 1.8.2 : *Write a TCP or UDP client and sever program to do the following :*
Client>java client localhost/IP Port <enter>
Enter text: This is my text to be changed by the SERVER <enter>
Response from server : revres EHT YB DEGNAHC EB OT TXET YM SI SIHt Client>exit **GTU : Winter-12, Summer-16, Marks 7**

Solution : Step 1 : Write a client program as follows

```
/**********************************************************
          Client Program
**********************************************************/
import java.io.*;
import java.net.*;
class C
{
 public static void main(String args[]) throws Exception
 {
```

```
 String Str;
 String Str1;
 String Addr=args[0];
 String[] Hostport=Addr.split("/");     //Handling commandline localhost/port
 int port=Integer.parseInt(Hostport[1]);
 BufferedReader input_user = new BufferedReader(new InputStreamReader(System.in));
 Socket s1=new Socket(Hostport[0],port);
 DataOutputStream out_server=new DataOutputStream(s1.getOutputStream());
 BufferedReader in_server=new BufferedReader(new
InputStreamReader(s1.getInputStream()));
 System.out.println("\n Enter text: ");
 Str=input_user.readLine();
 out_server.writeBytes(Str+"\n");
 Str1=in_server.readLine();
 System.out.println("Response From server:  "+ Str1);
 s1.close();
}
}
```

Step 2 : Write a server program as follows -

```
/*********************************************************
Server Program which sends acknowledgement to the client
*********************************************************/
import java.io.*;
import java.lang.*;
import java.net.*;
class S
{
 public static void main(String args[]) throws Exception
 {
  String str;
  String newstr="";
  String reverse="";
  char ch1, ch2=' ';
  ServerSocket s2=new ServerSocket(1234);
  while(true)
  {
   Socket s3=s2.accept();
   BufferedReader in_client=new BufferedReader(new
      InputStreamReader(s3.getInputStream()));
   DataOutputStream out_client=new  DataOutputStream(s3.getOutputStream());
   str=in_client.readLine();
   for(int i = 0; i<str.length(); i++)
   {
     ch1 = str.charAt(i);
     if(ch1>='A'&&ch1<='Z')
       ch2 = Character.toLowerCase(ch1);
```

```
    if(ch1>='a'&&ch1<='z')
      ch2 = Character.toUpperCase(ch1);
    if(ch1 == ' ')
      ch2 = ' ';
   newstr = newstr+ch2;
  }
  for ( int i = newstr.length() - 1 ; i >= 0 ; i—)
      reverse = reverse + newstr.charAt(i);
   reverse=reverse+'\n';
   out_client.writeBytes(reverse);
  }
 }
}
```

Step 3 :

Output

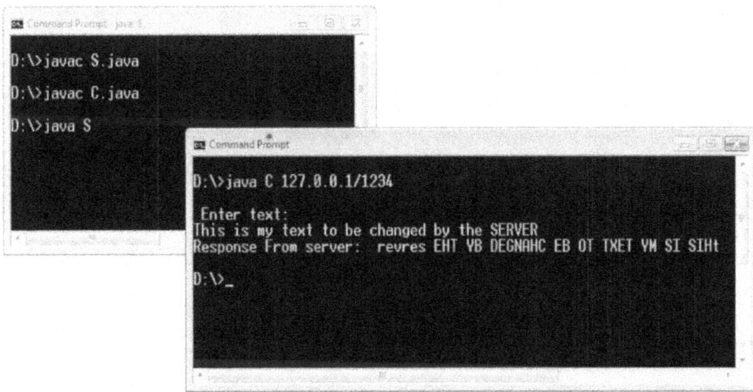

1.8.1 Methods for Types of IP Addresses

Different types of IP addresses can be identified using various methods as follows -

1. isLoopbackAddress()

This method is a Boolean method which returns true if the address given to it is a loop back address (i.e. 127.0.0.1). The following program shows use of this method.

Java Program

```
/*
This program shows the type of IP address

*/
import java.net.*;
class InetAdd5
{
 public static void main(String args[]) throws UnknownHostException
 {
   InetAddress addr=InetAddress.getByName("127.0.0.1");
```

```
   if(addr.isLoopbackAddress())
     System.out.println("Its a Loop back address"+addr);
   else
    System.out.println("Its not a Loop back address" +addr);

 }
}
```

Output

```
D:\test>javac InetAdd5.java

D:\test>java InetAdd5
Its a Loop back address/127.0.0.1
```

2. isAnyLocalAddress()

This is a Boolean method which returns true if the system has a local IP address.

3. isSiteLocalAddress()

This method returns true if the address is IPv6 site local address.

4. isMulticastAddress()

This method returns true if the address is a multicast address otherwise it returns false.

5. isMCGlobal()

This method returns true if the address is a multicast address with global scope, otherwise it returns false.

6. isMCNodeLocal()

This method returns true if the address is a multicast address with node-local scope, otherwise it returns false.

Review Question

1. *Write a TCP or UDP client and server program to do the following :*

   client > java client localhost/IP Port <enter>

   Enter text : Welcome to Gujarat Technological UNIVERSITY <enter>

   Response from server: ytisrevinu LACIGOLONHEt TARAJUg TO EMOCLEw

   client> exit. **GTU : Summer-16, Marks 7**

1.9 URL

GTU : Summer-13, Marks 4

For identifying the documents on the internet the uniform or universal resource locator i.e. URL is used.

There is variety of URL depending upon the type of resources.

1.9.1 URL Formats

- The general format of URL is -

Scheme:Address

That is

protocol://username@hostname/path/filename

- The scheme specifies the **communication protocol**. Different schemes have different schemes have different forms of addresses.
- Various schemes that are used are http, ftp, gopher, file, mailto, news and so on.
- The most commonly used protocol for web browser and web server communication is **Hypertext Transfer Protocol(HTTP).** This protocol is based on request-response mechanism. This protocol handles the documents that are created using e**X**tensible **H**ypertext **M**arkup **L**anguage (XHTML). Using **http** the **Address** part of URL can be written as follows -

//Domain_name/path_to_Document

- **file** is another most commonly used scheme in URL. This protocol allows to reside the document in the client's machine from which the web browser is making out the demand. Due to this the actual document is not available only for its visibility but it can be tested. Using **file** the Address part of URL can be written as follows -

file://path-to-document

- The **hostname** is the name of the server computer that stores the web documents.
- The default port number for the http protocol is 80.
- Any URL does not allow the spaces in it. But there are some special characters that can be present in the URL. These characters are - ampersand & or percentage % .

1.9.2 URL Paths

- The path to the web document is similar to the path to the particular file present in the folder. In this path the directory names and files are separated by the separator characters. The character that is used as a separator is **slash.** Unix system uses forward slash whereas the windows system makes use of backward slash. For example -

http://www.mywebsite.com/mydocs/index.html

- The URL path that includes all the directories along the path to the file is called the **complete path**.
- Sometimes the base URL path is specified in the configuration file of the server. In such a case we need not have to specify the complete path for accessing the particular file such a path is called the **partial path**.

- For example -

```
http://www.mywebsite.com
```

This indicates that the file mydocs/index.html is specified in the configuration file.

1.9.3 URL Class

The Java's URL class has various constructors. These constructors throw the exception **MalformedURLException**.

The syntax to specify the URL constructor is as follows -

```
URL(String URLString);

URL(String protocolName, String hos, int port, String path)

URL(String protocolName, String host, String path)
```

Various methods in URL class that are commonly used in Java programs are –

Method	Description
getProtocol()	This method returns the name of the protocol which is typically used. Generally http is the protocol being used.
getPort()	It returns the port number. For http the port number is 80.
getHost()	This method returns the host name.
getFile()	This method returns the name of the file which we want to access.

Following is a simple Java program which makes use of URL class for obtaining the protocol host name, file name being used in the URL.

Example 1.9.1 : *Write a Java program to obtain the name of the protocol, port number, host name and file name of the URL.*

Solution :

```
import java.net.*;
class MyURLDemo
{
    public static void main(String args[])throws MalformedURLException
    {
        URL obj=new URL("http://technicalpublications.org/index.php/");
        System.out.println("Protocol: " + obj.getProtocol());
        System.out.println("Port: " + obj.getPort());
        System.out.println("Host: " + obj.getHost());
        System.out.println("File: " + obj.getFile());
    }
```

```
}
```

Output

```
Protocol: http
Port: -1
Host: technicalpublications.org
File: /index.php/
```

Program Explanation : We get the protocol name as http, the host name as the name of the website and the corresponding file name. The port value as -1 indicates that it is not set explicitly.

Review Question

1. *Describe the URL class.* **GTU : Summer-13, Marks 4**

1.10 URLConnection

GTU : Winter-13, Marks 7

The class **URLConnection** is used for accessing the attributes of remote resource. These attributes are exposed by the HTTP protocol.

Using the **OpenConnection()** method of **URL** class we can examine the contents. This method is used to establish the connection with some specific web site. Hence to get the contents of the web page we used following statement -

```
URLConnection handle_connection=handle.openConnection();
```

Here **handle_connection** is an object of class **URLConnection**. Thus the **openConnection()** method returns object of **URLConnection**.

Using this object we can further get the access for desired webpage.

Here is a sample java program which accepts the URL of some web site. Then using **openConnection()** method we can get the information about that web page. This information could be current date or content type (such as text/html or image/gif or audio/midi and so on). In the following program we are displaying the contents of the web page on command prompt. Just observe the output of this program carefully.

Example 1.10.1 : *Write a Java Program to display the date, content-type, content length and contents of a web page on command prompt.*

Solution :

```
import java.net.*;

import java.io.*;
import java.util.Date;
class Get_Web_Page
{
 public static void main(String args[ ]) throws Exception
 {
```

```
  int ch;
  URL handle=new URL("http://www.yahoo.com");
  URLConnection handle_connection=handle.openConnection();
  long date_info;
  int length,i;
  date_info =handle_connection.getDate();
  System.out.println("Date: "+new Date(date_info));//Printing the current Date
  System.out.println("Content-Type: "+handle_connection.getContentType());
//printing the content types
   length=handle_connection.getContentLength();
  System.out.println("Content length: "+length);//printing the length of contents

  if(length!=0)
  {
    System.out.println("\n\t*******Contents of web page are*******\n\n");


          InputStream input_string=handle_connection.getInputStream();
    while((ch=input_string.read())!=-1)
    {

      System.out.print((char)ch);  //printing web page contents

     }//end of while
     input_string.close();
   }//end of if
  else
  {
    System.out.println("There are no Contents for this site");
  }
 }//end of main
}//end of class
```

Output

```
Date: Wed Feb 04 11:38:56 IST 2015
Content-Type: text/html
Content length: 1450

     *******Contents of web page are*******

<!DOCTYPE html>
<html lang="en-us"><head>
<meta http-equiv="content-type" content="text/html; charset=UTF-8">
  <meta charset="utf-8">
  <title>Yahoo</title>
....
....
....
```

```
    <img src="https://s.yimg.com/nn/img/yahoo-logo-201402200629.png" alt="Yahoo Logo">
    <h1 style="margin-top:20px;">Will be right back...</h1>
    <p id="message-1">Thank you for your patience.</p>
    <p id="message-2">Our engineers are working quickly to resolve the issue.</p>
    </td>
</tr>
</tbody></table>

</body></html>
```

Program Explanation :

In above program we have used

```
URL handle=new URL("http://www.yahoo.com");
URLConnection handle_connection=handle.openConnection();
```

In order to connect to the web site *"www.yahoo.com"*.

The **handle_connection** is the object variable being used for this purpose. Then using **getDate()** and **getContentType()** methods we can get the current date and content type and this information is displayed on the console.

Then in order to read the contents of the web site we have to create one input stream using InputStream with the help of following code -

```
InputStream input_string = handle_connection.getInputStream();
```

Then using the **read()** function we can read the contents character by character manner in the while loop.

```
ch=input_string.read()
```

The output of this program shows the contents of the web page "www.yahoo.com"

Review Question

1. *Describe the URL and URLConnection class with their use in network programming.*

GTU : Winter-13, Marks 7

Notes

2 JDBC Programming

Syllabus

The JDBC Connectivity Model, Database Programming : Connecting to the Database, Creating a SQL Query, Getting the Results, Updating Database Data, Error Checking and the SQLException Class, The SQLWarning Class, The Statement Interface, PreparedStatement, CallableStatement The ResultSet Interface, Updatable Result Sets, JDBC Types, Executing SQL Queries, ResultSetMetaData, Executing SQL Updates, Transaction Management.

Contents

*2.1 The JDBC Connectivity Model . . . . **Winter-13,** . . . . Marks 7*

2.2 The Java.sql Package

*2.3 Database Programming . . . . **Summer-13,** . . . . Marks 7*

2.4 Creating a SQL Query

2.5 Getting the Results

*2.6 Updating Database Data . . . . **Winter-11,** . . . . Marks 7*

2.7 Error Checking and SQLException Class

2.8 The SQLWarning Class

*2.9 The Statement Interface **Winter-13, 14,***

*. . . . . **Summer-11, 13, 16,** . . . . Marks 7*

2.10 The ResultSet Interface

*2.11 JDBC Types **Winter-11, 13,***

*. . . . . **Summer-12, 14, 16,** . . . . Marks 7*

2.12 Executing SQL Queries

2.13 ResultSetMetaData

2.14 Executing SQL Updates

2.15 Difference between executeQuery(), executeUpdate() and execute()

2.16 Transaction Management

2.1 The JDBC Connectivity Model

GTU : Winter-13, Marks 7

In this section we will discuss *"What is JDBC ?"*, *"How it works ?"* and then we will discuss the architecture of JDBC.

- JDBC stands for **Java DataBase Connectivity**. JDBC is nothing but an API (i.e. Application Programming Interface). It consists of various classes, interfaces, exceptions using which Java application can send SQL statements to a database. The SQL is a Structured Query Language used for accessing the database.
- JDBC is useful for both application developers and JDBC driver vendors.
- The JDBC specification is prepared by Sun Microsystems. Any third party vendor can design their own JDBC drivers using this specification. These JDBC drivers are then used by the application developers for getting connected to the database.
- JDBC is specially used for having connectivity with the RDBMS packages (such as Oracle or MYSQL) using corresponding JDBC driver.

2.1.1 How JDBC Works ?

Following is a way by which JDBC works -

1) First of all Java application establishes connection with the data source.
2) Then Java application invokes classes and interfaces from JDBC driver for sending queries to the data source.
3) The JDBC driver connects to corresponding database and retrieves the result.
4) These results are based on SQL statements which are then returned to Java application.
5) Java application then uses the retrieved information for further processing.

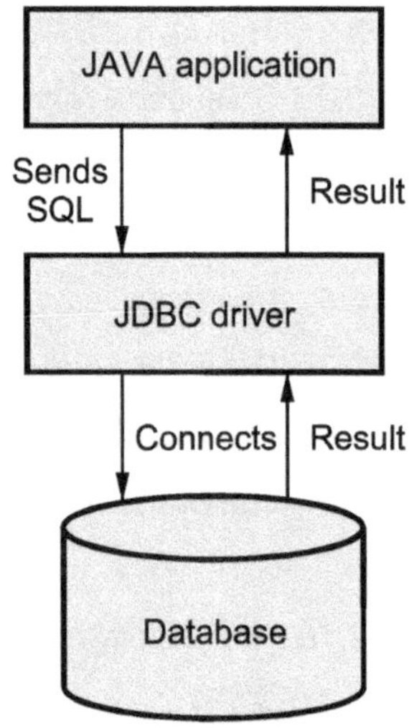

Fig. 2.1.1 Role of JDBC

2.1.2 JDBC Architecture

The JDBC architecture consists of two major components : **JDBC API** and **JDBC driver types**.

The **JDBC API** is a set of classes, interfaces and exceptions used for establishing connection with data source. This JDBC API is defined in the **java.sql** and **javax.sql**packages. We use following core JDBC classes and interfaces that belong to **java.sql** package.

- **DriverManager :** When Java application needs connection to the database it invokes the **DriverManager** class. This class then loads JDBC **drivers** in the memory. The DriverManager also attempts to open a connection with the desired database.
- **Connection :** This is an interface which represents connectivity with the data source. The **connection** is used for creating the **Statement** instance.
- **Statement :** This interface is used for representing the SQL statements. Some examples of SQL statements are
    - SELECT * FROM students_table;
    - UPDATE students_table set name='Neel' where roll_no='1';
    - DELETE from students_table WHERE roll_no='10';

There are two specialised Statement types : **PreparedStatement** and **CallableStatement**. The **PreparedStatement** represents the precompiled SQL statements.

For instance :

```
SELECT * from students_table WHERE name=?
```

The placeholder represented by ? is used in this type of statement. There are special type setter methods that assign the values to the placeholders before the SQL statement is executed.

CallableStatement represents the stored procedures. These are similar to **PreparedStatement.** In this type of Statements we can assign the methods for the types of output arguments.

- **ResultSet -** This interface is used to represent the database result set. After using SELECT SQL statement, the information obtained from the database can be displayed using **ResultSet.**
- **SQLException -** For handling SQL exceptions this interface is used.

Review Question

1. *Explain JDBC architecture.* **GTU : Winter-13, Marks 7**

2.2 The Java.sql Package

1. JDBC helps the client to store and retrieve the data to the databases.
2. JDBC allows the client to update the databases.

Following are the components that are used for establishing the connection with the database using JDBC .

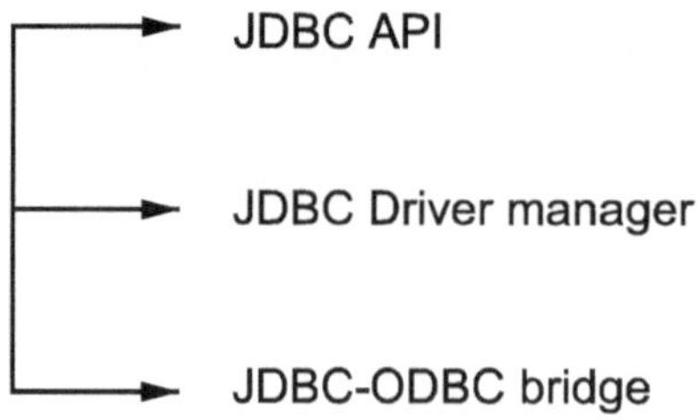

Fig. 2.2.1

The JDBC API classes are supported by the java package **java.sql**. Hence we must import **java.sql.*** in our program.

We have to use following statement for referring the JDBC-ODBC Bridge.

```
Class.forName("sun.jdbc.odbc.JdbcOdbcDriver") ;
```

There is a JDBC **Driver Manager** which connects your java application or servlet to the JDBC driver. We can try to connect our Java program to MS Access database with JDBC-ODBC Bridge using the **DriverManager.getConnection()** method, in which the first parameter is passed as jdbc:odbc:*your_database_name.* The JDBC-ODBC driver helps to translate the JDBC function calls into the ODBC function calls. The JDBC for any database can be implemented only when the ODBC driver is available. Note that JDBC-ODBC bridge is implemented in **sun.jdbc.odbc.**

2.3 Database Programming

GTU : Summer-13, Marks 7

Prerequisite : Before practicing the Programs in this chapter, make sure that following software are installed on your computer.

1. JDK - latest version for executing Java Programs.
2. Eclipse IDE
3. Apache Tomcat Server : It is better to install XAMPP or LAMP software as it contains all the necessary software such as Apache, Tomcat, MySQL, PHP, and PERL. Otherwise, simply Apach Tomcat Webcontainer can also be installed.
4. Microsoft Access
5. MySQL (Also install the mysql-connector in Tomcat's Lib Directory for connectivity between Java and MySQL).

Using Java program with the help of JDBC driver connection one can get connected to the databases. The Java program allows to connect to the database and insert, delete or modify the records in the databases. These databases can be created using MS-ACCESS, MYSQL, ORACLE, SQL Server and so on. Let us understand how to create a database in MS ACCESS and get connected to the database using Java program with the help of JDBC driver.

2.3.1 Connecting to Database

Step 1 : Create the database file in MS-ACCESS

1. Click on the MS Access in program menu, select the "Blank Access database" option and enter the file name : *My_database.mdb*

Step 2 : Create the DSN for your database

1. Open the Control Panel from Start->Settings, and double click on 'Administrative Tools' icon. Then click on the Data sources over there.

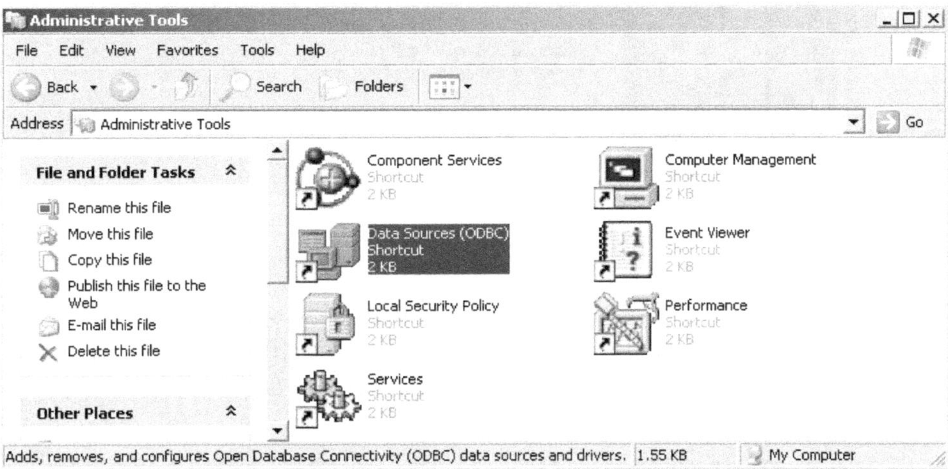

2. Once you double click the Data Sources you will get following window.

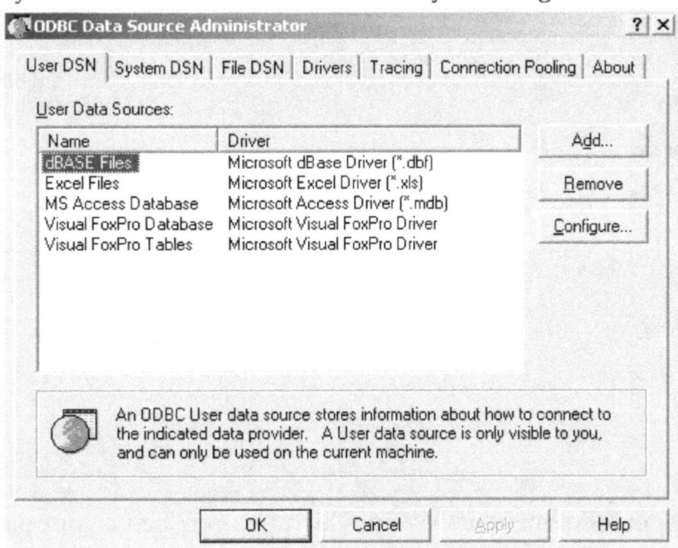

Just click on System DSN tab and click on the Add button. You will get the listing of various drivers as follows.

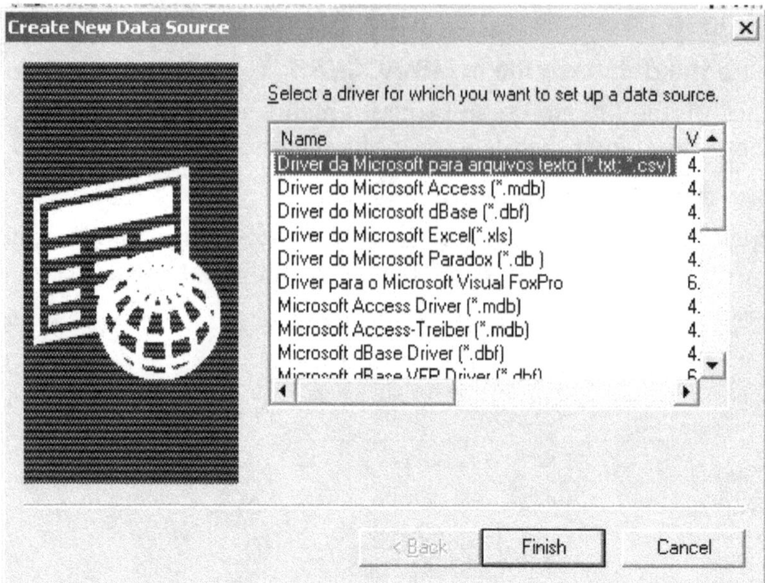

Select the Microsoft Access Driver(*.mdb) and then click on Finish button. You will get following window in which type the Data Source Name (DSN) as My_database. Write some description of your database for Description. Then click on the select button in order to select the database file for corresponding DSN.

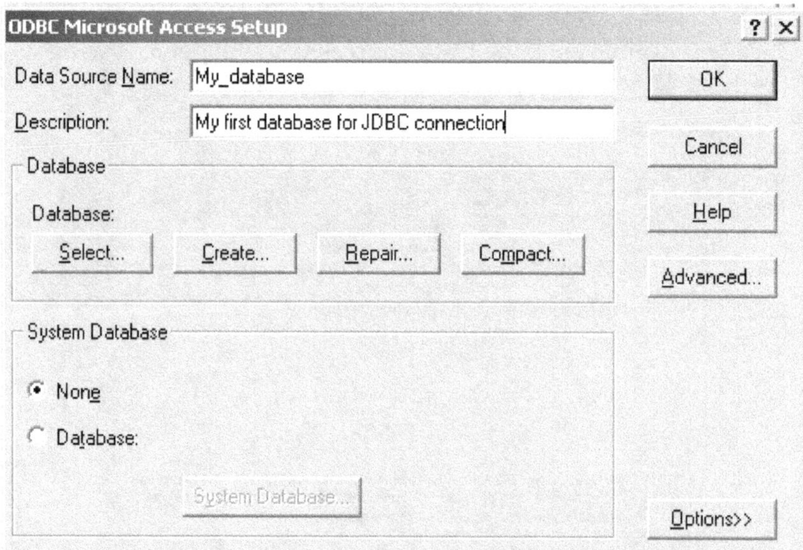

Then you will get following window in which you can locate your database file.

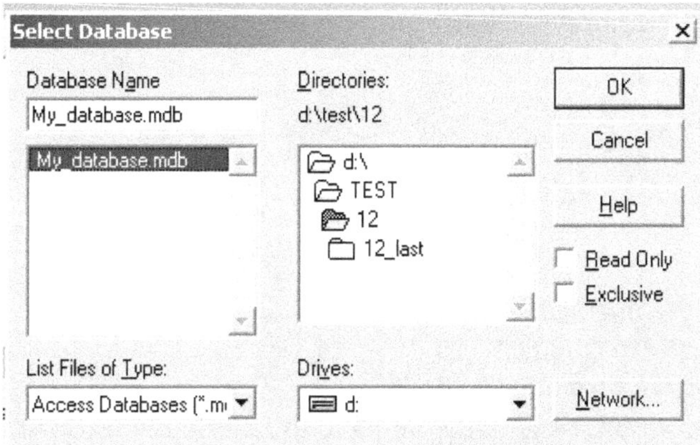

3. Then click on OK button again click OK for two more times. Thus the DSN is created for your database. The connection to this database can be done using the JDBC-ODBC driver with the help of following statement in our Java program

```
DriverManager.getConnection("jdbc:odbc:My_database"," "," ");
```

Now you very well recognise that the first parameter is the DSN. The second and third parameter specifies the user name and password. Right now we have kept it blank for our database. Let us now write simple Java program which simply connects to your database.

Java Program

```
import java.sql.*;
public class JDBCDemo
{
 public static void main(String [ ] args)
 {
   Connection con = null;
   try
   {
    Class.forName("sun.jdbc.odbc.JdbcOdbcDriver") ;
     con = DriverManager.getConnection("jdbc:odbc:My_database"," "," ");
    System.out.println("Connection Successful!");
    con.close();
   }
   catch (ClassNotFoundException e)
   {
    System.err.println("Exception: "+e.getMessage());
   }
   catch (SQLException e)
   {
```

This Java code is used to connect to database created in MS Access

```
    System.err.println("Exception: "+e.getMessage());
   }

  }
}
```

Output

```
C:\test>javac JDBCDemo.java
C:\test>java JDBCDemo
Connection Successful!
```

In the above program, essentially we have to handle two major Exceptions namely : **ClassNotFoundException** and **SQLException** with the help of try-catch block.

Example 2.3.1 : *Explain the JDBC URL with appropriate examples.*

GTU : Summer-13, Marks 7

Solution : JDBC URL with examples : The databases are referenced by Java runtime engine using JDBC URL. The syntax of these URLs depends on the database driver you are using.

The list of common drivers along with JDBC URL is

1. ODBC Driver

Syntax :

```
jdbc:odbc:<data source name>
```

Example :

```
jdbc:odbc:MyDataSource
```

2. MYSQL

Syntax :

```
jdbc:mysql://[host][:port]/[database]
```

Example :

```
jdbc:mysql://localhost:3306/Mydatabase
```

3. ORACLE

Syntax :

```
jdbc:oracle:<drivertype>:<user>/<password>@<database>
```

Example :

```
jdbc:oracle:thin:myuser/mypassword@localhost:mydatabse
```

2.4 Creating a SQL Query

The database can be created using SQL query as follows -

CREATE DATABASE *databasename;*

For example we can create a database named My_database as follows -

CREATE DATABASE My_database;

After creating the database, a table can be created within it. The query used for creating a table is

```
CREATE TABLE table_name
(
column_name1 data_type(size),
column_name2 data_type(size),
column_name3 data_type(size),
....
);
```

The *column_name* specifies the name of the columns of the table, *data_type* specifies the type of data the column field has. The *size* field specifies the *size* of the column in the table.

For example

```
CREATE TABLE My_table
(
Roll INT,
StudNameVARCHAR(20)
);
```

With the help of Java we can execute the query using following statement

```
Statement stat = con.createStatement();
ResultSetrs = stat.executeQuery("CREATE TABLE MY_table(Roll INT,StudName
VARCHAR(20))");
```

Here is a simple Java program that illustrates how to create a table using SQL statement

Java Program

```
import java.sql.*;
public class JDBCDemo1
{
 public static void main(String [ ] args)
 {
   Connection con = null;
   try
   {
    Class.forName("sun.jdbc.odbc.JdbcOdbcDriver") ;
    con = DriverManager.getConnection("jdbc:odbc:My_database"," "," ");
```

```
    System.out.println("Connection Successful!");
    Statement stat=con.createStatement();
     int result=stat.executeUpdate("CREATE TABLE My_table(Roll INT,StudName
     VARCHAR(20))");
    System.out.println("Table Created");
   stat.close();
    con.close();
  }
  catch (ClassNotFoundException e)
  {
    System.err.println("Exception: "+e.getMessage());
  }
  catch (SQLException e)
  {
    System.err.println("Exception: "+e.getMessage());
  }

 }
}
```

Program Explanation :

In the above program, as usual we are first establishing the connection with the database and then using following statements particular SQL statement can be executed.

```
Statement stat=con.createStatement();
    int result=stat.executeUpdate("CREATE TABLE My_table(Roll
                                  INT,StudName VARCHAR(20))");
```

First of all the object *stat* of **Statement** is created and then the **executeUpdate()** method of that object is written in which the complete SQL query is passed. Thus we can create the table in our database.

Output

```
c:\test>javac JDBCDemo1.java
c:\test>java JDBCDemo1
Connection Successful!
Table Created
```

2.5 Getting the Results

Using the **select** statement we can get the result from the database the result is obtained in the instance of **ResultSet.** The **executeQuery** function returns the ResultSet Object. The syntax of executeQuery is

```
ResultSet executeQuery(Strin SQL);
```

The **ResultSet** is basically an interface which provides access to the table of data generated by executing a statement. The table rows are retrieved in sequence using the name of the column field.

Following Java code is used for getting the result and displaying them

Prerequisite - i) Database is created ii) The table is stored in this database iii) Some record is inserted in the table.

JDBCDemo3.java

```
import java.sql.*;
public class JDBCDemo3 {
    public static void main(String [ ] args) {
        Connection con = null;
        try {
            Class.forName("sun.jdbc.odbc.JdbcOdbcDriver") ;
            con = DriverManager.getConnection("jdbc:odbc:My_database"," "," ");
            Statement stat=con.createStatement();
            String sql="SELECT * FROM My_table";
            ResultSet rs=stat.executeQuery(sql);

            System.out.println("Displaying the contents of the table...");
            while(rs.next())
            {
                int RollNo  = rs.getInt("Roll");
                String Name = rs.getString("StudName");
            //Display values
                System.out.print("Roll Number: " + RollNo);
                System.out.print(", Student Name: " + Name);
            }
            rs.close();
            stat.close();
            con.close();
        }
        catch (ClassNotFoundException e) {
            System.err.println("Exception: "+e.getMessage());
        }
        catch (SQLException e) {
            System.err.println("Exception: "+e.getMessage());
        }
    }
}
```

Output

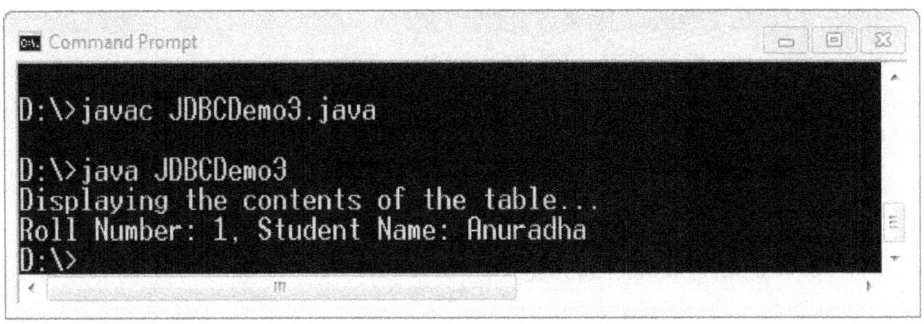

2.6 Updating Database Data

GTU : Winter-11, Marks 7

For updating data in the database the UPDATE query must be exeuted. The syntax of UPDATE command is

```
UPDATE table_name
SET column1 = value1, column2 = value2...., columnN = valueN
WHERE [condition];
```

The **condition** can be combined using AND and OR operators.

The steps to update the data in the database are as follows -

Step 1 : Create the instance for **Connection** class using **DriverManager's getConnection** method.

Step 2 : Then invoke the createStatement method in order to create the object for **Statement** class.

Step 3 : With the help of Statement class object the method **executeUpdate** will be invoked. The SQL query for UPDATE record can be passed as a parameter to **executeUpdate** method. The general syntax for executeUpdate is

```
public int executeUpdate(java.lang.String sql)
```

The **sql** represents the Query string using INSERT, DELETE or UPDATE.

The return value is integer which indicates number of rows affected.

Following is a Java program that updates the record stored in the table of a database.

JDBCDemo4.java

```
import java.sql.*;
public class JDBCDemo4 {
    public static void main(String [ ] args) {
        Connection con = null;
        try {
            Class.forName("sun.jdbc.odbc.JdbcOdbcDriver") ;
            con = DriverManager.getConnection("jdbc:odbc:My_database"," "," ");
            Statement stat=con.createStatement();

            String sql="UPDATE My_table " + "SET StudName='Anand' WHERE Roll=1";
            stat.executeUpdate(sql);

            sql="SELECT * FROM My_table";
            ResultSet rs=stat.executeQuery(sql);

            System.out.println("Displaying the contents of the table...");
            while(rs.next())
            {
                int RollNo = rs.getInt("Roll");
                String Name = rs.getString("StudName");
```

```
                //Display values
                    System.out.print("Roll Number: " + RollNo);
                    System.out.print(", Student Name: " + Name);
                }
                rs.close();
                stat.close();
                con.close();
            }
            catch (ClassNotFoundException e) {
                System.err.println("Exception: "+e.getMessage());
            }
            catch (SQLException e) {
                System.err.println("Exception: "+e.getMessage());
            }
        }
}
```

Output

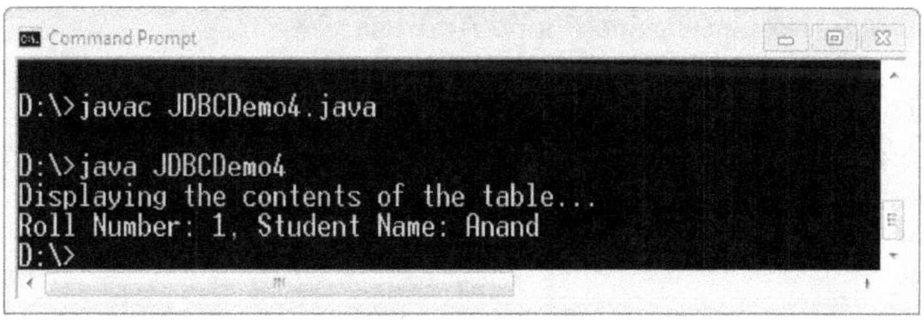

Example 2.6.1 : *Consider bank table with attributes AccountNo, CustomerName, Balance, Phone and Address. Write a database application which allows insertion, updation and deletion of records in Bank table. Print values of all customers whose balance is greater than 20,000.* **GTU : Winter-11, Marks 7**

Solution : Step 1 : Create a database in Microsoft Access. The name of the database is **bankdb** and the name of the table created is **banktable**.

The database will be

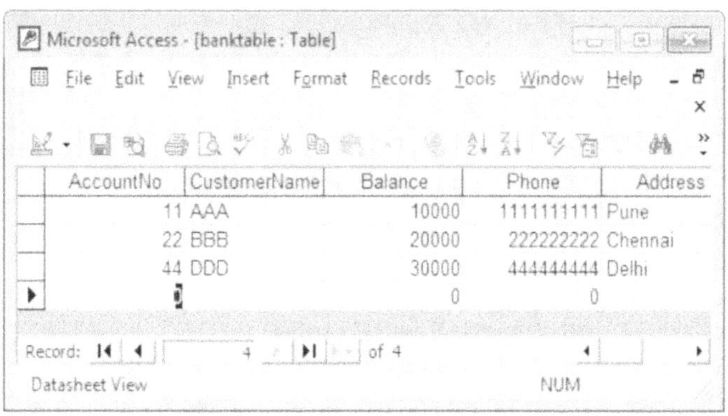

Step 2 : The java program for handling this database for given operations can be written as follows. Here we have taken the file name as **test.java**

```
import java.sql.*;
public class test
{
    public static void main(String [ ] args)
  {
      Connection con = null;
      int result;
      ResultSet rs = null;
      Statement stat=null;
  try
    {
          Class.forName("sun.jdbc.odbc.JdbcOdbcDriver");
          con = DriverManager.getConnection("jdbc:odbc:bankdb", " ", " ");
          stat = con.createStatement();
          result = stat.executeUpdate("INSERT INTO banktable" +
"(AccountNo,CustomerName,Balance,Phone,Address)" +
"VALUES(55,'EEE',40000,555555555,'Pune')");
          System.out.println("Values inserted in table!");
          result = stat.executeUpdate("DELETE FROM banktable WHERE AccountNo=33");
          System.out.println("Values deleted from table!");
          result = stat.executeUpdate("UPDATE banktable set AccountNo=100 WHERE
AccountNo=11");
          System.out.println("Values updated from table and updated record is as
follows....");
          rs = stat.executeQuery("SELECT * FROM banktable WHERE AccountNo=100");

          while (rs.next())
          {
                System.out.println("AccountNo: " + rs.getObject(1).toString());
                System.out.println("CustomerName: " + rs.getObject(2).toString());
                System.out.println("Balance: " + rs.getObject(3).toString());
                System.out.println("Phone: " + rs.getObject(4).toString());
                System.out.println("Address: " + rs.getObject(5).toString());
          }
          rs = null;
          System.out.println("Following records having salary>20000...");
          rs = stat.executeQuery("SELECT * FROM banktable WHERE Balance>20000");
          System.out.println("AccountNo   Name    Balance");
          while (rs.next())
          {
                if (rs != null)
                System.out.println(rs.getObject(1).toString() + "        " +
rs.getObject(2).toString() + "        " + rs.getObject(3).toString());
          }
```

```
    }
    catch (ClassNotFoundException e)
    {
        System.err.println("Exception: " + e.getMessage());
    }
    catch (SQLException e)
    {
        System.err.println("Exception: " + e.getMessage());
    }
    finally
    {
        try
        {
            if(rs!=null)
            {
                rs.close();
                rs=null;
            }
            if(stat!=null)
            {
                stat.close();
                stat=null;
            }
            if (con != null)
            {
                con.close();
                con = null;
            }

        }catch (SQLException e) { }
    }
}
}
```

2.7 Error Checking and SQLException Class

Error checking and exception handling is an important activity that needs to be handled while establishing the successful connection with the backend database.

When exception condition occurs, then an exception is thrown. The control is then redirected to the matching catch block. The code that is error-pro is placed within the try block.

The most useful class that deal with exception handling mechanism is **SQLException**.

Constructors

The constructor for SQLException class can be written as follows -

Constructor	Description
SQLException()	Create an object for SQLException with Null value.
SQLException(String cause)	Create an object for SQLException with the cause provided by the parameter.
SQLException(String cause, String SQLState)	Create an object for SQLException with the cause and SQLState provided by the parameter.

Methods

Various methods of this class that are commonly used are

Method	Description
getErrorCode( )	Gets the error number associated with the exception.
getMessage( )	Gets the JDBC driver's error message for an error.
getNextException( )	Gets the next Exception object in the exception chain.
printStackTrace( )	Prints the current exception, or backtrace to a standard error stream.
printStackTrace(PrintStream s)	Backtrace to the print stream.
printStackTrace(PrintWriter w)	Backtrace to the print writer.

The general format of throwing this exception is

```
try {
  // Your error-causing code
}
catch(Exception ex) {
  // Your exception handling code goes here
}
finally {
  // Your must-always-be-executed code goes between these
  // curly braces. Like closing database connection.
}
```

For example

```
try {
        Class.forName("sun.jdbc.odbc.JdbcOdbcDriver") ;
        con = DriverManager.getConnection("jdbc:odbc:My_database"," "," ");
        Statement stat=con.createStatement();
        String sql="SELECT * FROM My_table";
        ResultSet rs=stat.executeQuery(sql);
        Con = DriverManger.getConnection("jdbc:odbc:My_database","","");
        Statement stat=con.createStatement();
        String sql="SELECT * FROM My_table";
        ResultSet rs=stat.executeQuery(sql);
```

```
        System.out.println("Displaying the contents of the table...");
        ...
        ...
        }
        rs.close();
        stat.close();
        con.close();
    }
    catch (SQLException e) {
        System.err.println("Exception: "+e.getMessage());
    }
```

2.8 The SQLWarning Class

The **SQLWarning** class provides information on a database access warnings. Instead of having to catch this exception, we can use appropriate methods on **java.sql.Connection**

Constructor

Constructor	Description
SQLWarning()	Create an object for SQLWarning with Null value.
SQLWarning (String cause)	Create an object for SQLWarning with the cause provided by the parameter.
SQLWarning (String cause,String SQLState)	Create an object for SQLWarning with the cause and SQLState provided by the parameter.

Methods

Method	Description
SQLException getNextWarning()	Obtains the next warning in the chain if there is another exception.
String setNextWarning(SQLWarning w)	Sets the next warning in the chain of warnings attached to the current object.

2.9 The Statement Interface

GTU : Summer-13, 16, Winter-11, 13, 14, Marks 7

A Statement object is used for executing a static SQL statement and obtaining the results produced by it.

The Statement interface can not accept parameters.

Creation of Statement Object

The statement object can be created using the **createStatement()** method. Following is a illustrative Java code

```
try {
        Class.forName("sun.jdbc.odbc.JdbcOdbcDriver") ;
```

```
        con = DriverManager.getConnection("jdbc:odbc:My_database"," "," ");
        Statement stat=con.createStatement();
        ...
}
catch(SQLException ex) {
...
}
```

After creating the statement object one of the following three methods can be invoked.

1. **execute :** It Returns true if a **ResultSet** object can be retrieved; otherwise, it returns false. Use this method to execute SQL DDL statement. The general syntax is

```
bool execute(String SQL)
```

2. **executeUpdate :** It returns the number of rows affected by the execution of the SQL statement. Use this method to execute SQL statements using the INSERT, UPDATE or DELETE statement. The general syntax is

```
int executeUpdate(String SQL)
```

3. **executeQuery :** It returns a **ResultSet** object. Use this method when you expect to get a result set. Normally this statement is used with a SELECT statement. The general syntax is

```
ResultSet executeQuery(String SQL)
```

Closing Statement Object

Using a call to **close** method the Statement object can be closed. For instance

```
Stat.close();
```

There are two types of statements

1. Prepared statement 2. Callable statement

Let us discuss them in detail.

2.9.1 Prepared Statement

- The **java.sql.PreparedStatement** interface object represents a precompiled SQL statement.
- This interface is used to efficiently execute SQL statements multiple times. That is when we want to insert a record in a table by putting different values at runtime.
- This statement is derived from the Statement class.
- The PreparedStatement interface can be created by calling PrepareStatement() method.
- The prepareStatement() is available in **java.sql.Connection** interface.
- The prepareStatement() method takes SQL statement in java format.

```
prepareStatement("insert into student values(?,?)").
```

where each ? represents the column index number in the table. If table **student** has **rollnumber** and **name** columns, then 1st ? refers to **rollnumber**, 2nd ? refers to **name**.

- After that we need to set the value to each ? by using the setter method from PreparedStatement interface as follows :

```
setXXX(ColumnIndex,value)
```

- Various setter methods are

SQL datatype	Method used
char/varchar/varchar2	setString()
int/number	setInt()
float/number	setFloat()
double/Float	setDouble()
long/int	setLong()
int/short	setShort()
time	setTime()
datetime/date	setDate()

Following is a Java Program that makes use of Prepared Statement for inserting data in the table.

JDBCDemo5.java

```
import java.sql.*;
public class JDBCDemo5
{
 public static void main(String [ ] args)
 {
   Connection con = null;
   try
   {
      int rollnum=2;
      String name="Parth";
      Class.forName("sun.jdbc.odbc.JdbcOdbcDriver") ;
      con = DriverManager.getConnection("jdbc:odbc:My_database"," "," ");
      PreparedStatement ps=con.prepareStatement("INSERT INTO My_table VALUES(?,?)");
      ps.setInt(1,rollnum);
      ps.setString(2,name);
      int result=ps.executeUpdate();
      if(result!=0)
            System.out.println("Values inserted in the table");
      else
            System.out.println("Values are not inserted in the table");
      String sql="SELECT * FROM My_table";
      ps=con.prepareStatement(sql);
      ResultSet rs=ps.executeQuery();
      System.out.println("Displaying the contents of the table...");
      while(rs.next())
      {
```

```
            int RollNo  = rs.getInt("Roll");
            String Name = rs.getString("StudName");
           //Display values
           System.out.print("Roll Number: " + RollNo);
           System.out.println(", Student Name: " + Name);
      }
      rs.close();
      ps.close();
      con.close();
   }
   catch (ClassNotFoundException e)
   {
    System.err.println("Exception: "+e.getMessage());
   }
   catch (SQLException e)
   {
    System.err.println("Exception: "+e.getMessage());
   }

 }
}
```

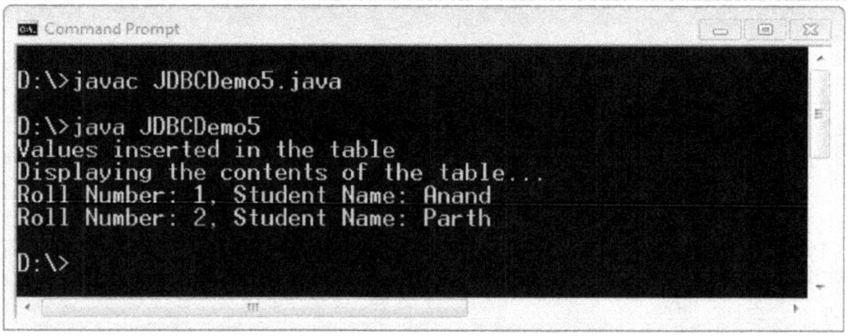

2.9.2 Callable Statement

The callable statement is used when we want to access the **database stored procedures**. The stored procedure is basically a block of code which is identified by unique name. Let us first understand how to create procedure

Creating Procedure

The procedure can be created using following syntax.

```
DELIMITER //
CREATE PROCEDURE procedureName(paramters_list)
BEGIN
SQL Statements to be executed
END //
```

Calling Procedure

When calling the stored procedure, the **CallableStatement** object is used. For this object three types of parameters are used.

Parameter	Description
IN	A parameter whose value is unknown when the SQL statement is created. Then the values can be associated with IN parameters with the setXXX() methods.
OUT	A parameter whose value is supplied by the SQL statement it returns. These values are obtained in OUT parameters with the getXXX() methods.
INOUT	A parameter that supplies input as well as accepts output parameter requires a call to the appropriate setXXX method

You can create an instance of a **CallableStatement** by calling the **prepareCall()** method on a connection object. Here is an example :
CallableStatement callableStatement = connection.prepareCall("{call myprocedure(?, ?)}");

Setting the values to Parameters

We can set the values to the paramters using setXX method. For example :

```
connection.prepareCall("{call myprocdeures(?, ?)}");

callableStatement.setInt(1, 10);
callableStatement.setString  (2, "AAA");
```

Executing the CallableStatement

Once you have set the parameter values you need to set, you are ready to execute the CallableStatement. Here is how that is done :

```
    ResultSet result = callableStatement.executeQuery();
```

Then using the instance of **ResultSet** we can display the result.

Following is a simple Java application program (illustrated in stepwise manner)that makes use of callable statement.

Step 1 : Create a database in MySQL with the table. Insert some values inside the table. The contents of the table are represented by following Screenshot

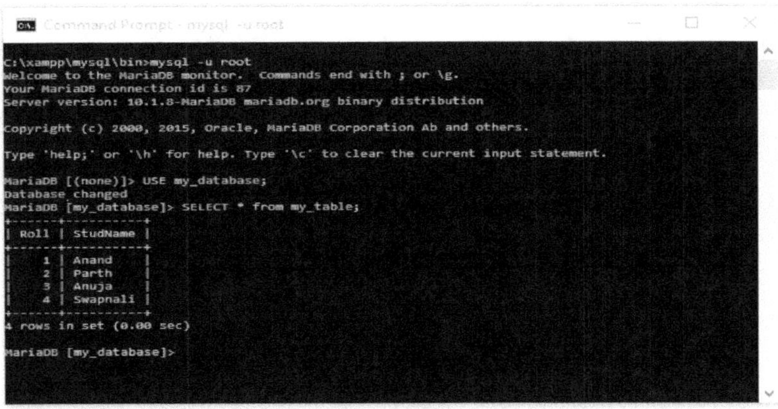

Step 2 : Then Create a procedure as follows -

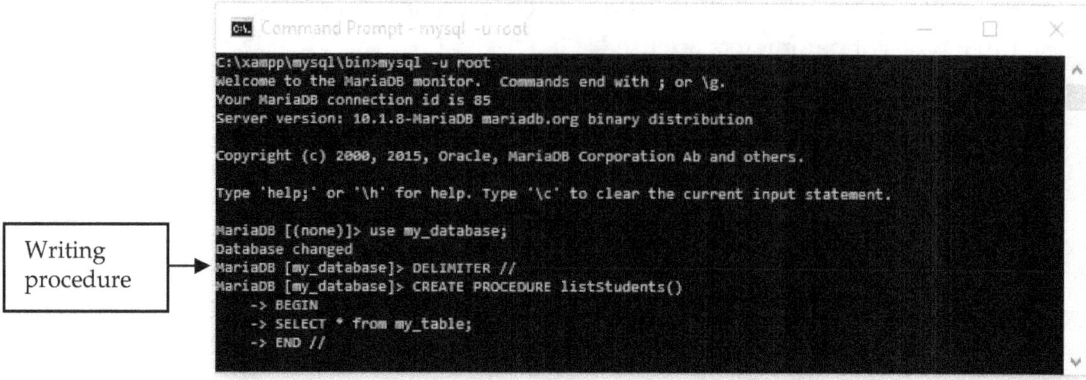

Step 3 : Before you start writing the application make sure that the driver for MySQL is present in the /tomcat/lib directory. It should be **mysql-connector-java-5.xx.xx-bin.jar** file.

If it is not present then it can be downloaded from the site

https://dev.mysql.com/downloads/connector/j/3.1html

Go for **Platform independent option** and select Zip or Tar file option depending upon your need.

I have executed this Java program in Eclipse. To create and run this Java program in Eclipse, I have followed following steps -

Step i : File -> New->Dynamic Web Project.

Step ii : Then I have given the Project Name as **CallableStmt**. Then Click Next-> Next and Finally click **Finish.**

Step iii : In the Project Explorer Window just Click on Java Resourcs. Select the **New → Class** option so that new Java Class template can be created. Name this class. I have given the name *JDBCDemo6.*

For the sake of understanding just refer following Screenshot

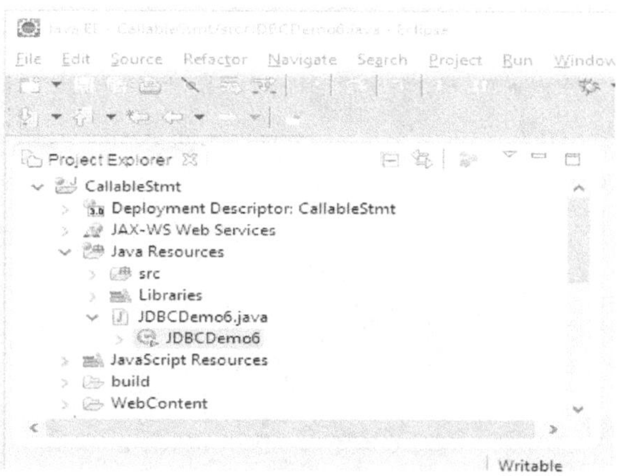

The Java code that makes use of Callable Statement for invoking the created procedure is as given below

JDBCDemo6.java

```
import java.sql.CallableStatement;
import java.sql.Connection;
import java.sql.DriverManager;
import java.sql.ResultSet;
import java.sql.SQLException;
public class JDBCDemo6 {
    public static void main(String[] args)
    {
        Connection con=null;
        try
        {
//Getting the driver for MyQL
            Class.forName("com.mysql.jdbc.Driver");
            con =
DriverManager.getConnection("jdbc:mysql://localhost/my_database","root","");
//Creating instance of CallableStatement using prepare call
//The procedure listStudents() created in Step 2 is invoked here
            CallableStatement cs=con.prepareCall("CALL listStudents()");
            ResultSet rs=cs.executeQuery();
            while(rs.next()){
                System.out.println(rs.getInt(1)+"\t"+rs.getString(2));
            }
        }catch(Exception e){
            e.printStackTrace();
        }
        finally {
            try {
                con.close();
            }catch(SQLException e){
                e.printStackTrace();
            }
        }
    }

}
```

Step 4 : Now it's the time to display the output.Just right click on JDBCDemo6.java and Click **Run As** option. Select "Java Application". The output will be displayed in the **Console** Window as listing of all the students information present in my_table of the database.

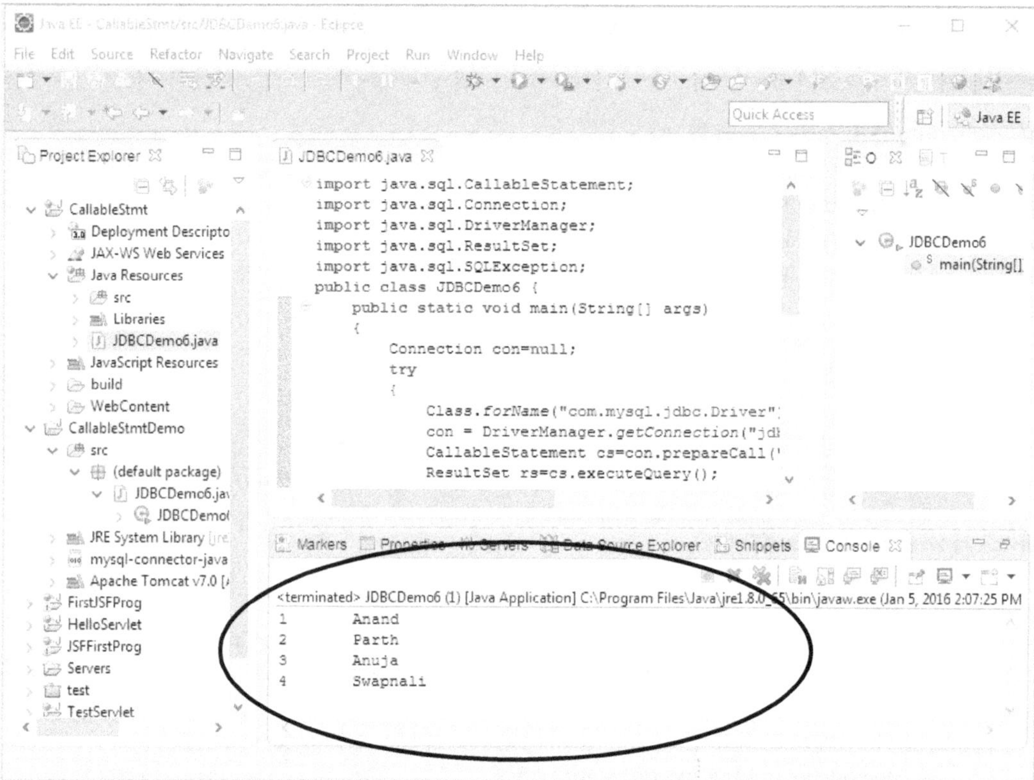

Review Questions

1. *Explain the use of callable statement and PreparedStatement with example.*

   GTU : Winter-11, Marks 7

2. *Explain the use of prepared statement object of the JDBC with an appropriate example.*

   GTU : Summer-13, Marks 7

3. *What is callable statement ? Show that how to use it to call a stored procedure running at database layer.* **GTU : Winter-13, Marks 7**

4. *Give the use of statement, prepared statement and callablestatement object and write the code to insert three records in student table using prepared statement.*

   GTU : Winter-14, Marks 7

5. *Show the use of PreparedStatement object to run precomplied SQL statement. Also write example of java snippet for Prepared Statement.* **GTU : Summer-16, Marks 7**

2.10 The ResultSet Interface

- The ResultSet interface is an important interface which is used to access the database table with general width and unknown length.

- The table rows are retrieved in sequence using **ResultSet** object. Within a row its column values can be accessed in any order.
- A ResultSet maintains a cursor pointing to its current row of data. Initially the cursor is positioned before the first row. The 'next' method moves the cursor to the next row.
- The ResultSet object can be created using **executeQuery()** method. For example

```
Statement statement = connection.createStatement();
ResultSet result = statement.executeQuery("select * from my_table");
```

2.10.1 Navigating Methods

Various commonly used navigating methods for ResultSet are as given in the following table.

Sr. No.	Methods	Description
1.	**public boolean first() throws SQLException**	Moves the cursor to the first row.
2.	**public void last() throws SQLException**	Moves the cursor to the last row.
3.	**public boolean previous() throws SQLException**	Moves the cursor to the previous row. This method returns false if the previous row is off the result set.
4.	**public boolean next() throws SQLException**	Moves the cursor to the next row. This method returns false if there are no more rows in the result set.
5.	**public int getRow() throws SQLException**	Returns the row number that the cursor is pointing to.

2.10.2 Reading the Result using ResultSet

There are various methods using which the data can be retrieved using the ResultSet object. These methods can be used with either column Name or with column Index. Few commonly used methods are

Sr. No.	Methods	Description
1.	public int getInt(int index)	Returns the integer value in the current row specified by the index.
2.	public int getInt(String Name)	Returns the integer value in the current row specified by the column Name.
3.	public Date getDate(int index)	Returns the Date value in the current row specified by index.
4.	Public Date getDate(String Name)	Returns the Date value in the current row specified by Name of the column.

Similar to **getInt** there are methods such as **getString, getBoolean, getByte, getFloat, getDouble** and so on.

2.10.3 Updating ResultSets

There are various methods for updating the ResuletSets denoted by **updateXXX().** Just similar to **getXX** method the update method makes use of Column Index and Column Name. These are as given below -

Sr. No.	Methods	Description
1.	Public void updateString(int *index*, String *new_val*)	Updates the string by *new_val* which is specified by *index* .
2.	Public void updateString(int *Name*, String *new_val*)	Updates the string by *new_val* which is specified by *Name* of the column.

The row values can be updated using the methods as given below

Sr. No.	Methods	Description
1.	public void updateRow()	Updates current row from database.
2.	public void deleteRow()	Deletes the current row from database.
3.	Public void insertRow()	Inserts the row in the database.

2.11 JDBC Types

GTU : Winter-11, 13, Summer-12, 14, 16, Marks 7

There are four types of JDBC drivers and those are -

1. **Type 1 :** JDBC-ODBCBridge
2. **Type 2 :** Native-API/Partly Java Driver
3. **Type 3 :** All JAVA/ Net Protocol driver for accessing middleware server.
4. **Type 4 :** All JAVA/ Native-Protocol Pure driver

Let us discuss them in detail -

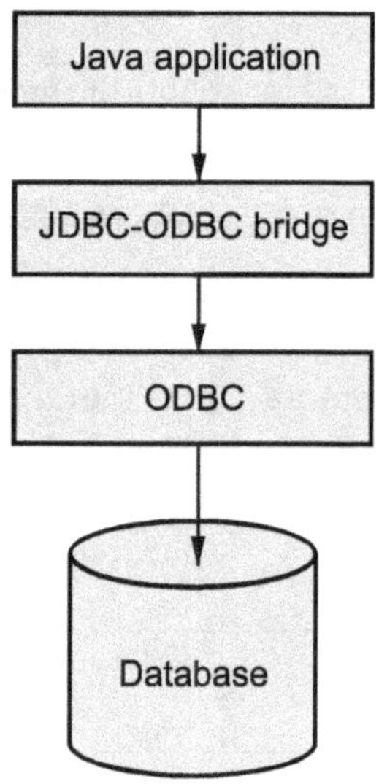

Fig. 2.11.1 JDBC-ODBC bridge

Type 1 : JDBC-ODBCBridge

This driver translates all the JDBC calls into ODBC(Open Database Connectivity) calls and send them to ODBC driver. Thus JDBC access is via ODBC driver. The ODBC is a generic API. In this scenario the client database code must be present on the client machine.

Merit

Using the JDBC-ODBC bridge access to any database is possible.

Demerits

1. This is slowest driver because the calls are sent to ODBC driver and then to the native database connectivity interface.
2. This type of driver is not suitable for large scale applications.
3. For using this type of driver the native database must be present on the client machine and the ODBC driver must be installed on the client's machine.

Type 2 : Native-API/Partly Java Driver

This driver translates all the JDBC calls into database-specific calls. This driver works specifically for particular database. For example MYSQL will have native MYSQL API. This type of driver directly communicates with the database server. Hence some binary code must be present on the client machine.

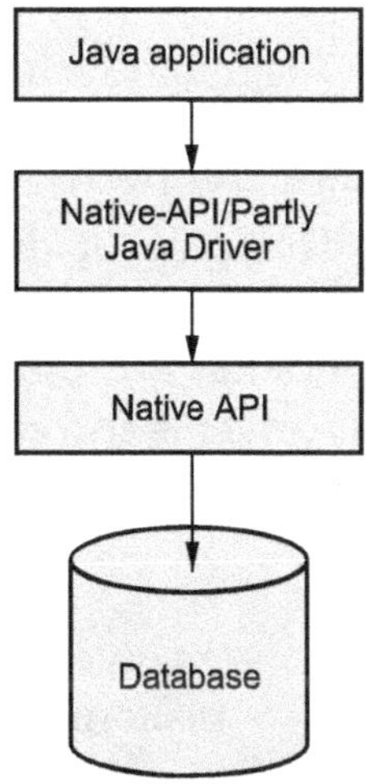

Fig. 2.11.2 Type - 2 driver

Merit

It gives better performance as comparison with type -1 driver because the JDBC call is directly converted to database specific call.

Demerits

1. The library of required databases must be loaded on the client machine.
2. This type of driver is not useful for the internet.
3. If some modifications in made in the database then the native API must also be modified because it is specific to a database.

Type 3 : All JAVA/ Net Protocol driver for accessing middleware server

In this type of driver all the JDBC calls are passed through the network to the middle-ware server. The middleware server then translates the request to the database-specific native-connectivity interface and then the request is sent to the database server.

This driver is a server-based driver. This is also known as a pure Java driver.

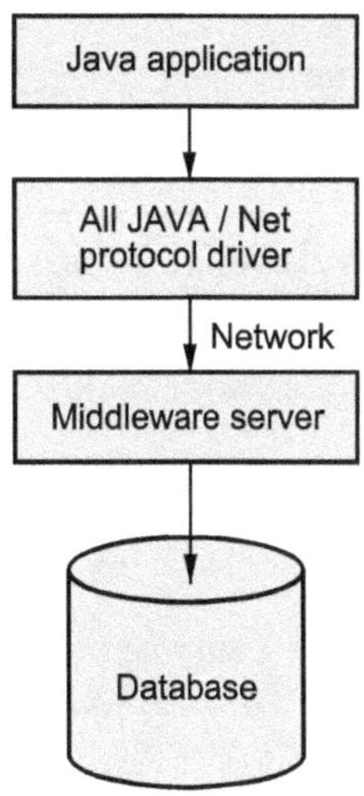

Fig. 2.11.3 Type - 3 driver

Merits

1. As it is server-based driver there is no need keep library of required databases on the client machine.
2. This driver is fully written in JAVA(hence is the name all Java) and hence it is portable and can be used on internet.
3. The performance of this driver can be optimized.

4. This driver supports many advanced features such as load balancing, caching and logging.
5. For this driver it is possible to access multiple databases using one driver.

Demerits

The middleware server application needs to be installed and maintained.

The record set has to traverse through the backend server.

Type 4 : All JAVA / Native-Protocol Pure driver

This type of driver converts the JDBC calls to network protocol used by the database directory so that the client application can directly communicate to the database server. This driver is also completely implemented in Java and hence it is referred as Pure Java driver.

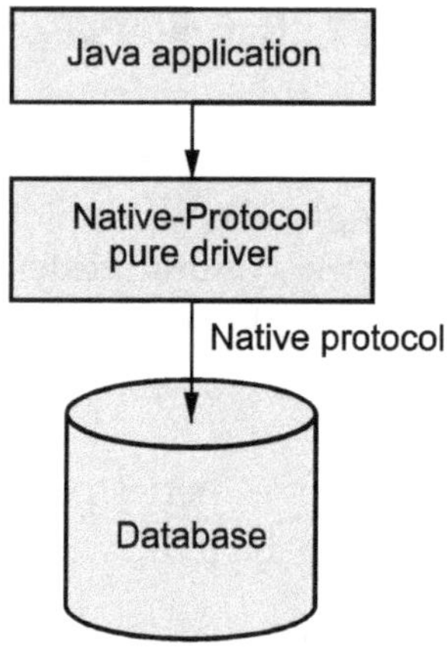

Fig. 2.11.4 Type - 4 driver

Merits

1. As this driver is completely written in Java, it is platform independent and can be used on Internet.
2. There is no translation layer in between such as to ODBC or to native API. Neither there is a need to send the call to middle ware server. Hence the performance of this type of driver is typically good.
3. There is no need to install specific software on the client machine.
4. These drivers can be downloaded dynamically.

Demerit

When the type 4 driver is used then for each database a specific driver is needed.

Review Questions

1. *Explain various types of JDBC drivers and comment on selection of driver.*

   GTU : Winter-11, Summer-14, Marks 7

2. *What is JDBC driver ? What is its role ? List the types of drivers and explain working of type-4 driver. Give different ways to create JDBC connection with example*

   GTU : Summer-12, Marks 7

3. *Describe type-4 JDBC driver with proper illustration.* **GTU : Winter-13, Marks 7**

4. *What is JDBC ? List out all various types of JDBC driver. Explain Thick and Thin driver. Write code snippet for each type of JDBC connection. Comment on selection of driver.*

   GTU : Summer-16, Marks 7

2.12 Executing SQL Queries

- The **executeQuery()** method is belonging to java.sql.Statement interface of JDBC.
- This method is used for SQL statements which retrieve some data from the database. For example is **SELECT** statement.
- This method is basically used for SELECT queries which fetch some data from the database. This method returns one **java.sql.ResultSet** object which contains the data returned by the query.
- This method throws the exception SQLException.
- The general syntax is

```
ResultSet executeQuery(String SQL)
```

2.13 ResultSetMetaData

- The metadata means data about data. That means information about data can be obtained using **ResultSetMetaData**. This information can be number of columns, name of columns, data type of columns and so on.
- Using the **getMetaData** method the object for ResultSetMetaData is returned. The general syntax for getMetaData is

```
public ResultSetMetaData getMetaData()
```

- This method throws **SQLEception**.
- Various commonly used methods ResultSetMetadata are -

Method	Description
public int getTableName(int index)	This method returns the name of the table for specified column index
public int getColumnCount()	It returns the number of columns present in the table.
public String getColumnName(int index)	It returns the name of the column for specified column index.
public String getColumnTypeName(int index)	It returns data type of the column for specified column index.

Following is a simple Java program created using Eclipse platform that makes use of **ResultSetMetaData**. Prior to this example, it is necessary to create database with some records present in it.

Step 1 : Open Eclipse IDE. Click on File->New->Dynamic Web Project.

Step 2 : I have created database in MYSQL. Name of my database is my_database, with table my_table.

Step 3 : Create a new Java Class file under **src** directory.

The Java program is as follows -

JDBCDemo7.java

```
import java.sql.*;
public class JDBCDemo7 {
    public static void main(String[] args) {
        Connection con=null;
        try {
            Class.forName("com.mysql.jdbc.Driver");
            con =
DriverManager.getConnection("jdbc:mysql://localhost/my_database","root","");
            PreparedStatement ps=con.prepareStatement("select * from my_table");
            ResultSet rs=ps.executeQuery();
// Obtain the object for ResultSetMetaData using getMetaData method
            ResultSetMetaData rsmd=rs.getMetaData();
    //Displaying metadata using methods of ResultSetMetaData
            System.out.println("Table Name: "+rsmd.getTableName(1));
            System.out.println("Total Number of columns: "+rsmd.getColumnCount());
            System.out.println("Name of First column: "+rsmd.getColumnName(1));
            System.out.println("Data Type of First column:
"+rsmd.getColumnTypeName(1));
            System.out.println("Name of Second column: "+rsmd.getColumnName(2));
            System.out.println("Data Type of Second column:
"+rsmd.getColumnTypeName(2));
            con.close();
            }catch(Exception e){ System.out.println(e);}
    }
}
```

Output

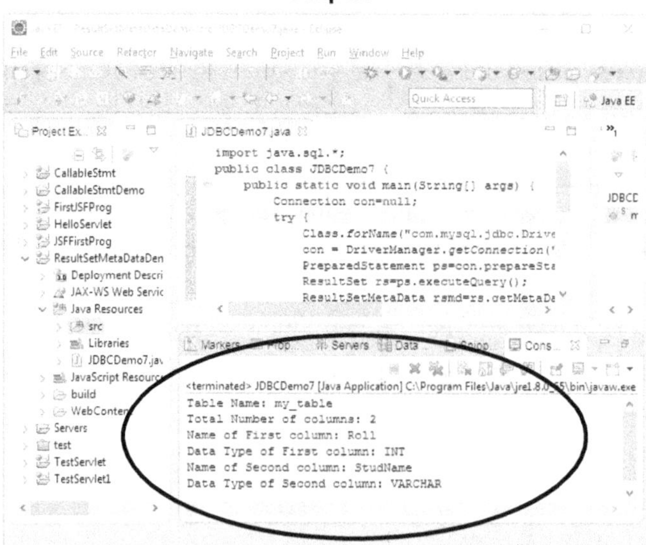

2.14 Executing SQL Updates

- The **executeUpdate()** method is used to update the database.
- This method makes used of all the Data Manipulation Language(DML) statements such as INSERT, DELETE, UPDATE or Data Definition Language(DDL) such as CREATE, ALTER and so on.
- This method returns an **int value** which represents the number of rows affected by the query. This value will be **0** for the statements which return nothing.
- This method throws the exception **SQLException.**
- The general syntax of this method is

```
int executeUpdate(String sql)
```

2.15 Difference between executeQuery(), executeUpdate() and execute()

executeQuery	executeUpdate()	execute()
This method is used to execute SQL statements in order to retrieve data from the database.	This method is used to execute SQL statements which are intended to update or modify the database.	This method can be used to execute any type of SQL statement.
This method returns a ResultSet object in which the result of the query is strored.	This method rerurns integer value that represent number of rows affected by the query.	This method returns the Boolean value. If this method returns TRUE then that means ResultSet object is returned. The value FALSE indicates query returned an int value or returns nothing.
This method is normally used to execute SELECT queries.	This method is used to execute non SELECT queries. That is- DML as INSERT, DELETE, UPDATE or DDL as CREATE, DROP	This method can be used to execute any type of SQL statement.

2.16 Transaction Management

- Transaction management is used to provide data integrity, correct application semantics and consistent view of data during concurrent access.
- The transaction management is described using the ACID properties. The word ACID stands for Atomicity, consistency, Isolation, and Durability.
    - **Atomicity** means either all operations get successful or none.
    - **Consistency** means the database must be at consistent state.
    - **Isolation** is a property which indicates isolation of one transaction from other.
    - **Durability** means after transaction been committed, it will remain as it is.

- In JDBC **Connection** interface is used that provides methods for transaction management.
- Various methods supported by **Connection** interface are

Method	Description
void setAutoCommit(boolean)	The true value indicates that each transaction is committed automatically. By default it is true. Programmer can set it to false for manual transaction.
void commit()	This method is used for committing the transaction
void rollback()	This method is for canceling the transaction.

- **Example**

Following is a Java application which makes use of transaction management. In the following example **setAutoCommit** method is used.

Step 1 : Open Eclipse IDE. Click on File->New->Dynamic Web Project.

Step 2 : Create a new Java Class file under **src** directory.

JDBCDDemo8.java

```
import java.sql.*;
public class JDBCDemo8 {
    public static void main(String args[])throws Exception
    {
        Connection con=null;
        Class.forName("com.mysql.jdbc.Driver");
        con = DriverManager.getConnection("jdbc:mysql://localhost/my_database","root","");
        con.setAutoCommit(false);
        Statement stmt=con.createStatement();
        stmt.executeUpdate("INSERT INTO my_table VALUES(5,'Shilpa')");
        stmt.executeUpdate("INSERT INTO my_table VALUES(6,'Kedar')");
        con.commit();
        con.close();
    }
}
```

Step 3 : For the **Output,** we can check the database table by executing SQL query on the MySQL prompt. Following screenshot illustrates it.

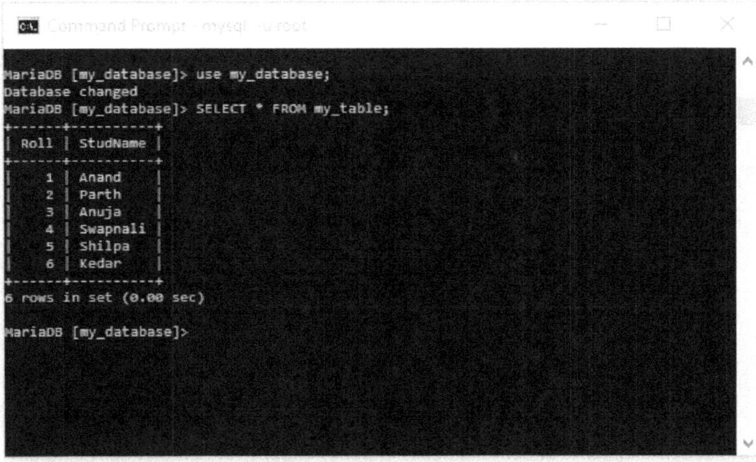

Advantages of using Transaction Management

1. Transaction management is used to increase performance.
2. It helps in maintaining the integrity in business logic.
3. The transaction management is used for transaction with distributed objects.

❑❑❑

Notes

3 Servlet API and Overview

Syllabus

Servlet Model : *Overview of Servlet, Servlet Life Cycle, HTTP Methods Structure and Deployment descriptor*

ServletContext and ServletConfig interface, Attributes in Servelt, Request Dispacher interface The Filter API: Filter, FilterChain, Filter Config

Cookies and Session Management : Understanding state and session, Understanding Session Timeout and Session Tracking, URL Rewriting

Contents

3.1 Overview of Servlet .... ***Summer-16,*** .... *Marks 2*

3.2 Deployment of Servlet

3.3 Architecture of Servlet

3.4 Servlet Life Cycle ***Dec.-11, May-12,***

.... ***Summer-13, 15, 16,*** .... *Marks 7*

3.5 HTTP Methods Structure .... ***Summer-16,*** .... *Marks 7*

3.6 Deployment Descriptor .... ***May-12,*** .... *Marks 7*

3.7 ServletContext and ServletConfig Interface

3.8 Attributes in Servlet

3.9 Request Dispatcher Interface

3.10 The Filter API .... ***May-12, Dec.-12, Winter-13,*** *Marks 7*

3.11 Cookies and Session Management .... ***Dec.-07, May-12,*** .... *Marks 7*

3.1 Overview of Servlet

GTU : Summer-16, Marks 2

Servlets are simple Java programs that run on the servers. Hence is the name Servlets! Servlets are most commonly used with HTTP (i.e. Hyper Text Transfer Protocol) hence sometimes servlets are also called as "HTTP Servlet". Servlets make use of the Java standard extension classes in the packages **javax.servlet** and **javax.servlet.http**. The servlets normally follows the framework standard.

Typical uses of servlets are

- Servlets can process and store the data submitted by an HTML form.
- Servlets are useful for providing the dynamic contents. For example retrieving and updating the databases.
- Servlets can be used in the cookies and session tracking. Cookies are small programs which can make use of the information submitted on currently accessed web pages. Similarly session tracking are the useful programs that keeps track of all previously accessed the web pages.

Let us first enlist the differences between Applets and Servlets.

Difference between Applets and Servlets

Applets	Servlets
Applets are the programs at the client side.	Servlets are the programs at the server side.
Applets can make request to servlets.	The servlets are intended to response the applets or HTML program.
Applets may have graphical user interface(GUI).	Servlets have no graphical user interface.
Applets are extend the web browser	Servlets are extend the web servers

Difference between Servlets and CGI

The main purpose of servlets is to add up the functionality to a web server. With the same intension CGI i.e. **Common Gateway Interface** is developed. The CGI is language-independent interface that allows a server to start an external process. These external processes further get information about the **request** using the command line arguments and its standard input stream. The **response** can then be given using standard output stream. Each request is answered in ***a separate process*** by ***a separate instance*** of the CGI program. The CGI programs can be written in Perl or C language. But servlets have many advantages over CGI -

1. There is **no need** to generate a **separate process** for serving each request in case of servlets.

2. A CGI program needs to be loaded and started on each CGI request. On the other hand, servlets **stay in the memory** while serving the requests.
3. Servlet creates a single instance to process all the requests. This processing can be done concurrently by this instance. This in turn saves the **memory** as well as an efficient request processing can be done. Hence **performance** of servlets is surely better than CGI.
4. Servlets can be run by the servlet engines hence secure use of untrusted servlets can be done. Thus servlets prove to be **more secure** than CGI.
5. Last but not the least, full functionality of Java class libraries is available to the servlets. Servlets can communicate with applets, HTML programs, databases or even with some RMI programs.

How Servlet Works ?

Before learning the actual servlet programming it is very important to understand how servlet works.

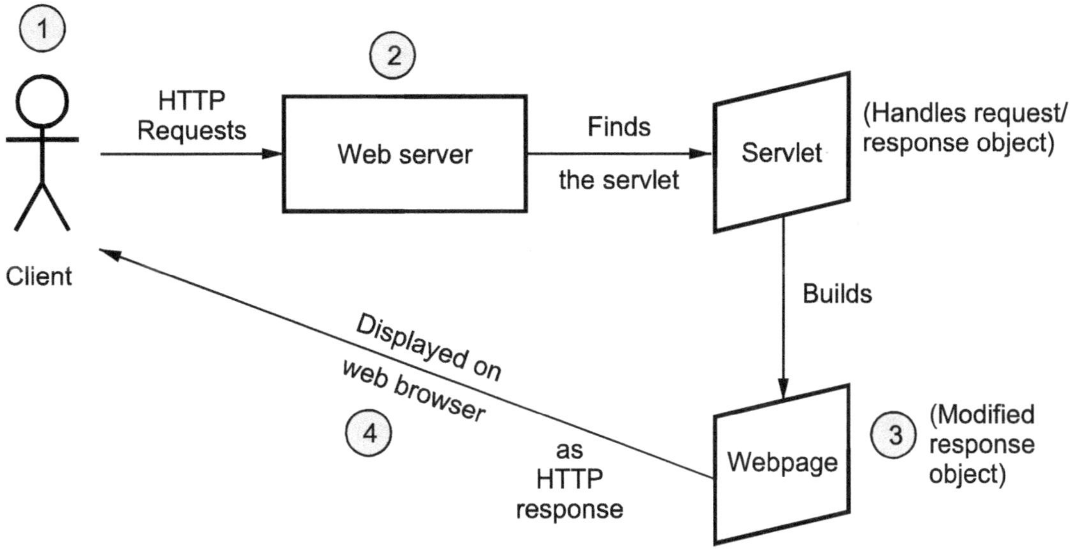

Fig. 3.1.1 How servlet works ?

1. When a client make a request for some servlet, he/she actually uses the **Web browser** in which request is written as a URL.
2. The web browser then sends this request to **Web server**. The web server first finds the requested servlet.
3. The obtained servlet gathers the relevant information in order to satisfy the client's request and builds a **web page** accordingly.
4. This web page is then **displayed** to the client. Thus the request made by the client gets satisfied by the servlets.

Review Question

1. *Differentiate the followings : Servlets vs CGI.* **GTU : Summer-16, Marks 2**

3.2 Deployment of Servlet

As we know, that if we want to go for serious server side programming then writing the servlets is the best choice. These servlets need a special environment in which they can be executed. For that matter, one commonly recommended *servlet container* is **Tomcat**. The Tomcat is an open-source product. It is maintained by **Jakarta Project** of **Apache Software Foundation**. The Tomcat is basically a servlet container that contains the class libraries, documentation and runtime support which is useful for executing and testing the servlets.

For the execution of servlets following software must be installed on your PC -

- **JDK :** As servlets are basically Java files we should have JDK installed.
- **Tomcat :** Tomcat is servlet container using which servlet can be executed.

3.3 Architecture of Servlet

Here is simple Servlet which can be written in Notepad and saved using .java extension.

Java Program [FirstServlet.java]

```
import java.io.*;
import javax.servlet.*;
import javax.servlet.http.*;

public class FirstServlet extends HttpServlet
{
 public void doGet(HttpServletRequest request,HttpServletResponse response)
 throws IOException,ServletException
 {
  response.setContentType("text/html");
  PrintWriter out=response.getWriter();
  out.println("<html>");
  out.println("<head>");
  out.println("<title>My First Servlet</title>");
  out.println("<body>");
  out.println("<h1>Hello How are U?</h1>");
  out.println("<h2>I am enjoying this Servlet Application</h2>");
  out.println("<h3>See You later!</h3>");
  out.println("</body>");
  out.println("</html>");
}
}
```

In the above program, we have imported following files,

```
import java.io.*;
import javax.servlet.*;
import javax.servlet.http.*;
```

Out of these files **java.io** package is useful for taking care of I/O operations. The **javax.servlet** and **javax.servlet.http** are important packages containing the **classes** and **interfaces** that are required for the operation of servlets. The most commonly used interface from **javax.servlet** package is **Servlet**. Similarly most commonly used class in this package is **GenericServlet**. The **ServletRequest** and **ServletResponse** are another two commonly used interfaces defined in **javax.servlet** package.

In the **javax.servlet.http** package **HttpServletRequest** and **HttpServletResponse** are two commonly used interfaces. The **HttpServletRequest** enables the servlet to read data from the HTTP request and **HttpServletResponse** enables the servlet to write data to HTTP response. The **cookie** and **HttpServlet** are two commonly used classes that are defined in this package.

We have given class name FirstServlet which should be derived from the class **HttpServlet**. (Sometimes we can derive our class from **GenericServlet**).

Then we have defined **doGet method** to which the HTTP request and response are passed as parameters. The commonly used basic exceptions for the servlets are **IOException** and **ServletException.**

The MIME type is specified as using the **setContentType**() method. This method sets the content type for the HTTP response to type. In this method "text/html" is specified as the MIME type. This means that the browser should interpret the contents as the HTML source code.

Then an output stream is created using **PrintWriter()**. The **getWriter()** method is used for obtaining the output stream. Anything written to this stream is sent to the client as a response. Hence using the object of output stream 'out', we can write the HTML source code in **println** method as HTTP response.

3.3.1 How to Execute Servlet ?

For obtaining the output of above given servlet, follwing steps are followed -

Step 1 :

We will first compile it. The servlet can be compiled using any of the following two methods -

Method 1 : Compile the java servlet code using javac by specifying the class path using following command at the command prompt -

```
C:\test>javac FirstServlet.java – classpath
"C:\Tomcat 5.5\apache-tomcat-5.5.27\common\lib\servlet-api.jar"
```

Note that FirstServlet.java is the name of my servlet for which I want to obtain the output. The **servlet-api.jar** file contains all the required interfaces and classes needed for executing the servlet.

Method 2 : You can set the **CLASSPATH** using environment variable as follows.

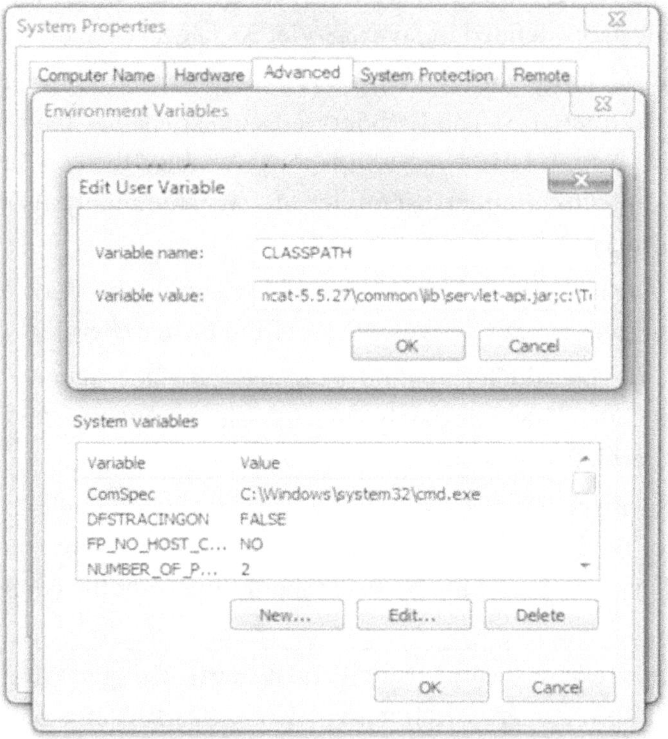

Then simply type the following command at the command prompt for compiling FirstServlet.java as -

```
C:\test>javac FirstServlet.java
```

Step 2 : The class file **FirstServlet.class** gets generated by this method.

Now we will deploy this servlet in the Tomcat. For that, we have to **copy** the generated class file FirstServlet.class to the directory -

```
C:\Tomcat 5.5\apache-tomcat-5.5.27\webapps\servlets-examples\WEB-INF\classes
```

Step 3 : Now open the **web.xml** file present in the current directory. In my case, I have one

web.xml file at the path

```
C:\Tomcat 5.5\apache-tomcat-5.5.27\webapps\servlets-examples\WEB-INF
```

Open this web.xml file in Notepad. Edit it by adding following statements –

```
...
...
<servlet>
    <servlet-name>FirstServlet</servlet-name>
    <servlet-class>FirstServlet</servlet-class>
  </servlet>
...
...
...
<servlet-mapping>
    <servlet-name>FirstServlet</servlet-name>
    <url-pattern>/servlet/FirstServlet</url-pattern>
  </servlet-mapping>
```

These are two segments of code that must be added in **web.xml** file after generating class file.

Step 4 :

Now start the Tomcat by clicking the **startup.bat**. Then open some web browser and type the URL :

http://localhost:4040/servlets-examples/servlet/FirstServlet

and you will get the following output :

Output

3.4 Servlet Life Cycle

GTU : Dec.-11, May-12, Summer-13, 15, 16, Marks 7

In the life cycle of servlet there are three important methods. These methods are

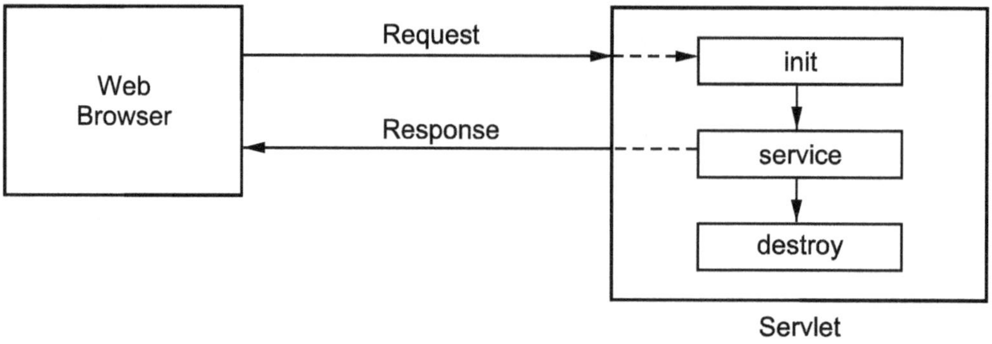

Fig. 3.4.1 Life cycle of servlet

- The client enters the URL in the web browser and makes a request. The browser then generates the HTTP request and sends it to the Web server.
- Web server maps this request to the corresponding servlet.
- The server basically invokes the **init()** method of servlet. This method is called only when the servlet is loaded in the memory for the first time. Using this method initialization parameters can also be passed to the servlet in order to configure itself.
- Server can invoke the service for particular HTTP request using **service()** method. The servlets can then read the data provided by the HTTP request with the help of **service()** method.
- Finally server unloads the servlet from the memory using the **destroy()** method.

Following is a simple servlet in which these three methods viz. init(), service() and destroy() are used -

Java Program [LifeCycle.java]

```
import javax.servlet.*;
import javax.servlet.http.*;
import java.io.*;

public class LifeCycle extends GenericServlet
{
  public void init(ServletConfig config) throws ServletException
  {
    System.out.println("init");
  }
```

```
  public void service(ServletRequest request, ServletResponse response)
  throws ServletException, IOException
   {
     System.out.println("from service");
     PrintWriter out = response.getWriter();
     out.println("Twinkle Twinkle Little Stars.");
     out.print("How I wonder what you are.");
   }
  public void destroy()
  {
     System.out.println("destroy");
   }
}
```

In the above program we have first of all used an **init()** method to which object of the **ServletConfig** interface is passed. This interface allows the servlet to get the initialization parameters.

Then we have used the **service()** method to which the ServletRequest and ServletResponse parameters are passed for making the HTTP request and getting the HTTP response from the sevlet. The output stream is created using **getWriter()** and along this output stream some messages are written. These messages will then be displayed on the web browser when the servlet gets executed.

Finally the **destroy()** function is written in order to unload the servlet from the memory.

We will -

1. Compile this program and copy the class file in the class folder of Tomcat.
2. Edit the web.xml by mentioning the servlet name and servlet mapping.
3. Start the Tomcat server.
4. Open the web browser and request for the above servlet using the URL.

You will then get following output.

Output

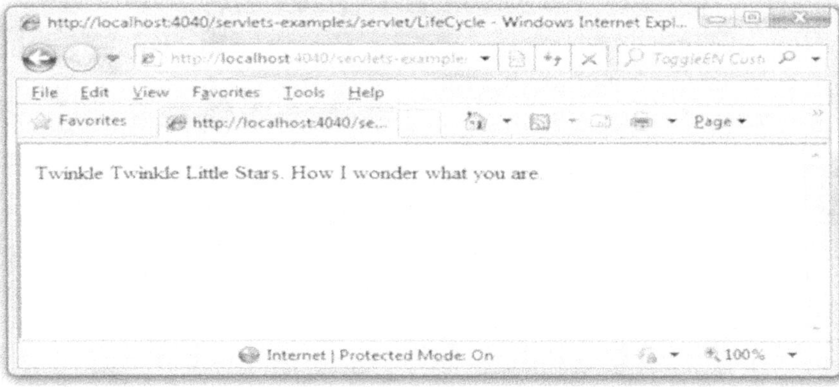

Your Tomcat console is running behind and it is interesting to know that as soon as you load this servlet, **init** method is invoked and then the service method is invoked. Just go to the window in which Tomcat is running you will get following output.

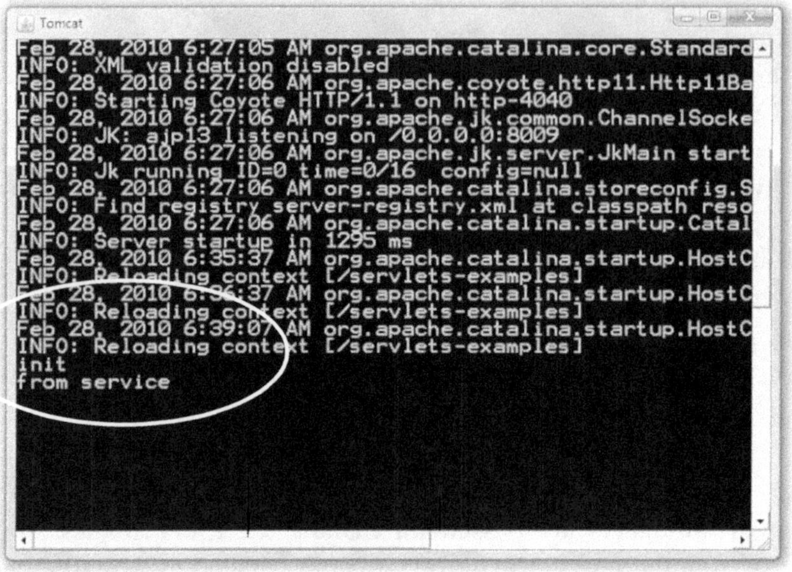

If you try to shut down the Tomcat server you will get the message "destroy" which we have given in the destroy method of above program.

Review Questions

1. *Discuss servlet life cycle methods. Explain the role of web container.* **GTU : Dec.-11, Marks 7**
2. *Explain the servlet life cycle with life cycle methods.* **GTU : May-12, Summer-13, Marks 7**
3. *Explain servlet life cycle with example to demonstrate every state.* **GTU : Summer-15, Marks 7**
4. *List and Explain various stages of Servlet life cycle. Explain role of web container.* **GTU : Summer-16, Marks 7**

3.5 HTTP Methods Structure

GTU : Summer-16, Marks 7

The **javax.servlet.http** package contains a number of interfaces and classes and their functionality makes it easy to build servlets. These servlets then work with HTTP requests and responses.

3.5.1 Interface

The following table describes the interfaces that are provided in this package

Interface	Description
HttpSession	The session data can be read or written using this interface.
HttpServletRequest	The servlet can read the information from the HTTP request using this interface.
HttpServletResponse	The servlet can write the data to HTTP response using this interface.
HttpSessionBindingListener	This interface tells the object about its binding with the particular session.

1. The *HttpSession*

At every HTTP session, the state information is gathered. The servlet can read or write this information using **HTTPSession** interface. This interface is implemented by the server.

Various methods used by this interface are as given below -

Method	Description
String getId()	This method returns the session ID.
Object getAttribute(String *attribute_name*)	The value of the attribute *attribute_name* in the current session is returned.
Enumeration getAttributeNames()	Returns the attribute names.

2. The *HttpServletRequest*

The **HTTPServletRequest** is used to obtain the information from client's HTTP request.

Method	Description
String getMethod()	It returns the HTTP method for the client request.
String getPathInfo()	Returns the path information about the servlet path.
HttpSession getSession()	Returns the current session.
String getHeader(String *fields*)	It returns the value of header fields.
Cookie [ ] getCookies()	It returns the information in the cookies in the request made.
String getAuth Type()	It returns the type of Authentication.

3. The *HttpServletResponse*

This **HtttpServletResponse** interface is used to formulate an HTTP response to the client. Various methods are -

Method	Description
void addCookie(Cookie *cookie)*	This method is used to add cookie in the response.
String encodeURL(String url)	This method is used to encode the specified URL.
Boolean containsHeader(String *f*)	This method returns **true** if the response header contains the field *f*
void sendError(int *code*)	This method sends error code to the client.

4. The *HttpSessionBindingListener*

When particular listener gets bound or unbound from a value within **HttpSession** object then this class is required. It extends the **HttpSessionEvent**. Various methods that can be defined by this interface are -

Method	Description
Object getValue()	This function returns the value of bounded or unbounded attribute.
String getName()	This function returns the name being bound or unbound.
HttpSession getSession()	This function returns the session to which the listener can be bound or unbound.

3.5.2 Classes

The following table describes the classes that are provided in this package

Class	Description
Cookie	This class is used to write the cookies
HttpServlet	It is used when developing servlets that receive and process HTTP requests
HttpSessionEvent	This class is used to handle the session events
HttpSessionBindingEvent	When a listener is bound to a value

1) The Cookie class

A cookie is a small piece of information that is stored in the client's machine. Sometimes Cookies are useful to keep track of the user using the client machine. Various methods used by this class are –

Class	Description
String getValue()	This function returns a value of the cookie.
void setValue(String s)	This function sets the value to the cookie.
String getName()	This function returns the name.

2) The HttpServlet class

The **HttpServlet** class extends **GenericServlet**. It is used when developing servlets that receive and process HTTP requests. Various methods of this class are -

Class	Description
void doGet(HttpServletRequest req, HttpServletResponse res)	This method performs HTTP get request.
void doPost(HttpServletRequest req, HttpServletResponse res)	This method performs HTTP Post request.
void doPut(HttpServletRequest req, HttpServletResponse res)	This method performs HTTP Put request.
void service(HttpServletRequest req, HttpServletResponse res)	This method is invoked for processing HTTP request and response.

3) The HttpSessionEvent

This method encapsulates the session event.

4) HttpSessionBindingEvent

The **HttpSessionBindingEvent** class extends **HttpSessionEvent**. It is generated when a listener is bound to a value. The **getSession()** method obtains the session to which the listener is being bound or unbound.

Example 3.5.1 : *Write servlet displayed following information of client.*
i) Client Browser *ii) Client IP address* *iii) Client Port No*
iv) Server Port No *v) Local Port No.* *vi) Method used by client for form submission*
vii) Query String name and values **GTU : Summer-16, Marks 7**

Solution :

```
import java.io.IOException;
import java.io.PrintWriter;
import javax.servlet.ServletException;
import javax.servlet.http.HttpServlet;
import javax.servlet.http.HttpServletRequest;
import javax.servlet.http.HttpServletResponse;
public class DisplayInfo extends HttpServlet
{
  protected void doGet(HttpServletRequest request, HttpServletResponse response)
        throws ServletException, IOException {
     PrintWriter out=response.getWriter();
              response.setContentType("text/html");
              out.print("Client's Browser: "+request.getHeader("user-agent"));
              out.print("<br/>Client's IP Address: "+request.getRemoteAddr());
              out.print("<br/>Client Port NO: "+request.getRemotePort());
              out.print("<br/>Server Port NO: "+request.getServerPort());
              out.print("<br/>Local Port NO: "+request.getLocalPort());
```

```
            out.print("<br/>Method Used By Client: "+request.getMethod());
            out.print("<br/>QueryString: "+request.getQueryString());
    }
}
```

Output

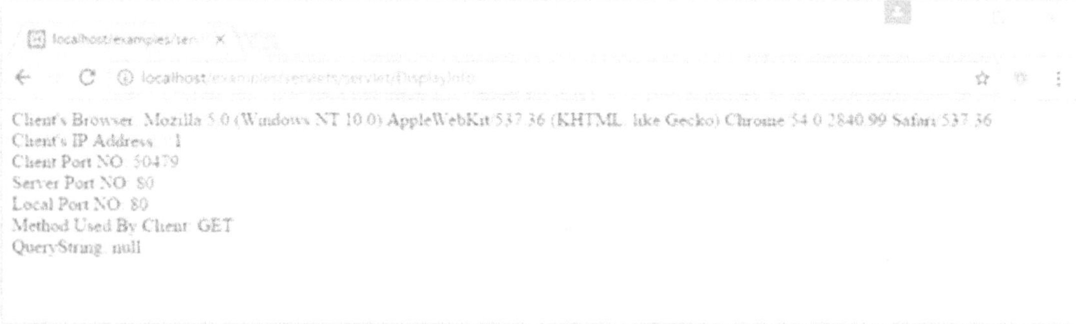

3.6 Deployment Descriptor

GTU : May-12, Winter-14, Marks 7

- The deployment descriptor is a file that describes how the web application should be deployed.
- The deployment descriptor is written in XML syntax.
- The web application deployment descriptor is named as **web.xml**
- This file is located in a WEB-INF subdirectory at the web application root.
- The contents of this file direct a deployment tool to deploy a module or application with the specified security settings, and describes other specific configuration requirements and container options.

For example :

web.xml

```
<?xml version="1.0" encoding="ISO-8859-1"?>
...
  <description>
   Servlet and JSP Examples.
  </description>
  <display-name>Servlet and JSP Examples</display-name>

  <!-- Define example filters -->
  <filter>
    <filter-name>Timing filter</filter-name>
    <filter-class>filters.ExampleFilter</filter-class>
    <init-param>
      <param-name>attribute</param-name>
      <param-value>filters.ExampleFilter</param-value>
```

```
    </init-param>
  </filter>

  <!-- Define example application events listeners -->
  <listener>
    <listener-class>listeners.ContextListener</listener-class>
  </listener>
  <listener>
    <listener-class>listeners.SessionListener</listener-class>
  </listener>

  <!-- Define servlets that are included in the example application -->

  <servlet>
   <servlet-name>ServletToJsp</servlet-name>
   <servlet-class>ServletToJsp</servlet-class>
  </servlet>
  <servlet>


  <servlet-mapping>
    <servlet-name>ChatServlet</servlet-name>
    <url-pattern>/jsp/chat/chat</url-pattern>
  </servlet-mapping>

...

  <!-- Security roles referenced by this web application -->
  <security-role>
   <role-name>role1</role-name>
  </security-role>
  <security-role>
   <role-name>tomcat</role-name>
  </security-role>

  <!-- Environment entry examples -->
  <!--env-entry>
   <env-entry-description>
     The maximum number of tax exemptions allowed to be set.
   </env-entry-description>
   <env-entry-name>maxExemptions</env-entry-name>
   <env-entry-type>java.lang.Integer</env-entry-type>
   <env-entry-value>15</env-entry-value>
  </env-entry-->
....
  <welcome-file-list>
```

```
    <welcome-file>index.html</welcome-file>
    <welcome-file>index.xhtml</welcome-file>
    <welcome-file>index.htm</welcome-file>
    <welcome-file>index.jsp</welcome-file>
  </welcome-file-list>

</web-app>
```

- While creating the servlet we must modify the deployment descriptor file as follows

```
<web-app>
  <servlet>
    <servlet-name>Servlet1</servlet-name>
    <servlet-path>myServlet</servlet-path>
  </servlet>
  <servlet-mapping>
    <servlet-name>Servlet1</servlet-name>
    <url-pattern>/myservlet</url-pattern>
  </servlet-mapping>
</web-app>
```

- By above modification in web.xml we are actually registering the servlet with the tomcat.
- The **servlet** has two child tags - **servlet-name** and **servlet-path**. The servlet-path specifies the path for the servlet class.
- The **servlet-mapping** has two child tags, **url-pattern** and **servlet-name**. The **url-pattern** specifies the type of urls for which, the servlet given in servlet-name should be called.

Example 3.6.1 : *Write a servlet which counts the number of digits into an integer received as parameter. Give the necessary web.xml file to deploy the servlet.*

GTU : May-12, Marks 7

Solution :

Step 1 : Write the servlet program for counting the number of digits in the number. It is as follows -

```
import java.io.*;
import javax.servlet.*;
import javax.servlet.http.*;
import java.util.*;

public class DigitServlet extends HttpServlet
{
 public void doGet(HttpServletRequest request,HttpServletResponse response)
```

```
throws ServletException, IOException
 {
  PrintWriter pw = response.getWriter();
  Enumeration enumeration = getServletConfig().getInitParameterNames();
     //obtaining number as a parameter from web.xml file
  String num=getServletConfig().getInitParameter("Number");
  int n=Integer.parseInt(num);
  pw.println("The Number is: "+n);
  int count=0;
  while(n>=1)
  {
     n=n/10;
     count++;
  }
  pw.print("The total number of digits in number are: "+count);
 }
}
```

Step 2 : Open the **web.xml** file present in the WEB-INF folder. It will be edited as -

```
<?xml version="1.0" encoding="ISO-8859-1"?>
<!--
...
...
<servlet>
      <init-param>
            <param-name>Number</param-name>
            <param-value>1234</param-value>
       </init-param>
       <servlet-name>DigitServlet</servlet-name>
      <servlet-class>DigitServlet</servlet-class>
</servlet>
...
...
<servlet-mapping>
           <servlet-name>DigitServlet</servlet-name>
           <url-pattern>/servlets/servlet/DigitServlet</url-pattern>
 </servlet-mapping>
```

Step 3 : The output will be -

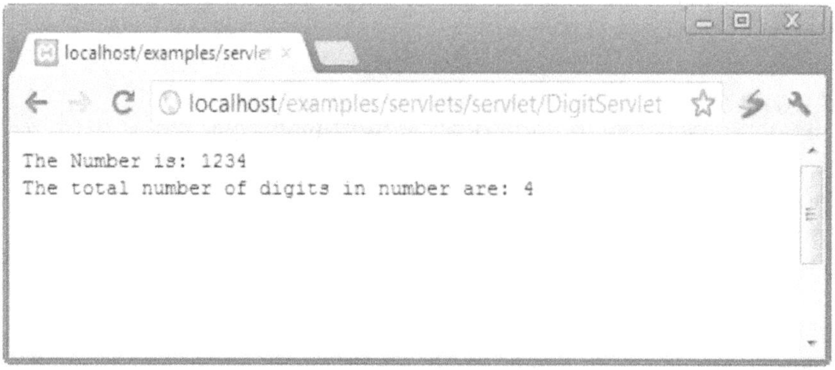

Example 3.6.2 : *Write a web application using servlet to compute an area of a circle. Get the radius from the client. Write necessary web.xml file.*

GTU : Winter-13, Marks 7

Solution : Step 1 : Create an HTML document for client side. Using this HTML document client can enter the radius for computation of area of circle.

```
<html>
 <head>
  <title>Client Form</title>
 </head>
 <body>
   <form action="http://localhost/examples/servlets/servlet/CircleArea" method="get">
    Enter Radius of the Circle: <input type="text" name="Radius"><br />
   <input type="submit" value="Submit" />
  </form>
 </body>
</html>
```

Step 2 : Create the following servlet program in which the value of radius is read and the area of the circle is computed and will be displayed on the web page.

```
import java.io.*;
import java.net.*;
import javax.servlet.*;
import javax.servlet.http.*;
public class CircleArea extends HttpServlet
{
 protected void doGet(HttpServletRequest request, HttpServletResponse response) throws
ServletException, IOException
 {
  String radius=request.getParameter("Radius");
  int r=Integer.parseInt(radius);
  response.setContentType("text/html;charset=UTF-8");
  PrintWriter out = response.getWriter();
```

```
   out.println("<html>");
   out.println("<head>");
   out.println("<title>Servlet Sum</title>");
   out.println("</head>");
   out.println("<body>");

   double a=3.14*r*r;
   out.println("The area of circle is "+a);
   out.println("</body>");
   out.println("</html>");
   out.close();
 }
}
```

Step 3 : Edit **web.xml** in the WEB-INF folder as follows -

```
...
<servlet>
      <servlet-name>CircleArea</servlet-name>
      <servlet-class>CircleArea</servlet-class>
   </servlet>
...
   <servlet-mapping>
      <servlet-name>CircleArea</servlet-name>
      <url-pattern>/servlets/servlet/CircleArea</url-pattern>
   </servlet-mapping>
```

Step 4 : The output will be as follows -

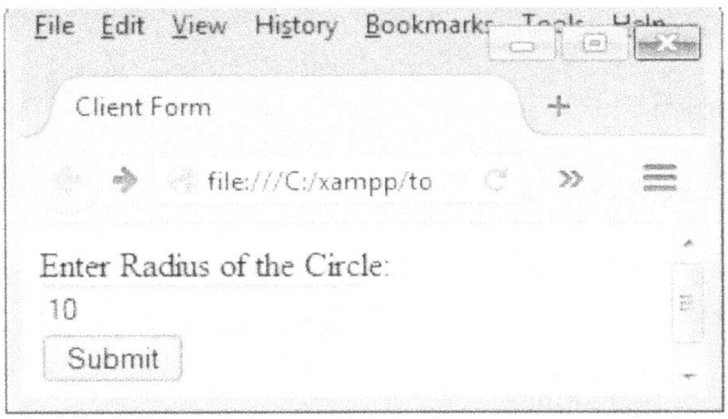

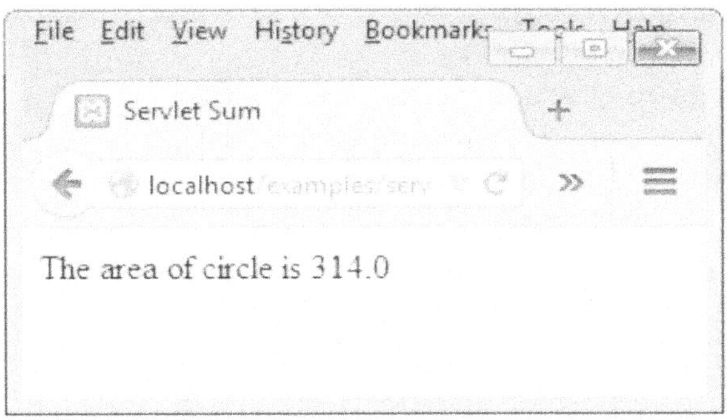

Example 3.6.3 : *Write a servlet which accept two numbers using POST methods and display the maximum of them.* **GTU : Winter-14, Marks 7**

Solution : Step 1 : The HTML document for inputting two numbers is as follows -

NumbersInput.html

```
<html>
<head>
<body>
<div align="center">
   <br> <br>
   <form action="http://localhost/examples/servlets/servlet/MaxNumber" method="post">
      Enter First Number:
      <input type="text" value="" name="Number1" size='5'>
      <br/><br/> Enter Second Number:
      <input type="text" value="" name="Number2" size='5'>
      <br/> <br/> <br/>
      <input  type="submit" value="Submit">
   </form>
</div>
</body>
</html>
```

Step 2 : The servlet code that handles the Post method and finds the maximum of the two input numbers is as follows -

MaxNumber.java

```
import java.io.*;
import javax.servlet.*;
import javax.servlet.http.*;

public class MaxNumber extends HttpServlet
{
   protected void doPost(HttpServletRequest req, HttpServletResponse res) throws
ServletException, IOException
   {
      res.setContentType("text/html");
      PrintWriter out=res.getWriter();

      // get request parameters for userID and password
      int a = Integer.parseInt(req.getParameter("Number1"));
      int b = Integer.parseInt(req.getParameter("Number2"));

      if (a>b)
           out.println("<h4>The maximum number is:"+a+"</h4>");
      else
           out.println("<h4>The maximum number is:"+b+"</h4>");
```

```
    }
}
```

Step 3 :

The output is as follows –

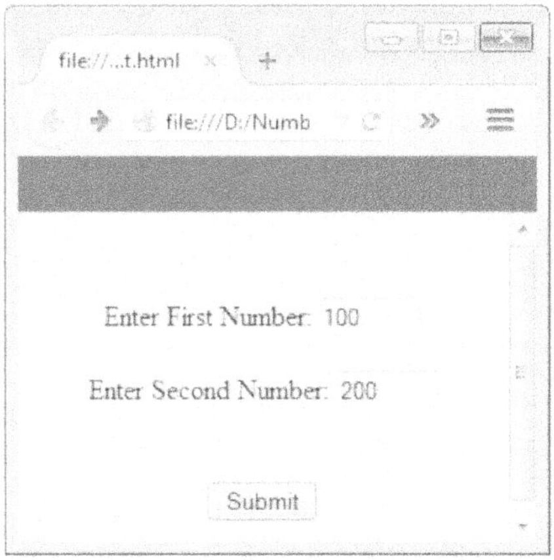

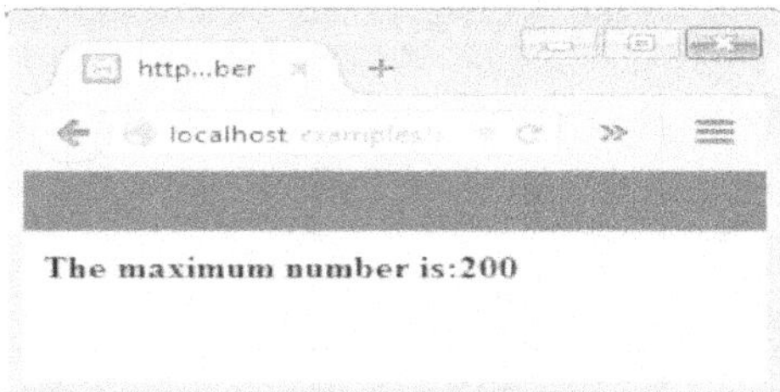

3.7 ServletContext and ServletConfig Interface

This package is used to implement the servlet. Out of many other interfaces and classes defined in this package the most important interface is **Servlet** . All the servlet must implement this interface. The interfaces and classes that are defined in this package are enlisted below -

3.7.1 Interfaces

Interface	Description
Servlet	This interface defines all the life cycle methods.
ServletConfig	This interface obtains the initialization parameters.
ServletContext	Using this interface the events can be logged.
ServletRequest	This interface is useful in reading the data from the client request.
ServletResponse	This interface is useful in writing the data to the client response.

1. The Servlet Interface

This interface defines all the life cycle methods such as **init(),destroy()** and **service()**. All the servlets must implement this interface. Some of the methods provided by this interface are -

Method	Description
void init(ServletConfig s)	This method is called for initialising the servlet. The initialisation parameter is obtained from the **ServletConfig** interface.
void destroy()	This method is called when the servlet has to be unloaded.
ServletConfig getServletConfig()	This method is used to obtain the initialisation parameters.
void Service(ServletRequest req, ServletResponse res)	This method is used to implement the service that a servlet should provide. The clients request is processed and a response is given.
String getServletInfo()	This method is used to obtain description of the servlet.

2. The ServletConfig Interface

This interface is used to obtain the initialisation parameters. Various methods that are used by this interface are -

Method	Description
String getServletName()	This method is used to obtain the name of the servlet.
String getInitParameter(String *p*)	This method returns the value of the parameter *p*
Enumeration getinitParamernames()	This method returns the names of initialisation parameters.
ServletContext getServletContext()	This method returns the context for the servlet.

3. The ServletContext Interface

This is the interface that enables the servlet to log events and access information about their environment. Various methods of this interface are -

Method	Description
Object getAttribute(String *attribute_name*)	The value of the attribute *attribute_name* in the current session is returned.
void setAttribute(String *attribute_name*, object *value*)	The *attribute_name* is passed to the object *value.*
String getServerInfo()	This method returns the information about the server.
String log(String *str*)	Writes the *str* to the servlet log.
String getMimeType(String *file*)	It returns the MIME type of the file.

4. The ServletRequest Interface

The **ServletRequest** interface helps in gathering the information about the client. Various methods in ServletRequest are

Method	Description
Object getAttribute(String *attribute_name*)	The value of the attribute *attribute_name* in the current session is returned.
int getContentlength()	It returns the content size of the request.
String getContentType()	It returns the type of the request.
getInputStream()	This method is used to read the binary data from the request.
getProtocol()	Returns the name of the protocol used.
getReader()	This method is useful for reading the text from the request.
getServerName()	It returns the name of the server on which the servlet is running.
int getServerPort()	It returns the port number of the server.

5. The ServletResponse Interface

This interface helps the servlet to formulate the response for the client's request. Various methods of this interface are -

Method	Description
String getCharacterEncoding()	This method returns the character encoding.
ServletOutputStream getOutputStream()	This method returns outputstream which is used to write the data for responding.
PrintWriter getWriter()	This method is used to write the character data to the response.
void setContentLength(int *size*)	This method sets the length of the content equal to the *size*.
void setContentType(String *Type*)	This methods sets the type of the content

3.7.2 Classes

The **javax.servlet** package contains following classes.

Class	Description
GenericServlet	This class implements the **Servlet** and **ServletConfig** interfaces.
ServletInputStream	This class provides the input stream for reading the client's request.
ServletOutputStream	This class provides the output stream for writing the client's response.
ServletException	This class is used to raise the exception when an error occurs.

1. The *GenericServlet* Class

This class is useful for implementing the life cycle methods. It implements the **servlet** and **ServletConfig** interfaces. It is called "Generic" because it does not assume that the protocol it will process will be HTTP. If we want to write our own protocol, then we must extend this class.

2. The *ServletInputStream* class

The **ServletInputStream** class extends the **InputStream**. This class provides an input stream which is used by a servlet for reading the data from a client request. For reading the bytes from a client the method used is **readLine**.

3. The ServletOutputStream class

The **ServletOutputStream** class extends the **OutputStream**. This class provides an output stream which is used by a servlet for writing the data for a client response. It also defines **print** and **println** method.

4. The ServletException class

The **javax.servlet** defines two **servlets ServletException** and **UnavailableException**

3.8 Attributes in Servlet

- The attributes in servlet is used to pass the information from one servlet to another.
- It is treated as objects.
- The attributes can be SET and GET from one of the following scopes.
  1. Request
  2. Session
  3. Application
- There are four attribute methods that are commonly used -

public void setAttribute(String name,Object object)	Sets the given object in the application scope.
public Object getAttribute(String name)	Returns the attribute for the specified name.
public Enumeration getInitParameterNames()	Returns the names of the context's initialization parameters as an Enumeration of String objects.
public void removeAttribute(String name)	Removes the attribute with the given name from the servlet context.

Attributes in Application Scope

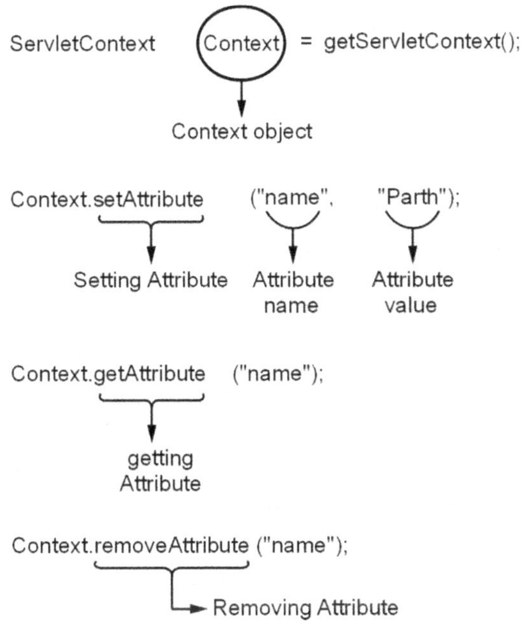

Fig. 3.8.1

Following is an servlet example which represents how to use attributes to set and pass the value to another servlet.

Step 1 : Create a servlet that sets the value to an attribute. Following servlet sets the attribute as **name** and set some name value to it.

SetAttribDemo.java

```
import java.io.*;
import javax.servlet.*;
import javax.servlet.http.*;
public class SetAttribDemo extends HttpServlet{
public void doGet(HttpServletRequest req,HttpServletResponse res)
{
      try {
         res.setContentType("text/html");
         PrintWriter out=res.getWriter();
         ServletContext context=getServletContext();
         context.setAttribute("name","Parth");

         out.println("<h2> Welcome!!!</h2>");
         out.println("<a href='GetAttribDemo'>Click Here to Continue...</a>");
         out.close();
      }catch(Exception e){}

   }
}
```

Step 2 : The value set to the attribute can be read using getAttribute method. Following servlet retrieves the value being set in the step 1.

GetAttribDemo.java

```
import java.io.*;
import javax.servlet.*;
import javax.servlet.http.*;

public class GetAttribDemo extends HttpServlet {
    public void doGet(HttpServletRequest req,HttpServletResponse res) {
        try {
            res.setContentType("text/html");
            ServletContext context=getServletContext();
            String n=(String)context.getAttribute("name");
            PrintWriter out=res.getWriter();
            out.println("<b>Welcome "+n+"</b>");
            out.close();
        }catch(Exception e){}

    }
}
```

Step 3 : Open suitable browser and invoke the servlet to set the value.

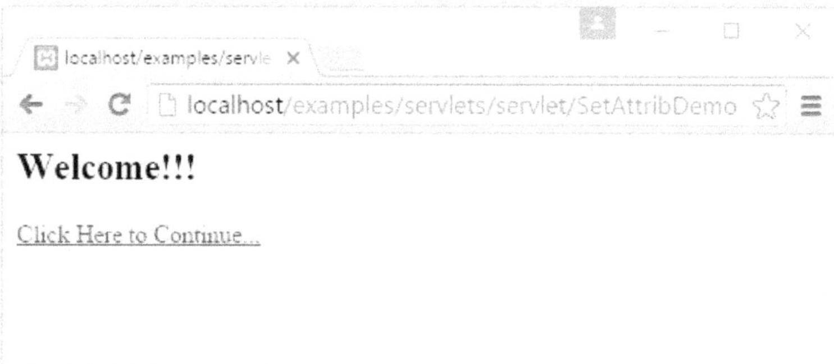

After clicking the hyperlink "Click Here to Continue" we will get

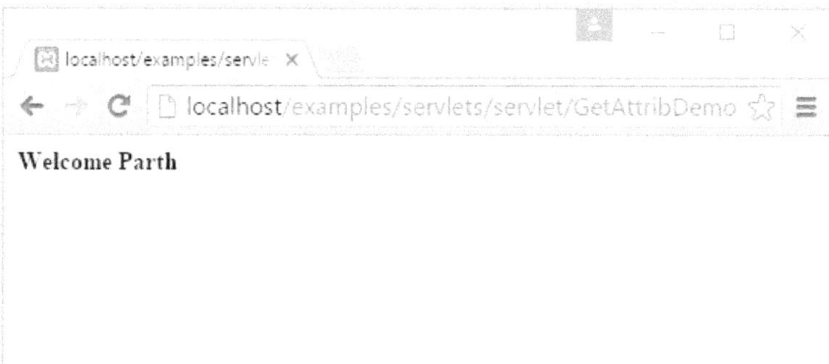

3.9 Request Dispatcher Interface

- The **RequestDispatcher** interface enables your servlet to "call" one servlet from inside another servlet. That means using RequestDispatcher we can dispatch the request to any source such as HTML, Servlet, JSP,image and so on.
- The other servlet is called as if an HTTP request was sent to it by a browser.
- There are two important methods that are used by the RequestDispatcher interface and these are -

Methods	Description
void forward(ServletRequest request, ServletResponse response)	forwards a request from a servlet to another resource (servlet, JSP file, or HTML file) on the server
void include(ServletRequest request, ServletResponse response)	includes the content of a resource (servlet, JSP page, HTML file) in the response

Following servlet shows the use of forward and include methods using RequestDispatcher interface.

Step 1 : Write an HTML document for entering user name and password.

Input.html

```
<!doctype html>
<html>
<head>
<title> Demo For Request Dispatcher</title>
<body>
<form method ="post" action="http://localhost/examples/servlets/servlet/Validate">
User:<input type ="text" name="user" ><br/>
Password:<input type ="password" name="pwd"> <br/><br/>
<input type="submit" value="Submit">
</form>
</body>
```

Step 2 : Following servlet retrieves the user name and password and validate the password. If the password is valid then the request is forwarded to **MainPage.java** and if the password is not valid then message about the "Incorrect Password" will be displayed.

Validate.java

```
import java.io.*;
import javax.servlet.*;
import javax.servlet.http.*;

public class Validate extends HttpServlet {
    protected void doPost(HttpServletRequest request,HttpServletResponse response)
                    throws ServletException,IOException {
```

```
        response.setContentType("text/html;charset=UTF-8");
        PrintWriter out=response.getWriter();

        try {

            String name=request.getParameter("user");
            String password=request.getParameter("pwd");
            if(password.equals("mypassword123") )
            {
                RequestDispatcher rd=request.getRequestDispatcher("MainPage");
                rd.forward(request,response);
            }
            else
            {
                out.println("<b> You have entered incorrect password</b>");
                RequestDispatcher rd=request.getRequestDispatcher("input.html");
                rd.include(request,response);
            }

        }finally {
            out.close();
        }
    }
}
```

Step 3 : On entering the valid password, the request will be forwarded to Main Page. The Main page will display the Welcome message.

MainPage.java

```
import java.io.*;
import javax.servlet.*;
import javax.servlet.http.*;

public class MainPage extends HttpServlet {
    protected void doPost(HttpServletRequest request,HttpServletResponse response)
        throws ServletException, IOException {

            response.setContentType("text/html;charset=UTF-8");
            PrintWriter out=response.getWriter();
            try {
                out.println("<h2> Welcome to Main Page</h2>");

            } finally {
                out.close();
            }
        }
}
```

Step 3 : Compile both the **Validate.java** and **MainPage.java.** Copy the class files to the classes folder of WEB-INF directory. Modify the Web.xml file as follows –

```
<?xml version="1.0" encoding="ISO-8859-1"?>
...
  <servlet>
      <servlet-name>Validate</servlet-name>
      <servlet-class>Validate</servlet-class>
   </servlet>
   <servlet>
      <servlet-name>MainPage</servlet-name>
      <servlet-class>MainPage</servlet-class>
   </servlet>

   <servlet-mapping>
      <servlet-name>Validate</servlet-name>
      <url-pattern>/servlets/servlet/Validate</url-pattern>
   </servlet-mapping>
   <servlet-mapping>
      <servlet-name>MainPage</servlet-name>
      <url-pattern>/servlets/servlet/MainPage</url-pattern>
   </servlet-mapping>
</web-app>
Start the Tomcat web server.
```

Open the suitable web browser and invoke the HTML document as given in Step 1.

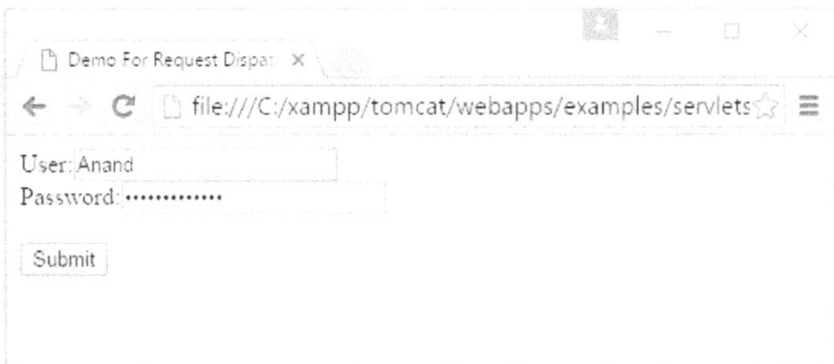

On providing correct password we will get following page.

Difference between forward and include methods

Sr. No.	Forward()	Include()
1.	The client request will get forwarded to the forwarding page.	By this method, another file will be included in the current file.
2.	Once the control returned to the client the output can not be modified.	Once the control is returned to the client, any activity such as calling another servlet or another RequestDispatcher object can be performed.
3.	This method is normally used when further processing is given to another web resource.	This method is normally used to include another web resource such as banner contents, copyright information and so on.
4.	This is faster to execute.	This is slower to execute.

3.10 The Filter API

GTU : May-12,Dec.-12, Winter-13, Marks 7

Servlet Filters are nothing but the Java Classes. The filters are basically used for -

1. **Request :** Using the client sends a request for accessing the back end, the filters intercept this request.
2. **Response :** The filters help in manipulating the response which is send from the back end to the client.

Various types of filters are -

- Authentication filter
- Encryption filter
- Image Conversion filter
- Logging filter
- Data compression filter

Working of Filter

Step 1 : The request sent by the client reaches to the web container. The web container checks if any filter has URL pattern that matches the requested URL.

Step 2 : The web container matches locates the first filter with matching URL pattern and filter code will be executed. If another filter also has the matching URL pattern then that filter code is also executed. This continues until there are no unmatched filter remain.

Step 3 : Then the request is passed to the target servlet .

Step 4 : The target servlet then returns the response back to the filter. The last filter which processed the request becomes the first filter to process the response.

Step 5 : Finally the response is sent to the client.

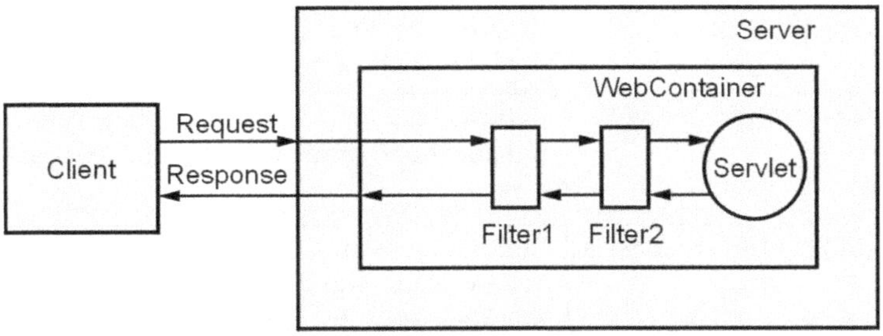

Fig. 3.10.1 Use of filter

3.10.1 Filter

Filters are deployed in the web descriptor file(**web.xml**) of Tomcat server. When the tomcat starts the web application it creates the instance of each filter which is deployed in the web descriptor file.

The **javax.servlet.Filter** implements three methods and these methods are used by the servlet filter. These methods are as given below -

1. public void doFilter (ServletRequest, ServletResponse, FilterChain)

This method is called by the container each time a request/response pair is passed through the chain.

2. public void init(FilterConfig filterConfig)

This method is called by the web container to indicate to the filter that it is being placed into service.

3. public void destroy()

This method is called by the web container to indicate to the filter that it is taken out from the service.

3.10.2 FilterChain Interface

The FilterChain object is responsible for invoking the next filter or resource in the chain. This object is passed to the **doFilter** method of Filter interface. The method in the FilterChain interface is

public void doFilter(HttpServletRequest request, HttpServletResponse response)

This method passes the control to the next filter or resource.

3.10.3 FilterConfig

A filter configuration object used by a servlet container to pass information to a filter during initialization.Various methods supported by FilterConfig interface are

String getFilterName()	Returns the filter-name of this filter as defined in the deployment descriptor.
String getInitParameter(String name)	Returns a String containing the value of the named initialization parameter, or null if the parameter does not exist
Enumeration getInitParameterNames()	Returns the names of the filter's initialization parameters as an Enumeration of String objects, or an empty Enumeration if the filter has no initialization parameters.
ServletContext **getServletContext**()	Returns a reference to the ServletContext in which the caller is executing.

Simple Filter Application

Step 1 :

Write a simple Filter using the Java servlet. It is as given below.

Java Program[Filter1.java]

```
import java.io.*;
import java.util.*;
import java.net.*;
import javax.servlet.*;
import javax.servlet.http.*;

import java.util.Enumeration ;
public final class Filter1 implements Filter
{
 private FilterConfig filtercon = null;
 PrintWriter out;
 public void init(FilterConfig filterConfig)
  throws ServletException
 {
  filtercon = filterConfig;
 }

 public void destroy()
 {
 // called method is destroyed here
 }

 public void doFilter(ServletRequest request, ServletResponse response,FilterChain chain)
 throws IOException, ServletException
 {
    HttpServletResponse res;
    String ipAddress = request.getRemoteAddr();
```

```
        res = (HttpServletResponse ) response;
        out = response.getWriter();
        out.println("<h3>This is my Servlet Filter</h3>");
        out.println("IP "+ ipAddress + ", Time "+ new Date().toString());
        out.println("<hr/>");
        out.println("<i>The website is under construction.</i>");
        out.println("<i>Sorry for inconvenience!!!</i>");
        return;
    }
}
```

Step 2 :

Compile the above code by using javac command. The class file will get generated. Now copy this class file to <your_tomcat_directory>/webapps/ROOT/WEB-INF/classes

Step 3 :

Open the **web.xml** file in Notepad. This **web.xml** file is at the location <your_tomcat_directory>/webapps/ROOT/WEB-INF/

Edit is as follows -

```
<?xml version="1.0" encoding="ISO-8859-1"?>

<!DOCTYPE web-app
  PUBLIC "-//Sun Microsystems, Inc.//DTD Web Application 2.3//EN"
  "http://java.sun.com/dtd/web-app_2_3.dtd">

<web-app>
...
...
...

<filter>
  <filter-name>Filter1</filter-name>
  <filter-class>Filter1</filter-class>
</filter>
<filter-mapping>
  <filter-name>Filter1</filter-name>
  <url-pattern>/*</url-pattern>
</filter-mapping>
</web-app>
```

Step 4 :

Save this web.xml file and then close it. Now open the web browser and type the URL for the servlet **Filter1.** The output will be as follows -

Output

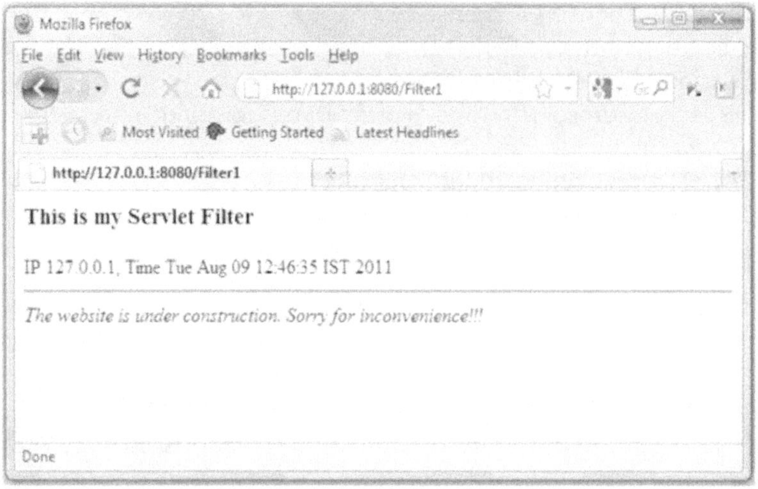

3.10.4 Uses of Filter

1. Filters are used to log the IP addresses of the computers from which the request originates.
2. Filters are useful for recording all the incoming requests.
3. For data validation purpose the filters can be used.
4. Filters are used for encryption and decryption of data.
5. During data compression, filters are used.

Review Questions

1. *What is filter ? What is its use ? List different filter interfaces with their important methods.* **GTU : May-12, Marks 7**
2. *Enlist and explain the need of filters with a program.* **GTU : Dec.-12, Marks 7**
3. *What is servlet filters ? Give the necessary API for filters and explain their use.* **GTU : Winter-13, Marks 7**

3.11 Cookies and Session Management **GTU : Dec.-07, May-12, Marks 7**

3.11.1 Understanding State and Session

- Basically there are two types of protocols : Stateful and stateless protocol. In **stateful protocol**, part of data is exchanged between client and server and these protocols always keep track of communication sessions. On the other hand **stateless protocol** is a protocol in which neither client not server keeps track of the state of communication session. **HTTP** is a **stateless protocol** in which each request is independent of the previous request. And HTTP is a protocol using which user can interact with the server via web browser and it cannot remember previously held communications but sometimes there is serious need to keep track of previous communication sessions. This can be achieved by **session tracking**.

- The **session tracking technique** is a mechanism by which we can keep track of previous sessions between server and the browser.

For sending all state information to and fro between browser and server, usually an ID is used. This ID is basically a **session-ID**. Thus session-ID is passed between the browser and server while processing the information. This method of keeping track of all the information between server and browser using session-ID is called **session tracking**.

3.11.2 Session Tracking

In servlets, for creating the sessions **getSession()** method can be used. This method returns the object which stores the bindings with the names that use this object. And these bindings can be managed using **getAttribute()**, **setAttribute()**, **removeAttribute()** methods. Actually in session tracking two things are playing an important role -

- One is **HttpServletRequest** interface which supports **getSession()** method.
- The another class is **HttpSession** class which supports the binding managing functions such as **getAttribute()**, **setAttribute()**, **removeAttribute()** and **getAttributeNames()**.

Let us first discuss the servlet program which returns the number of previous sessions established between client and server. Note that any client can communicate with the server using some web browser only!

Example 3.11.1 : *Write a servlet program to keep track of number of times user is visiting the page. Display the count appropriately*

Solution :

Servlet Program(SessionServletDemo)

```
import java.io.*;
import java.util.*;
import javax.servlet.*;
import javax.servlet.http.*;
public class SessionServletDemo extends HttpServlet
{
 public void doGet(HttpServletRequest req,HttpServletResponse res)
 throws ServletException,IOException
 {
  res.setContentType("text/html");
  HttpSession session=req.getSession();
  String heading;
```

```
 Integer cnt=(Integer)session.getAttribute("cnt");
 if(cnt==null)
 {
  cnt=new Integer(0);
  heading="Welcome You are accessing the page for the First Time";
 }
else
{
 heading="Welcome once again!";
 cnt=new Integer(cnt.intValue()+1);
}

session.setAttribute("cnt",cnt);
PrintWriter out=res.getWriter();
out.println("<html>");
out.println("<head>");
out.println("</head>");
out.println("<body>");
out.println("<center>");
out.println("<h1>"+heading);
out.println("<h2> The number of previous access= "+cnt);
out.println("</center>");
out.println("</body>");
out.println("</html>");
}
}
```

Output

To get an output we will use following steps -

1. Compile the Servlet (i.e. a java program) using **javac**. This will generate a class file.
2. Copy this class file to C:*your tomcat directory**examples-folder**WEB-INF**classes*
3. Edit the **web.xml** file present at C:*your tomcat directory**examples-folder**WEB-INF* like this

```
...
<servlet>
     <servlet-name>SessionServletDemo</servlet-name>
     <servlet-class>SessionServletDemo</servlet-class>
   </servlet>
...
<servlet-mapping>
                  <servlet-name>SessionServletDemo</servlet-name>
                  <url-pattern>/servlet/SessionServletDemo</url-pattern>
</servlet-mapping>
```

4. Open the web browser and give the URL for **SessionServletDemo**. Following output can be seen.

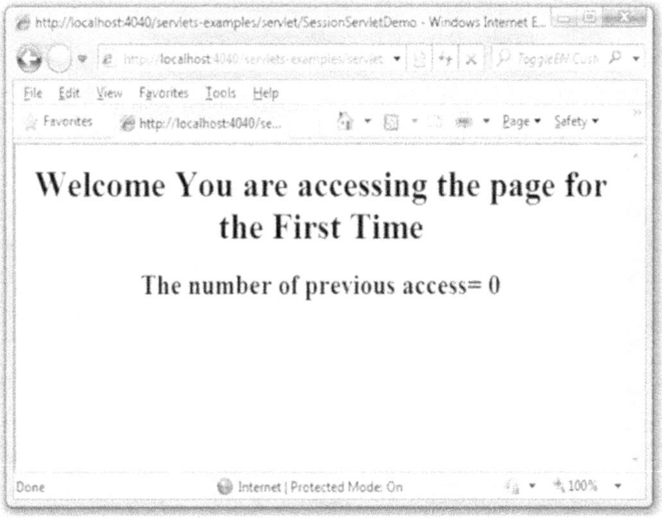

If you simply refresh your browser either by pressing F5 or clicking the refresh button then you will get following kind of output.

Our class *SessionServletDemo* is inherited from **HttpServlet** class. And inside the **doGet()** method we can create an object *session* of **HttpSession** class. This method returns the current session for the corresponding request.

The **getAttribute(string** *atrribute***)** returns the value associated with the *attribute.* We can pass this *attribute* as a parameter to this method. If there is no attribute present then this method returns null. The data type of getAttribute() method is **void**.

The setAttribute(**string** *attribute,* **object** *value*) is a method which assigns the *value* passed as the object value to the *attribute* name. The data type of this method is **void**.

3.11.3 Understanding Session Timeout

The length of time that a session lasts before the server invalidates it is an important component of any web application.

In Tomcat 4.1.x, the default timeout period for a session is 30 minutes. If any requests that are associated with the session have been inactive for that period, the session times out. If the user decides to return to the web application after 30 minutes, using the same browser, then a new session is created for him.

There are two methods to set the session timeout.

Method 1 : Using Deployment Descriptor

We can set the session timeout period with the help of deployment descriptor i.e. **web.xml** by using

<session-config>

For example – Following is a web.xml in which the session timeout is set to 15 minutes.

```
<?xml version="1.0" encoding="ISO-8859-1"?>
<!DOCTYPE web-app
  PUBLIC "-//Sun Microsystems, Inc.//DTD Web Application 2.3//EN"
     "http://java.sun.com/dtd/web-application_2_3.dtd"
>

<web-app>

<!-- filter, listener, servlet, and servlet-mapping elements precede session-config -->
...
...

 <session-config>
  <session-timeout>15</session-timeout>
 </session-config>

</web-app>
```

Method 2 : Using setMaxInactiveInterval()

We can manually set the session timeout for particular session as follows –

```
HttpSession session = request.getSession();
session.setMaxInactiveInterval(15*60);
```

The above setting is applicable on session which calls the "**setMaxInactiveInterval()**" method, and session will be killed by container if client doesn't make any request after 15 minutes. Note that the setMaxInactiveInterval() method will accept the value in "seconds"

3.11.4 URL Rewriting

This is more precise technique in which information is embedded into URL. For instance.

```
GET    / introduction.html    HTTP P.1

HOST   www.mywebpage.com
```

Browser **Requests** → **Server**

The server then repsonds by putting **sid=xf1234ad** in response body.

```
HTTP/1.1                200 OK
<html>
<a   href = introduction.html; sid=xf1234ad>
     Click here to go to Next page </a>
     : : :
</html>
```

Browser ← **Response** **Server**

The browser will demand for the required web page by putting the same URL string in the request.

```
GET      /introduction.html   sid=xf1234ad    HTTP/1.1
```

Browser **Request** → **Server**

When browser makes requests for another page same URL is embedded. There by server will come to know that the request is related to previous page and the work in same session will get co-related.

We can send the name-value pair from one page to another using URL rewriting method. In this method the token of name-value pair can be added at the end of URL. The URL writing occurs in the following format

URL?name1=value1&name2=value2

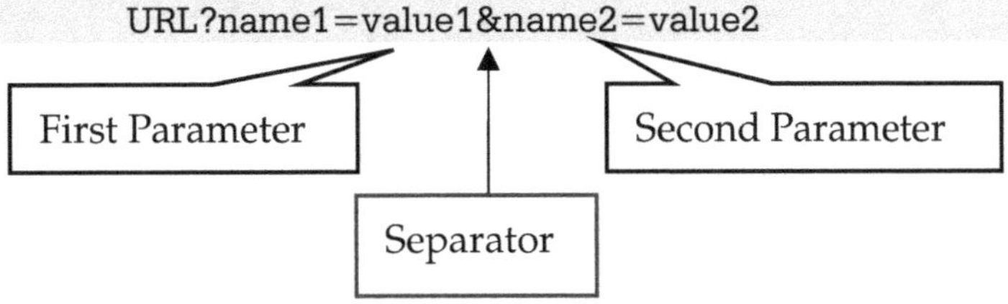

The parameter sent by the URL is obtained at the server side by **getParameter** method. The syntax of this method is

String **getParameter**(String)

Example 3.11.2 : *Write a servlet that Welcomes the user by his/her name only if the valid password is entered by the user. Make use of URL rewriting method*

Step 1 : Create a registration form. I have named it as registration.html. The code for it is as follows

registration.html

```
<!doctype html>
<html>
<head>
<title> Demo For URL Rewriting </title>
<body>
<form method ="post" action="http://localhost/examples/servlets/servlet/firstpg">
User:<input type ="text" name="user" ><br/>
Password:<input type ="password" name="pwd"> <br/><br/>
<input type="submit" value="Submit">
</form>
</body>
```

Step 2 : Create a servlet program that reads the user name and password values entered by the user. This servlet also compares the entered password with the valid password. If the user enters valid password, then the request is redirected to another servlet page. Otherwise *wrong password* message will be displayed. The first servlet is

firstservlet.java

```
import java.io.*;
import javax.servlet.*;
import javax.servlet.http.*;
public class firstpg extends HttpServlet {
 protected void doPost(HttpServletRequest request, HttpServletResponse response)
        throws ServletException, IOException {

    response.setContentType("text/html;charset=UTF-8");
    PrintWriter out = response.getWriter();
    String uname = request.getParameter("user");
    String pass = request.getParameter("pwd");
    if(pass.equals("password"))
    {
      response.sendRedirect("secondpg?user_name="+uname+"");
    }
    else
     out.println("<i> You have entered wrong password!!!</i>");
  }
}
```

Step 3 : If user enters the valid password, then he/she is redirected to main page. This page welcomes him/her by his/her name. The code for this servlet is as follows –

secondpg.java

```
import java.io.*;
import javax.servlet.*;
import javax.servlet.http.*;
public class secondpg extends HttpServlet {
 protected void doGet(HttpServletRequest request, HttpServletResponse response)
        throws ServletException, IOException {

     response.setContentType("text/html;charset=UTF-8");
     PrintWriter out = response.getWriter();
     String user = request.getParameter("user_name");
     out.println("<h3>Welcome "+user+" to main page!!!</h3>");
  }
}
```

Step 4 : Compile the java files created in step 2 and step 3. Copy the class files to **classes** folder of Tomcat's WEB-INF folder. Modify the web.xml file as follows –

```
<?xml version="1.0" encoding="ISO-8859-1"?>
...
  <servlet>
     <servlet-name>firstpg</servlet-name>
     <servlet-class>firstpg</servlet-class>
  </servlet>
  <servlet>
     <servlet-name>secondpg</servlet-name>
     <servlet-class>secondpg</servlet-class>
  </servlet>

  <servlet-mapping>
     <servlet-name>firstpg</servlet-name>
     <url-pattern>/servlets/servlet/firstpg</url-pattern>
  </servlet-mapping>
  <servlet-mapping>
     <servlet-name>secondpg</servlet-name>
     <url-pattern>/servlets/servlet/secondpg</url-pattern>
  </servlet-mapping>
</web-app>
```

Start the Tomcat web server.

Open the suitable web browser and invoke the HTML document as given in Step 1. The output will be

On clicking Submit button we will get the following page on valid password

3.11.5 Cookies

> Cookies are some little information that can be left on your computer by the other computer when we access an internet.

Generally this information is left on your computer by some advertising agencies on the internet. Using the information stored in the cookies these advertising agencies can keep track of your internet usage. For the applications like on-line purchase systems once you enter your personal information such as your name or your e-mail ID then it can be remembered by these systems with the help of cookies. Sometimes cookies are very much dangerous because by using information from your local disk some malicious data may be passed to you. So it is upto you how to maintain your own privacy and security. Below is simple HTML form in which a servlet is invoked. This servlet creates a cookie by the name My_Cookie and stores the value entered by you in the textbox of HTML form. You can further get the information stored in the cookie by another servlet program *getCookieServlet*. Hence we will write three programs -

1. Our normal HTML script in which some value is entered in the textbox.

2. The servlet program named mycookieservlet which will set a cookies and take the value entered by you in the HTML form.
3. The another servlet program named *getCookieServlet* which helps us to view the cookie.

HTML Program

```
<html>
<head>
<title>Demo of Cookie</title>
</head>
<body>
<form name="form1" method="post"
action="http://localhost:8080/examples/servlet/mycookieservlet">
<h3> Enter the value for my Cookie: </h3>
<input type=text name="txt_data" size =30 value=" ">
<input type=submit  value="Submit">
</form>
</body>
</html>
```

Servlet Program [mycookieservlet.java]

```
import java.io.*;
import javax.servlet.*;
import javax.servlet.http.*;
public class mycookieservlet extends HttpServlet
{
public void doPost(HttpServletRequest req,HttpServletResponse res)
throws ServletException, IOException
{
String txt_data = req.getParameter("txt_data");
// Create cookie.
Cookie cookie = new Cookie("My_Cookie", txt_data);
// Adding cookie to HTTP response.
res.addCookie(cookie);
// Write friendly output to browser.
res.setContentType("text/html");
PrintWriter out = res.getWriter();
out.println("<h2>MyCookie has been set to: ");
out.println(txt_data);
out.println("<br><br><br>");
out.println("This page shows that the cookie has been added");
out.close();
}
}
```

We have first created an object of Cookie class using which the cookie can be added using addCookie() method.

Servlet Program[getcookieservlet.java]

```
import java.io.*;
import javax.servlet.*;
import javax.servlet.http.*;
public class getCookieServlet extends HttpServlet
{
 public void doGet(HttpServletRequest req,HttpServletResponse res)
 throws ServletException,IOException
{
Cookie[ ] my_cookies=req.getCookies();
res.setContentType("text/html");
PrintWriter out=res.getWriter();
out.println("<b>");
int n=my_cookies.length;
for(int i=0;i<n;i++)
{
String name=my_cookies[i].getName();
String value=my_cookies[i].getValue();
out.println("name= "+name);
out.println("and value= "+value);
}
out.close();
}
}
```

In the above program using **getName()** and **getValue()** functions we can get the name of the cookie as well as the value of the cookie respectively. The output of all the above given three programs is as given below -

Output

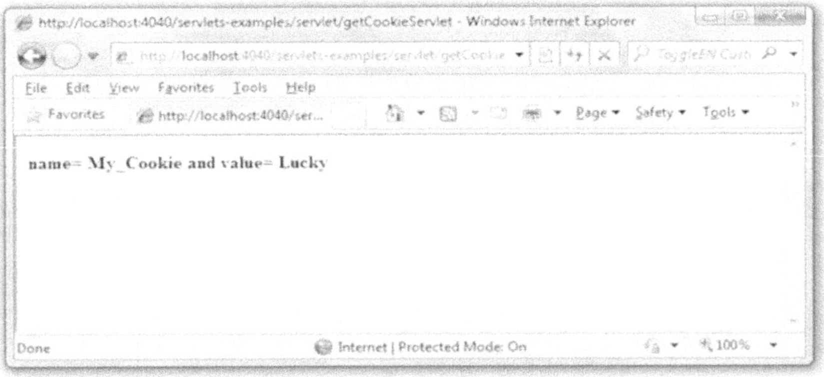

Review Questions

1. *Develop any servlet application which demonstrates use of session management.*

GTU : Dec.-07, Marks 7

2. *What are Cookies ? Write a servlet that reads and prints all the precious cookies and add a cookie with your name.* **GTU : May-12, Marks 7**

❑❑❑

Notes

4 Java Server Pages

Syllabus

JSP Overview : *The Problem with Servlets, Life Cycle of JSP Page, JSP Processing, JSP Application Design with MVC, Setting Up the JSP Environment*

JSP Directives, JSP Action, JSP Implicit Objects

JSP Form Processing, JSP Session and Cookies Handling, JSP Session Tracking

JSP Database Access, JSP Standard Tag Libraries, JSP Custom Tag, JSP Expression Language, JSP Exception Handling, JSP XML Processing.

Contents

4.1 JSP Overview

4.2 Problems With Servlets . . . . **Summer-14, 16,** · · · · · · · · · · · · · · · *Marks 7*

4.3 Life Cycle of JSP Page . . . . **Winter-14, Summer-16,** · · · · · · · · *Marks 7*

4.4 Anatomy of JSP Page

4.5 JSP Application Design with MVC . . . . . **Summer-13, 14,** · · · · · · · · · · · · · · *Marks 7*

4.6 Setting up JSP Environment

4.7 Declarations

4.8 JSP Directives . . . . **Winter-13, Summer-15,** · · · · · · · · *Marks 7*

4.9 Code Snippets

4.10 JSP Action . . . . **Dec.-12,** · *Marks 7*

4.11 JSP Implicit Objects . . . . **May-12,** · *Marks 7*

4.12 JSP Form Processing . . . . **May-12, Summer-16,** · · · · · · · · · · · *Marks 7*

4.13 JSP Cookies Handling

4.14 JSP Session Tracking

4.15 JSP Database Access . . . . **Dec.-12, Summer-13, 16,** · · · · · · · *Marks 7*

4.16 JSP Standard Tag Libraries **Dec.-11, May-12, Winter-13, 14,**
. . . . **Summer-14, 16,** · · · · · · · · · · · · · · · *Marks 7*

4.17 JSP Custom Tag

4.18 JSP Expression Language . . . . **May-12, Summer-15,** · · · · · · · · · · · *Marks 7*

4.19 JSP Exception Handling

4.20 JSP XML Processing . . . . **Summer-13, 15, Winter-13, 14,** · · *Marks 7*

4.1 JSP Overview

JSP stands for Java Server Pages. It is a server side scripting language.

4.1.1 Advantages of Java Server Pages(JSP)

Following are some advantages of Java Server Pages -

1. JSP is useful for server side programming.
2. JSP can be used along with servlets. Hence business logic for any application can be developed using JSP.
3. Dynamic contents can be handled using JSP because JSP allows scripting and element based programming.
4. JSP allows creating and using our own custom tag libraries. Hence any application specific requirements can be satisfied using custom tag libraries. This helps the developer to develop any kind of application.
5. JSP is a specification and not a product. Hence developers can develop variety of applications and add up to performance and quality of software products. Due to this many companies are ready to invest in JSP technology.
6. JSP is an essential component of J2EE. Hence using JSP it is possible to develop simple as well as complex applications.

4.2 Problems With Servlets

GTU : Summer-14, 16, Marks 7

- In one and only one class, the servlet alone has to do various tasks such as
  - o Acceptance of request
  - o Processing of request
  - o Handling of business logic
  - o Generation of response.

Hence there are some problems that are associated with servlets -

1. For developing a servlet based application, knowledge of Java as well as HTML code is necessary.
2. While developing any web based application, if a look and feel of web based application needs to be changed then the entire code needs to be changed and recompiled.
3. There are some **web page development tools** available using which the developer can develop web based applications. But the servlets do not support such tools. Even if such tools are used for a servlet, we need to change embedded HTML code manually, which is a time consuming, error prone and complicated process.

4.2.1 Comparison between JSP and Servlet

Sr. No.	JSP	Servlet
1.	JSP is a scripting language that generates dynamic content.	Servlets are the Java programs that can be compiled to generate dynamic content.
2.	JSP runs slower than servlet.	Servlet runs faster than JSP.
3.	In Model View Controller JSP acts as view.	In Model View Controller servlet acts as controller.
4.	JSP can build custom tags.	There is no facility of creating custom tags.
5.	JSP can directly call Java beans.	Servlets have no facility of calling Java Bean.
6.	It is easier to code in JSP.	The servlets are basically complex Java programs.

Review Questions

1. *Compare JSP with Servlet.* **GTU : Summer-14, Marks 7**
2. *Differentiate the followings : JSP vs Servlet.* **GTU : Summer-16, Marks 2**

4.3 Life Cycle of JSP Page

GTU : Winter-14, Summer-16, Marks 7

JSP pages can be processed using **JSP container** only. Following are the steps that need to be followed while processing the request for JSP page -

I. Client makes a request for required JSP page to the server. The server must have JSP container so that JSP request can be processed. For instance: Let the client makes a request for *xyz.jsp* page.

II. On receiving this request the JSP container searches and then reads the desired JSP page. Then this JSP page is straightaway converted to corresponding **servlet**. Basically any JSP page is a combination of template text and JSP element. Every **template text** is translated into corresponding **println** statement.

For instance :

```
<html>
<head>
<title>Demo</title>
...
```

→

```
out.println("<html>");
out.println("<head>");
out.println("<title>Demo</title>");
...
```

Every **JSP element** is converted into corresponding **Java code**. This phase is called **translation phase**. The output of translation phase is a servlet. For instance: our *xyz.jsp* gets converted to *xyzServlet.java*.

III. This servlet is then compiled to generate the servlet class file. Using this class the response can be generated. This phase is called **request processing phase**.

IV. The JSP container thus **executes** the servlet class file.

V. A requested page is then returned to the client as a **response**. Refer Fig. 4.3.1.

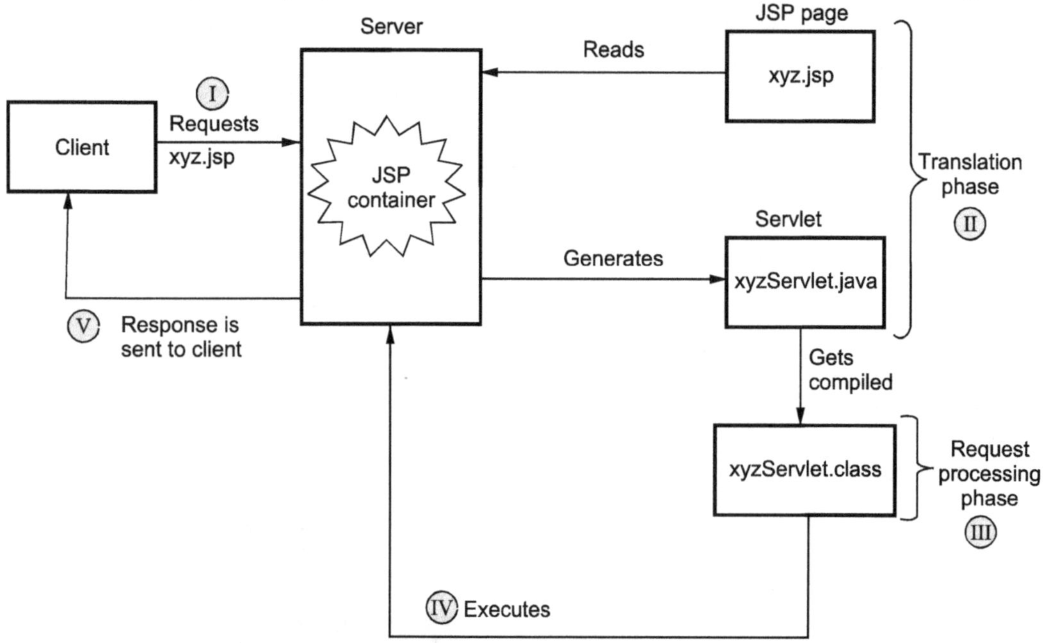

Fig. 4.3.1 JSP processing

Review Questions

1. *Explain the life cycle of JSP.* **GTU : Winter-14, Marks 7**
2. *List and explain various stages of JSP life cycle. Briefly give the function of each phase.* **GTU : Summer-16, Marks 7**

4.4 Anatomy of JSP Page

JSP page is a simple web page which contains the **JSP elements** and **template text**. The template text can be scripting code such as HTML,WML,XML or a simple plain text. Various JSP elements can be action tags, custom tags, JSTL library elements. These JSP elements are responsible for generating dynamic contents.

JSP code

```
<%@ page language="java" contentType="text/html" %> <-------- JSP element
    <html>
        <head>
            <title>Demo for Template Text</title>
        </head>
        <body bgcolor="gray">                               <---------Template text
            <h1>Twinkle Twinkle little stars</h1>
            <h2>How I wonder what you are!!!</h2>
            <li>like a diamond in the sky</li>
            <p>
```

```
        <% out.print(" JSP is eqaul to HTML and JAVA "); %> <-----------JSP element

    </p>                                  } <-----------Template text
    <h3>Today's Date is:

        <%= new Date().toString() %>        <----------------JSP element
      </h3>
    </body>        } <-----------------------Template text
</html>
```

When JSP request gets processed template text and JSP elements are merged together and sent to the browser as a response.

4.5 JSP Application Design with MVC

GTU : Summer-13, 14, Marks 7

- JSP is a technology in which the request processing, business logic and presentations are separated out.

The design model of JSP application is called **MVC model**. The MVC stands for **Model-View-Controller**. The basic idea in MVC design model is to separate out design logic into three parts - **modelling, viewing** and **controlling**.

Any server application is classified in three parts such as **business logic**, **presentation** and **request processing**.

The **business logic** means the coding logic applied for manipulation of application data. The **presentation** refers to the code written for look and feel of the web page. For example: background color, font style, font size, placing of controls such as text boxes, command buttons and so on. The request processing is nothing but a combination of business logic and presentation. The request processing is always done in order to generate the response.

According to the MVC design model, the Model corresponds to business logic, View corresponds to presentation and Controller corresponds to request processing.

Advantages of using MVC design Model

The use of MVC architecture allows the developer to keep the separation between business logic, presentation and request processing. Due to this separation it becomes easy to make **changes** in presentation without disturbing the business logic. The changes in presentation are often required for accommodating the new presentation interfaces.

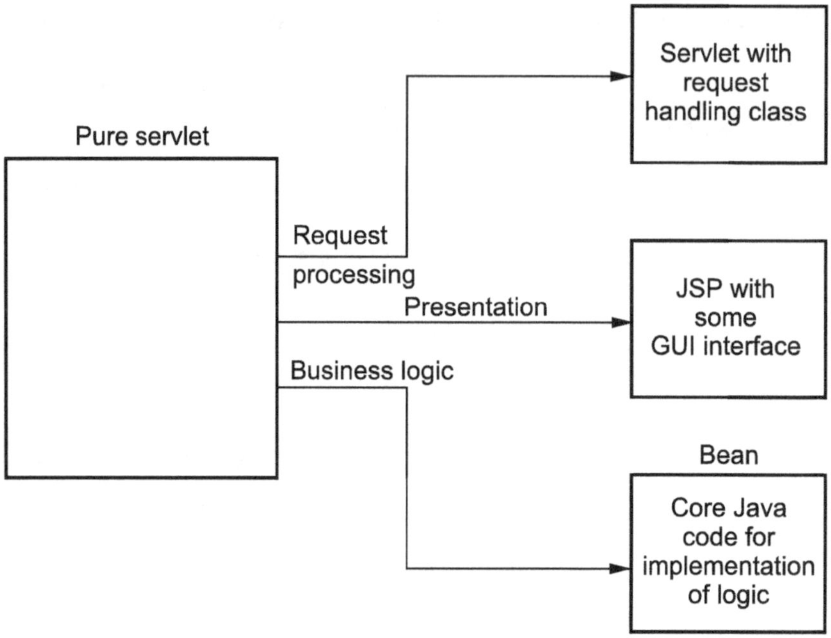

Fig. 4.5.1 Separation of request processing, presentation and business logic

Advantages of MVC Architecture

1. Separation of three components such as **model, view** and **controller**. Hence **parallel development** of the code for these three components is possible.
2. The code can be **reusable**.
3. It is easy to **maintain and enhance the project** code using this architecture.
4. One can attach **multiple views** to model in order to have **different presentations**.
5. The developer working on view model need not have to know about controller model and vise versa. That means the development teams can **work independently** as per their skill.

Review Questions

1. *What do you mean by MVC architecture ? Explain its role in modern applications and list its advantages.* **GTU : Summer-13, Marks 7**
2. *Draw and explain JSP architecture.* **GTU : Summer-14, Marks 7**

4.6 Setting up JSP Environment

For execution of JSP pages following installations are needed.

1. **Java Development Kit :** Download and install the latest version of JDK.

2. **Tomcat WebServer :** The Tomcat is a web container provided by Apache Web server which can be freely downloaded on your computer. Set the environment variable.

```
TOMCAT_HOME= <your tomcat installation directory path>
```

Note that before running any JSP page it is essential to start the tomcat by double clicking the startup.bat file present in the tomcat directory.

Example : Write a simple JSP page for displaying the message "This is my first JSP page!!!"

We follow these steps to get the JSP page displayed -

Step 1 : First of all open some text editor like Notepad and type the following code.

hello.jsp

```
<%@ page language="java" contentType="text/html" %>
<%@ page import ="java.util.*" %>
<html>
<!-- This is basic JSP page -->
<title>JSP Demo </title>
<body>
<%-- Displaying the message on the browser --%>
        <% out.println("This my first JSP page!!!"); %>
    </body>
</html>
```

Create a separate directory at the path c:\your_tomcat_directory\webapps\jsp-examples and store the above code in this newly created directory.

I have created a directory named **HelloDemo** in which I have stored the above program by the name **hello.jsp**. Note that while saving the file using Notepad editor with the extension jsp, you must select the **all files** option if you don't do that then the file may get saved as hello.jsp.txt because the default extension for the notepad files is .txt

For the sake of understanding, just look at the following screenshot to know the location of the your JSP pages -

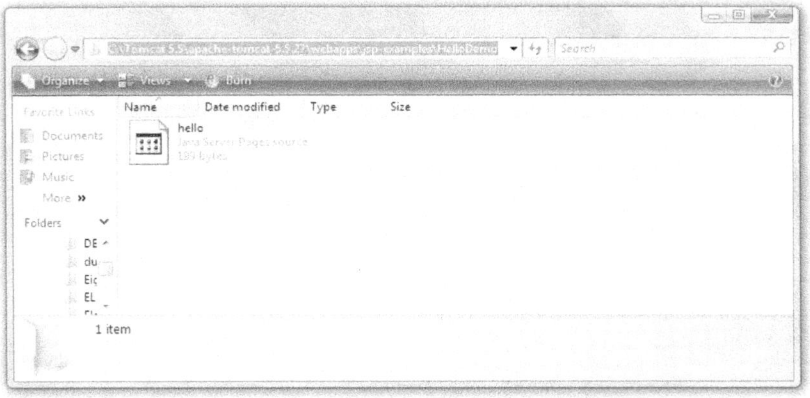

Step 2 : Start the Tomcat Web server by typing the command **startup** at the command prompt.

Step 3 : Open some suitable web browser like Firefox or Internet Explorer. Type the path for the JSP page using the prefix **http://localhost:portnumber.** The default port for Tomcat web server is 8080. But we can install Tomcat to some other port for convenience. The output for the JSP page written in step 1 is as follows -

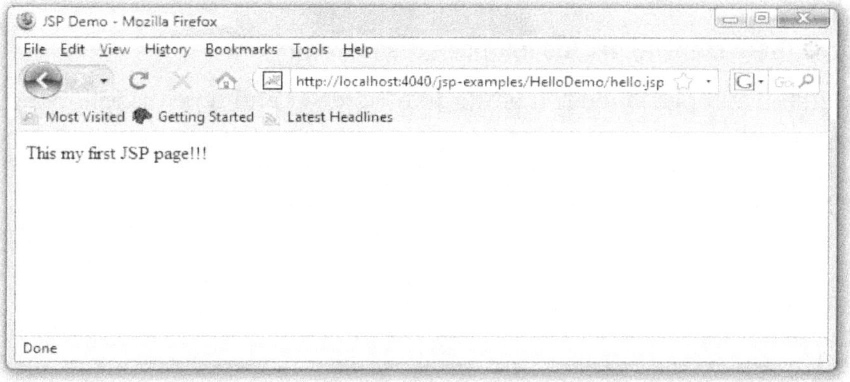

Code explanation

The first line is the **page directive** statement

```
<%@ page language="java" contentType="text/html" %>
```

using this line we are specifying that the language used in this script is Java and the contentType specifies the MIME type which is **text/html.**

Then on the next line we have imported the Java library package **java.util** using import statement -

```
<%@ page import ="java.util.*" %>
```

We can specify the JSP comments in two ways

```
<!—HTML style comment statement -->
<%-- JSP comment statement --%>
```

As JSP is commonly used along with HTML, it also supports the HTML comments.

For displaying the message on the web browser we have written the message using the Java statement

```
out.println("This my first JSP page!!!");
```

Normally any Java code must be written within <% and %>

Then all the corresponding tags are closed.

4.7 Declarations

The JSP page that we write is turned into class definition. So when we declare a variable or method in JSP inside **Declaration Tag**. We can declare static member,instance variable and methods inside **Declaration Tag**. Syntax of Declaration Tag

```
<%! Declaration code %>
```

For example -

```
<html>
  <head>
    <title>JSP Declaration Demo</title>
  </head>
  <%!
    String msg = "Hello";
  %>
 <body>
    Message is:
    <% out.println(msg); %>
 </body>
</html>
```

Output

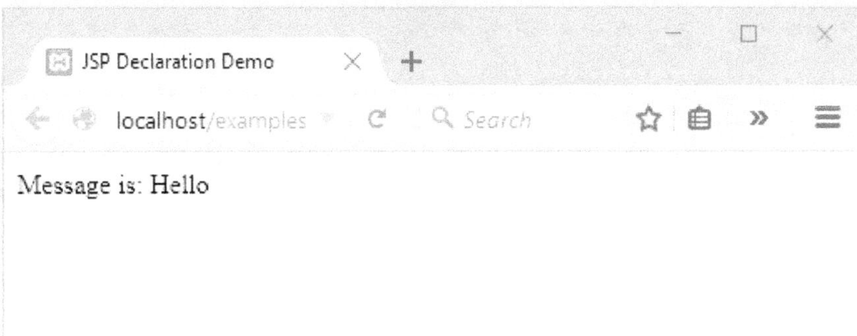

The above JSP code contains the declaration within <%!   %> tag.

We can declare a function of a method in JSP just similar to variable. Following JSP example illustrates the use of function declaration and definition.

MethodDemo.jsp

```
<%@ page language="java" contentType="text/html" %>
    <%!
        String msg="Hello";
    %>
    <%! public String MyFunction(String msg)
    {
            return msg;
    }
```

```
    %>
<html>
    <head>
        <title> Use of Method </title>
    </head>
    <body>
        <% out.print("Before function call: "+msg); %>
    <br/>
        After function call: <%= MyFunction("Technical Publications") %>
    </body>
</html>
```

Output

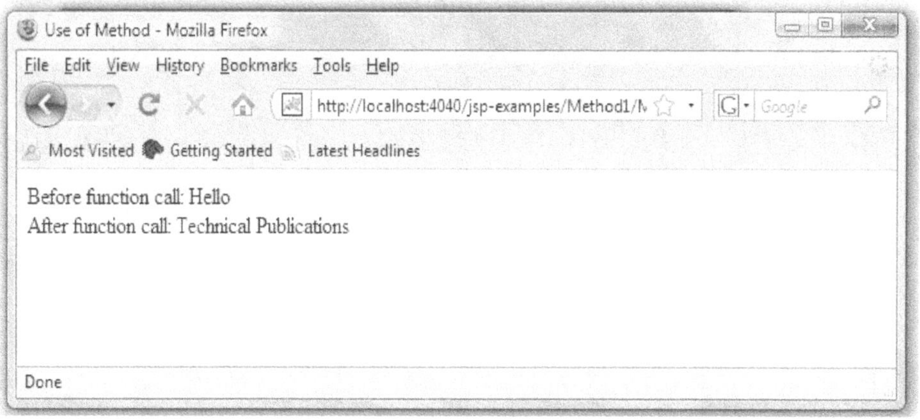

Let us see one more example of JSP page that uses the **Date** from **java.util.Date** package.

Dt.jsp

```
<%@ page language="java" contentType="text/html" %>
<%@ page import="java.util.*" %>
<%!
    String ShowTime()
    {
        Date d=new Date();
        String msg="Hello ";
        if(d.getHours()< 12)
        {
            msg+="It's morning now!!!";
        }
        else if(d.getHours()<18)
        {
            msg+="It's afternoon now!!";
        }
        else
```

```
        {
            msg+="It's evening now!!";
        }
        return msg;
    }
%>
<html>
    <head>
        <title>Date Demo</title>
    </head>
    <body>
        <h3><%= ShowTime() %></h3>
    </body>
</html>
```

In above program we have used an object of Date() using which the **getHours()** function is invoked. Appropriate message will get displayed on the web browser using the system time.

Hence the output can be obtained on the web browser as follows -

Output

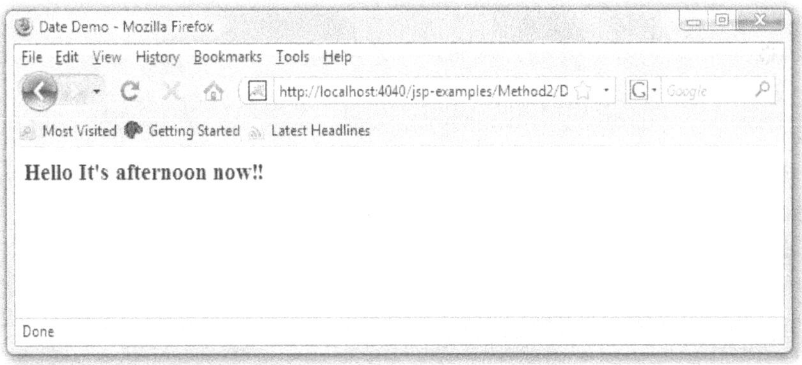

4.8 JSP Directives

GTU : Winter-13, Summer-15, Marks 7

JSP directives control the processing of entire JSP Page. It gives direction to the server regarding the processing of a page.

Syntax

```
<%@ directive name [attribute name="value" attribute name="value" ........]%>
```

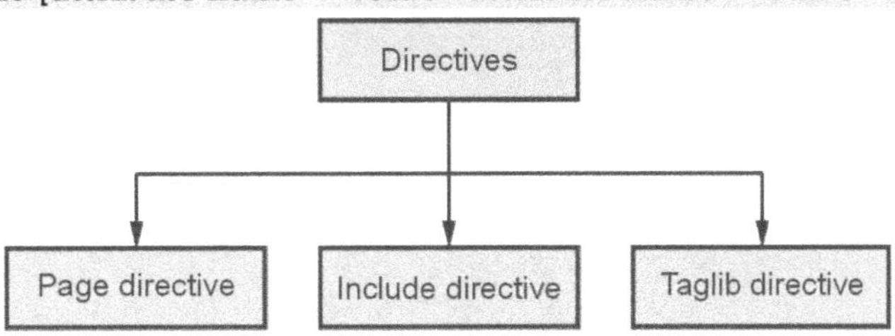

1. **Page Directive :** The page directive is used to provide the information about the page. Various attributes of Page directive are -

   i) import ii) language iii) contentType

   iv) extends v) session vi) buffer

   vii) autoFlush viii) isThreadSafe ix) info

   x) errorPage xi) IsErrorPage

For example -

```
<%@page import="java.io.*" %>
<%@page language="java" %>
<%@page contentType="text/html" %>
```

2. **Include Directive :** Include directive is used to copy the content of one JSP page to another. It's like including the code of one file into another.

For example

```
<% @include file=calculate.jsp %>
```

3. **Taglib Directive :** This directive basically allows user to use Custom tags in JSP. The custom tags are those which are created by user.

For example -

```
<%@ taglib uri="mytaglib" prefix="sampletag" %>
```

Example 4.8.1 : *Write a JSP program to display current date and time.*

Solution :

DateDemo.jsp

```
<%@ page language="java" contentType="text/html" %>
<%@ page import ="java.util.*" %>
<html>
<body>Today's Date is:
        <%= new Date().toString() %>
</body>
</html>
```

Output

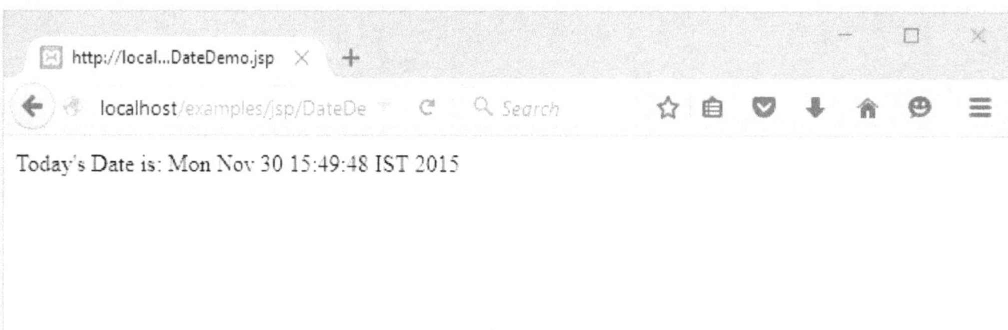

Review Questions

1. *Show the use of JSP page directive tag with its attributes.* **GTU : Winter-13, Marks 7**
2. *Explain the JSP i) Page ii) Include iii) Taglib directive with attribute, description. Also write example of java snippet for each directive.* **GTU : Summer-15, Marks 7**

4.9 Code Snippets

The code that appears between the <% and %> delimiters is called a *scriptlet*. Scriptlets are nothing but java code **enclosed within** <% and %> tags**.**

The every thing other than a JSP statement in the JSP is called template text. For example

Templatetext.jsp

```
<%@ page language="java" contentType="text/html" %>
    <html>
        <head>
            <title>Demo for Tempplate Text</title>
        </head>
        <body bgcolor="gray">
            <h1>Twinkle Twinkle little stars</h1>
            <h2>How I wonder what you are!!!</h2>
            <li>like a diamond in the sky</li>
            <p>
                <% out.print("JSP is eqaul to HTML and JAVA "); %>
            </p>
    </body>
</html>
```

In the above code the boldfaced code is a template text. The output for the above code will be

Output

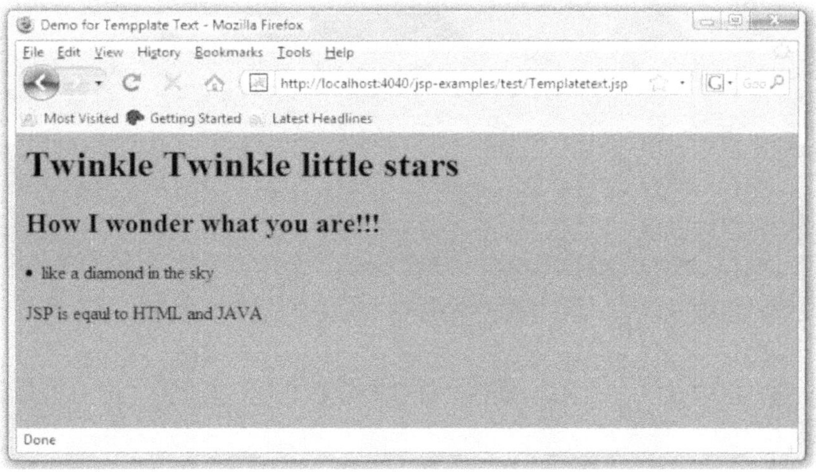

Another example of Scriplet is given by following JSP code

Scriptletdemo.jsp

```
<%@ page language="java" contentType="text/html" %>
    <html>
        <head>
            <title>Introduction to scriptlet</title>
        </head>
        <body>
            <strong>
                <% out.println(" Value of i is:");%>
                <% for(int i=1;i<5;i++) {
                 out.print("<br/>");
                 if(i%2==0)
                 {
                     out.print("<i/>");
                     out.println("Even value is: "+i);
                 }
                 else
                 {
                     out.print("<i/>");
                     out.println("Odd value is: "+i);
                 }
            }%>
        </strong>
    </body>
</html>
```

Output

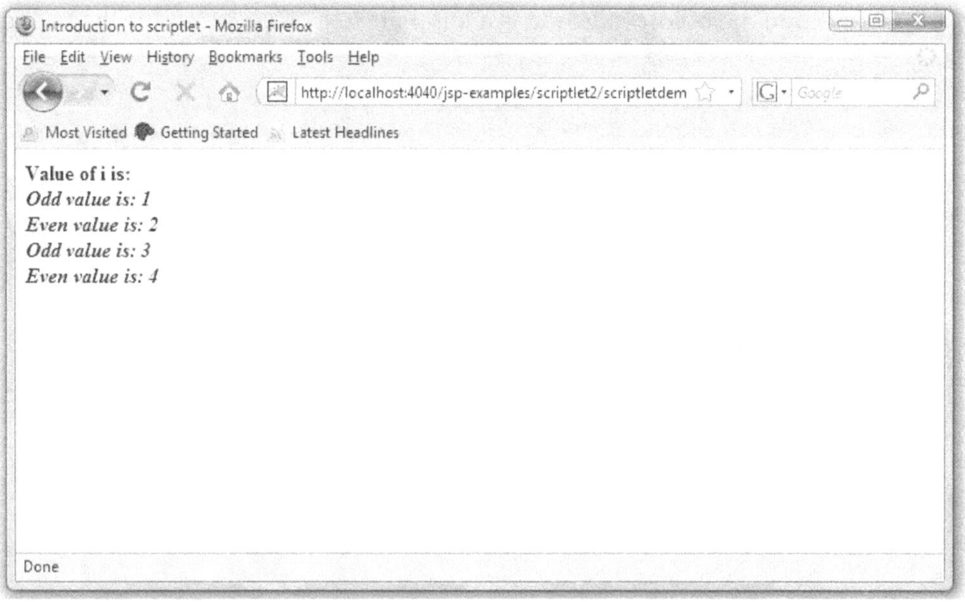

4.10 JSP Action

GTU : Dec.-12, Marks 7

The elements which are used to access the bean in a page is called **JSP action elements**. JSP defines three types of actions

1. Standard action
2. Custom action
3. JSP standard Tag Library (JSTL).

In this section we will discuss standard action tags only. The other types of actions will be discussed in later part of this chapter.

4.10.1 Standard Action

The standard actions are those actions that can be defined by the JSP specification itself. Following is a list of standard actions

Action Element	Description
<jsp:useBean>	This tag is used to instantiate the object of java bean.
<jsp:setProperty>	This tag is used to set the property value for the java bean.
<jsp:getProperty>	This tag is used to get the property value from the java bean.
<jsp:include>	This tag works as a subroutine. It includes the response from servlet or JSP when request is being processed.
<jsp:param>	For adding the specific parameter to the request this tag is used. Normally this tag is used inside <jsp:include> or <jsp:forward>
<jsp:forward>	This tag helps in forwarding the current request to servlet or to JSP page.
<jsp:plugin>	This tag is used to generate HTML code and to embed the applet into it.
<jsp:attribute>	This tag sets the value of the action attribute
<jsp:element>	This tag generated the XML elements dynamically.
<jsp:text>	This tag is used to handle template text. When JSP pages are written as XML documents then this tag is used.
<jsp:body>	This tag is used to set the body element.

Let us now discuss the standard actions by creating appropriate JSP pages.

a) Include action

We have already discussed the use of **<jsp:useBean>,<jsp:setProperty>** and **<jsp:getProperty>** actions in earlier section. Let us now see how to use **<jsp:include>** action. Using the **<jsp:include>** action we can include different files in current jsp pages. In the following example we have created one main JSP page *Include_action.jsp* which will include one html file *test_include.html* and one JSP page *test_jsp.jsp*. The *test_include.html* page is for showing the static contents and *test_jsp.jsp* page is for showing the dynamic contents. Let us first see the main JSP page named *Include_action.jsp*

Include_action.jsp

```
<html>
    <head>
        <title> Include action Demo </title>
    </head>
    <body>
        <h1>This page contains include action</h1>
        <jsp:include page="test_include.html" />
        <jsp:include page="test_jsp.jsp" />
    </body>
</html>
```

Now the static html page can be

test_include.html

```
<html>
<body>
    Hello How are you?
</body>
</html>
```

Now the JSP page for displaying dynamic content is

test_jsp.jsp

```
<html>
    <body>
    <br>Time is <%= new java.util.Date().getHours()%>
    : <%= new java.util.Date().getMinutes()%>
    </body>
</html>
```

For getting the output, open the web browser and open our main JSP page **Include_action.jsp**, it is as follows -

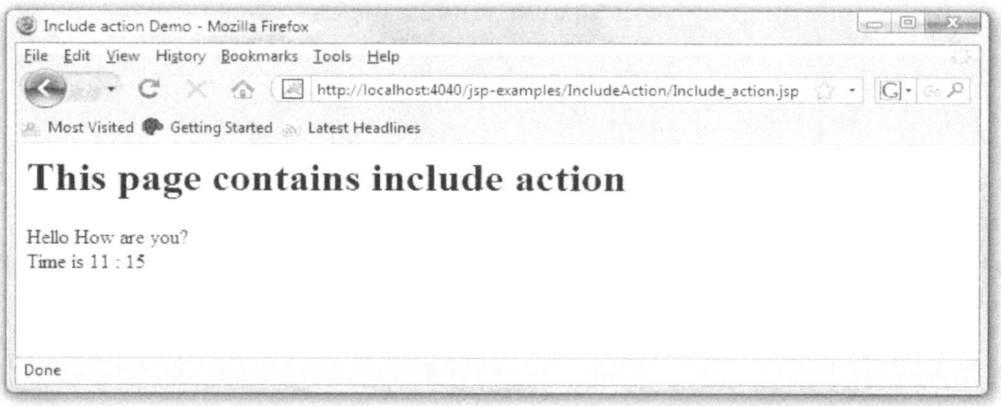

Note that **include action** and **include directive** are two different entities but both of these are for the same purpose and that is to include some external file in the current JSP page.

To understand this difference clearly let us have a look at the use of **include directive** in the JSP page. Again we will use three different file out of which one main file is named as **Include_directive.jsp** in which we are making use of **include directive** and other two files will remain the same.

Include_directive.jsp

```
<html>
    <head>
        <title> Include action Directive </title>
    </head>
    <body>
        <h1>This page contains include Directive</h1>
        <%@ include file="test_include.html" %>
        <%@ include file="test_jsp.jsp" %>
    </body>
</html>
```

test_include.html

```
<html>
<body>
    Hello How are you?
</body>
</html>
```

Now the JSP page for displaying dynamic content is

test_jsp.jsp

```
<html>
    <body>
    <br>Time is <%= new java.util.Date().getHours()%>
    : <%= new java.util.Date().getMinutes()%>
    </body>
</html>
```

Output

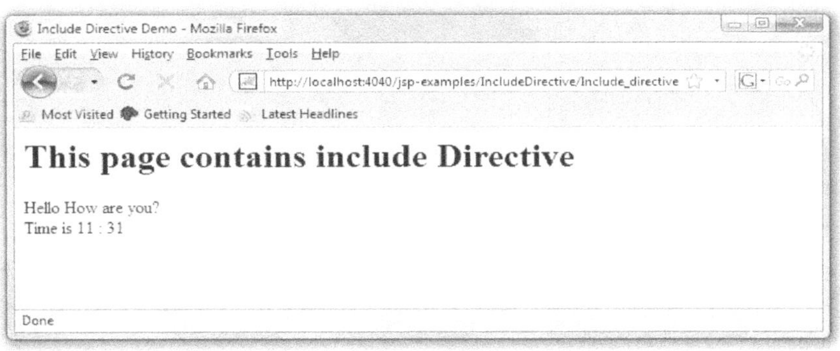

b) Forward action

Using forward action we can forward the current request to corresponding JSP page or servlet. Here is a simple demonstration in which we have created two web pages the first one is a main JSP page named as **first.jsp** in which we are using JSP action forward. And forwarding the current request to an HTML page which is named as **Second.html**

first.jsp

```
<html>
    <head>
        <title> Forward action Demo </title>
    </head>
    <body>
        <h1>This page contains forward action</h1>
        <jsp:forward page="Second.html" />
    </body>
</html>
```

Second.html

```
<html>
<body>
    <strong>You are forwarded to Second page!!</strong>
</body>
</html>
```

For getting the output open the web page and open the main JSP page that is **first.jsp** and you will get the following output -

Output

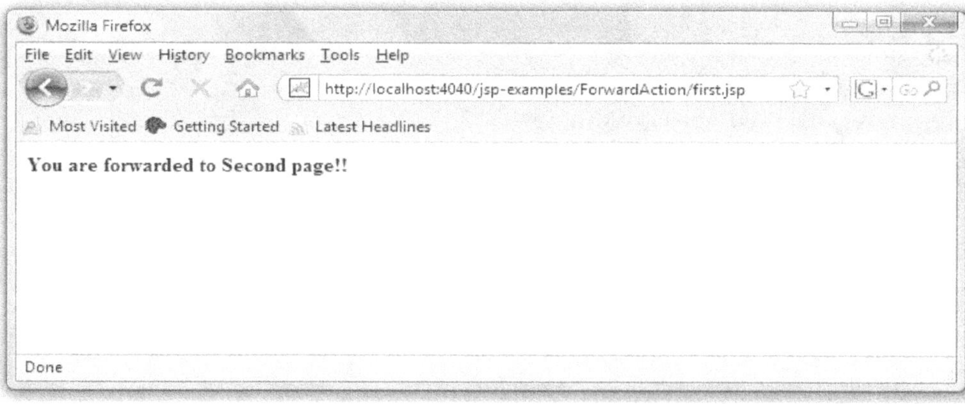

c) Plugin action

The plugin action is used to embed an applet or a bean. In this section we will discuss how to embed an applet in the JSP page using **jsp:plugin**. We will follow these steps to use plugin action.

Step 1 :

Let us write an applet program as follows -

ColorDemo.java

```
import java.awt.*;
import java.applet.*;
public class ColorDemo extends Applet
{
 public void paint(Graphics g)
 {
  setBackground(Color.cyan);
  setForeground(Color.red);
  g.drawString("Its a colorful Applet",50,30);
  Color newColor=new Color(255,255,0);
   //creating red+green=yellow color
  g.setColor(newColor);
  g.drawString("Its a colorful Applet",50,70);
 }
}
```

compile this code using the command

```
javac ColorDemo.java
```

Then corresponding class file i.e. ColorDemo.class gets generated. Now create a folder named **PluginAction** in your tomacat directory in the subfolder webapps/jsp-examples. Copy this class path in the **PluginAction** directory.

Step 2 : Now create a JSP page in **PluginAction** folder in which we are using the jsp action plugin. It is as follows -

Plugin_action.jsp

```
<jsp:plugin type="applet" code="ColorDemo" codebase=
"/jsp-examples/PluginAction" width = "190" height = "190">
      <jsp:fallback>
            <strong>Sorry!!! Applet can not be loaded.</strong>
      </jsp:fallback>
</jsp:plugin>
```

Note that in the above given JSP page we have used **<jsp:plugin>** where **type** is **applet** because we want to insert applet in JSP page. The type can also be **bean** for inserting a bean component. Then **code** denotes the name of the applet class. We have created applet class in step 1 and its name is **ColorDemo** hence we put the same name for the **code**. Then comes a **codebase** whose value is the directory name in which java class is located. Here the class file refers to the applet class file which we have created in Step 1.

Step 3 : For getting the output, open the web browser and open the jsp file Plugin_action.jsp and you can see that the desired applet is getting loaded -

Output

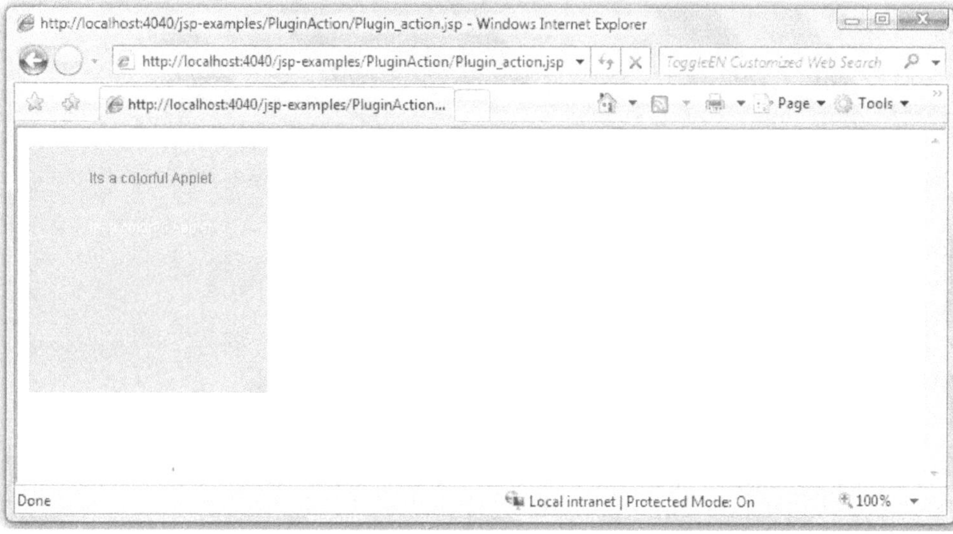

Review Question

1. *Enlist and explain the purpose and use of action tag in JSP.* **GTU : Dec.-12, Marks 7**

4.11 JSP Implicit Objects

GTU : May-12, Marks 7

The implicit objects are **predefined variables** used to access request and application data. These objects are used by the scripting elements. Following is a list of implicit objects -

Variable name	Class/Interface name	Meaning	Sample methods
application	javax.servlet.ServletContext	This object provides the resources shared within a web application.	log() getServerinfo()
config	javax.servlet.ServletConfig	It helps in passing the information to servlet or JSP page during initialization.	getInitParameter() getServletName()
request	javax.servlet.http.HttpServletRequest	It provides the methods for accessing the information made by current request.	getContentLength() getLocalAddr() getServerName()

response	javax.servlet.http.HttpServletResponse	It provides the methods related to adding cookies, sessions or setting header.	addCookie() addHeader() flushBuffer() getContentType() setContentType()
out	javax.servlet.jsp.JspWriter	It provides the methods related to I/O	clear() newLine()
page	java.lang.Object	This variable is assigned to instance of JSP implementation class. It is rarely used variable.	
pageContext	javax.servlet.jsp.PageContext	It provides access to several JSP page attributes	getPage() getRequest() getResponse() getSession()
session	javax.servlet.http.HttpSession	This variable is used to access the current client's session.	getId() getCreationTime()
exception	java.lang.Throwable	This object is for handling error pages and contain information about runtime error.	

Review Question

1. *Explain the JSP implicit objects with their use.* **GTU : May-12, Marks 7**

4.12 JSP Form Processing

GTU : May-12, Summer-16, Marks 7

Form is very common way of interaction in web sites. JSP makes form processing very easy. The <form> tag is used so that user can enter the form data. The two important methods GET and POST are used to send the form data to the JSP page.

GET Method

The GET method sends the encoded user information separated by the ? character appended to the page URL.

```
http://localhost/myhtmlfile?key1=value1&key2=value2
```

This is a default method type.

We should avoid using GET method to send password or other sensitive information to the server.

POST Method

POST method is more reliable method of sending information to the server. This method sends the information as a separate message.

JSP handles this type of requests using getParameter() method to read simple parameters.

JSP handles form data using the following methods.

Method	Description
getParameter()	returns the value of a form parameter.
getParameterValues()	returns multiple values, for example checkbox.
getParameterNames()	returns a complete list of all parameters.
getInputStream()	read binary data stream coming from the client.

Following is a simple example that demonstrates the form processing by JSP page.

Example 4.12.1 : *Write a JSP page that displays the user form containing the two fields-user name and city.*

Solution :

Step 1 :

Input.html

```
<html>
<body>
<form action="http://localhost/examples/jsp/FormDemo/MyFormProcess.jsp"
method="GET">
    Name: <input type="text" name="name">
<br />
    City: <input type="text" name="city" />
<input type="submit" value="Submit" />
</form>
</body>
</html>
```

Step 2 :

MyFormProcess.jsp

```
<html>
<body>
<h2>Displaying Form Data</h2>
<b>Name:</b><%= request.getParameter("name")%><br/>
<b>City:</b><%= request.getParameter("city")%>
</body>
</html>
```

Step 3 : Open the input.html file in the web browser and enter some data. The data can be sent to the JSP page for displaying.

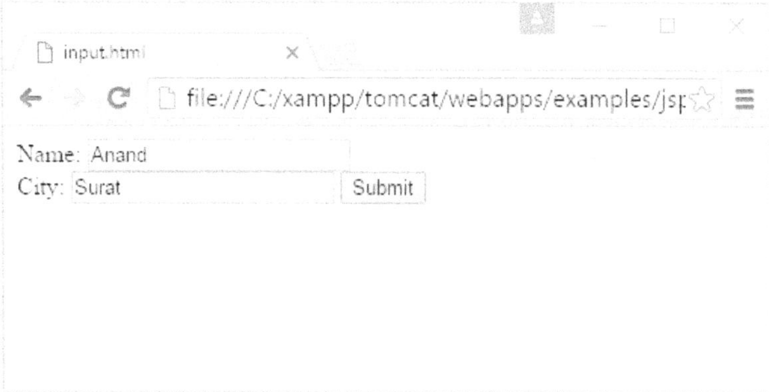

Example 4.12.2 : *Write a JSP page that prints your resume in well formatted form.*

GTU : May-12, Marks 7

Solution :

Step 1 : Create an HTML file for creating a form. User will submit his resume by filling up the form. The HTML document will be -

<input.html>

```
<html>
<head>
 <title>Resume</title>
</head>
<body>
<form method="post" action="resume.jsp">
<table>
<tr>
<td>Name:</td>
<td><input type="text" name="user"></td>
</tr>
<tr>
<td>Address:</td>
```

```
<td><input type="text" name="addr"></td>
</tr>
<tr>
<td>Email:</td>
<td><input type="text" name="email"></td>
</tr>

<tr>
<td>Phone:</td>
<td><input type="text" name="ph"></td>
</tr>
<tr>
<td>Qualification:</td>
<td><input type="text" name="qualify"></td>
</tr>
<tr>
<td>Experience:</td>
<td><input type="text" name="expr"></td>
</tr>
</table>
<tr>
<input type="submit" value="Submit">
</tr>
</form>
</body>
```

Step 2 : The jsp code will display the information submitted by the user in proper format. The JSP code will be as follows -

<resume.jsp>

```
<%@ page language="java" contentType="text/html" %>
<html>
<body>
<h3>RESUME</h3>
<table border="1">
 <tr>
  <td>Name:</td><td><b>${param.user}</b></td>
 </tr>
 <tr>
  <td>Address:</td><td><b>${param.addr}</b></td>
 </tr>
 <tr>
  <td>Email:</td><td><b>${param.email}</b></td>
 </tr>
 <tr>
  <td>Phone:</td><td><b>${param.ph}</b></td>
 </tr>
```

```
<tr>
 <td>Qualification:</td><td><b>${param.qualify}</b></td>
</tr>
<tr>
 <td>Experience:</td><td><b>${param.expr}</b></td>
</tr>

</table>
</body>
</html>
```

Example 4.12.3 : *Write small web application which takes marks of three subject and pass to servlet. Servlet forward to model class having method getClass() and getPercentage(). Display class and percentage in .jsp page.* **GTU : Summer-16, Marks 7**

Solution : Step 1 : Write an HTML form in which the marks for three subjects can be accepted

```
Input.html
<html>
<head>
  <title>WEB APPLICATION</title>
</head>
<body>
<form id="form1" method="post"
action="http://localhost/examples/servlets/servlet/Computations"> <br />
  Subject1: <input type="text" name="subject1" value="" /> <br/>
  Subject2: <input type="text" name="subject2" value="" /> <br/>
  Subject1: <input type="text" name="subject3" value="" /> <br/>
  <p><input type="submit" name="submit" value="Submit" /></p>
</form>
</body>
</html>
```

Step 2 : Following is a servlet that receives the marks for three subjects. These values are forwarded to another servlet.

Computations.java

```
import java.io.*;
import javax.servlet.*;
import javax.servlet.http.*;
public class Computations extends HttpServlet
{
    protected void doPost(HttpServletRequest request,HttpServletResponse response)
throws ServletException,IOException
    {
        response.setContentType("text/html;charset=UTF-8");
        PrintWriter out=response.getWriter();
        RequestDispatcher rd=request.getRequestDispatcher("MainPage");
```

```
            rd.forward(request,response);
            out.close();
    }
}
```

Step 3 : Following servlet contains methods getClass() and getPercentage() for calculation of class and percentage marks.

```
import javax.servlet.*;
import javax.servlet.http.*;
import java.io.*;
public class MainPage extends HttpServlet
{
 public void service(HttpServletRequest req, HttpServletResponse res) throws
ServletException, IOException
  {
   res.setContentType("text/html");
   PrintWriter out = res.getWriter();

   String str1 = req.getParameter("subject1");
   double num1 = Double.parseDouble(str1);
   String str2 = req.getParameter("subject2");
   double num2 = Double.parseDouble(str2);
   String str3 = req.getParameter("subject3");
   double num3 = Double.parseDouble(str3);

   out.println("Mark1: " + num1);
   out.println("<br>Marks2: " + num2);
   out.println("<br>Marks3: " + num3);
   double result;
   String cls;
   result=getPercentage(num1,num2,num3);
   cls=getClass(result);
   ServletContext context=getServletContext();
   req.setAttribute("Percentage",result);
   req.setAttribute("Class",cls);
   RequestDispatcher rd=req.getRequestDispatcher("/Display.jsp");
  rd.forward(req,res);
   out.close();
  }
  public double getPercentage(double m1,double m2,double m3)
  {
      double result;
      result=(m1+m2+m3)/3;
      return result;
  }
  public String getClass(double result)
  {
```

```
        if(result<40)
            return "Fail";
        else if((result>=40)&&(result<50))
            return "Pass_Class";
        else if((result>=50)&&(result<60))
            return "First_Class";
        else
            return "Distinction";
    }
}
```

Step 4 : The percentage and class computed in above servlet is then transferred to the JSP page for the display of result. The code for this JSP page is

Display.jsp

```
<%@ page import="java.io.*"%>
<html>
<head>
</head>
<body>
  <h2>Final Results ...</h2>
  <%
  Object ob1 = request.getAttribute("Percentage");
  out.println("<p>Percentage = "+ob1+"</p>");
  Object ob2 = request.getAttribute("Class");
  out.println("<p>Class = "+ob2+"</p>");
  %>
</body>
</html>
```

Step 5 : The web.xml file is updated by the names of servlets and after starting the tomcat server, the results can be obtained in web browser as follows -

Output

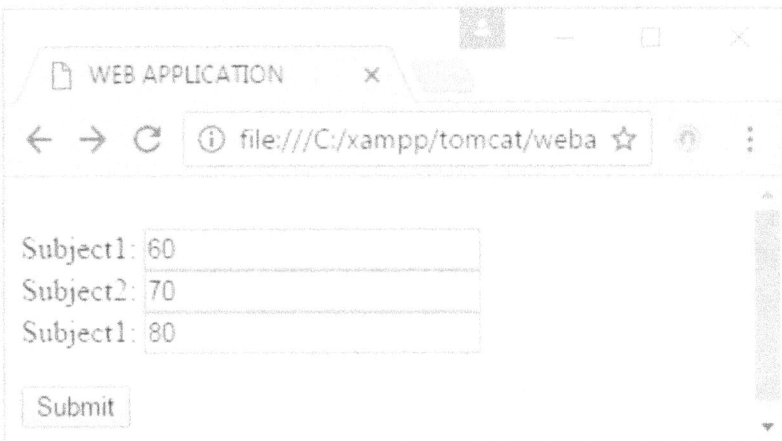

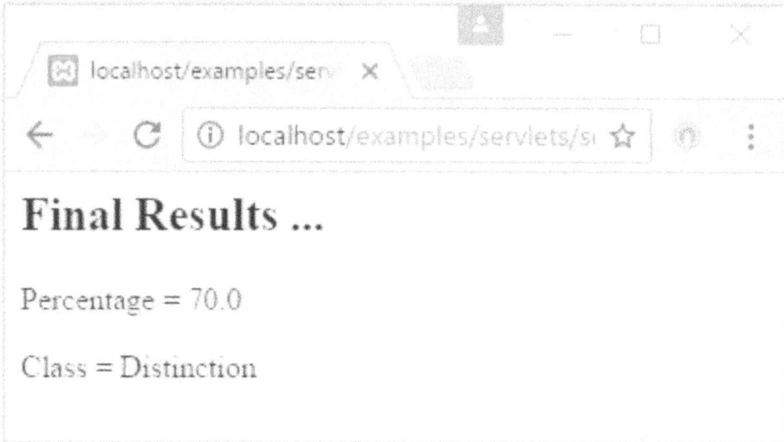

4.13 JSP Cookies Handling

- Cookies are the small text files that are stored in the client's computer.
- These are basically used to keep track of the users who browse the web. The information stored in the cookie is generally **name, age, id, city** and so on.
- The server script sends a set of cookies to the browser. The browser stores this information on the local machine and makes use of this information next time when the browser is browsing the web.
- Cookies are usually set in HTTP header.
- Various methods used in handling the cookies are -

  1. Create Cookie
  2. Read Cookie
  3. Delete Cookie

We will discuss these methods along with the JSP code

1. Create cookie

Step 1 : In JSP the cookie is created using the constructor named **Cookie**. It requires two parameters - name and value. For example

```
Cookie cookie= new Cookie("name", "value");
```

Step 2 : Then we can set the validity period for the cookie using the method setMaxAge. For example to set the cookie alive for 24 hour we will write the code as

```
cookie.setMaxAge(60*60*24);
```

Step 3 : Now our cookie is ready to send over. We can add the cookie in HTTP response header as follows

```
response.addcookie(cookie);
```

2. Read cookie

Step 1 : First the cookie is retrieved using **getCookies**() method

```
Cookie[] cookies = request.getCookies();
```

Step 2 : Then using **getName**() and **getValue**() methods the cookies are read.

3. Delete cookie

Step 1 : Read the already created cookie and store it in cookie object

```
Cookie cookie = new Cookie("name","");
```

Step 2 : Then set its period of existence as 0 by **setMaxAge** method. This means the cookie is actually deleted.

```
cookie.setMaxAge(0);
cookie.setValue("");
```

Step 3 : Add this cookie back to response header.

```
response.addCookie(cookie);
```

Implementation of Cookie in JSP

Step 1 : Create an html file to read the values from the user

Input.html

```
<html>
<body>
<form method = "post" action="Createcookie.jsp">
Username<input type = "text" name = "name">
City<input type = "text" name = "city">
<input type = "submit" name = "submit" value = "submit" >
</form>
</body>
</html>
```

Step 2 : Create the cookie as follows

Createcookie.jsp

```
<%@ page language="java" import="java.util.*"%>
<%
String name=request.getParameter("name");
String city=request.getParameter("city");

Cookie namecookie = new Cookie ("name",name);
Cookie citycookie = new Cookie ("city",city);

response.addCookie(namecookie);
response.addCookie(citycookie);
```

```
namecookie.setMaxAge(60*60*24);
citycookie.setMaxAge(60*60*24);
%>
<h3>
<a href="Readcookie.jsp">Click here to continue...</a>
</h3>
```

Step 3 : Read the created cookie

Readcookie.jsp

```
<h3>Reading the Cookie</h3>
<%
Cookie[] cookies = request.getCookies();
for (int i=0; i<cookies.length; i++)
{
    out.println("Cookie_Name:"+cookies[i].getName()+"<br>");
    out.println("Cookie_Value:"+cookies[i].getValue()+"<br>");
}
%>
<a href="Deletecookie.jsp">Click here to Delete the Cookie!!!</a>
```

Step 4 : For deletion of cookie following is JSP implementation

Deletecookies.jsp

```
<%
Cookie namecookie = new Cookie("name","");
namecookie.setMaxAge(0);
namecookie.setValue("");
response.addCookie(namecookie);

Cookie citycookie = new Cookie("city","");
citycookie.setMaxAge(0);
citycookie.setValue("");
response.addCookie(citycookie);
%>
<h3>Cookie is Deleted!!</h3>
<a href="Readcookie.jsp">Click here to check the deletion...</a>
```

Step 5 : Start the tomcat and Check the output on suitable web browser.

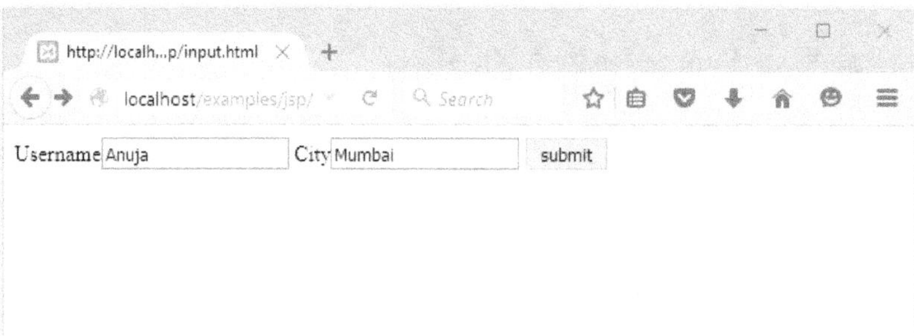

Click **submit** button

If we click for deletion of the cookie, then the cookie gets deleted.

By clicking the hyperlink we can check that cookie is actually getting deleted.

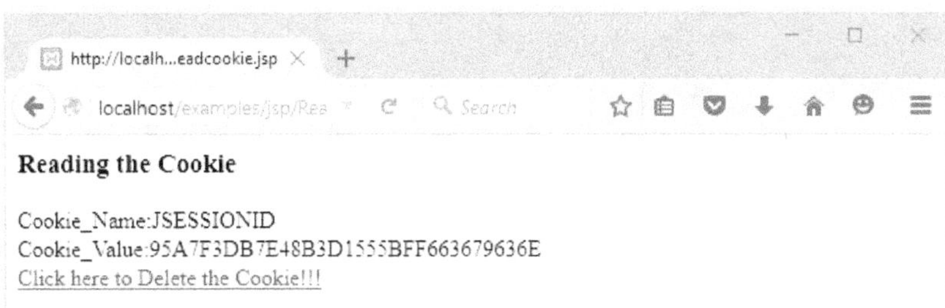

4.14 JSP Session Tracking

As HTTP is a stateless protocol, we can not maintain or restore the user's data in the next session. Hence to store the user's data across multiple HTTP requests, the session tracking mechanism is used.

For tracking the session, JSP makes use of **HTTPSession** object. A new HTTPSession object is instantiated for each new client automatically.

The JSP session tracking requires to turn off the page directive session attribute to false.Then the JSP engine exposes the HTTPSession object to JSP author through **session** object.

Various important methods supported by session object are as given below

Method	Description
public Object getAttribute(String name)	This method returns the object bound with the specified name in this session, or null if no object is bound under the name.
public Enumeration getAttributeNames()	This method returns the names of all the objects bound to this session.
public long getCreationTime()	This method returns the time when this session was created, measured in milliseconds since midnight January 1, 1970 GMT.
public boolean isNew()	This method returns true if the user does not yet know about the session.
public String getId()	This method returns a string containing the unique identifier assigned to this session.
public long getLastAccessedTime()	This method returns the last time the user sent a request associated with this session, as the number of milliseconds since midnight January 1, 1970 GMT.
public void removeAttribute(String name)	This method removes the object bound with the specified name from this session.
public void setAttribute(String name, Object value)	This method binds an object to this session, using the name specified.

Following is a JSP document that uses the **session object** for tracking the session.

SessionDemo.jsp

```
<%@ page import="java.io.*,java.util.*" %>
<html>
<head>
<title>Session Tracking Demo</title>
</head>
<body>
```

```
<h3>"Welcome to my website"</h3>
<%
  Integer visitCount = new Integer(0);
  String visitCountKey = new String("visitCount");
  // Check if this is new comer on your web page.
  if (session.isNew())
  {
       out.print("<p> You are accessing this site for the First Time!!</p>");
       session.setAttribute(visitCountKey, visitCount);
  }
  visitCount = (Integer)session.getAttribute(visitCountKey);
  visitCount = visitCount + 1;
  session.setAttribute(visitCountKey, visitCount);
%>
   You have visited this site for <% out.print(visitCount); %> times.
</body>
</html>
```

Output

4.15 JSP Database Access

GTU : Dec.-12, Summer-13, 16, Marks 7

While accessing JSP database from JSP page we should have some database package installed. In this section we will consider the connectivity of JSP with the MYSQL database. We will follow following steps to get access the database using JSP page with some assumptions -

Assumptions

- TOMCAT web server is installed.
- MYSQL server is installed.
- JDK is installed.

Step 1 : Create a database named students in MYSQL using following command.

```
mysql>CREATE DATABASE students;
```

Then create a table named **students_table** in the **students** database as follows -

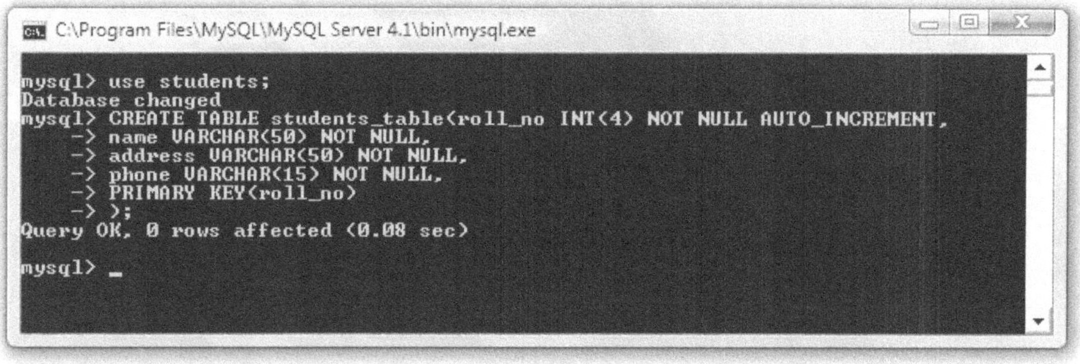

If you would like to see the structure of created table then give following command -

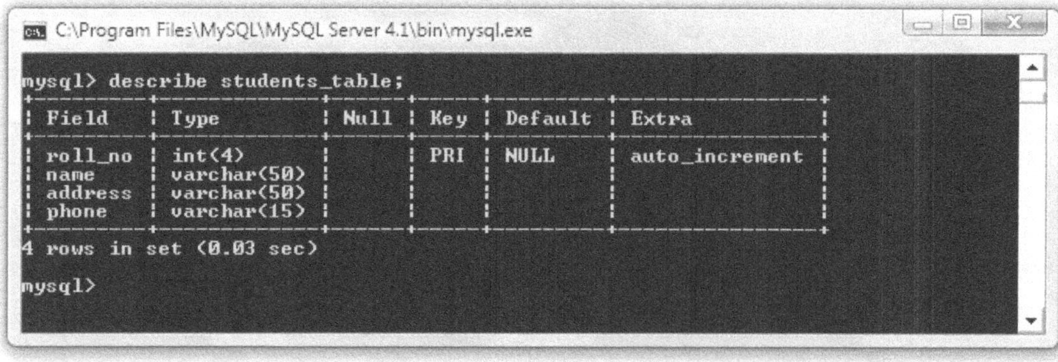

Step 2 : For establishing the connectivity between JSP and MYSQL using JDBC driver what we need is to download the MYSQL JDBC connector. Download this connector from **http://www.mysql.com/products/connector/j/** Just pick up the mirror and download the ZIP file if you are working on the Windows operating system.(*I have downloaded **Connector J3.1**, which is most suitable version as I am using Tomcat 5.5 with MYSQL 4.1*). Then from the extracted folder just copy the jar file named **mysql-connector-java-3.1.14-bin.jar** to the C:/*your_tomcat_directoy*/common/lib. For understanding the exact location for copying this file just refer the following snapshot.

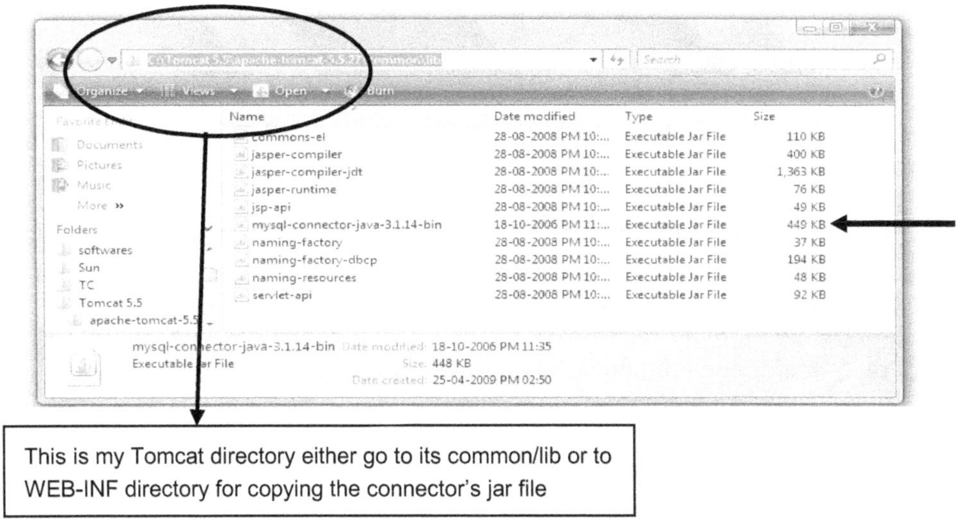

Then just set the CLASSPATH using the environmental variables. For that purpose go to Control Panel->System->System Properties->environmental variables and set the CLASSPATH as shown below -

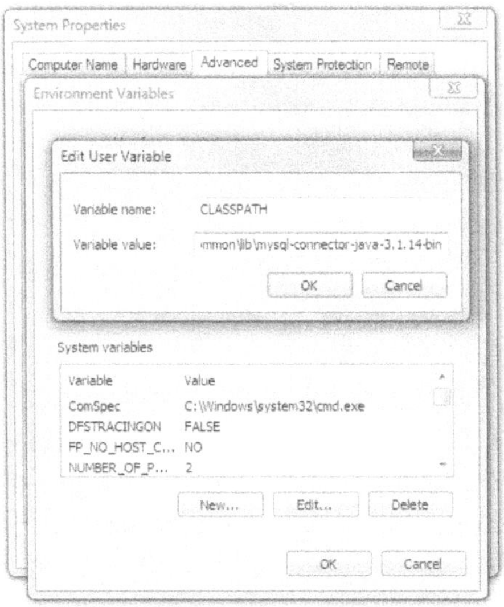

Step 3 : After setting the CLASSPATH, restart the Tomcat Web server using the **startup.bat** file at the command prompt. Created a folder **DBDemo** and write the following JSP program in c:/*your_tomcat_directory*/jsp-examples/DBDemo

StudentForm.jsp

```
<%@ page language="java" import="java.sql.*" %>
<%@ page import="java.io.*" %>
  <%
  Connection conn=null;
  ResultSet rs=null;
  Statement stmt=null;
  Class.forName("com.mysql.jdbc.Driver").newInstance();
  conn=
  DriverManager.getConnection("jdbc:mysql://localhost:3306/students","root","system");
  out.write("Connected to mysql!!!");
  stmt=conn.createStatement();
  if(request.getParameter("action") != null)
  {
      String Studname=request.getParameter("Studname");
      String Studaddress=request.getParameter("Studaddress");
      String Studphone=request.getParameter("Studphone");
      stmt.executeUpdate("insert into students_table(name,address,phone) values('
      "+Studname+" ',' "+Studaddress+" ',' "+Studphone+" ')" );
      rs=stmt.executeQuery("select * from students_table");
  %>
      <html>
      <body>
      <center>
          <h2>Student List</h2>
          <table border="1" cellspacing="0" cellpadding="0">
          <tr>
              <td><b>Roll No</b></td>
              <td><b>Student Name</b></td>
              <td><b>Address</./b></td>
              <td><b>Phone</./b></td>
          </tr>
              <%
              int num=1;
              while(rs.next()){
              %>
              <tr>
               <td><%=num%></td>
               <td><%=rs.getString("name")%></td>
               <td> <%=rs.getString("address")%></td>
               <td> <%=rs.getString("phone")%></td>
```

```
            </tr>
            <%
            num++;
            }
            rs.close();
            stmt.close();
            conn.close();
            %>
        </table>
</center>
</body>
</html>
<%}else{%>
<html>
<head>
<title>Student Registartion Demo</title>
<script language="javascript">
  function validation(Form_obj)
     {
     if(Form_obj.Studname.value.length==0){
     alert("Please,fill up the remaining information!!");

     Form_obj.Studname.focus();
     return false;
     }
     if(Form_obj.Studaddress.value.length==0){
     alert("Please,fill up the remaining information!!");
     Form_obj.Studaddress.focus();
     return false;
     }
     if(Form_obj.Studphone.value.length==0){
     alert("Please,fill up the remaining information!!");
     Form_obj.Studphone.focus();
     return false;
     }
     return true;
     }
     </script>
</head>
<body>
```

```
            <center>
            <form action="StudentForm.jsp" method="post"
            name="entry" onSubmit="return validation(this)">
                <input type="hidden" value="list" name="action">
                <table border="3" cellpadding="0" cellspacing="0">
                    <tr>
                    <td>
                    <table>
                        <tr>
                        <td colspan="2" align="center">
                        <h2>Student Entry Form</h2></td>
                        </tr>
                        <tr>
                        <td colspan="2"> </td>
                        </tr>
                        <tr>
                        <td>Student Name:</td>
                        <td><input name="Studname"
                        type= "text" size="50"></td>
                        </tr>
                        <tr>
                        <td>Address:</td>
                        <td><input name="Studaddress" type="text"
                        size="50"></td>
                        </tr>

                        <td>Phone:</td>
                        <td><input name="Studphone"
                        type="text" size="15"></td>
                        </tr>

                        <tr>
                        <td colspan="2" align="center">
                        <input type="submit" value="Submit"></td>
                        </tr>
                    </table>
                    </td>
                    </tr>
                </table>
            </form>
            </center>
        </body>
    </html>
<%}%>
```

6

Output

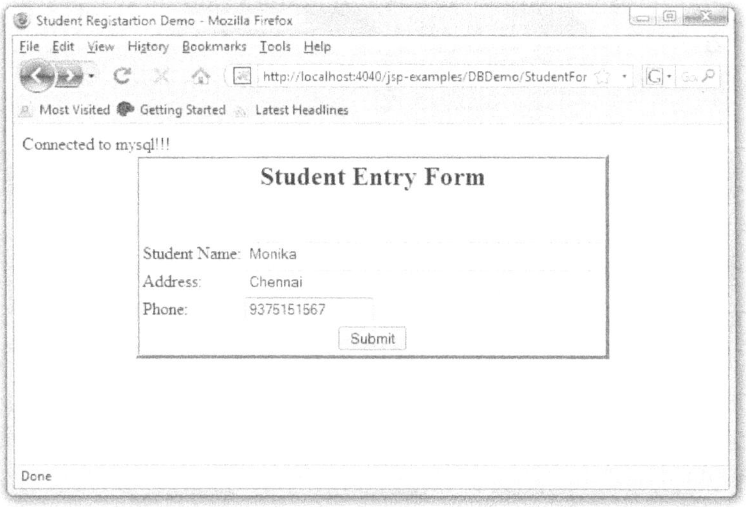

Just click the Submit button and you will get the display of all the records from the students_table.

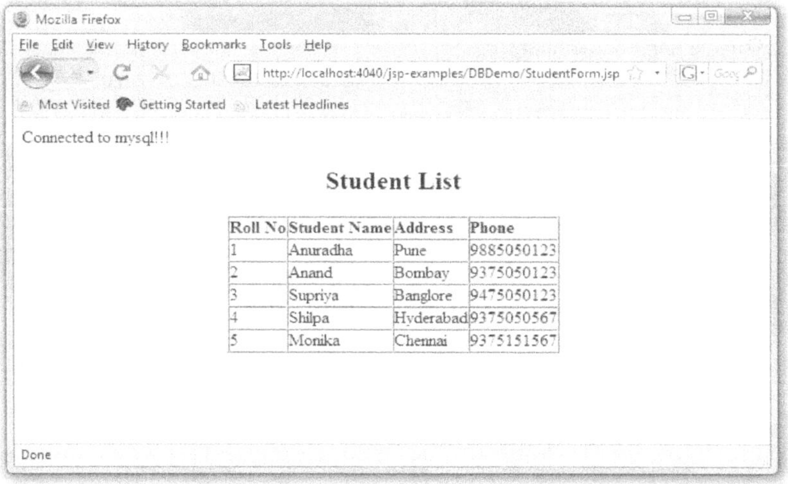

We can verify this table using backend database MYSQL as follows -

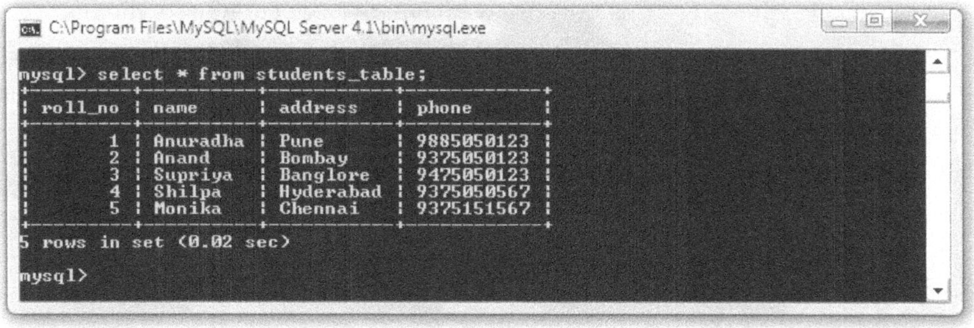

Code explanation

In above code, I have marked some steps by numbering them out. Let us understand these steps -

1. In this step required JDBC classes and interfaces such as **Connection**, **ResultSet**, **Statement** are initialised. These classes and interfaces are defined in the package **java.sql.***. That is why we must import them hence at the beginning of the program we did this job!
2. Here the object of the JDBC driver is instantiated. We have already downloaded the MYSQL JDBC connector. Hence the we specify it as

```
Class.forName("com.mysql.jdbc.Driver").newInstance();
```

3. Then using **DriverManager** class we are getting connected to the MYSQL database. Note that this **DriverManager** class is defined in **java.sql.*** package.Using getConnection method we are actually getting connected to the MYSQL database.

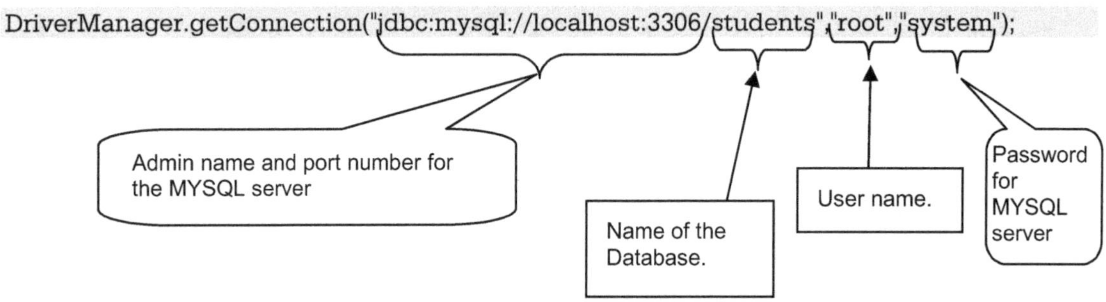

Note that the above given parameters in **getConnection** method may vary as per your database name, login name for your SQL server and the password. Then, a **createStatement** is used. It creates on object using which SQL statements can be sent to database.

4. Now we are retrieving the fields from the **form**(*this form is created on the same JSP page*) using **request.getParameter** method.
5. We then insert the values in the table using Insert query using **executeUpdate** method.

   After inserting the values the table in the database can be displayed using the **Select *** query. For this purpose we have used **executeQuery** method.
6. An HTML form is created in which various input fields such as students' name, address and phone number are given. User can enter the required values in these fields. These values can be further used by **Insert** query.

The above code also has a provision of validating the user input. If we forget to give any information then it will display the alert as follows -

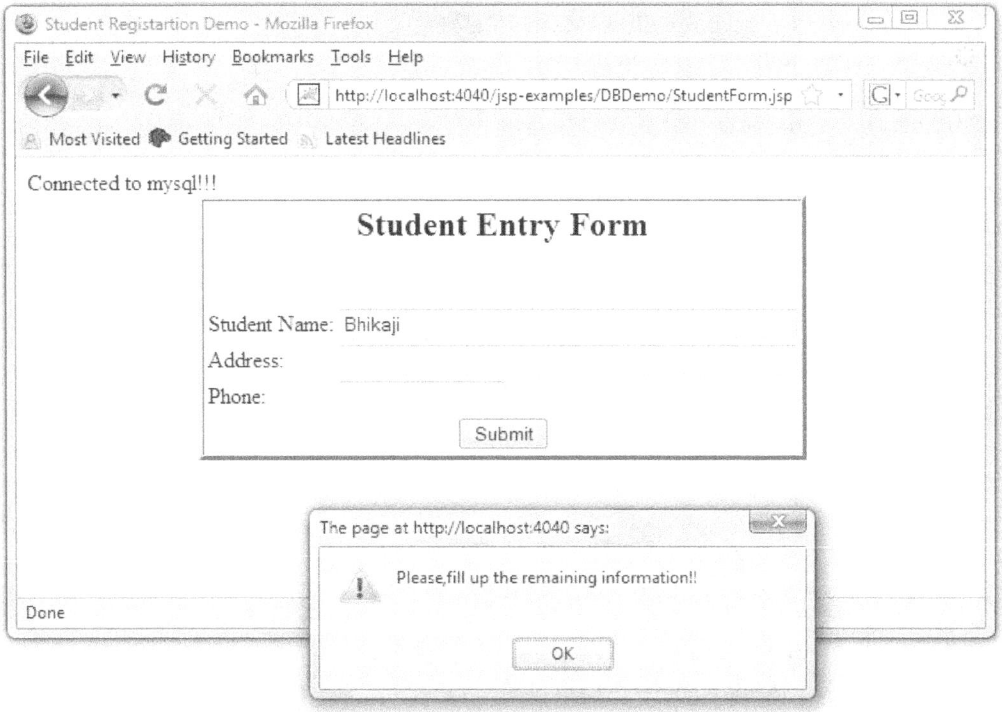

Example 4.15.1 : *Write a program that lists all books and the authors for those books from technical library database [Assume database schema].*

Solution : Assumption :

1. The database named **books** is created.
2. The table in the books database is **books_info** which is as given below –

ISBN	name	author
1	DSF	Tannebaum
11	DC	Kelvin
22	OS	Peterson
42	Unix Programming	Bach
55	Java Server Pages	Hans Bergsten
57	DAA	Coreman

input.jsp

```
<%@ page language="java" import="java.sql.*" %>
<%@ page import="java.io.*" %>
<%@ page import="java.sql.Connection" %>
<%@ page import="java.sql.DriverManager" %>
```

```
<%@ page import="java.sql.ResultSet"%>
<%@ page import="java.sql.ResultSetMetaData" %>
<%@ page import="java.sql.Statement" %>
<%
    Connection conn=null;
    ResultSet rs=null;
    Statement stmt=null;
    Class.forName("com.mysql.jdbc.Driver").newInstance();
    conn=DriverManager.getConnection("jdbc:mysql://localhost:3306/books","root","system
");
    out.write("Connected to mysql!!!");
    stmt=conn.createStatement();
    rs=stmt.executeQuery("select * from books_info");
%>
    <html>
    <body>
    <center>
    <h2>Books List</h2>
    <table border="1" cellspacing="0" cellpadding="0">
    <tr>
     <td><b>ISBN</b></td>
     <td><b>Book Name</b></td>
     <td><b>Author</.b></td>
    </tr>
    <%
      while(rs.next())
      {
    %>
    <tr>
     <td><%=rs.getString("ISBN")%></td>
     <td><%=rs.getString("name")%></td>
     <td> <%=rs.getString("author")%></td>
    </tr>
    <%
    }
    rs.close();
    stmt.close();
    conn.close();
    %>
    </table>
    </center>
    </body>
    </html>
```

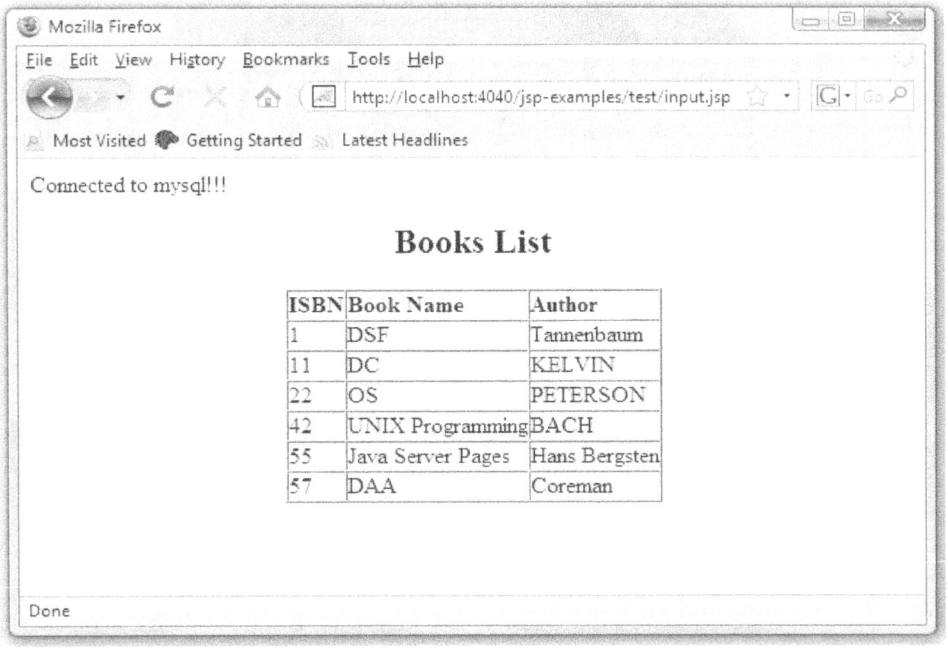

Example 4.15.2 : *Create a JSP to check the status of a bus ticket reservation from the server database. Status will be marked with character R-Reserved, W-waiting, C-Cancelled.*

Solution :

Step 1 : Create a database using some suitable database package database. The name of my database is **test** inside which I have created a table **mytab** containing three fields - id, Name and Status.

Step 2 : Write a JSP code as follows -

```
<%@ page language="java" import="java.sql.*" %>
<%@ page import="java.io.*" %>
    <%
    Connection conn=null;
    ResultSet rs=null;
    Statement stmt=null;
    Class.forName("com.mysq.l.jdbc.Driver");
    conn=DriverManager.getConnection("jdbc:mysql://localhost:3306/test"
                                        "root","system);
    out.write("Connected to database!!!");
    stmt=conn.createStatement();
    rs=stmt.executeQuery("select * from mytab");
    %>
        <html>
        <body>
```

```
<center>
    <h2>Reservation Chart</h2>
    <table border="1" cellspacing="0" cellpadding="0">
    <tr>
        <td><b>ID</b></td>
        <td><b>Name</b></td>
        <td><b>Status</.b></td>
    </tr>
        <%
        int num=1;
        while(rs.next()){
        %>
        <tr>
         <td><%=num%></td>
         <td><%=rs.getString("name")%></td>
         <td> <%=rs.getString("Status")%></td>
        </tr>
        <%
        num++;
        }
        rs.close();
        stmt.close();
        conn.close();
        %>
    </table>
</center>
</body>
</html>
```

Step 4 : Open some suitable web browser to see the output

Output

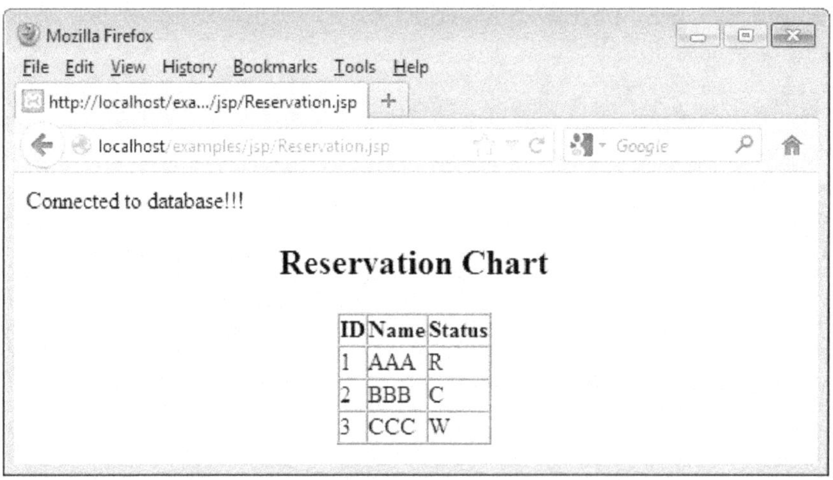

4.15.1 Use of Prepared Statement

The prepared statement is a precompiled statement. The SQL processor parses and analyses the statement and produces the execution plan. Following is a simple demo for the use of prepared statement.

Step 1 : Create a database, and table in the database using following commands

```
C:\Program Files\MySQL\MySQL Server 4.1\bin\mysql.exe

mysql> USE employees;
Database changed
mysql> CREATE TABLE employees_table(id INT(4) NOT NULL AUTO_INCREMENT,
    -> name VARCHAR(50) NOT NULL,
    -> address VARCHAR(50) NOT NULL,
    -> designation VARCHAR(20) NOT NULL,
    -> salary VARCHAR(15) NOT NULL,
    -> PRIMARY KEY(id)
    -> );
Query OK, 0 rows affected (0.01 sec)

mysql> describe employees_table;
+-------------+-------------+------+-----+---------+----------------+
| Field       | Type        | Null | Key | Default | Extra          |
+-------------+-------------+------+-----+---------+----------------+
| id          | int(4)      |      | PRI | NULL    | auto_increment |
| name        | varchar(50) |      |     |         |                |
| address     | varchar(50) |      |     |         |                |
| designation | varchar(20) |      |     |         |                |
| salary      | varchar(15) |      |     |         |                |
+-------------+-------------+------+-----+---------+----------------+
5 rows in set (0.00 sec)

mysql>
```

Thus the database **employees** gets created in which **employees_table** is created.

Step 2 : Now we will write a simple JSP program in which the **prepared statement** is used for getting connected with MYSQL.

EmployeeForm.jsp

```
<%@ page language="java" import="java.sql.*" %>
<%@ page import="java.io.*" %>
    <%
    Connection conn=null;
    ResultSet rs=null;
    PreparedStatement pstmt=null;
    Class.forName("com.mysql.jdbc.Driver").newInstance();
    conn=DriverManager.getConnection("jdbc:mysql://localhost:3306/employees","root","system");
    out.write("Connected to mysql!!!");
    if(request.getParameter("action") != null)
    {
        String Empname=request.getParameter("Empname");
        String Empaddress=request.getParameter("Empaddress");
        String Empdesig=request.getParameter("Empdesig");
        String Empsalary=request.getParameter("Empsalary");
        String myquery="insert into
        employees_table(name,address,designation,salary) values (?,?,?,?)";
        pstmt= conn.prepareStatement(myquery);
```

```
        pstmt.setString(1,Empname);
        pstmt.setString(2,Empaddress);
        pstmt.setString(3,Empdesig);
        pstmt.setString(4,Empsalary);
        pstmt.executeUpdate();
        rs=pstmt.executeQuery("select * from employees_table");
%>
        <html>
        <body>
        <center>
            <h2>Employee List</h2>
            <table border="1" cellspacing="0" cellpadding="0">
            <tr>
                <td><b>Id</b></td>
                <td><b>Employee Name</b></td>
                <td><b>Address</.b></td>
                <td><b>Designation</.b></td>
                <td><b>Salary</.b></td>
            </tr>
                <%
                int num=1;
                while(rs.next()){
                %>
                <tr>
                 <td><%=num%></td>
                 <td><%=rs.getString("name")%></td>
                 <td> <%=rs.getString("address")%></td>
                 <td> <%=rs.getString("designation")%></td>
                 <td> <%=rs.getString("salary")%></td>
                </tr>
                <%
                num++;
                }
                rs.close();
                pstmt.close();
                conn.close();
                %>
            </table>
        </center>
        </body>
        </html>
        <%}else{%>
        <html>
        <head>
        <title>Employee Details</title>
        <script language="javascript">
```

```
function validation(Form_obj)
    {
    if(Form_obj.Empname.value.length==0){
    alert("Please,fill up the remaining information!!");
    Form_obj.Empname.focus();
    return false;
    }
    if(Form_obj.Empaddress.value.length==0){
    alert("Please,fill up the remaining information!!");
    Form_obj.Empaddress.focus();
    return false;
    }
    if(Form_obj.Empdesig.value.length==0){
    alert("Please,fill up the remaining information!!");
    Form_obj.Empdesig.focus();
    return false;
    }
    if(Form_obj.Empsalary.value.length==0){
    alert("Please,fill up the remaining information!!");
    Form_obj.Empsalary.focus();
    return false;
    }
    return true;
    }
    </script>
</head>
<body>
    <center>
    <form action="EmployeeForm.jsp" method="post"
    name="entry" onSubmit="return validation(this)">
        <input type="hidden" value="list" name="action">
        <table border="3" cellpadding="0" cellspacing="0">
            <tr>
            <td>
            <table>
                <tr>
                <td colspan="2" align="center">
                <h2>Employee Entry Form</h2></td>
                </tr>
                <tr>
                <td colspan="2"> </td>
                </tr>
                <tr>
                <td>Employee Name:</td>
                <td><input name="Empname" type= "text" size="50"></td>
                </tr>
```

```
                        <tr>
                        <td>Address:</td>
                        <td><input name="Empaddress" type="text" size="50"></td>
                        </tr>

                        <tr>
                        <td>Designation:</td>
                        <td><input name="Empdesig" type="text" size="20"></td>
                        </tr>

                        <td>Salary:</td>
                        <td><input name="Empsalary" type="text" size="15"></td>
                        </tr>

                        <tr>
                        <td colspan="2" align="center">
                        <input type="submit" value="Submit"></td>
                        </tr>
                     </table>
                     </td>
                     </tr>
                  </table>
               </form>
               </center>
            </body>
         </html>
<%}%>
```

Output

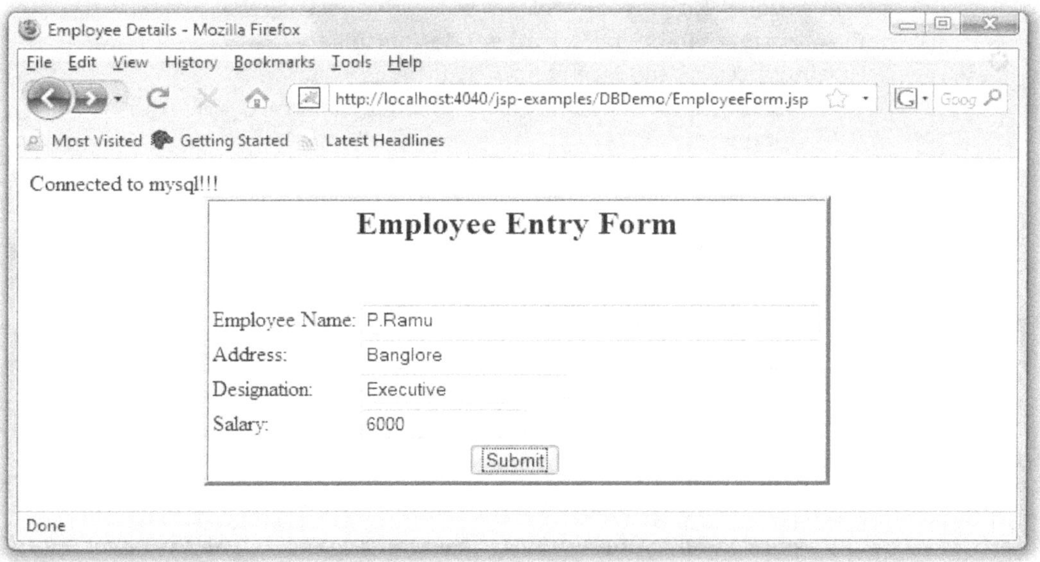

Press submit button and following output will be obtained

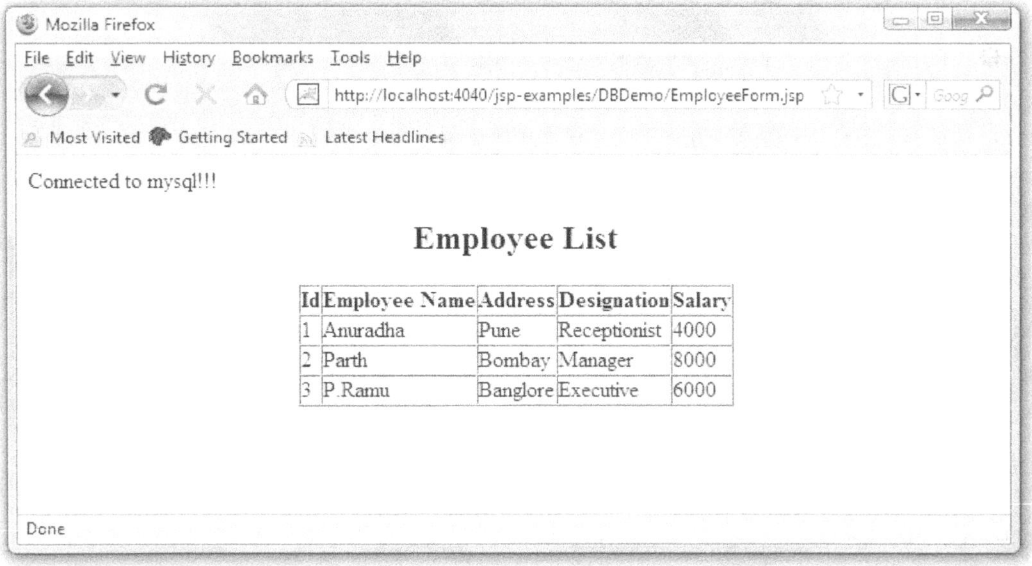

4.15.2 ResultSetMetaData

Metadata is data that describes other data. For example, ResultSetMetadata describes the result set, such as the number of columns in the result set, the data types of those columns, their names, or nullability, and so on.

The resultset interface is used to represent the database result set. After using SELECT SQL statement, the information obtained from the database can be displayed using **ResultSet**. Using the object of resultset we can scroll forward or backward. The ResultSetMetadata interface is used to retrieve number of columns , size of each column in the table, name of the table to which that column belongs to, whether the column is nullable or not and so on.

Following JSP code shows the process of getting and accessing the metadata using **ResultSetMetaData.**

Assumptions:

i) We have got JDBC driver installed for MYSQL

ii) We have already created one database named **students** having the table **students_table**. The table contains some records. The structure of table is like this-

Field	Type	Null	Key	Default	Extra
roll_no	int(4)		Pri	NULL	auto_increment
name	VARCHAR(50)				

address	VARCHAR(50)
phone	VARCHAR(15)

Following is a JSP script that displays metadata.

input.jsp

```
<%@ page language="java" import="java.sql.*" %>
<%@ page import="java.io.*" %>
<%@ page import="java.sql.Connection" %>
<%@ page import="java.sql.DriverManager" %>
<%@ page import="java.sql.ResultSet"%>
<%@ page import="java.sql.ResultSetMetaData" %>
<%@ page import="java.sql.Statement" %>
<%
    Connection conn=null;
    ResultSet rs=null;
    Statement stmt=null;
    Class.forName("com.mysql.jdbc.Driver").newInstance();
    conn=DriverManager.getConnection
("jdbc:mysql://localhost:3306/students","root","system");
    out.write("Connected to mysql!!!");
    stmt=conn.createStatement();

    rs=stmt.executeQuery("select * from students_table");
    ResultSetMetaData rsMetaData = rs.getMetaData();
    int n = rsMetaData.getColumnCount();
    out.write("<br/>"+"Obtaining column information using resultSet MetaData
"+"<br/>");
    out.write("Total number of columns in the table are "+ n+"<br/>");
    for (int i = 1; i <= n; i++)
    {
    out.write("column number: " + i+"<br/>");
   // indicates the designated column's normal maximum width
    out.write("Size of column: "+rsMetaData.getColumnDisplaySize(i)+"<br/>");
   // displays column's name.
      out.write("Name of column:"+rsMetaData.getColumnName(i)+"<br/>");
   // displays column's table name.
      out.write("Name of parent table:"+rsMetaData.getTableName(i)+"<br/>");
   // indicates whether the designated column is automatically incrementable
     out.write("Auto increment?: "+rsMetaData.isAutoIncrement(i)+"<br/>");

  }

 rs.close();
 stmt.close();
 conn.close();
%>
```

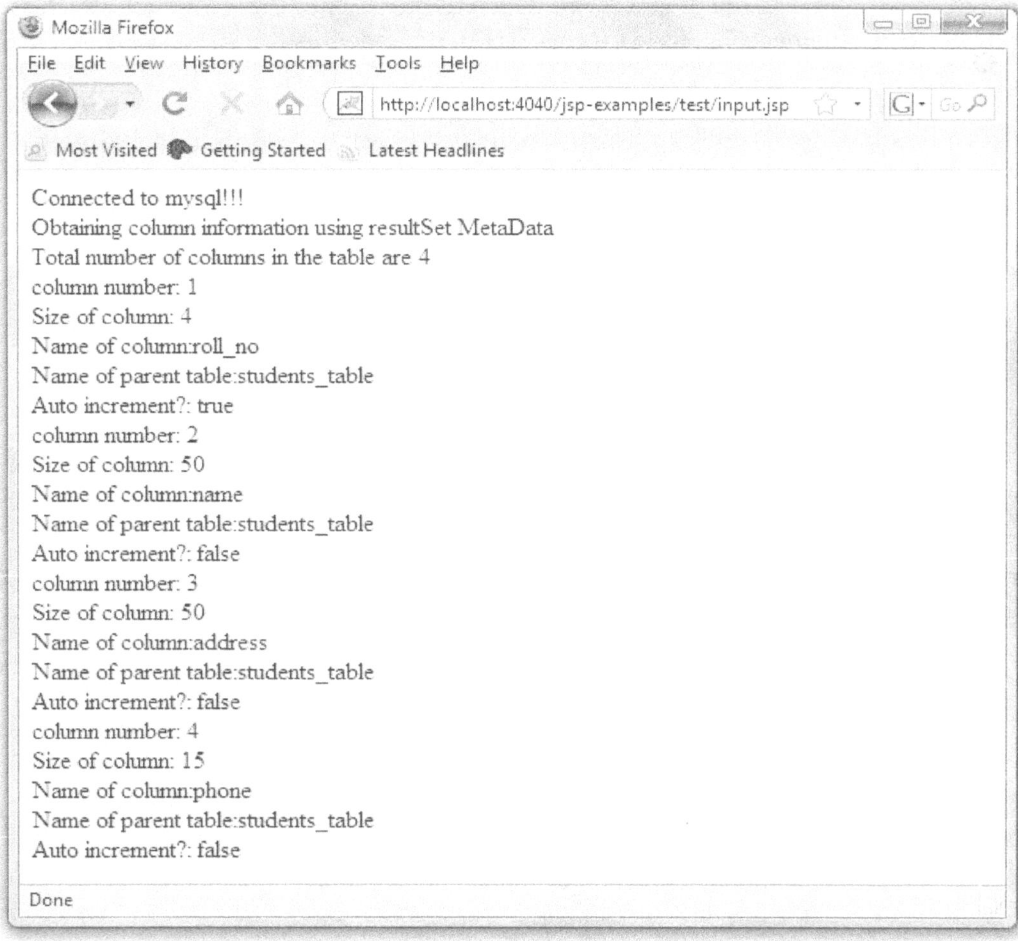

4.15.3 More Examples on Database Connectivity

Example 4.15.3 : *Write a JSP page to display your semester mark sheet. Give the necessary files to deploy it.* **GTU : Summer-13, Marks 8**

Solution :

Step 1 : Create a database and store the table MarkList within it. The content of the database table will be

Seatno	Name	Subject1	Subject2	Subject3	Status
111	AAA	40	50	60	Pass
222	BBB	5	20	22	Fail
333	CCC	55	77	88	Pass

Step 2 : Create an HTML document using which user can enter the seatno for which the marklist is to be obtained. The code for this HTML document is -

inputform.html

```
<html>
<head><title> mark sheet</title></head>
<body>
<center>
<h1>Student Mark Sheet</h1>
</center>
<form action="Marksheet.jsp" method="POST">
Enter Seat Number:<input type="text" name="seatno">
<input type="submit" value="Submit"><br><br>
</form>
</body>
</html>
```

Step 3 : The JSP code for displaying marksheet is as follows -

```
<%@ page language="java" import="java.sql.*" %>
<%@ page import="java.io.*" %>
    <%
    Connection conn=null;
    ResultSet rs=null;
    Statement stmt=null;
    Class.forName("sun.jdbc.odbc.JdbcOdbcDriver");
    conn=DriverManager.getConnection("jdbc:odbc:MarksheetDB","","");
    stmt=conn.createStatement();
    String sno=request.getParameter("seatno");
    String query=new String("SELECT * FROM MarkList WHERE seatno=  "+sno);
    rs=stmt.executeQuery(query);
    %>
    <html>
    <body>
     <center>
          <h2>Mark Sheet</h2>
          <table border="1" cellspacing="0" cellpadding="0">
               <tr>
                    <td><b>SeatNo</b></td>
                    <td><b>Name</b></td>
                    <td><b>Subject1</b></td>
                    <td><b>Subject2</b></td>
                    <td><b>Subject3</b></td>
                    <td><b>Status</b></td>

               </tr>
                    <%
```

```
            while(rs.next())
            {
            %>
            <tr>
             <td><%=rs.getString("seatno")%></td>
             <td><%=rs.getString("name")%></td>
             <td> <%=rs.getString("Subject1")%></td>
             <td> <%=rs.getString("Subject2")%></td>
             <td> <%=rs.getString("Subject3")%></td>
             <td> <%=rs.getString("Status")%></td>
            </tr>
            <%

            }
            rs.close();
            stmt.close();
            conn.close();
            %>
        </table>
    </center>
    </body>
    </html>
```

Example 4.15.4 : *Explain JDBC driver types. Write a Java bean to connect to database and insert in the database. Query will be passed as a message to bean.*

GTU : Dec.-12, Marks 7

Solution : JDBC Driver Type : Refer section 2.11.

Program for connecting to database using Bean

Step 1 : Create a database in MS-ACCESS named EMPDB. Create a table named EmpTable. Create two fields named empid and empname in this table. Store some suitable values. Then create a DSN connection using Control Panel->ODBC.

Step 2 : Create a folder named MyDBConn. Store following java program in it. This is actually a bean program named as bean.java

```
package MyDBConn;
import java.io.*;
import java.sql.Connection;
import java.sql.DriverManager;
import java.sql.Statement;
import java.sql.ResultSet;
public class bean
{
```

```
  private int empid;
  private String empname;
  private Connection connection=null;
  String connectionURL = "jdbc:odbc:EmpDB";

  public bean()
  {
     try {
              Class.forName("sun.jdbc.odbc.JdbcOdbcDriver");
              // Connecting to the database
              connection = DriverManager.getConnection(connectionURL,"","");
              }catch(Exception e){
              System.out.println("Exception is ;"+e);
              }

  }
  public void setempid(int empid)
    {
        this.empid = empid;
    }

    public int getempid()
    {
        return (this.empid);
    }

    public void setempname(String empname)
    {
        this.empname = empname;
    }

    public String getempname()
    {
        return (this.empname);
    }

  public void insert()
  {

    try
    {
       String query = "insert into EmpTable(empid,empname)
values('"+empid+"','"+empname+"')";
              Statement stmt = connection.createStatement();
              stmt.executeUpdate (query);
```

```
            stmt.close ();
        }catch(Exception e){
            System.out.println("Exception is ;"+e);
        }
    }

}
```

Compile this program using javac. The class file is generated in the folder MyDBConn.

Step 3 : Copy this folder(i.e. MyDBConn) to classes folder of WEB-INF of your tomcat directory.

Step 4 : Write following JSP program which invokes the bean program created in Step 2.

< BeanJSPDB.jsp>

```
<%@ page language="Java" import="java.sql.*" %>

<html>
  <head><title>Input Form</title></head>
<body>
<h3>Connecting to Database using Bean</h3>
<form name="form1" method="POST">
 EmpID:<input type="text" name ="empid"> <br/>
 Emp Name:<input type="text" name ="empname"> <br/>
 <br/><br/>
 <input type = "submit" value="Submit">

 <jsp:useBean id="beanObj" class="MyDBConn.bean" scope="page">
   <jsp:setProperty name="beanObj" property="*"/>
 </jsp:useBean>
</form>

<% beanObj.insert();%>

</body>
</html>
```

Create some folder say DBConnect in jsp directory of example directory of your tomcat folder.

Type the URL http://localhost/examples/jsp/DBConnect/BeanJSPDB.jsp. Using the input form you can insert the data in the database.

Example 4.15.5 : *Write a student bean class with property student_name, enrollment_no, address and cpi. Write jsp page to set and display all property.*

GTU : Summer-16, Marks 7

Solution : Bean Program[StudentBean.java]

```
public class StudentBean implements java.io.Serializable
{
  private String name = null;
  private int enrollment_no = 0;
  private String address = null;
  private double cpi = 0.0;

  public StudentBean() {
  }
  public String getName(){
    return name;
  }
  public int getEnrollment_no(){
    return enrollment_no;
  }
  public String getAddress(){
    return address;
  }
  public double getCpi(){
    return cpi;
  }
  public void setName(String name){
    this.name = name;
  }
  public void setEnrollment_no(int enrollment_no){
    this.enrollment_no = enrollment_no;
  }
  public void setAddress(String address){
    this.address = address;
  }
  public void setCpi(double cpi){
    this.cpi = cpi;
  }
}
```

JSP Program[DisplayStudent.jsp]

```
<html>
<head>
<title>BEAN and JSP Example</title>
</head>
<body>
<jsp:useBean id="students" class="StudentBean">
<jsp:setProperty name="students" property="name"  value="AAA"/>
<jsp:setProperty name="students" property="enrollment_no" value="10"/>
<jsp:setProperty name="students" property="address" value="Pune"/>
```

```
<jsp:setProperty name="students" property="cpi" value="9.2"/>
</jsp:useBean>
<p>Student Name:
  <jsp:getProperty name="students" property="name"/>
</p>
<p>Student Enrollment Number:
  <jsp:getProperty name="students" property="enrollment_no"/>
</p>
<p>Student Adrress:
  <jsp:getProperty name="students" property="address"/>
</p>
<p>Student CPI:
  <jsp:getProperty name="students" property="cpi"/>
</p>
</body>
</html>
```

4.16 JSP Standard Tag Libraries

GTU : Dec.-11, May-12, Winter-13, 14, Summer-14, 16, Marks 7

The JSTL Expression Language or EL is used by JSP programmer in order to avoid the usage of java code for accessing data. The EL statements are always used with in {...} along with a prefix **$**. Here is a simple example in which EL expression is used in JSP page. First of all HTML page is displayed from which user name is obtained and using JSP page we are displaying the entered username.

Input.html

```
<html>
    <body>
        <form method=post action="ELDemo.jsp">
            <input type=text name='text1'>
            <input type=submit value="submit">
        </form>
    </body>
</html>
```

ELDemo.jsp

```
<%@ page contentType="text/html" %>
<%@ taglib prefix="c" uri="http://java.sun.com/jsp/jstl/core" %>
<html>
        You have entered string
        <strong><c:out value="${param.text1}" /></strong>
    </html>
</body>
```

Output

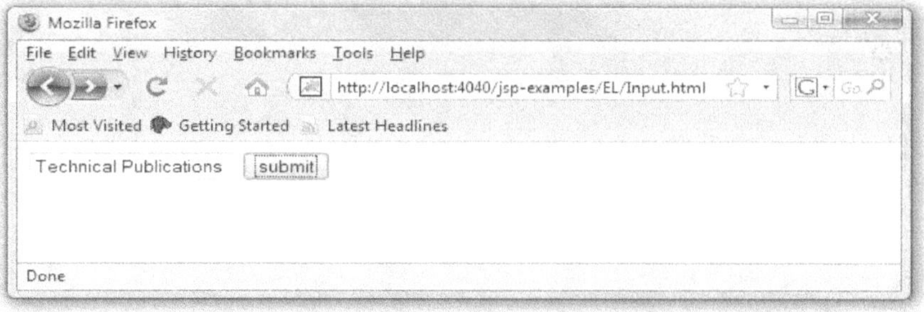

Various **keywords** used in EL expression are

and	ge	mod
div	gt	ne
empty	instanceof	not
eq	le	null
false	lt	

Various **operators** that can be used are

Arithmetic Operators	+ – * / or **div** % or **mod**
Logical Operators	&& or **and** || or **or** ! or **not**
Relational Operators	== or **eq** != or **ne** < or **lt** <= or **le** > or **gt** >= or **ge**

Sometimes we can compute the expression directly like this ${1+3+5} which will be evaluated as 9.

4.16.1 Core Tag Library

The core tag is used nearly in all the web applications. This tag is useful for performing basic input and output, for looping operation or for evaluating expressions. Various tags used in core library are -

1. <c:out>
2. <c:set>
3. <c:if>
4. <c:choose>
5. <c:when>
6. <c:otherwise>
7. <c:forEach>
8. <c:forTokens>
9. <c:url>
10. <c:redirect>
11. <c:param>
12. <c:import>

Let us understand the use of core tag with the help of programming examples.

First.jsp

```
<%@ page contentType="text/html" %>
<%@ taglib prefix="c" uri="http://java.sun.com/jsp/jstl/core" %>
<html>
<body>
<form method=post action="first.jsp">
Name <input type=text name="text1" value=""><br><br>
<input type=submit value="Enter">
</form>
Name:<c:out value="${param.text1}" /><br>
</body>
</html>
```

Output

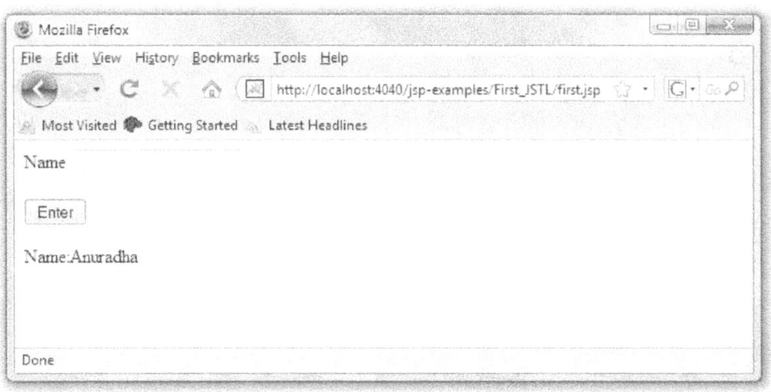

Code explanation

In above written JSP code we have used **taglib** directive with prefix **c**. Note that we must specify the **uri="http://java.sun.com/jsp/jstl/core"** for every core tag and prefix **"c"** .

We have used **<c:out** for outputting the value written in the text box of the form.

Let us see the use of <c:set> tag.

Second.jsp

```
<%@ page contentType="text/html" %>
<%@ taglib prefix="c" uri="http://java.sun.com/jsp/jstl/core" %>
<html>
<body bgcolor=pink>
<form  method=post  action=Second.jsp>
  <select name="combo1">
  <option value="">Select
   <option value="Apple">Apple
   <option value="Mango">Mango
   <option value="Banana">Banana
   <option value="Guava">Guava
</select>
<input type=submit value="Enter">
</form>
<c:set var="fruit"  value="${param.combo1}"  />
I like <strong> <c:out value="${fruit}" /> </strong> very much!!!
<br>
</body>
</html>
```

Output

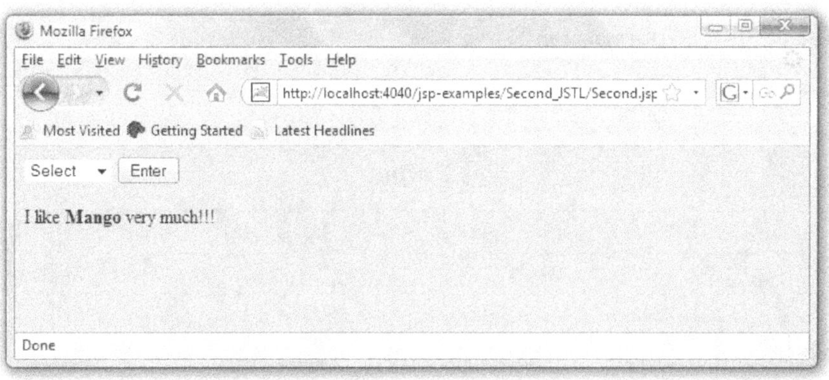

Let us now see the use of tag **<c:if>**

Third.jsp

```
<%@ page contentType="text/html" %>
<%@ taglib prefix="c" uri="http://java.sun.com/jsp/jstl/core" %>
```

```
<html>
<body bgcolor=pink>
<form method=post action=Third.jsp>
   <select name="combo1">
   <option value="">Select
     <option value="Apple">Apple
     <option value="Mango">Mango
     <option value="Banana">Banana
     <option value="Guava">Guava
  </select>
<input   type=submit value="Enter">
</form>
<c:set var="fruit"   value="${param.combo1}"   />

<c:if test="${fruit == 'Apple'}" >
I like <strong><c:out value="${fruit}" /></strong> very much!!!
</c:if>

<c:if test="${fruit == 'Mango'}" >
I like <strong><c:out value="${fruit}" /></strong> very much!!!
</c:if>

<c:if test="${fruit == 'Banana'}" >
I like <strong><c:out value="${fruit}" /></strong> very much!!!
</c:if>

<c:if test="${fruit == 'Guava'}" >
I like <strong><c:out value="${fruit}" /></strong> very much!!!
</c:if>

<br>
</body>
</html>
```

Output

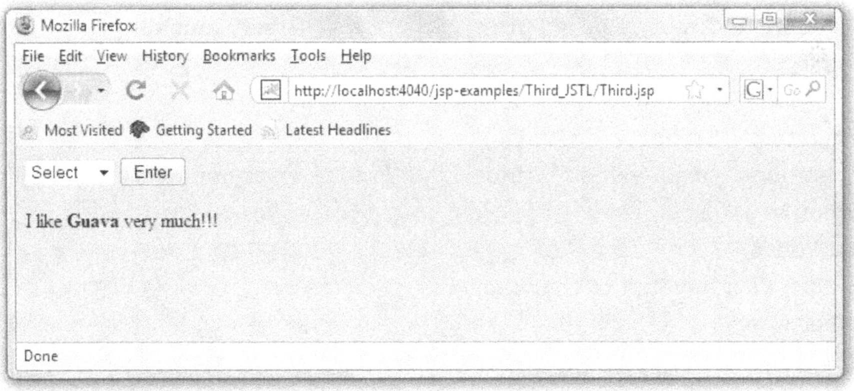

We can have select any item using **<c:choose>** tag. The <c:choose> contains the <c:when test> and <c:otherwise> tags for specifying the selection criteria. In the following example we will see how to make use of these tags. For a <c:when> tag the **test** is a standard variable being used.

Forth.jsp

```
<%@ page contentType="text/html" %>
<%@ taglib prefix="c" uri="http://java.sun.com/jsp/jstl/core" %>
<html>
<body bgcolor=pink>
<form method=post action=Forth.jsp>
  <select name="combo1">
  <option value="">Select
    <option value="Apple">Apple
    <option value="Mango">Mango
    <option value="Banana">Banana
    <option value="Guava">Guava
  </select>
<input   type=submit value="Enter">
</form>
<c:set var="fruit"  value="${param.combo1}"   />
<c:choose>
    <c:when test="${fruit == 'Apple'}" >
            I like <strong><c:out value="${fruit}" /></strong> very much!!!
    </c:when>

    <c:when test="${fruit == 'Mango'}" >
    I like <strong><c:out value="${fruit}" /></strong> very much!!!
    </c:when>

    <c:when test="${fruit == 'Banana'}" >
    I like <strong><c:out value="${fruit}" /></strong> very much!!!
    </c:when>

    <c:when test="${fruit == 'Guava'}" >
    I like <strong><c:out value="${fruit}" /></strong> very much!!!
    </c:when>
    <c:otherwise>
            Select any fruit of your choice
    </c:otherwise>
    </c:choose>
```

```
    <br>
    </body>
</html>
```

Output

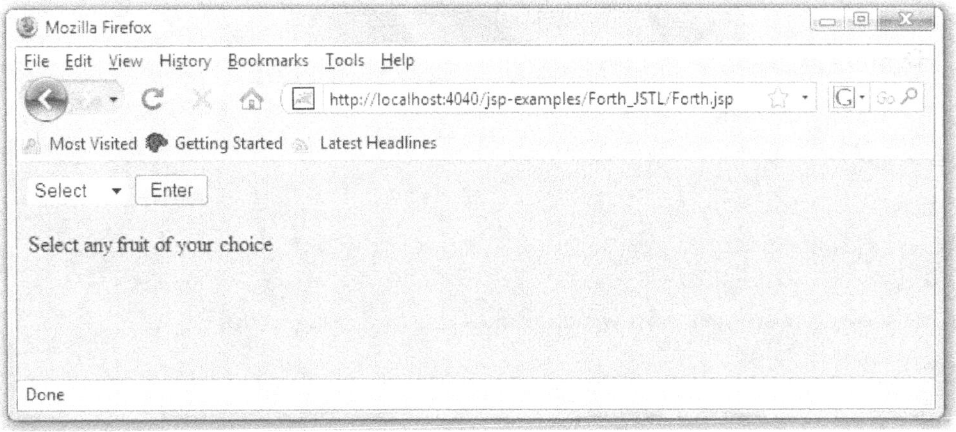

Let us now see the use of **<c:forEach>** tag. This tag is specially used to denote the looping condition. Following code shows its demonstration.

Fifth.jsp

```
<%@ page contentType="text/html" %>
<%@ taglib prefix="c" uri="http://java.sun.com/jsp/jstl/core" %>
<html>
<body>
<% pageContext.setAttribute("Fruits",new String[] {"Apple","Mango","Banana","Guava"}
);%>
<b>The various fruits are...</b>
<c:forEach   var="i"  items="${Fruits}"  varStatus="n">
<br/>
  <c:out value="${n.index}"  />
  <c:out value="${n.current}" />
</c:forEach>
</body>
</html>
```

In above code we have used <c:forEach> tag in which **items** denote the current String, var is a symbolotic name for array varStatus is the symbolic name for current status. Using **index** we can display the index of each item in an array. By default array starts from index 0 and **current** is used to display the current element. The output will be

Output

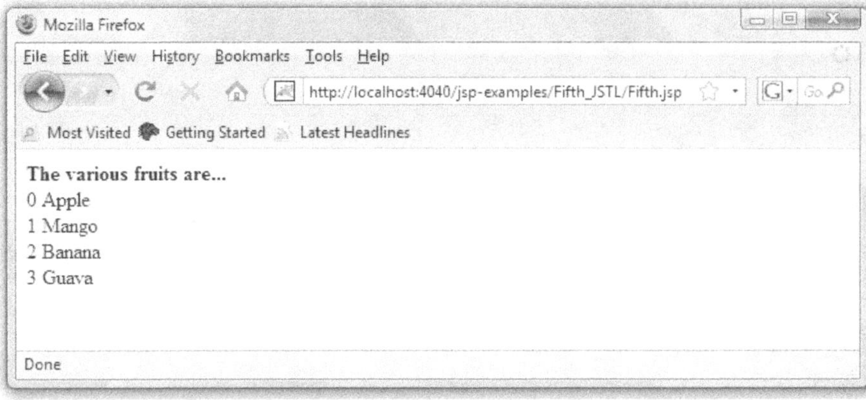

Let us see one more program which makes use of the tag **<c:forEach>**

for_loop.jsp

```
<%@ page contentType="text/html" %>
<%@ taglib prefix="c" uri="http://java.sun.com/jsp/jstl/core" %>
<html>
    <body>
        <b>The natural numbers are...</b>
        <c:forEach   var="i" begin="1" end="10">
            <br/>
            <c:out value="${i}" />
            </c:forEach>
    </body>
</html>
```

Output

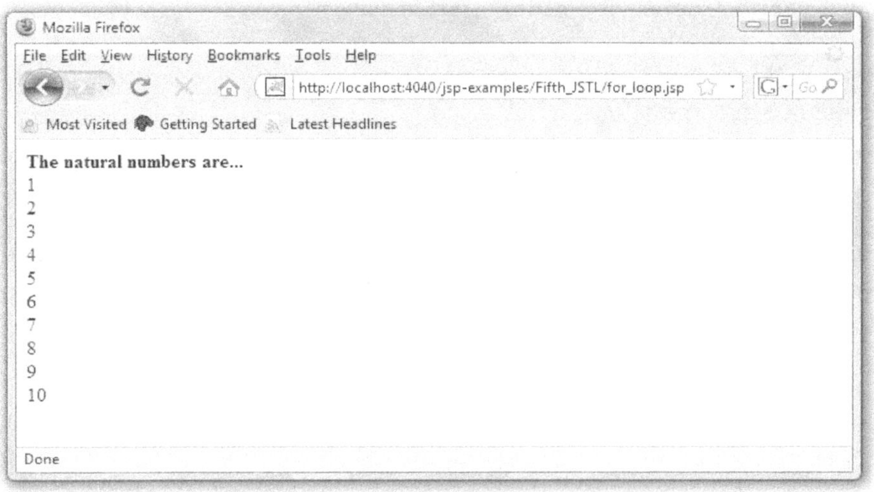

There is another simple token **<c:forTokens>**. Using this token each instance of a string from given sentence can be separated out.

TokenDemo.jsp

```
<%@ page contentType="text/html" %>
<%@ taglib prefix="c" uri="http://java.sun.com/jsp/jstl/core" %>
<c:set var="i" value="c5-Sun Empire;Anuradha;Puntambekar;Pune;"/>
<html>
<body>
<table border="3">
  <tr>
  <th>Address</th>
  <th>Name</th>
  <th>Surname</th>
  <th>City</th>
  </tr>
  <tr>
<c:forTokens items="${i}" delims=";" var="tok" >
<td><c:out value="${tok}" /></td>
</c:forTokens>
</tr>
</table>
</body>
</html>
```

In above code, we have taken a variable i to which some string containing many substrings is assigned. These substrings are separated out by the delimiter ; Then using the token **<c:forToken>** we tokenise the string using **items= "${i}".** We must assign the separator to the **delim** so that while parsing the given string for separating out the tokens, the **delim** value is treated as a separation symbol and only token strings can be extracted. Following output itself explains the above program -

Output

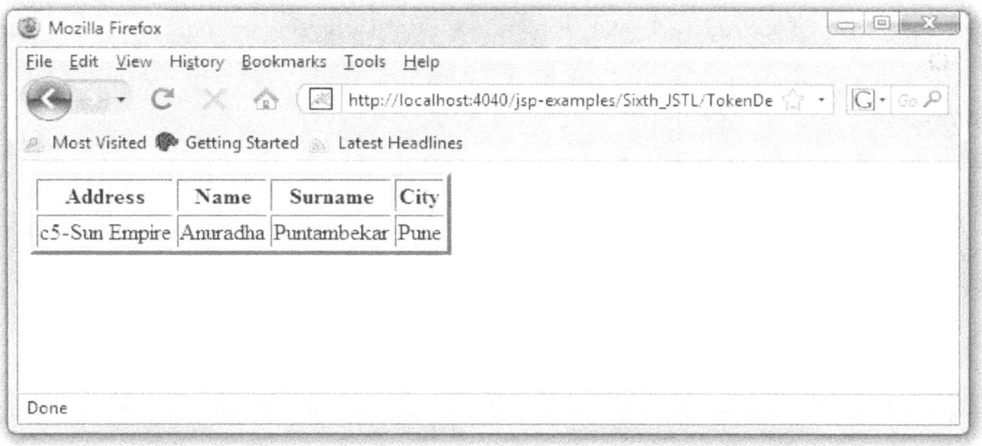

Now we will discuss the tag **<c:url>** As the name suggests this tag is used to navigate to the desired page using the URL. Here is its demonstration -

urldemo.jsp

```
<%@ page contentType="text/html" %>
<%@ taglib prefix="c" uri="http://java.sun.com/jsp/jstl/core" %>
<html>
    <body>
        <c:import url="MyPage.html" />
        <c:out value="Thank you for using this demo..." />
        </body>
</html>
```

MyPage.html

```
<html>
<body>
<h1>The visitors of this site are always wonderful persons!!</h1>
</body>
</html>
```

Output

To make use of **<c:redirect>** tag just make slight change in the above JSP page as follows -

urldemo.jsp

```
<%@ page contentType="text/html" %>
<%@ taglib prefix="c" uri="http://java.sun.com/jsp/jstl/core" %>
<html>
    <body>
    <c:redirect url="http://localhost:4040/jsp-examples/Seventh_JSTL/MyPage.html" />
    <c:out value="Thank you for using this demo..." />
    </body>
</html>
```

MyPage.html

```
<html>
    <body>
        <h1>The visitors of this site are always wonderful persons!!</h1>
    </body>
</html>
```

The **Output** itself is self explanatory. Note that the string specified using **<c:out>** tag i.e. "Thank you for using this demo..." will not be displayed at all. That means using <c:redirect> we get navigated to designated page from the source web page and contents of source web page will not be displayed. Here is your output

Let us now see how to make use of the tag **<c:param>**. This tag is useful to send some parameter to another page. We have written one main JSP page on which we have given a redirecting link to the **NewPage.jsp** and while navigating to this web page we have sent a parameter **MyName** by assigning some name value to it.

ParamDemo.jsp

```
<%@ page contentType="text/html" %>
<%@ taglib prefix="c" uri="http://java.sun.com/jsp/jstl/core" %>
<c:redirect url="http://localhost:4040/jsp-examples/Eighth_JSTL/NewPage.jsp" >
<c:param name="MyName" value="Parth" />
</c:redirect>
```

NewPage.jsp

```
<%@ taglib prefix="c" uri="http://java.sun.com/jsp/jstl/core" %>
<html>
    <body>
        <strong> Just look at the address bar of your Web browser </strong>
        <c:out value="${param.MyName}" />
    </body>
</html>
```

Output

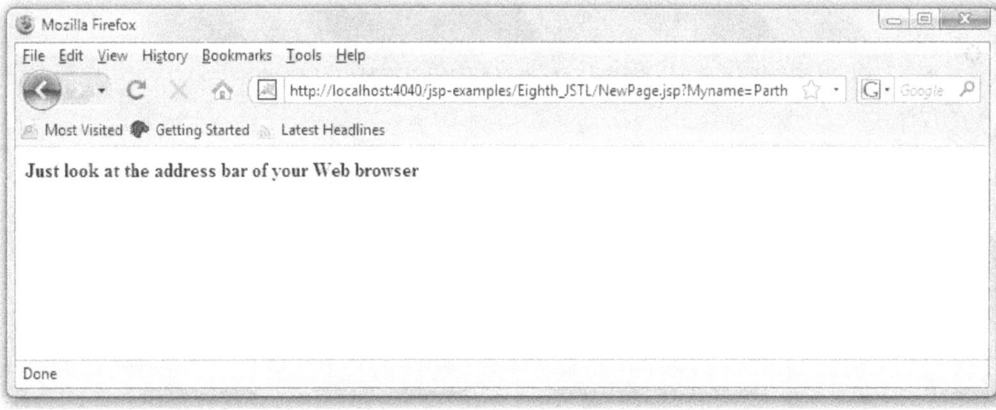

Finally we will discuss a simplest core tag which is very much similar to **<c:url>** tag and i.e. **<c:import>** tag. Following code makes use of <c:import> tag.

ImportDemo.jsp

```
<%@ page contentType="text/html" %>
<%@ taglib prefix="c" uri="http://java.sun.com/jsp/jstl/core" %>
<html>
<body>
    <c:import url="http://localhost:4040/jsp-examples/Nineth_JSTL/MyPage.html" />
    <c:out value="Thank you for using this demo..." />
</body>
</html>
```

MyPage.html

```
<html>
    <body>
        <h1>The visitors of this site are always wonderful persons!!</h1>
    </body>
</html>
```

Output

Example 4.16.1 : *Write line(s) of code in JSP for following.*
i) Session read and write.
ii) URL rewriting sending and retrieving parameter(s)
iii) URL redirection
iv) Print "hello world" as output
v) Include the other JSP file statically
vi) Expression to display date as output
vii) Method of setting the JSP parameters to user in JSTL

GTU : Summer-16, Marks 7

Solution : (I)

```
<%
  String name = request.getParameter( "username" );
  session.setAttribute( "User", name );
%>
 <%= session.getAttribute( "User" ) %>
```

(II)

```
out.println("<a href="" + response.encodeURL("/mypage.html") + "">Example</a>");
```

(III)

```
<%
  // New location to be redirected
  String website = new String("http://www.myexamples.com");
  response.setStatus(response.SC_MOVED_TEMPORARILY);
  response.setHeader("Location", website);
%>
```

(IV)

```
<% out.println("Hello World"); %>
```

(V)

```
<jsp:include page="myPage.html"/>
```

(VI) Refer example 4.8.1

(VII)

```
<%@ taglib prefix="c" uri="http://java.sun.com/jsp/jstl/core" %>
<html>
<body>
<c:import url="MyPage.html" />
<c:out value="Thank you for using this demo..." />
</body>
</html>
```

4.16.2 Function Tag Library

The standard functions can be used using the JSTL library. Following is the syntax used for including the JSTL functions library -

```
<%@ taglib prefix="fn" uri="http://java.sun.com/jsp/jstl/functions" %>
```

Various funcitons are -

Tag	Purpose
fn:contains()	For checking if the input string contains the desirted substring or not.
fn:endsWith()	For checking if an input ends with specific substring or not.
fn:join()	For joining all the elements of an array of substring.
fn:split()	This tag is used to split the substring into the array of two substrings.
fn:replace()	This tag is used to replace the string by the desired new string.
fn:substring()	It returns the substring of the given string.
fn:toUpperCase()	It converts all the characters of the string to the upper case.
fn:toLowerCase()	It converts all the characters of the string to the lower case.
fn:trim()	It removes the white space from both the ends of the string.
fn:length()	It returns the number of characters present in the string.

Example : Conversion of given string to upper case

JSP Document[funtag.jsp]

```
<%@ taglib uri="http://java.sun.com/jsp/jstl/core" prefix="c" %>
<%@ taglib uri="http://java.sun.com/jsp/jstl/functions" prefix="fn" %>
<html>
<head>
<title>JSTL Functions Tag Demo</title>
</head>
<body>

<c:set var="str1" value="I LOVE INDIA"/>
<c:set var="str2" value="${fn:toLowerCase(str1)}" />
<p><b>Original :</b> ${str1}</p>
<p><b>Conversion :</b> ${str2}</p>

</body>
</html>
```

Output

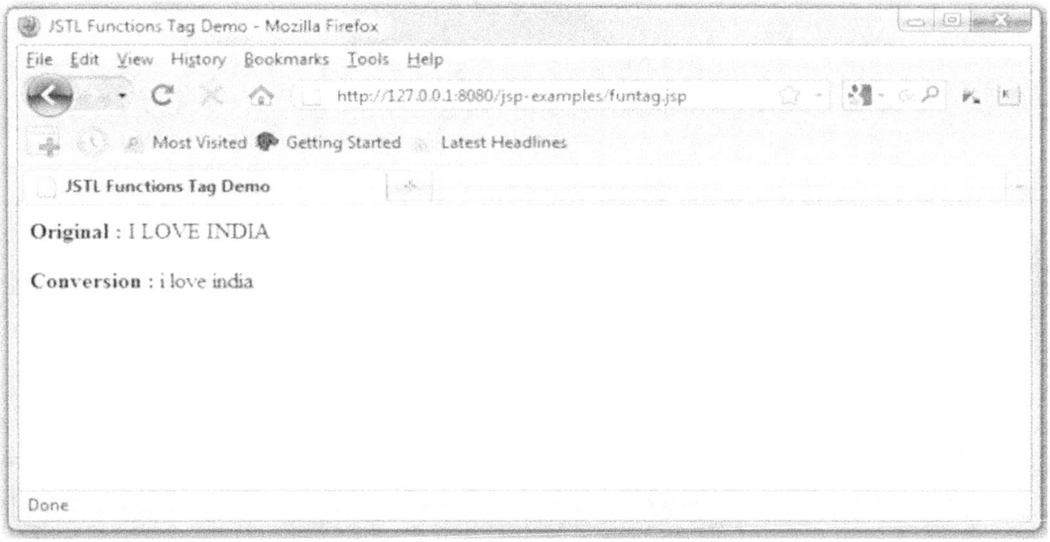

Example : Finding the substring of the given string

JSP Document[funtag1.jsp]

```
<%@ taglib uri="http://java.sun.com/jsp/jstl/core" prefix="c" %>
<%@ taglib uri="http://java.sun.com/jsp/jstl/functions" prefix="fn" %>
<html>
<head>
<title>JSTL Functions Tag Demo</title>
</head>
<body>

<c:set var="str1" value="I like Programming"/>
<c:set var="str2" value="${fn:substring(str1, 2,6)}" />
<p><b>string is:</b>${str1}</p>
<p><b>sub string is:</b>${str2}</p>

</body>
</html>
```

Output

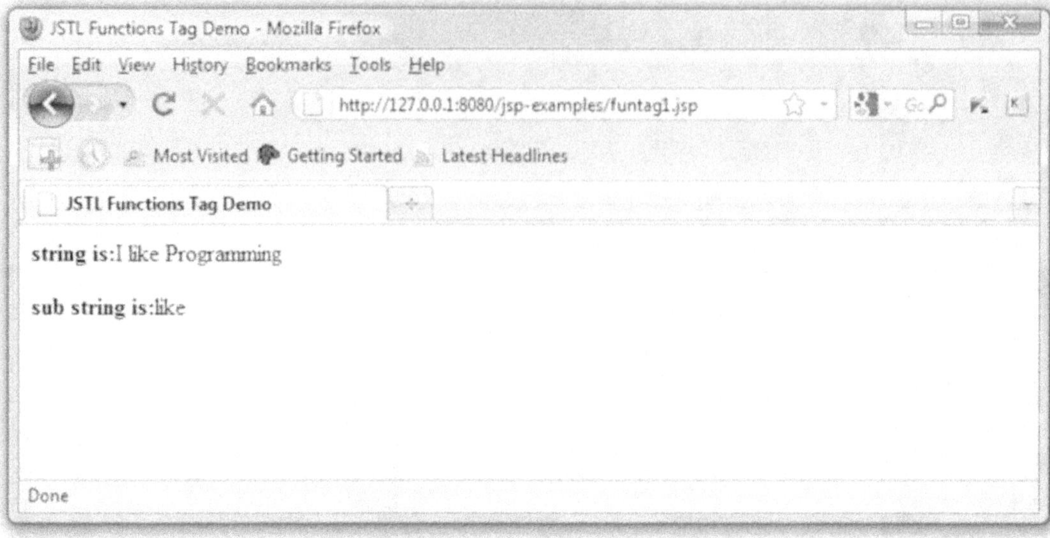

Example : Replacing the string by another new string

JSP Document[funtag2.jsp]

```
<%@ taglib uri="http://java.sun.com/jsp/jstl/core" prefix="c" %>
<%@ taglib uri="http://java.sun.com/jsp/jstl/functions" prefix="fn" %>
<html>
<head>
<title>JSTL Functions Tag Demo</title>
</head>
<body>

<c:set var="str1" value="I like Programming."/>
<c:set var="str2" value="${fn:replace(str1,'Programming', 'Reading')}" />

<p><b>string is:</b>${str1}</p>
<p><b>New string is:</b>${str2}</p>
</body>
</html>
```

Output

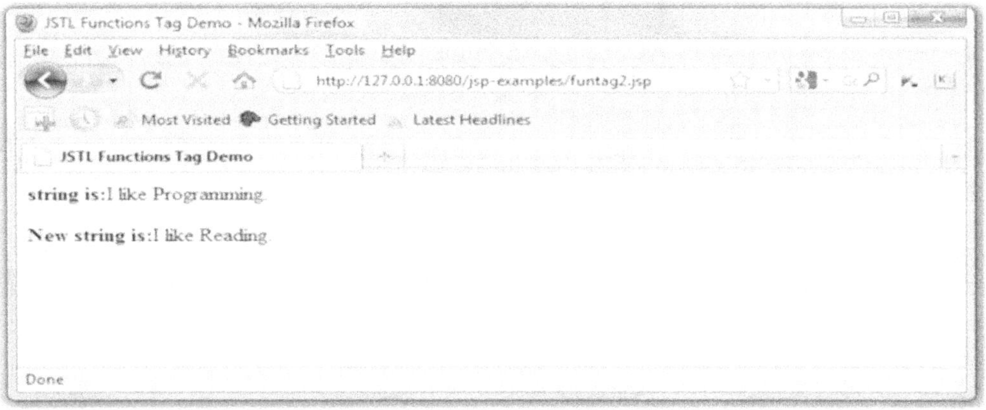

4.16.3 SQL Tag Library

The SQL tag library is used to connect to the relational database such as MYSQL,Oracle and so on.

For including this tag in the JSP document following line must be added in the beginning.

```
<%@ taglib uri="http://java.sun.com/jsp/jstl/sql" prefix="sql"%>
```

Various tags used in sql tag library are –

Tag	Purpose
<sql:setDataSource>	Creates a simple DataSource. You can specify the driver name, user name and password for the target database.
<sql:query>	This tag is used for specifying the SQL query.
<sql:update>	Using this tag you can insert, delete or update the records of the existing database.

Following is a simple example in which we connect to the SQL database from JSP using the sql tag library. Just follow the following steps -

Step 1 : Open the command prompt and type the command

```
mysql –u root –p
Enter password: **********
```

Then the mysql prompt will appear. Type following commands for creating a table inside the test database -

```
mysql> use test;
Database changed
mysql> create table Employees
   -> (id int not null,
   -> age int not null,
   -> name varchar(255)
   -> );
```

```
Query OK, 0 rows affected (0.39 sec)

mysql> insert into Employees VALUES(1,20,'Shilpa');
Query OK, 1 row affected (0.07 sec)

mysql> insert into Employees VALUES(2,35,'Supriya');
Query OK, 1 row affected (0.00 sec)

mysql> insert into Employees VALUES(3,22,'Monika');
Query OK, 1 row affected (0.00 sec)
```

Step 2 : Now create a JSP document by typing following code in the Notepad.

JSP Document

```
<%@ taglib uri="http://java.sun.com/jsp/jstl/core" prefix="c" %>
<%@ taglib uri="http://java.sun.com/jsp/jstl/sql" prefix="sql"%>
<html>
<head>
<title>JSTL sql Tag Demo</title>
</head>
<body>

<sql:setDataSource var="DB" driver="com.mysql.jdbc.Driver"
url="jdbc:mysql://localhost/test"
   user="root"  password="mypassword"/>

<sql:query dataSource="${DB}" var="Rec">
SELECT * from Employees;
</sql:query>
<center>
<h2>Employee Database</h2>
<table border="1">
<tr>
<th>ID</th>
<th>Name</th>
<th>Age</th>
</tr>
<c:forEach var="row" items="${Rec.rows}">
<tr>
<td><c:out value="${row.id}"/></td>
<td><c:out value="${row.name}"/></td>
<td><c:out value="${row.age}"/></td>
</tr>
</c:forEach>
</table>
```

```
</center>

</body>
</html>
```

Step 3 : Open some suitable web browser and type the URL for the JSP document and you will get the following output.

Output

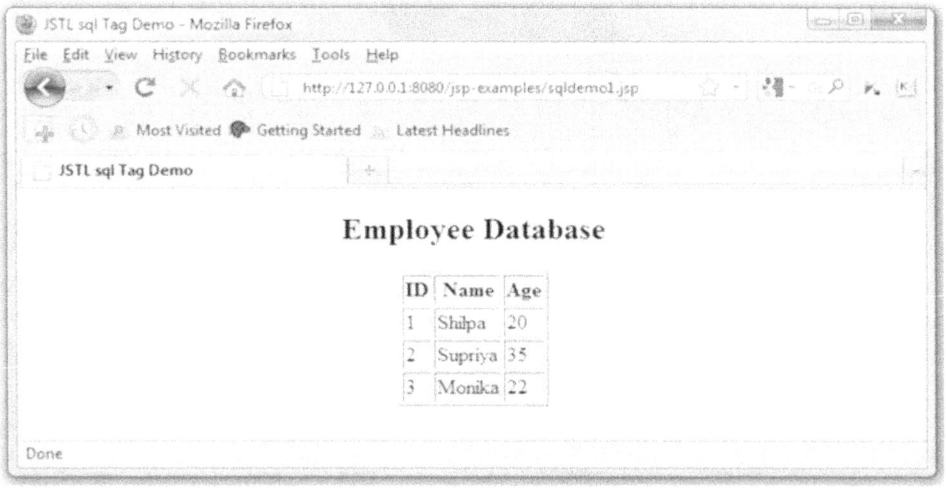

Program Explanation :

- In the above code at the beginning we have included the tag lib as

```
<%@ taglib uri="http://java.sun.com/jsp/jstl/sql" prefix="sql"%>
```

- Then using **<sql:setDataSource>** tag we have established the connection of JSP document with the MySQL. The driver **mysql.jdbc.Driver** is needed to establish a connection with MySQL. The user name is 'root/ and password is 'mypassword' for the MYSQL which I installed right now.
- The variable for data source is created(named DB) using the <sql:query> statement. Then using this variable- the rows of each record set are accessed and the corresponding result is displayed on the web browser. The output it self is self explanatory.

Review Questions

1. *Explain JSP tag library with examples.* **GTU : Dec.-11, Winter-14, Marks 7**
2. *Explain the features of core tag library for JSP.* **GTU : May-12, Marks 7**
3. *Explain the JSP core tag library* **GTU : Winter-13, Marks 7**
4. *Write a note on - SQL tag library.* **GTU : Summer-14, Marks 7**

4.17 JSP Custom Tag

- Tag extension is a new feature available in JSP 1.1. It is also called as **custom tag**. The tag extensions allow the authors to add their own custom tags that perform custom actions.
- The tag extensions are similar to the HTML or XML tags which are embedded in JSP page. These tags have some special meaning to a JSP engine at translation time. These tags help to invoke the **application functionality** without the embedding the Java code in JSP.

4.17.1 Tag Extensions API

In addition to the pre-defined JSP actions, developers can add their own **custom actions** using tag extensions with the help of **Tag Extension API.**

Developers write a Java class that implements one of the **Tag interfaces** and provide a **tag library XML description file** that specifies the tags and the java classes that implement the tags.

4.17.2 Tag Handlers

- The **tag handler** is a Java class which responds to the events raised by the container. These events get raised when the **custom tag or tag extension** is encountered.
- Every tag handler class must extend the **TagSupport** class. This class is supported by the **tag extension API**
- The **TagSupport** supports following methods -
  1. **doStartTag()** is used to process the start tag.
  2. **doEndTag()** is for processing the end tag.
  3. **getId()** is for getting the value of Id attribute.
  4. **setId()** is for setting the value of Id attribute.
  5. **getParent()** is for returning the parent tag instance.
- The **doStartTag()** method may return following -
  1. **SKIP_BODY :** The body between the SKIP_BODY tag is not processed.
  2. **EVAL_BODY_INCLUDE :** Evaluate the body of the tag enclosed within this tag.
  3. **EVAL_BODY_TAG :** Evaluate the body of the tag and push the result onto stream.
  4. **EVAL_PAGE :** This indicates that the rest of the JSP file should be processed.

5. **SKIP_PAGE :** This indicates that no further processing should be done. That means the control leaves the JSP page.

- Following are some steps that can be adopted to create the custom tag and embed it in the JSP code.

Step 1 : Creation of Tag handler.

Step 2 : Creation of Tag Library Descriptor (TLD)

Step 3 : Creation of JSP with registration and use of tags declared in TLD

Let us understand these steps with some illustrating example.

Step 1 : The tag handler is a Java class which responds to the events raised by the container. These events get raised when the custom tag is encountered. Every tag handler class must extend the **TagSupport**. This class is supported by JSPAPI. Let us create a tag handler class.

Go to the path c:*your_tomcat_directory*\jsp-examples\WEB-INF\classes and create one folder say **CustomTag** and store a java file named **firstTag.java.** This file is as given below-

firstTag.java

```
package CustomTag;
import java.io.*;
import javax.servlet.http.*;
import javax.servlet.jsp.*;
import javax.servlet.jsp.tagext.*;
import java.util.*;
public class firstTag extends TagSupport
{
    public int doStartTag() throws JspException
    {
        try
        {
            JspWriter out= pageContext.getOut();
            out.print("Hello!!!This is my first custom tag");
        }
        catch(Exception e)
        {
            throw new JspException(e.getMessage());
        }
        return EVAL_PAGE;
    }
}
```

In above Java program our class is extended from the interface **TagSupport** which has following methods -

- doStartTag() for processing the start tag.
- doEndTag() for processing the end tag.
- getId() for getting the value of Id attribute.
- setId() for setting the value of Id attribute.
- getParent() for returning the parent tag instance.

And so on…

The **doStartTag** method returns EVAL_PAGE which means continue evaluating the page. This is valid return value. This method throws an exception JspException. In this Java program we are simply displaying the message "Hello!!!This is my first custom tag".

Before compiling this program set the class path using the Environment variables. For that purpose go to Control Panel, click System, and open its properties and set the CLASSPATH as

```
C:\your_tomcat_directory\common\lib\servlet-api.jar;C:\your_tomcat_directory\
common\lib\jsp-api.jar
```

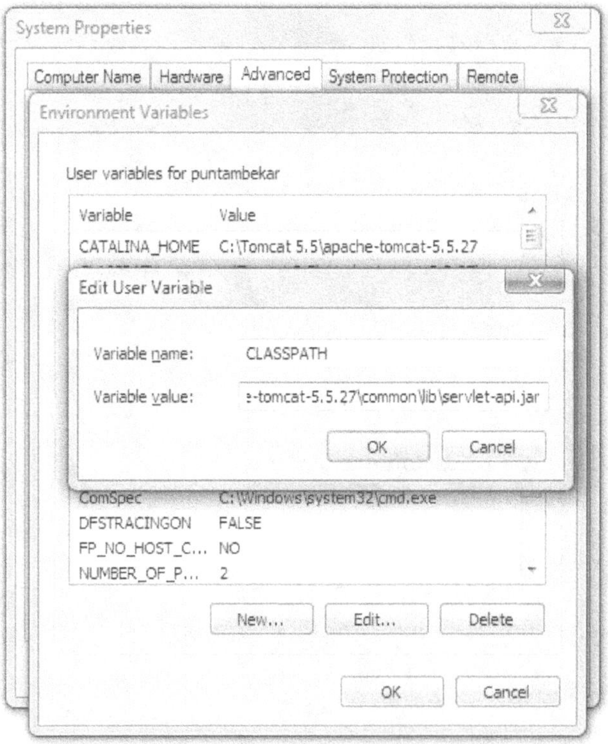

Then using **javac** command the class file can be generated -

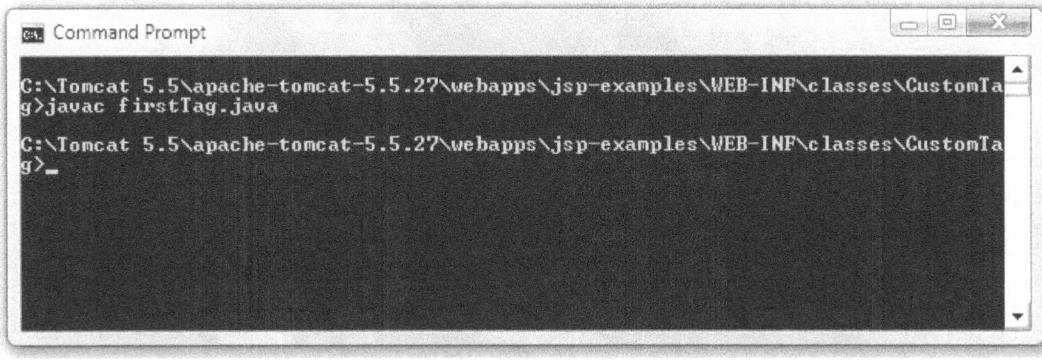

Step 2 : Now we will create a .tld file. For that purpose switch to the path c:*your_tomcat_directory*\jsp-examples\WEB-INF and write the following file which is named as **MyTag.tld**

```
<?xml version="1.0" encoding="ISO-8859-1" ?>
<!DOCTYPE taglib PUBLIC "-//Sun Microsystems, Inc.//DTD JSP Tag Library 1.2//EN"
"http://java.sun.com/j2ee/dtd/web-jsptaglibrary_1_2.dtd">
<taglib>
    <tlib-version>1.0</tlib-version>
    <jsp-version>1.2</jsp-version>
    <short-name>MyTag</short-name>
    <tag>
        <name>MyFirstTag</name> <---- tag name which will be referred in JSP
        <tag-class>CustomTag.firstTag</tag-class>  <------java class created in step 1
        <body-content>empty</body-content> <---without body content
    </tag>
</taglib>
```

Step 3 : Now we have to register custom tag from **MyTag.tld** file with the JSP page. We can do this using the **taglib** directive. Following JSP page registers **MyTag.tld**. Go to the path c:*your_tomcat_directory*\jsp-examples and create a folder say **CustTagDemo** and create following JSP page in that folder.

custtag.jsp

```
<%@ taglib uri="/WEB-INF/MyTag.tld" prefix="my" %>
<html>
    <body>
    <h1>Welcome Following sentence is written using custom tag...</h1>
    <br/>
    <my:MyFirstTag />
    </body>
</html>
```

In above JSP page we have specified the **MyTag.tld** file using **taglib** directive statement. The prefix is a small word that can be used as a prefix to the tag. i.e.

```
<my:MyFirstTag />
```

Recall that the tag name which we have used as **MyFirstTag** is already defined in **MyTag.tld** file as a name element and this is an empty tag. As soon as browser encounters this tag name from **MyTag.tld** file it searches the tag class. The tag class is nothing but a compiled Java program written step 1. This Java program simply performs the task of displaying the message "Hello!!! This is my first custom tag".

Finally open a web browser and specify the **custtag.jsp** page and obtain the output as -

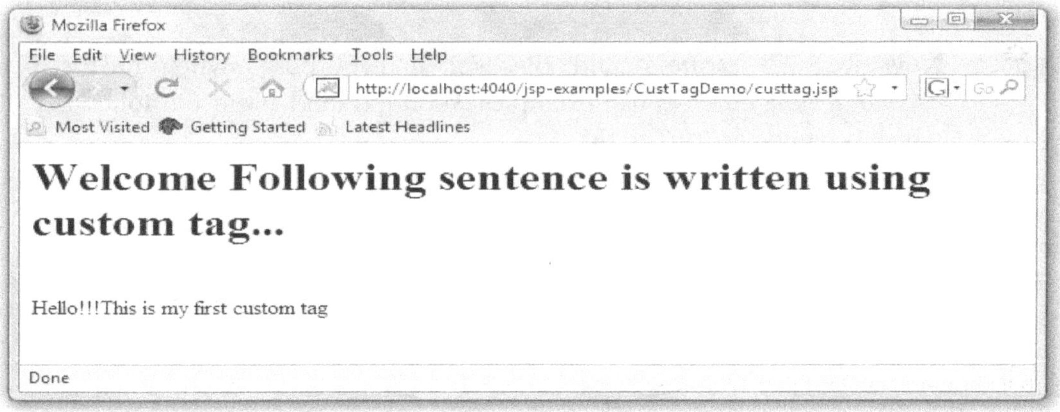

Thus we can embed the user defined tags in the JSP page along with the standard tags. We can further define the custom tag along with the attribute values. In the following demonstration we will learn how to create custom tag that supports the attribute values -

Step 1 : Create one folder named **CustomTag1** at the path c:*your_tomcat_directory*\jsp-examples\WEB-INF\classes. In that folder create a Java file named **firstTag1.java** which is as given below -

firstTag1.java

```
package CustomTag1;
import java.io.*;
import javax.servlet.http.*;
import javax.servlet.jsp.*;
import javax.servlet.jsp.tagext.*;
import java.util.*;
public class firstTag1 extends TagSupport
{
    private int n;
    public int getN()
    {
```

The get and set methods are added to read and set the attribute values

```
            return n;
        }
        public void setN(int i)
        {
            n=i;
        }
        public int doStartTag() throws JspException
        {
            try
            {
                JspWriter out= pageContext.getOut();
                int num=n*n;
                out.print("Square value is of "+n+"is "+num);    // computing the square value
            catch(Exception e)
            {
                throw new JspException(e.getMessage());
            }
            return EVAL_PAGE;
        }
}
```

compile the above program using the following command

```
javac firstTag1.java
```

Step 2 : Now go to the path c:*your_tomcat_directory*\jsp-examples\WEB-INF and create a TLD file. I have named this TLD file as **MyTagAtt.tld** and it is as given below -

MyTagAtt.tld

```
<?xml version="1.0" encoding="ISO-8859-1" ?>
<!DOCTYPE taglib PUBLIC "-//Sun Microsystems, Inc.//DTD JSP Tag Library 1.2//EN"
"http://java.sun.com/j2ee/dtd/web-jsptaglibrary_1_2.dtd">
<taglib>
    <tlib-version>1.0</tlib-version>
    <jsp-version>1.2</jsp-version>
    <short-name>MyTag1</short-name>
    <tag>
        <name>MyAttrib</name>   <---------Tag name is MyAttrib
        <tag-class>CustomTag1.firstTag1</tag-class>
        <body-content>empty</body-content>


        <attribute>
            <name>n</name>      } Attribute name is defined here. It is n
        </attribute>
    </tag>
</taglib>
```

Step 3 : Now create a JSP file and register the TLD file with this JSP. Let us store the JSP page named **custtagAtt.jsp** at the path c:*your_tomcat_directory*\\jsp-examples by creating a folder named **CustTagDemo1**. This page will be

custtagAtt.jsp

```
<%@ taglib uri="/WEB-INF/MyTagAtt.tld" prefix="my" %>
<html>
    <body>
    <h3>Finding square value of give number...</h3>
    <br/>
    <my:MyAttrib n="10"/>
    </body>
</html>
```

Use of Custom tag with attribute

Now in order to get an output, open the a web browser and just specify your JSP page and you will get the output as follows –

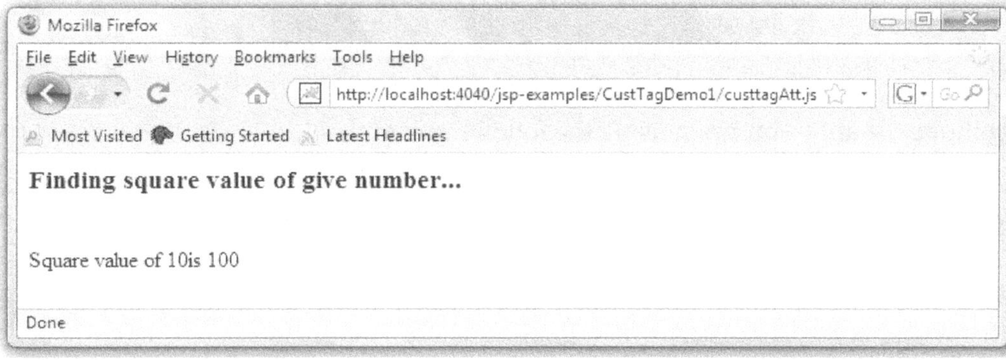

4.18 JSP Expression Language

GTU : May-12, Summer-15 Marks 7

The expression tag is used to represent the expression in JSP page. The syntax of writing expression is -

```
<%= Java Expression %>
```

For example -

```
<html>
  <head>
    <title>JSP Expression Demo</title>
  </head>

 <body>
    Value of Expression is:
    <%= (10*20) %>
 </body>
</html>
```

Output

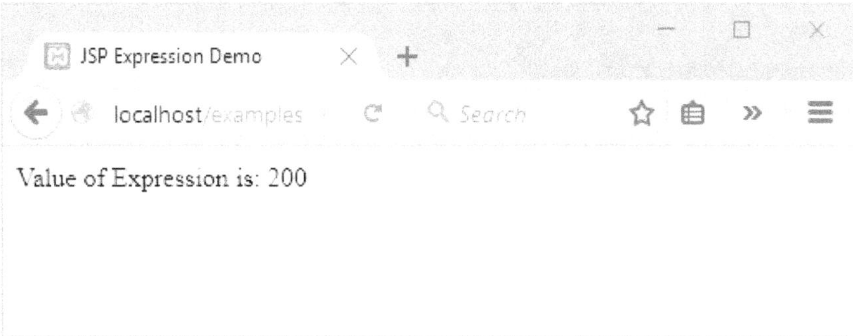

Review Question

1. *Discuss the Expression Language features of JSP and mention various implicit objects available in the EL with description.* **GTU : Summer-15, Marks 7**

4.19 JSP Exception Handling

Exception handling is a process of handling the runtime errors. Basically Exception is an object which is thrown at runtime. Exception handling is a process of handling the errors gracefully without crashing the program.

For handling the exception, **errorPage** is created and **isErrorPage** attribute is set to true.

Following is a simple example that illustrates how to use exception handling mechanism in JSP.

Example 4.19.1 : *Write a JSP program to handle the divide by zero error by exception handling mechanism.*

Solution :

Step 1 : Create an HTML form for inputting the numbers

```
<html>
<body>
<form action="http://localhost/examples/jsp/ExceptionDemo/Computation.jsp">
Enter First Number:<input type="text" name="a" /><br/><br/>
Enter Second Number:<input type="text" name="b" /><br/><br/>
<input type="submit" value="divide"/>
</form>
</body>
</html>
```

Step 2 : Create a JSP page that will perform the division operation.

Computation.jsp

```
<%@ page errorPage="error.jsp" %>
<%

String num1=request.getParameter("n1");
String num2=request.getParameter("n2");

int a=Integer.parseInt(num1);
int b=Integer.parseInt(num2);
int c=a/b;
out.print("division of numbers is: "+c);

%>
```

Step 3 : Create an error handling page named error.jsp as follows –

error.jsp

```
<%@ page isErrorPage="true" %>
<h3>Sorry for the exception!</h3>
Exception is: <%= exception %>
```

Output

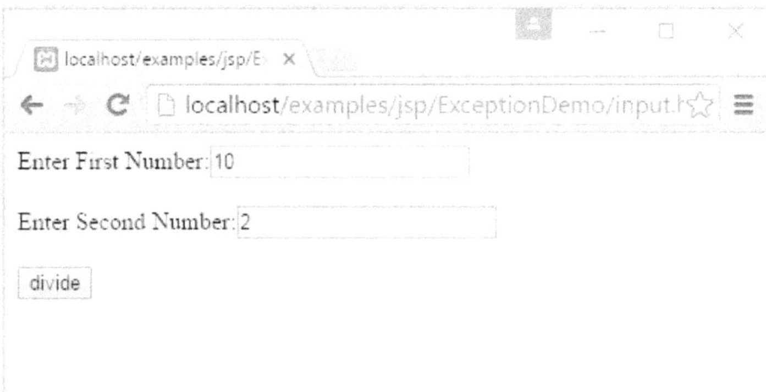

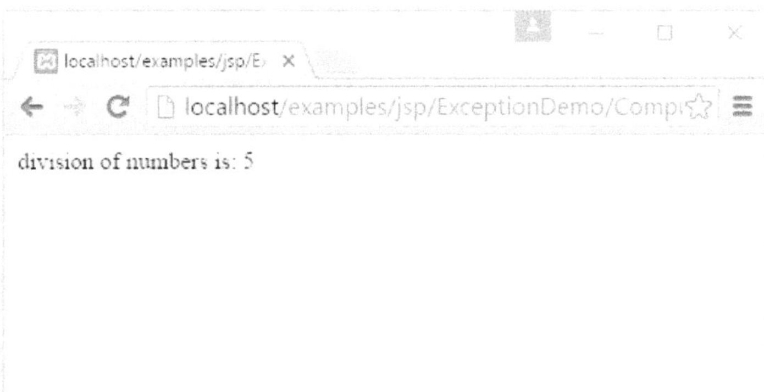

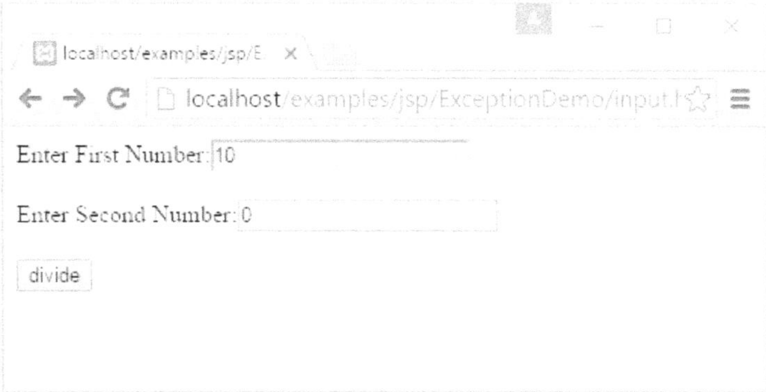

4.20 JSP XML Processing

GTU : Summer-13, 15, Winter-13, 14, Marks 7

- The XML tags are useful for creating and manipulating the XML documents through the JSP.
- Use of XML tags in JSP is similar to the use of core tag. For example if we have <x:if>,<x:out> and so on.
- Following is a syntax for including JSTL tag library in the JSP program.

```
<%@ taglib prefix="x" uri="http://java.sun.com/jsp/jstl/xml" %>
```

- Before proceeding with use of **xml tags** you need to copy following two XML and XPath related libraries into <your tomcat Installation Directory>/common/endorsed
    - **XercesImpl.jar :** Download it from http://www.apache.org/dist/xerces/j/
    - **xalan.jar :** Download it from http://xml.apache.org/xalan-j/index.html
- Various xml tags are enlisted in the following table -

Tags	Purpose
<x:out>	It displays the result of XPath expression.
<x:parse>	It is used to parse the XML file.
<x:set>	It sets the variable to the XPath expression.

<x:if>	The XPath expression is evaluated using the if condition. If the condition is true then the body part is executed otherwise it is ignored.
<x:forEach>	It is similar to the for loop which loops around the xml nodes.
<x:choose>	This tag is used to choose the particular operation when specific condition gets satisfied.
<x:when>	It is the subtag of <x:choose>. It is used when the condition is true.
<x:otherwise>	It is the subtag of <x:choose>. It is used when the condition is false.
<x:param>	This tag is used to set the parameter in XSLT stylesheet.

Example : Following XML tag named **<x:parse>** is used in JSP for displaying the contents of the XML document. The steps that need to be followed are -

Step 1 : Create a simple XML document named **Person.xml**. It is as follows -

Person.xml

```
<Person>
<student>
<name>Parth</name>
<marks>70</marks>
</student>

<student>
<name>Shilpa</name>
<marks>90</marks>
</student>

<student>
<name>Sagar</name>
<marks>40</marks>
</student>

<student>
<name>Shivani</name>
<marks>55</marks>
</student>
</Person>
```

Step 2 : Now create a JSP file in which the above defined XML document is invoked and is accessed using the <x:parse> tag. The code is as follows -

JSP Document[XMLProg1.jsp]

```
<%@ taglib prefix="c" uri="http://java.sun.com/jsp/jstl/core" %>
<%@ taglib prefix="x" uri="http://java.sun.com/jsp/jstl/xml" %>

<html>
<head>
 <title>JSTL XML Tags Demo</title>
```

```
</head>
<body>
<h3>Student Information</h3>
<c:import var="stud" url="http://127.0.0.1:8080/jsp-examples/XMLDemo/Person.xml"/>
<x:parse xml="${stud}" var="display"/>
<b>The first record is</b>:
<br>
<x:out select="$display/Person/student[1]/name" />
<br>
<x:out select="$display/Person/student[1]/marks" />
<br>------------------------------------------------<br>
<b>The second record is</b>:
<br>
<x:out select="$display/Person/student[2]/name" />
<br>
<x:out select="$display/Person/student[2]/marks" />

</body>
</html>
```

Step 3 : Open some web browser and type the URL for this JSP document and you will get the following output -

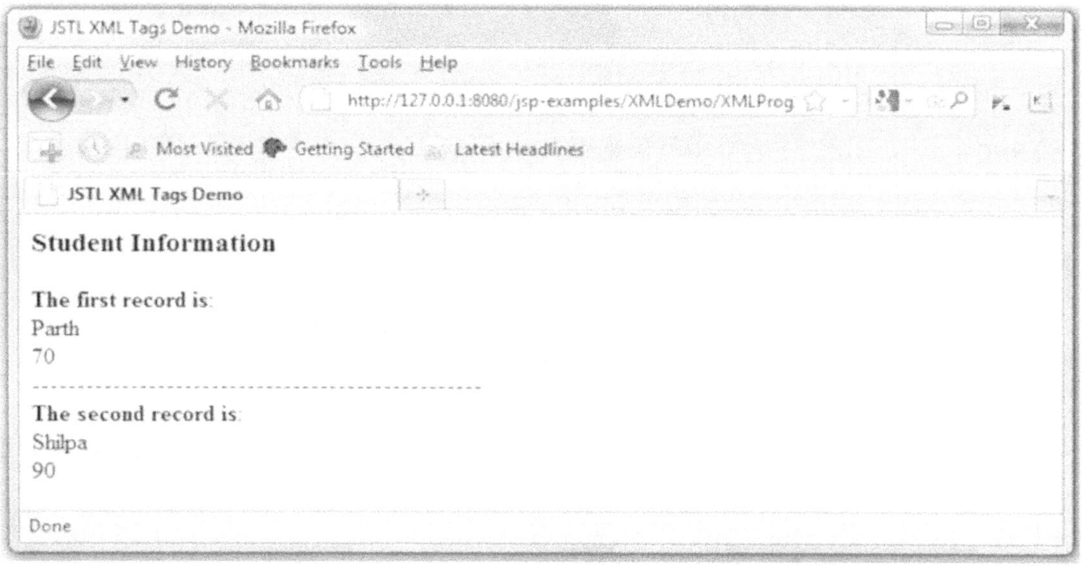

Program Explanation :

In the JSP document we have to define both the tags in the beginning i.e. **core tag** and the **xml tag**.Then using the **<c:import>** tag we can refer to the desired XML document. This XML document is then referred by some variable. In above example we have defined the variable **stud.** Then **<x:parse>** tag is used to parse the XML document. We then use the **<x:out>** tag to display desired nodes of the XML document. The output given in the step 3 is self explanatory.

Review Questions

1. *What is XML tag library ? Explain the XML core tags and show their use.* **GTU : Summer-13, Marks 7**
2. *Explain the JSP XML tag library.* **GTU : Winter-13, Marks 7**
3. *Write JSTL program to parse and display text of XML file.* **GTU : Winter-14, Marks 7**
4. *Explain various tags in JSTL with example i) SQL ii) Functions.* **GTU : Summer-15, Marks 7**
5. *Explain various tags in JSTL with example i) core ii) XML* **GTU : Summer-15, Marks 7**

❑❑❑

5 Java Server Faces 2.0

Syllabus

Introduction to JSF, JSF request processing Life cycle, JSF Expression Language, JSF Standard Component, JSF Facelets Tag, JSF Convertor Tag, JSF Validation Tag, JSF Event Handling and Database Access, JSF Libraries: PrimeFaces

Contents

5.1 Introduction to JSF

5.2 JSF Architecture

5.3 Writing First JSF Program

5.4 JSF Page Structure

*5.5 JSF Request Processing Life Cycle . . . . **Summer-16,** · · · · · · · · · · · · · Marks 7*

5.6 Form Handling

5.7 Managed Bean

5.8 JSF Expression Language

5.9 JSF Standard Component

5.10 JSF Facelets Tag

5.11 JSF Convertor Tag

5.12 JSF Validation Tag

5.13 JSF Event Handling

5.14 Database Access

5.15 JSF Libraries : PrimeFaces

5.1 Introduction to JSF

- Java Server Faces (JSF) is a web application framework used to develop the web applications with rich user interface.
- This Framework is based on **Model View Controller (MVC)** architecture. There are other technologies that make use of MVC pattern are JSP, Spring, ASP.NET and so on.
- It simplifies the construction of User Interface (UI) components. These UI components can establish communication with databases or event handlers.
- In JSF, the UI components can be created with the help of Application Programming Interface (API).

5.1.1 JSF Versions

The first version of JSF version was introduced in 2004. There are different versions of JSF that are enlisted in the following table.

Version	Year	J2EE Version
JSF 1.0	2004	J2EE 1.4
JSF 1.2	2006	J2EE 5
JSF 2.0	2009	J2EE 6
JSF 2.2	2013	J2EE 7
JSF 2.3	Expected in 2017	

5.1.2 Advantages and Disadvantages

Advantages of JSF

1. It is component based web framework. Hence the web application can be developed quickly.
2. It allows to create reusable components. This increases the productivity and consistency.
3. It allows implementation of custom components.
4. It has great support for EL expression that improves the user interface code readability.
5. It has inbuilt Template Layout Feature.
6. Validation and Converter implementation is easy.
7. Most of the things in JSF can be done using annotations (@)
8. JSF Primeface has good pre-built component suite and it has component.

Disadvantages of JSF

1. This framework is not suitable for high performance applications.
2. It allows very little control over generated HTML/CSS or JavaScript pages.

5.1.3 User Interface Component Model

JavaServer Faces UI components are the building blocks of a JavaServer Faces view.

A component can be simple, such as a textbox, button, or can be compound, such as a table, composed of multiple components.

JavaServer Faces technology provides a rich, flexible component architecture that includes the following :

- A set of **javax.faces.component.UIComponent** classes for specifying the state and behavior of UI components
- A rendering model that defines how to render the components in various ways
- A conversion model that defines how to register data converters onto a component
- An event and listener model that defines how to handle component events
- A validation model that defines how to register validators onto a component
- A navigation model that defines page navigation and the sequence in which pages are loaded

Review Question

1. *What is JSF ? Explain advantages and disadvantages of using JSF.*

5.2 JSF Architecture

- User submits the request to the application server using web browser. This request is received by JSF Faces Servlet. This servlet is a part of JSF library and it need not be written. It basically acts as a **controller.** It routes the request to appropriate page. It can read config.xml file or managed bean.
- The managed bean contains the form data which can access the backend data or database to retrieve desired data for processing the request. The managed bean acts as a **Model.**
- The Faces Servlet will determine and route the request to appropriate page for display information. Typically these web pages are in the xhtml files. This part acts as a **view**
- Finally the web page is rendered and sent to the web browser of the user.

- Following Fig. 5.2.1 represents this working scenario.

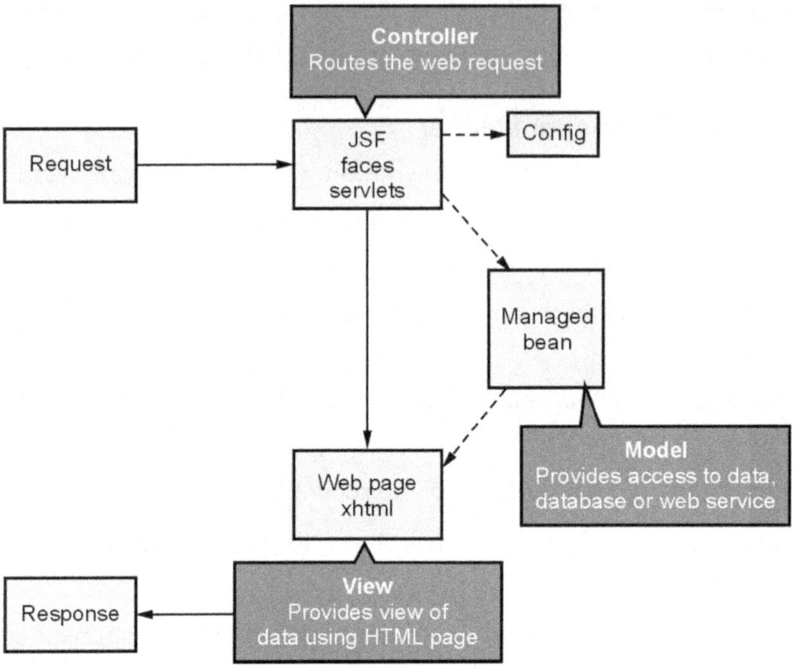

Fig. 5.2.1 JSF architecture

> **Review Question**
>
> 1. *Explain the JSF architecture with supporting block diagram.*

5.3 Writing First JSF Program

Before executing the JSF application program following software must be installed and exercised.

> **Environment Set up for Creating JSF Applications**
>
> 1. Install JDK
> 2. Install Tomcat
> 3. Install Eclipse

Here is a stepwise demonstration for creating the simple First JSF application program.

Step 1 : Open Eclipse. Click **File** menu. **Select New->Dynamic Web Project**. Specify some suitable name to the project. I have given the name as **FirstJSFProg**. Make sure that the **Target runtime** option represents the name of Apache Tomcat Server. If it is not then click on New Runtime button and select the suitable version of Apache Tomcat.

Then move on to the **Configuration** option on the same window. Click the **Modify** ... command button.

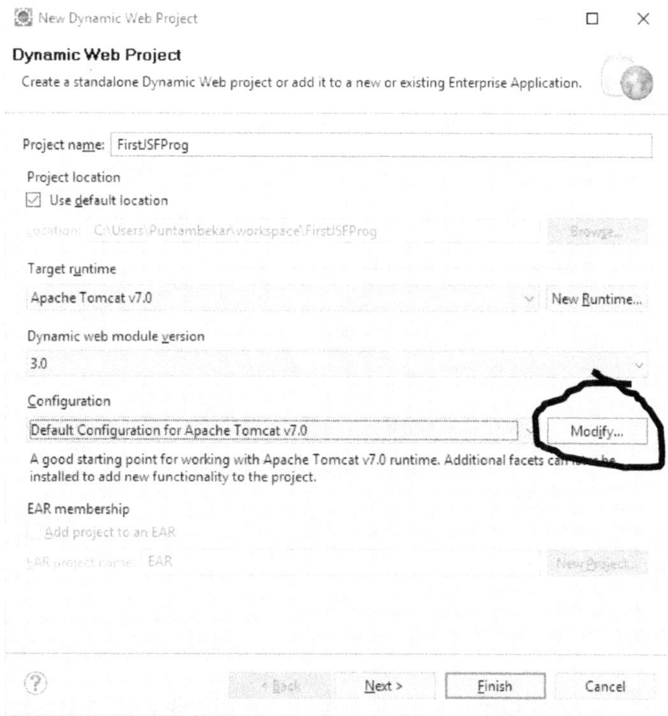

Select the option for Java Server Faces

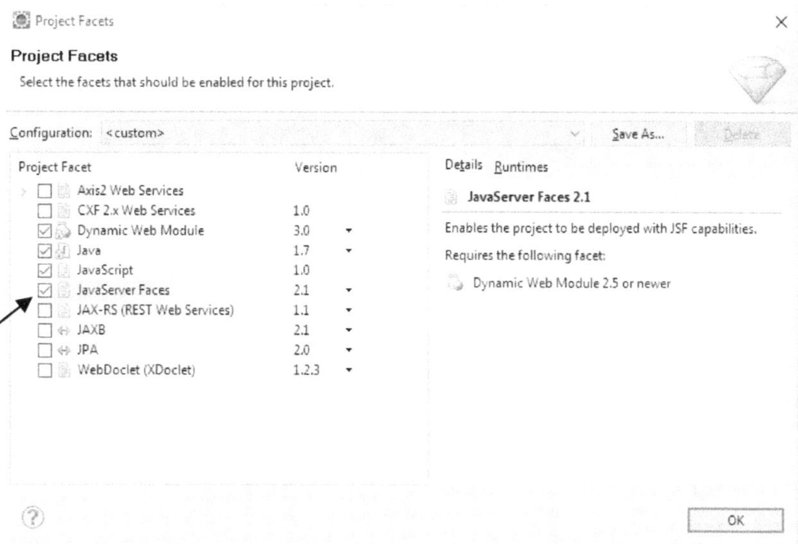

Click OK button. Then Click Next button. Keep the source folder as **src** as it is and simply click Next button. Check the *Generate web.xml* deployment option on the next window. The screenshot is as follows -

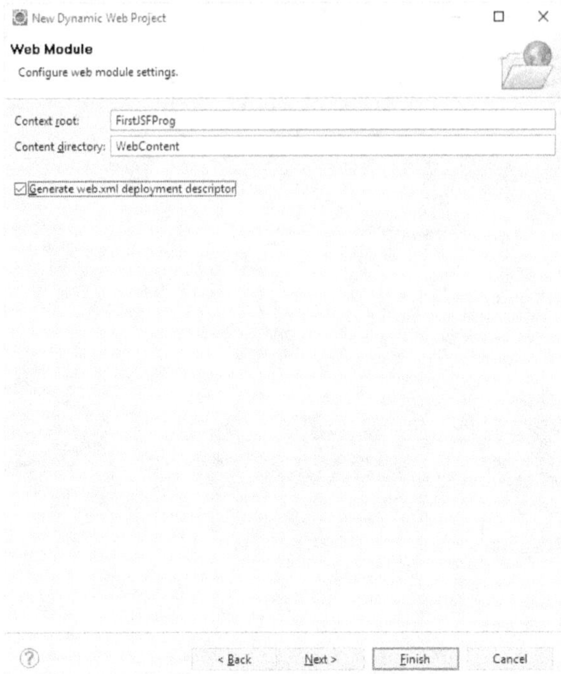

Step 2 : Then the JSF Capabilities Window will be displayed. Initially, it will not show any library, just click on the Floppy icon to download library, click on I Accept check box and the required library file for JSF will get downloaded. You can then see the name of this library make it checked.

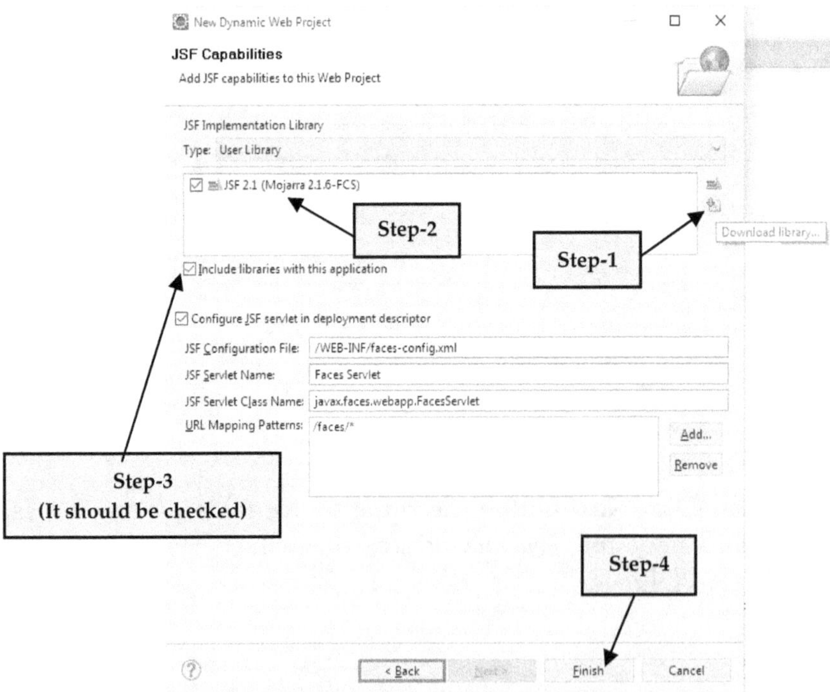

On clicking Finish button the library files will get installed for your current project application.

Step 3 : In the Project Explorer window the name of your project will be displayed. Click on it. RightClick on the **WebContent** folder. Select New->HTML file. Type suitable filename. I have named this file as **myBigHello.xhtml**. Click Next and select suitable template type and finally click **Finish** button. Write the code as follows –

myBigHello.xhtml

```
<?xml version="1.0" encoding="ISO-8859-1" ?>
<!DOCTYPE html PUBLIC "-//W3C//DTD XHTML 1.0 Strict//EN"
"http://www.w3.org/TR/xhtml1/DTD/xhtml1-strict.dtd">
<html xmlns="http://www.w3.org/1999/xhtml"
      xmlns:c="http://java.sun.com/jsf/core"
      xmlns:ui = "http://java.sun.com/jsf/facelets"
      xmlns:h = "http://java.sun.com/jsf/html">
<head>
<meta http-equiv="Content-Type" content="text/html; charset=ISO-8859-1" />
<title>MY JSF PAGE</title>
</head>
<h:body>

     <h:outputLabel value="Hello!!! This is my First JSF Page"></h:outputLabel>

</h:body>
</html>
```

Step 4 : Right click on the xhtml file which you have created just now in the Project Explorer window and choose **Run As-> Run on Server**. The Tomcat server will then be started and the output will be displayed on the browser window. Here is the output screen shot.

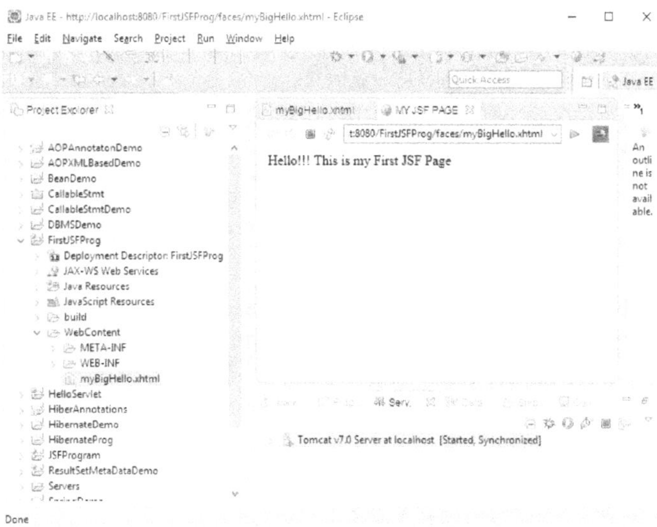

5.4 JSF Page Structure

The most common configuration for creating JSF page is to use **.xhtml file extension**. In this file the HTML page with **special JSF tags** is used.

The typical page structure of JSF page is

```
//Specify JSF Namespace at the beginning as follows
<!DOCTYPE html PUBLIC "-//W3C//DTD XHTML 1.0 Transitional//EN"
"http://www.w3.org/TR/xhtml1/DTD/xhtml1-transitional.dtd">
<html xmlns="http://www.w3.org/1999/xhtml"
xmlns:h="http://xmlns.jcp.org/jsf/html"
xmlns:f="http://xmlns.jcp.org/jsf/core"
xmlns:ui="http://xmlns.jcp.org/jsf/facelets">

 . . .

<html>
    ...
    Special JSF tags
    ...
    //You can use CSS or JavaScript or JQuery for adding more web related features

</html>
```

At the beginning of the JSF page we must specify the JSF namespace. Following table shows various JSF namespaces

JSF Component	Tag used	JSF Namespace
Core component	f	http://xmlns.jcp.org/jsf/core
HTML component	h	http://xmlns.jcp.org/jsf/html
Facelets components	ui	http://xmlns.jcp.org/jsf/facelets
Composite components	cc	http://xmlns.jcp.org/jsf/composite

5.5 JSF Request Processing Life Cycle

GTU : Summer-16, Marks 7

Various phases of request processing life cycle are

1. **Restore View :** This is the first phase in JSF Request processing life cycle. This phase is used for constructing **view** to display in the front end. This **view** is stored in **FacesContext** instance and using the information in this instance single request is processed.
2. **Apply Request Values :** After the component tree is restored, each component in the tree extracts its new value from the request parameters by using its decode method. The value is then stored locally on the component. If the conversion of the value fails, an error message associated with the component is generated and queued on **FacesContext**. This message will be displayed during the render response phase, along with any validation errors resulting from the **process validations phase**.

3. **Process Validations :** During this phase, the Java Server Faces implementation processes all validators registered on the components in the tree. It examines the component attributes that specify the rules for the validation and compares these rules to the local value stored for the component.

   If the local value is invalid, the JavaServer Faces implementation adds an error message to the FacesContext instance, and the life cycle advances directly to the render response phase so that the page is rendered again with the error messages displayed

4. **Update Model Values :** If the Java Server Faces implementation finds that the data is valid then, it moves over the component tree and set the server side object properties to component's local values. If the local data cannot be converted to the types specified by the bean properties, the life cycle advances directly to the render response phase so that the page is rerendered with errors displayed.

5. **Invoke Application :** In this phase, the JSF handles the application level events.

   If the application needs to redirect to a different web application resource or generate a response that does not contain any JavaServer Faces components, it can call FacesContext.responseComplete.

6. **Render Response :** During this phase, the JavaServer Faces implementation directs for rendering the page to the JSP container if the application is using JSP pages.

   After the content of the view is rendered, the response state is saved

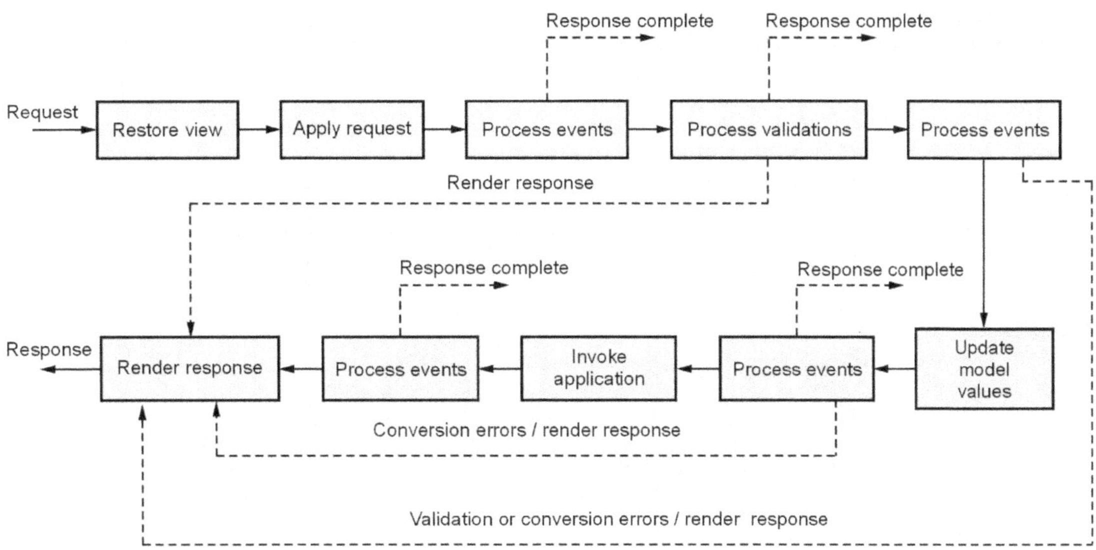

Fig. 5.5.1 Request processing life cycle

Review Questions

1. *Explain different phases of JSF Request Processing Life Cycle.*
2. *Draw the JSF request processing life cycle and briefly give the function of each phase.*

GTU : Summer-16, Marks 7

5.6 Form Handling

In JSF applications the HTML Forms are used to get the input from the user. For example - we have used many types of applications in which the forms are used. For instance : user registration form, login form and so on.

To build a form, we need a main form container. The form container can be created using h:form. Once the form container is set up, you can add multiple entries like input text, text area, checkboxes, radio buttons, drop-down lists and other form elements. These components can be added using the tags like **h:inputText, h:commandButton** and so on.

Let us understand the basics of creating a form and some form components with the help of following illustrating example.

Example 5.6.1 : *Create a form for displaying student ID, student Name*

Solution :

Step 1 : Open Eclipse. Click File menu. Select **New->Dynamic Web Project**. Specify some suitable name to the project. I have given the name as **JSFFormDemo.** Make sure that the Target runtime option represents the name of Apache Tomcat Server. If it is not then click on **New Runtime** button and select the suitable version of Apache Tomcat.

Then move on to the Configuration option on the same window. Click the **Modify** ... command button. And select JSF library.

Step 2 : In the Project Explorer window the name of your project will be displayed. Click on it. RightClick on the WebContent folder. Select New->HTML file. Type suitable filename. I have named this file as myform.xhtml. Click Next and select suitable template type and finally click Finish button. Write the code as follows –

myform.xhtml

```
<?xml version="1.0" encoding="ISO-8859-1" ?>
<!DOCTYPE html PUBLIC "-//W3C//DTD XHTML 1.0 Strict//EN"
"http://www.w3.org/TR/xhtml1/DTD/xhtml1-strict.dtd">
<html xmlns="http://www.w3.org/1999/xhtml"
      xmlns:c="http://java.sun.com/jsf/core"
      xmlns:ui = "http://java.sun.com/jsf/facelets"
      xmlns:h = "http://java.sun.com/jsf/html">
<h:head>
```

```
  <title>Form Demo</title>

</h:head>
  <h:body>
    <h:form>
      Student ID: <h:inputText id="id" value ="#{studentID}" />
      <br/><br/>
      Student Name: <h:inputText id="studName" value ="#{studentName}" />
      <br /><br/>
      <h:commandButton value="Submit" />
    </h:form>
  </h:body>
</html>
```

Step 3 : Right click on the **myform.xhtml** and click **Run As-> Run on Server** option. In a separate window web browser will be displayed with form components as text box and command button.

Output

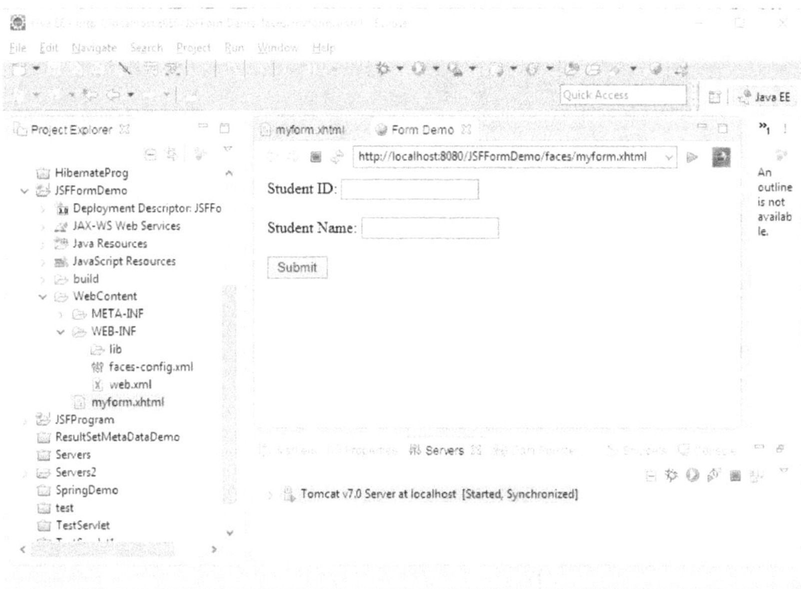

5.7 Managed Bean

Managed bean is nothing but a simple Java class. This class is used to hold the form data. When the front end input form accepts the user data and when the user submits this form then the input data is actually stored in the managed bean. This managed bean can also contain some **business logic.** The information stored in this managed bean can be used by another JSF page to display the response to the user. Following figure illustrates this idea

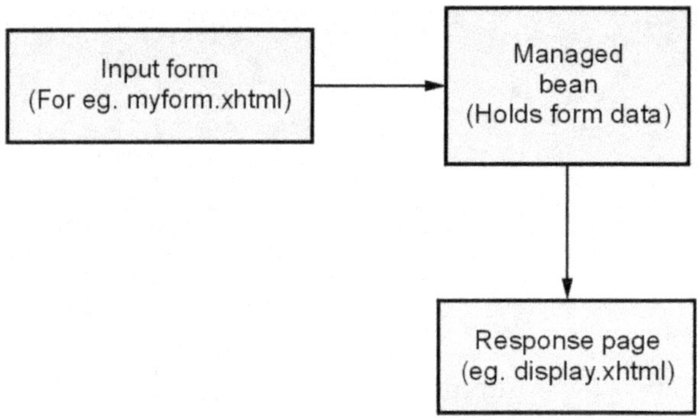

Fig. 5.7.1 Role of managed beans

Let us understand the working of managed bean with the help of simple JSF application program

Step 1 :

I have already created one form in previous section named **myform.xhtml**. modify it little bit (Refer step 1 and 2).The code for this file is as follows

myform.xhtml

```
<?xml version="1.0" encoding="ISO-8859-1" ?>
<!DOCTYPE html PUBLIC "-//W3C//DTD XHTML 1.0 Strict//EN"
"http://www.w3.org/TR/xhtml1/DTD/xhtml1-strict.dtd">
<html xmlns="http://www.w3.org/1999/xhtml"
      xmlns:c="http://java.sun.com/jsf/core"
      xmlns:ui = "http://java.sun.com/jsf/facelets"
      xmlns:h = "http://java.sun.com/jsf/html">
<h:head>
  <title>Form Demo</title>

</h:head>
  <h:body>
   <h:form>
     Student ID: <h:inputText value ="#{myStudBean.studentID}" />
     <br/><br/>
     Student Name: <h:inputText value ="#{myStudBean.studentName}" />
     <br /><br/>
     <h:commandButton value="Submit" action="display" />
   </h:form>
  </h:body>
</html>
```

Program Explanation : Note that in above program, at the beginning we have specified the JSF name spaces using **xmlns**. Then the head and body sections of the page are defined. The head section is delimited by <h:head> </h:head> tags in which simply the title of the page is specified.

The body section of the JSF page is written within <h:body></h:body> inside which we are creating a form using the tag <h:form>.

The three form components are created – two text boxes- to get the input from the user and one command button to submit the form. Just note the way we have specified the UI components of this form.

We are submitting the value of the text boxes as

```
#{<beanName>.<property>}
```

I will be creating the bean Java class file in next step (i.e. Step 3).

Here the bean name is **MyStudBean** class but while specifying the value to **inputText** we always take the first letter of bean class in lower case. For example - in order to refer the bean property **studentID** we will mention it as follows

```
value ="#{myStudBean.studentID}"
```

The push button is created using **<h:commandButton>** tag. The action for this button is to invoke the response file. As I have named it as **display.xhtml** (I will be creating it in step 4) we will simply mention it as

```
action="display"
```

Step 2 : In the Project Explorer window, Right click on your project, click New and create a Package. I have created a package named **com.mypackage** under **src** directory of my project **JSFFormDemo**

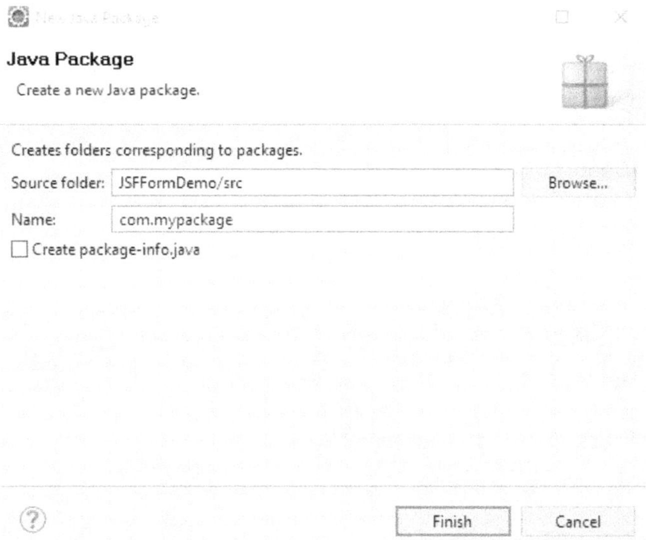

Click on Finish button.

Step 3 : Go to Project Explorer window once again, right click on the package you have created and select **New->Class** and type suitable bean class name. I have named by bean as **MyStudBean**. Here is the Screen shot for it

Click on **Finish** button. Now the java class file will get opened up. Type following code for it

MyStudBean.java

```
package com.mypackage;
import javax.faces.bean.ManagedBean;
@ManagedBean
public class MyStudBean {
    private int studentID;
    private String studentName;

    //defining getter/setter methods
    public int getStudentID() {
        return studentID;
    }
    public void setStudentID(int studentID) {
        this.studentID = studentID;
    }
    public String getStudentName() {
        return studentName;
    }
    public void setStudentName(String studentName) {
        this.studentName = studentName;
    }
}
```

Program Explanation : In the beginning we have used annotation **@ManagedBean** in order to denote the managed bean class. For that purpose we have imported the required javax file.

Bean is nothing but a Java class with getter and setter method for the properties. In above program, I have used two properties studentID and studentName (Keep the first letter of the properties in lower case). Set and get the values for these methods using setPropertyName and getPropertyName. The set method will be used by our input form (created in Step 1) in order to set the values entered in the text boxes. The get method will be used by our response page (created in step 4) to retrieve the values entered by the user. That it!!!

Step 4 : Now it's the time to create the response page. I am creating a response page named **display.xhtml** under the WebContent directory. For creation of it follow these steps -

Go to Project explorer window, Right click on WebContent folder click **New->Other->File** Specify the file name. In my case it is **display.xhtml**. Here is the code for it

display.xhtml

```
<?xml version="1.0" encoding="ISO-8859-1" ?>
<!DOCTYPE html PUBLIC "-//W3C//DTD XHTML 1.0 Strict//EN"
"http://www.w3.org/TR/xhtml1/DTD/xhtml1-strict.dtd">
<html xmlns="http://www.w3.org/1999/xhtml"
      xmlns:c="http://java.sun.com/jsf/core"
      xmlns:ui = "http://java.sun.com/jsf/facelets"
      xmlns:h = "http://java.sun.com/jsf/html">
<h:head>
  <title>Form Demo</title>

</h:head>
  <h:body>
   <h3>You have entered following data...</h3>
   Student ID: #{myStudBean.studentID} <br/>
   Student Name: #{myStudBean.studentName}
   </h:body>
</html>
```

Program Explanation : The beginning of this file is with specification of JSF Namespaces. Followed by typical Head and Body Section. The data from the bean class can be retrieved using

```
#{<beanName>.<property>}
```

For retrieving the data from the bean class **getStudentID** and **getStudentName** methods will be invoked.

Step 5 : Before running the application make sure that your files are appropriately placed. Just refer the following Project explorer window as a guideline.

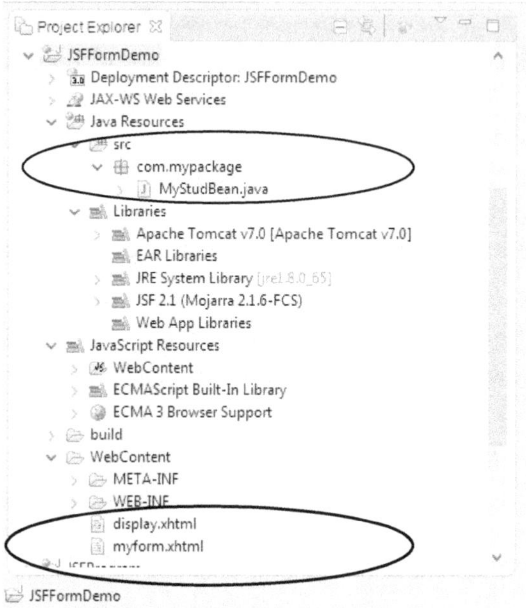

Step 6 : Go to Project Explorer window right click on **myform.xhtml** Click Run As-> **Run On Server**. The output will be displayed on a Web browser window. First of all the form for inputting the data will appear, just input any desired data and click submit button. Refer following screen shot

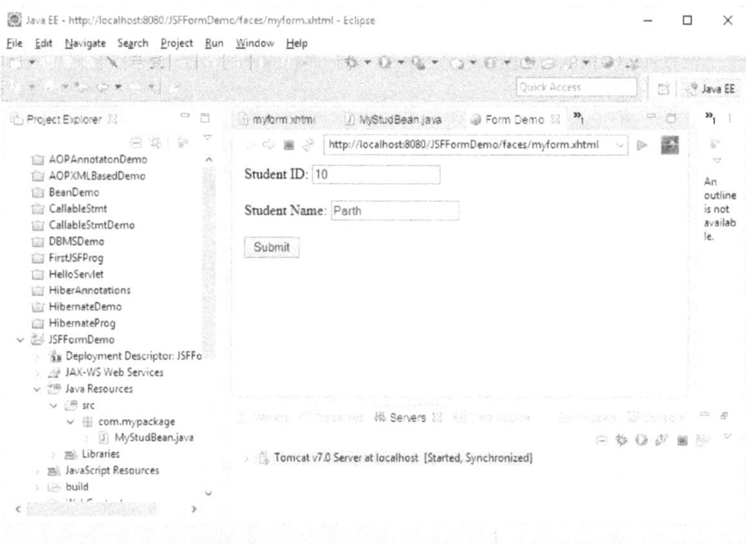

After clicking the Submit button, the response page will be displayed showing what you have entered as input. Here is the screen shot for the same.

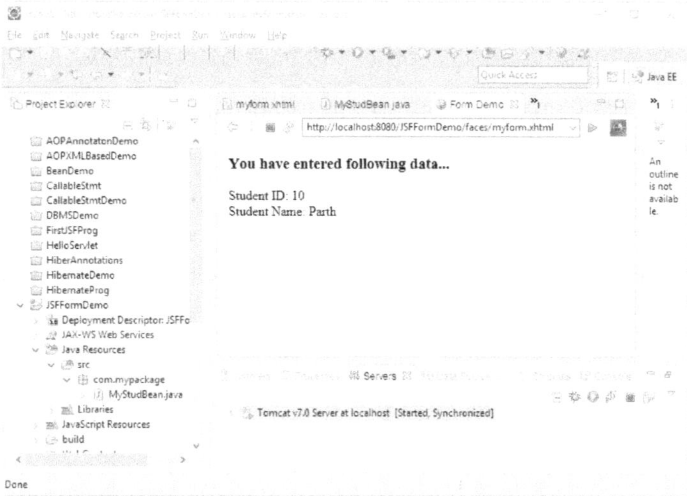

Review Question

1. *Explain the concept and used of managed bean with the help of JSF application program.*

5.8 JSF Expression Language

JSF expression language allows the user to access the data dynamically from the Java Bean component (by using get method defined in Bean class)

JSF provides a rich expression language. We can write normal operations using #{operation-expression} notation.

The Expression language can be denoted using the following syntax -

```
#{expression}
```

The expression can be of two types

1. **Property expression :** This is the kind of expression in which the property value defined in the managed bean class is specified. The syntax for this is -

```
#{<beanName>.<property>}
```

2. **Method expression :** This is the kind of expression in which the property value defined in the managed bean class is specified. The syntax for this is -

```
#{<beanName>.<method>}
```

Let us understand the use of expression language in JSF with the help of illustrating example -

Example 5.8.1 : *Create JSF application which calculates the area of rectangle. Make use of Expression language.*

Solution :

Step 1 : Open Eclipse. Click **File** menu. Select **New->Dynamic Web Project**. Specify some suitable name to the project. I have given the name as **JSFELDemo**. Make sure that the Target runtime option represents the name of Apache Tomcat Server. If it is not then click on New Runtime button and select the suitable version of Apache Tomcat.

Then move on to the Configuration option on the same window. Click the Modify ... command button.And select JSF library.

Step 2 : In the Project Explorer window the name of your project will be displayed. Click on it. RightClick on the WebContent folder. Select **New->Other -> File**. Type suitable filename. I have named this file as **input.xhtml**. Finally click Finish button. Write the code as follows -

input.xhtml

```
<?xml version="1.0" encoding="ISO-8859-1" ?>
<!DOCTYPE html PUBLIC "-//W3C//DTD XHTML 1.0 Strict//EN"
"http://www.w3.org/TR/xhtml1/DTD/xhtml1-strict.dtd">
<html xmlns="http://www.w3.org/1999/xhtml"
      xmlns:c="http://java.sun.com/jsf/core"
      xmlns:ui = "http://java.sun.com/jsf/facelets"
      xmlns:h = "http://java.sun.com/jsf/html">
<h:head>
  <title>Expression Language Demo</title>

</h:head>
  <h:body>
   <h:form>
     Enter Length: <h:inputText value ="#{calculateBean.length}" />
      <br/><br/>
     Enter Breadth: <h:inputText value ="#{calculateBean.breadth}" />
      <br /><br/>
      <h:commandButton value="Submit" action="result" />
   </h:form>
  </h:body>
</html>
```

Step 3 : Now create a bean Java class inside package created inside the **src** folder. I have created a bean class named **CalculateBean.java** . The code for this is

CalculateBean.java

```
package com.mypackage;
import javax.faces.bean.ManagedBean;
@ManagedBean

public class CalculateBean {
     private int length;
     private int breadth;

     public int getLength() {
```

```
        return length;
    }
    public void setLength(int length) {
        this.length = length;
    }
    public int getBreadth() {
        return breadth;
    }
    public void setBreadth(int breadth) {
        this.breadth = breadth;
    }
    public int calculatearea()
    {
        int area=length*breadth;
        return area;
    }
}
```

Program Explanation :

The two properties **length** and **breadth** are declared in the above bean program and get and set method for them are defined. One more method named **calculatearea** is defined in this bean program. This method is for computing the area of rectangle. We are going to invoke this method in the expression language. This expression language will be used in the response page which will be created in the next step.

Step 4 : Create a response file once again under **WebContent** folder. I have named it as **result.xhtml**. This is the file in which the expression language is defined. The code for this file is as follows

result.xhtml

```
<?xml version="1.0" encoding="ISO-8859-1" ?>
<!DOCTYPE html PUBLIC "-//W3C//DTD XHTML 1.0 Strict//EN"
"http://www.w3.org/TR/xhtml1/DTD/xhtml1-strict.dtd">
<html xmlns="http://www.w3.org/1999/xhtml"
      xmlns:c="http://java.sun.com/jsf/core"
      xmlns:ui = "http://java.sun.com/jsf/facelets"
      xmlns:h = "http://java.sun.com/jsf/html">
<h:head>
  <title>Form Demo</title>

</h:head>
  <h:body>
   <h4>You have entered following data...</h4>
   Length: #{calculateBean.length} <br/>
   Breadth: #{calculateBean.breadth}
```

```
    <br/><br/>
    <h4>Area of Rectangle is...</h4>
    Area: #{calculateBean.calculatearea()}
  </h:body>
</html>
```

Program Explanation :

This is the response page which will be invoked as soon as user clicks the Submit button. This page communicates with the managed bean and retrieve the property values and methods. **The expression language used in the above code is denoted by following code**

```
Length: #{calculateBean.length}  ←Value Expression
Breadth: #{calculateBean.breadth}← Value Expression

Area: #{calculateBean.calculatearea()}← Method Expression
```

Step 5 : Go to Project Explore window and right click on **input.xhtml**. Click **Run As ->Run On Server**. Enter suitable data in the form window. Here is the screenshot for the same.

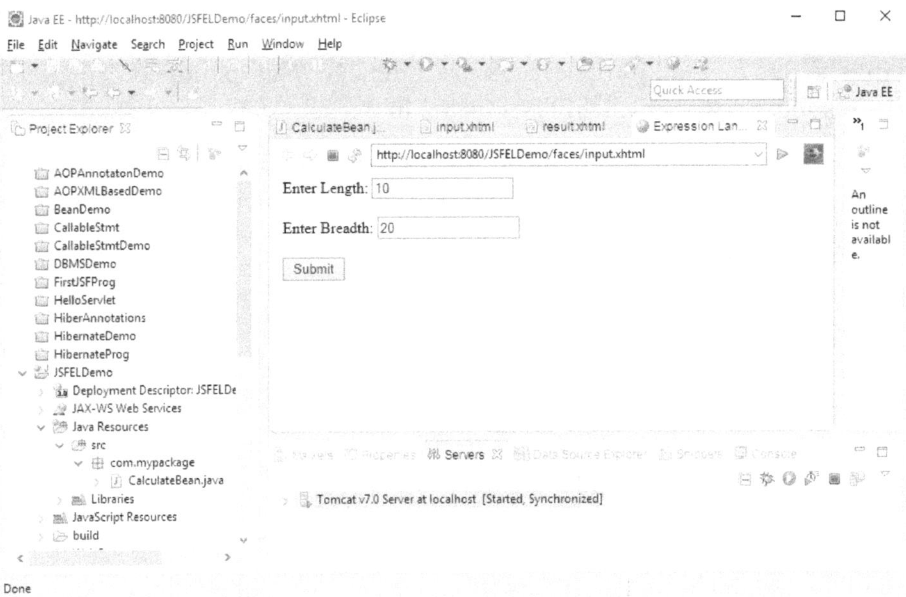

Click on Submit button and you will get the following output

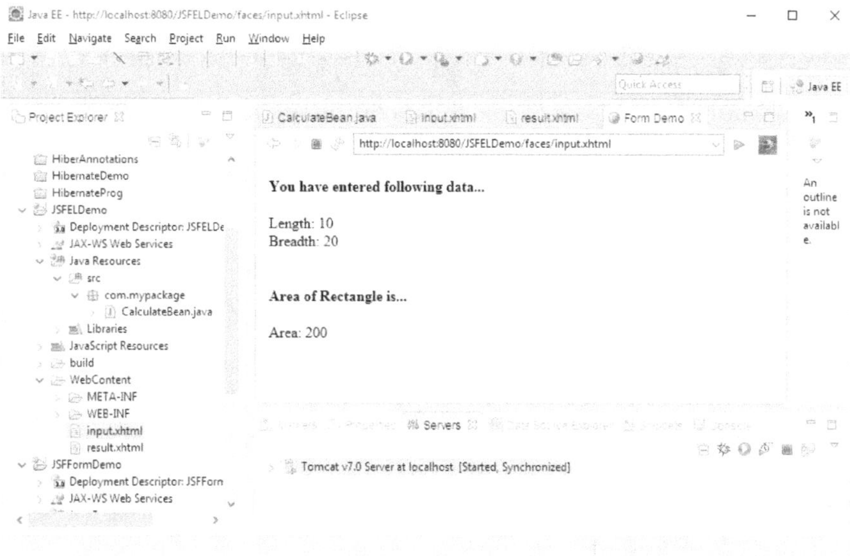

Review Question

1. *Explain JSF expression language with the help of suitable JSF program.*

5.9 JSF Standard Component

To build the HTML form, various JSF UI (User Interface) components are available. Following table describes such JSF UI components

JSF UI Component	Description
h:form	HTML form
h:inputText	Single line text input con
h:inputTextArea	Multiline text input control
h:inputSecret	Password input control
h:outputLabel	Label for another component for accessibility
h:outputLink	HTML anchor tag
h:outputText	Single line text output
h:commandButton	Push Button for Submit or Reset
h:selectOneListBox	Single select listbox
h:selectOneMenu	Single select menu
h:selectOneRadio	Radio buttons
h:selectBooleanCheckbox	Checkbox
h:selectManyCheckbox	Set of check boxes

h:selectManyListbox	Multiselect listbox
h:selectManyMenu	Multiselect menu

Following example shows how to use these components on the form.

Example 5.9.1 : *Create a Student Registration Form using standard components in JSF*

Solution :

Just follow the steps described in section 5.6 to create JSF application form and write following code.

myform.xhtml

```
<?xml version="1.0" encoding="ISO-8859-1" ?>
<!DOCTYPE html PUBLIC "-//W3C//DTD XHTML 1.0 Strict//EN"
"http://www.w3.org/TR/xhtml1/DTD/xhtml1-strict.dtd">
<html xmlns="http://www.w3.org/1999/xhtml"
      xmlns:f="http://java.sun.com/jsf/core"
      xmlns:ui = "http://java.sun.com/jsf/facelets"
      xmlns:h = "http://java.sun.com/jsf/html">
<h:head>
  <title>Form Demo</title>

</h:head>
  <h:body>
   <h:form>
   <h2> Student Registration Form</h2>
```

Text Box

```
     Student ID: <h:inputText id="id" value ="#{studentID}" />
     <br/><br/>
     Student Name: <h:inputText id="studName" value ="#{studentName}" />
     <br /><br/>
     City:<h:selectOneMenu value="#{studentCity.country}">
     <f:selectItem itemValue="Mumbai" itemLabel="Mumbai" />
     <f:selectItem itemValue="Pune" itemLabel="Pune" />
     <f:selectItem itemValue="GandhiNagar" itemLabel="GandhiNagar" />
     <f:selectItem itemValue="Hyderabad" itemLabel="Hyderabd" />
         </h:selectOneMenu>
```

Select one item from Menu

```
         <br/><br/><br/>
         Sex:
         <h:selectOneRadio value="#{studentSex.data}">
         <f:selectItem itemValue="Male" itemLabel="Male" />
         <f:selectItem itemValue="Female" itemLabel="Female" />
         </h:selectOneRadio>
```

Radio Button

```
         <br/>
         Hobby:
         <h:selectManyCheckbox value="#{studentHobby.data}">
         <f:selectItem itemValue="Sports" itemLabel="Sports" />
```

```
            <f:selectItem itemValue="Reading" itemLabel="Reading" />
            <f:selectItem itemValue="Music" itemLabel="Music" />
            <f:selectItem itemValue="Other" itemLabel="Other" />
            </h:selectManyCheckbox>
            <br/><br/>
        <h:commandButton value="Submit" />
    </h:form>
  </h:body>
</html>
```

Multiple Section Checkbox

Command Button

Output

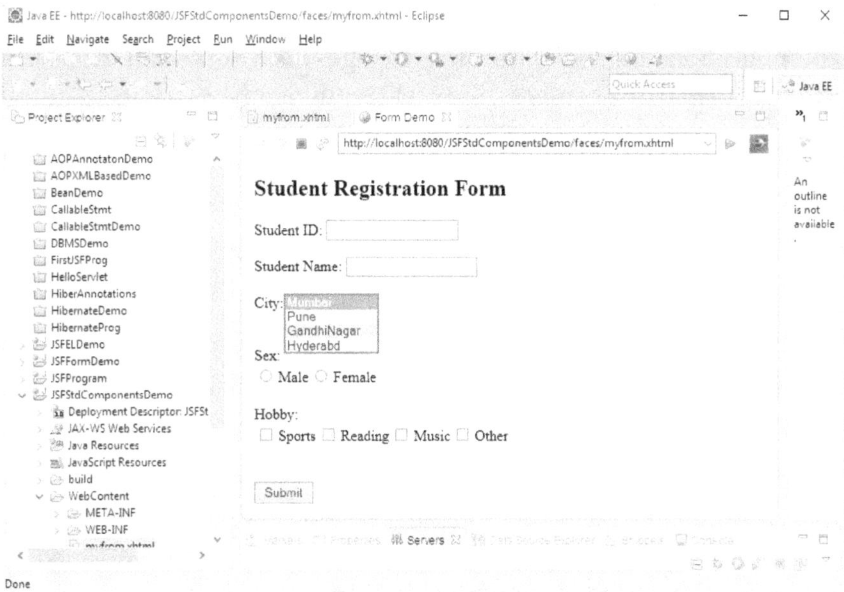

The sample code fragments for using other standard components are -

SelectOneListBox

```
<h:selectOneListbox value="#{bean.property}">
  <f:selectItem itemValue="1" itemLabel="Item 1" />
  <f:selectItem itemValue="2" itemLabel="Item 2" />
</h:selectOneListbox>
```

SelectManyListBox

```
<h:selectManyListbox value="#{bean.property}">
  <f:selectItem itemValue="1" itemLabel="Item 1" />
  <f:selectItem itemValue="2" itemLabel="Item 2" />
</h:selectManyListbox>
```

outputText

```
<h:outputText value="my display message" />
```

inputSecret

```
<h:inputSecret value="password" />
```

graphicsImage

```
<h:graphicImage  value=Image file path/>
```

> **Review Question**
>
> 1. *List and explain the purpose of at least five JSF standard components.*

5.10 JSF Facelets Tag

The Web application contains various web page. Each web page has some standard layout and style to display the contents. Typical layout of any web page is as follows

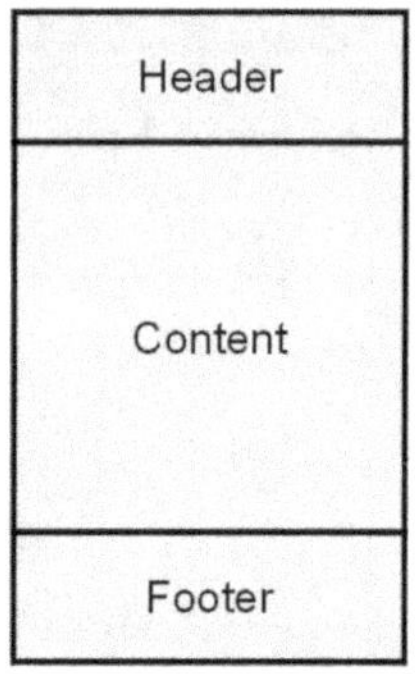

Fig. 5.10.1 Layout of web page

To display the contents of the web page at header, footer or content section we can make use of facelet tag.

Following are four facelet tags are used to build the template.

Sr. No.	Facelet	Purpose
1.	ui:insert	Used in template file, it defines content that is going to replace by the file that load the template. The content can be replace with "ui:define" tag.
2.	ui:define	Defines content that is inserted into template with a matching "ui:insert" tag.
3.	ui:include	Similar to JSP's "jsp:include", includes content from another XHTML page.
4.	ui:composition	If used with "template" attribute, the specified template is loaded, and the children of this tag defines the template layout; Otherwise, it's a group of elements, that can be inserted somewhere. In addition, JSF removes all tags "outside" of "ui:composition" tag.

Following is an illustration that shows use of facelet tag.

Step 1 : Open Eclipse. Create Dynamic Web Project. Ensure that the Apache Tomcat and JSF library are made available for the project. (We have already discussed these steps in earlier section).

Step 2 : Create a folder named *template* under WebContent directory. Created following xhtml files in the template folder

Step 3 : Create an xhtml file for the main page or home page. I have named it as **welcome.xhtml**

```
<?xml version="1.0" encoding="UTF-8"?>
<!DOCTYPE html PUBLIC "-//W3C//DTD XHTML 1.0 Transitional//EN"
"http://www.w3.org/TR/xhtml1/DTD/xhtml1-transitional.dtd">
<html xmlns="http://www.w3.org/1999/xhtml"
   xmlns:h="http://java.sun.com/jsf/html"
   xmlns:ui="http://java.sun.com/jsf/facelets">

<h:body>

     <ui:composition template="myPageLayout.xhtml">
</ui:composition>

   </h:body>

</html>
```

Program Explanation : This page invokes the **myPageLayout.xhtml** file for defining the layout of the page. Here the facelet tag **ui:composition** is used with **template** attribute so that the specified template is loaded.

Step 3 : The template for the web page layout is created in **myPageLayout.xhtml**. The code is as follows -

myPageLayout.xhtml

```
<?xml version="1.0" encoding="UTF-8"?>
<!DOCTYPE html PUBLIC "-//W3C//DTD XHTML 1.0 Transitional//EN"
"http://www.w3.org/TR/xhtml1/DTD/xhtml1-transitional.dtd">
<html xmlns="http://www.w3.org/1999/xhtml"
   xmlns:h="http://java.sun.com/jsf/html"
   xmlns:ui="http://java.sun.com/jsf/facelets">

<h:head>
</h:head>

  <h:body>
     <div style="border-width:1px; border-color:black; border-style:solid;">
          <ui:insert name="header" >
          <ui:include src="header.xhtml" />
```

```
        </ui:insert>
    </div>
    <br/><br/>
    <div style="border-width:1px; border-color:black; border-style:solid;">
        <ui:insert name="content" >
        <ui:include src="content.xhtml" />
        </ui:insert>
    </div>
    <br/><br/>
  <div style="border-width:1px; border-color:black; border-style:solid;">
        <ui:insert name="footer" >
      <ui:include src="footer.xhtml" />
        </ui:insert>
  </div>
  </h:body>
</html>
```

Program Explanation : In this template, it defines a standard web layout :

1. By specifying the **style** inside the **<div>** tag. The border to the contents is applied by this style.
2. By using **ui:insert** tag to define three replaceable sections : header, content and footer.
3. By using **ui:include** tag to Includes contents of one xhtml page into another xhtml page. For defining the header **header.xhtml**, for content layout **content.xhtml** and for footer **footer.xhtml** files must be created.

Here are they.

Step 4 :

header.xhtml

```
<?xml version="1.0" encoding="UTF-8"?>
<!DOCTYPE html PUBLIC "-//W3C//DTD XHTML 1.0 Transitional//EN"
"http://www.w3.org/TR/xhtml1/DTD/xhtml1-transitional.dtd">
<html xmlns="http://www.w3.org/1999/xhtml"
   xmlns:ui="http://java.sun.com/jsf/facelets"
   >
  <body>
      <ui:composition>
            <h1>This is header section</h1>
      </ui:composition>
  </body>
</html>
```

content.xhtml

```
<?xml version="1.0" encoding="UTF-8"?>
```

```
<!DOCTYPE html PUBLIC "-//W3C//DTD XHTML 1.0 Transitional//EN"
"http://www.w3.org/TR/xhtml1/DTD/xhtml1-transitional.dtd">
<html xmlns="http://www.w3.org/1999/xhtml"
  xmlns:ui="http://java.sun.com/jsf/facelets"
  >
  <body>
    <ui:composition>
        <h1>This is a content section </h1>
    </ui:composition>
  </body>
</html>
```

footer.xhtml

```
<?xml version="1.0" encoding="UTF-8"?>
<!DOCTYPE html PUBLIC "-//W3C//DTD XHTML 1.0 Transitional//EN"
"http://www.w3.org/TR/xhtml1/DTD/xhtml1-transitional.dtd">
<html xmlns="http://www.w3.org/1999/xhtml"
  xmlns:ui="http://java.sun.com/jsf/facelets"
  >
  <body>
    <ui:composition>
        <h1>This is a footer Section</h1>
    </ui:composition>
  </body>
</html>
```

Program Explanation : The above created three xhtml files are very simple files with only one facelet tag used <ui:composition>. This tag defines the template layout.

Step 5 : The Project Explorer screenshot helps you to locate the positions of these files in the Web application created in Eclipse.

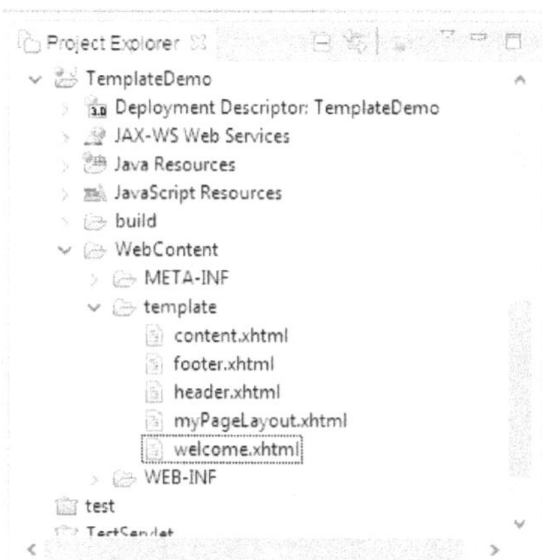

Step 6 : Right click on the main web page to run it on Server. The output will be

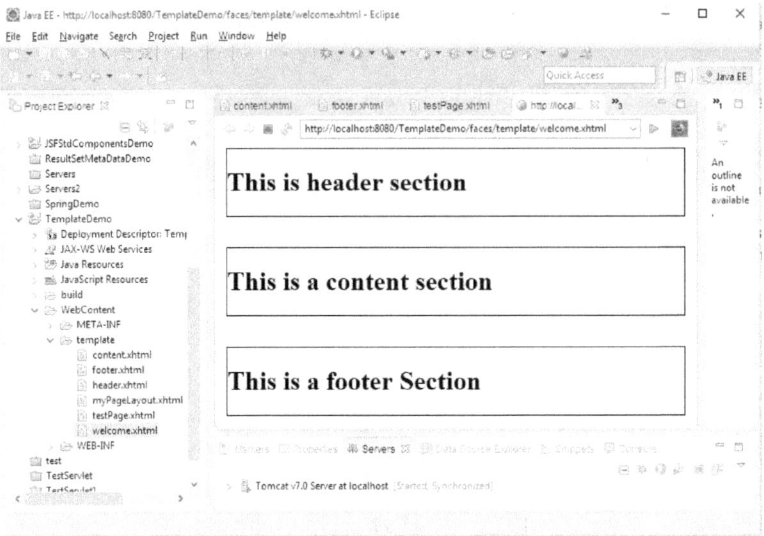

Step 7 : Now create one more page in order to insert the contents in our already created layout (Refer above output). I have created file **testPage.xhtml,** for insertion of contents.

testPage.xhtml

```
<?xml version="1.0" encoding="UTF-8"?>
<!DOCTYPE html PUBLIC "-//W3C//DTD XHTML 1.0 Transitional//EN"
"http://www.w3.org/TR/xhtml1/DTD/xhtml1-transitional.dtd">
<html xmlns="http://www.w3.org/1999/xhtml"
    xmlns:h="http://java.sun.com/jsf/html"
    xmlns:ui="http://java.sun.com/jsf/facelets"
    >
  <h:body>
     <ui:composition template="myPageLayout.xhtml">
          <ui:define name="content">
               <h2> test page contents  </h2>
          </ui:define>

          <ui:define name="footer">
               <h2>test page footer</h2>
          </ui:define>

     </ui:composition>

  </h:body>

</html>
```

Program Explanation : In this xhtml file the <ui:define> tag is used to **define the contents to be inserted in a template** with the help of **name** attribute.

Note that, we have just changed the content and footer section of the template and the header section remain untouched. Following Project Explorer window shows where to create this file.

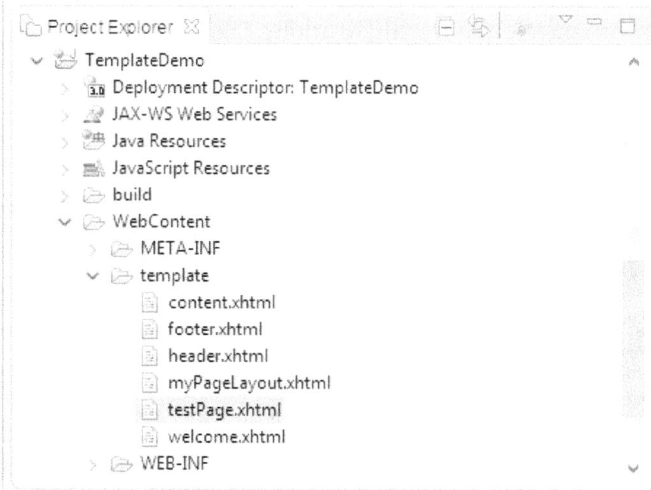

Right click on this file to run it on server and you will get following output.

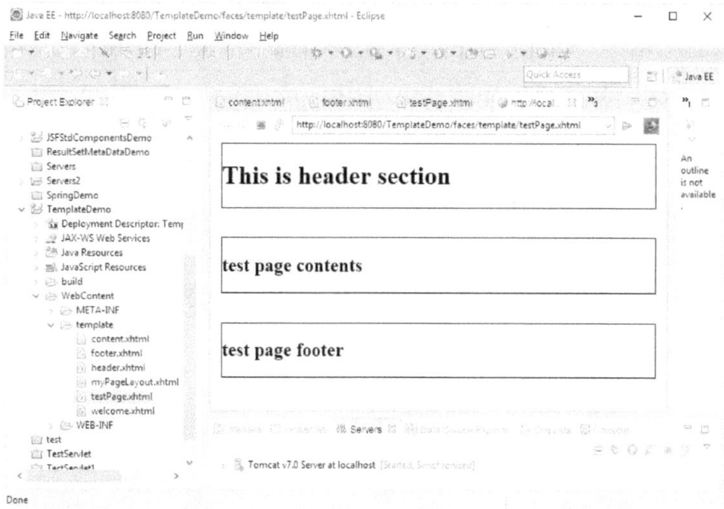

Review Question

1. *Explain the JSF facelet tags and their use.*

5.11 JSF Convertor Tag

During the web application, the data entered by the user need to be converted into their appropriate types. There are various inbuilt converter tags available in JSF. These are of following types -

1. Convert number tag
2. Convert date time tag
3. Converters

Let us discuss them with necessary illustrations.

Convert Number Tag

This tag is defined by **<f:convertNumber>.** Various attributes are associated with this tag. These are as described below -

Sr. No.	Attribute	Purpose
1.	pattern	It is for specific formatting pattern
2.	minIntegerDigits	For defining minimum number of digits in integer part
3.	maxIntegerDigits	For defining maximum number of digits in integer part
4.	minFractionDigits	For defining minimum number of digits in fractional part
5.	maxIntegerDigits	For defining maximum number of digits in fractional part
6.	type	For representing percent, currency or number.
7.	CurrencySymbol	For converting the currency values currency symbol.
8.	groupingUsed	If grouping separators need to be used then this attribute is used.

Following is an example code that shows the use of Convert Number tag

test.xhtml

```
<?xml version="1.0" encoding="UTF-8"?>
<!DOCTYPE html PUBLIC "-//W3C//DTD XHTML 1.0 Transitional//EN"
"http://www.w3.org/TR/xhtml1/DTD/xhtml1-transitional.dtd">
<html xmlns="http://www.w3.org/1999/xhtml"
 xmlns:h="http://java.sun.com/jsf/html"
 xmlns:f="http://java.sun.com/jsf/core">
  <h:head>
    <title>Converter Tag Demo</title>
  </h:head>
  <h:body>
    <table border="1" cellspacing="2" cellpadding="2">
    <tr><th>Attribute</th><th>Value</th><th>Output</th></tr>
    <tr>
         <td>pattern as ##,###.000</td>
         <td>12345.6789</td>
         <td>
              <h:outputText value = "12345.678">
                   <f:convertNumber pattern = "##,###.000"/>
              </h:outputText>
         </td>
    </tr>
```

```
    <tr>
        <td>Currency as $</td>
        <td>100.20</td>
        <td>
            <h:outputText value = "$100.20">
            <f:convertNumber currencySymbol="$" type = "currency"/>
            </h:outputText>
        </td>
    </tr>

    </table>
    </h:body>
</html>
```

In above code we have used to convert tags namely **pattern** and **type**

Output

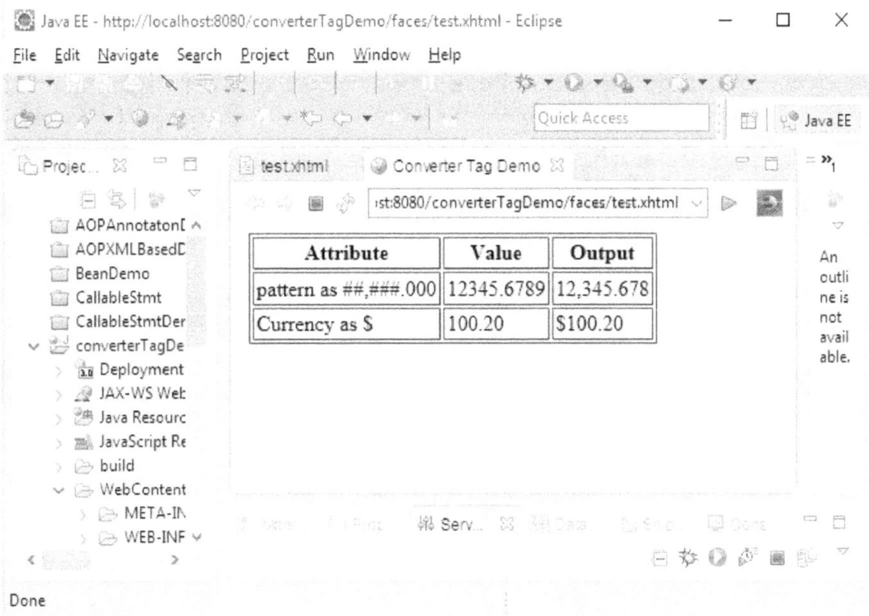

2. Convert Date Time Tag

- This Tag is used to convert the String to a Date or Time object and to Display it in different formats.
- This tag is denoted by **<h:convertDateTime>** tag
- This Tag has a dedicated set of Attribute Values for formatting both Date and Time Values.
- Following table shows the set of attributes

Sr. No.	Attribute	Meaning
1.	pattern	The formatting pattern of date or time. For example the pattern for date can be dd-mm-yy
2.	type	It can be date, time or both
3.	dateStyle	default,short,medium, long or full
4.	timeStyle	default,short,medium, long or full
5.	timeZone	It is used for specific formatting or parsing

Example

Step 1 : Create an **input.xhtml** for inputting the value

input.xhtml

```
<?xml version="1.0" encoding="UTF-8"?>
<!DOCTYPE html PUBLIC "-//W3C//DTD XHTML 1.0 Transitional//EN"
"http://www.w3.org/TR/xhtml1/DTD/xhtml1-transitional.dtd">
<html xmlns="http://www.w3.org/1999/xhtml"
  xmlns:h="http://java.sun.com/jsf/html"
  xmlns:f="http://java.sun.com/jsf/core">
  <h:head>
    <title>Converter Tag for Date/Time</title>
  </h:head>
  <h:body>
    <h:form>
      <h:inputText id="data" value="#{myBean.date}"
        label="Date" >
        <f:convertDateTime pattern="dd-mm-yyyy" />
      </h:inputText>
      <h:commandButton value="submit" action="display"/>
    </h:form>
  </h:body>
</html>
```

Program Explanation :

In above xhtml file, the value is entered in the text box and stored in the bean program using expression language #{myBean.date}

The **convertDateTime** tag is used to define the pattern for displaying the date. The pattern is dd-mm-yyyy.

Step 2 : Now we will create a simple Bean program in which the get and set methods for Date are defined. This **date** property is of the datatype Date.

myBean.java

```
package com.mypackage;
import java.util.Date;
```

```
import javax.faces.bean.ManagedBean;
import javax.faces.bean.SessionScoped;

@ManagedBean
@SessionScoped

public class myBean {
      private Date date;

      public Date getDate() {
            return date;
      }

      public void setDate(Date date) {
            this.date = date;
      }
}
```

Step 3 : Now the response file for displaying the date in the required format is created. The code for this is as follows -

display.xhtml

```
<?xml version="1.0" encoding="UTF-8"?>
<!DOCTYPE html PUBLIC "-//W3C//DTD XHTML 1.0 Transitional//EN"
"http://www.w3.org/TR/xhtml1/DTD/xhtml1-transitional.dtd">
<html xmlns="http://www.w3.org/1999/xhtml"
  xmlns:f="http://java.sun.com/jsf/core"
  xmlns:h="http://java.sun.com/jsf/html"
  xmlns:ui="http://java.sun.com/jsf/facelets">
  <h:body>
    <h2>Display of Date in required format:</h2>
    <br />
    #{myBean.date}
  </h:body>
</html>
```

Step 4 : Right click on the input file to run it on server. The output will be

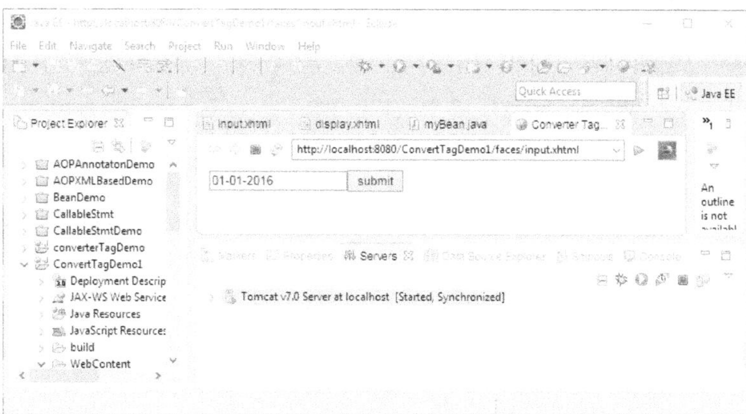

Click the submit button and following format of date will be displayed.

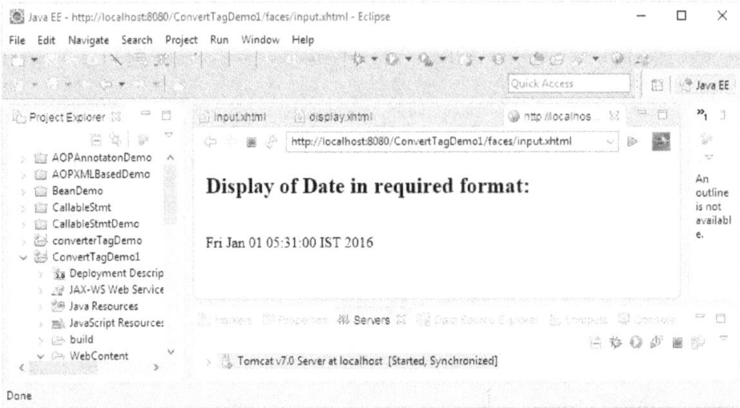

5.12 JSF Validation Tag

It is a common practice to validate the data entered by the user before being processed by the Server Web Application. JSF has various built in validation tags. Those are -

Validation Tag	Purpose
<f:validateLength>	It validates the length of the string.
<f:validateLongRange>	The range of numeric values is validated by this tag.
<f:validateDoubleRange>	The range of float values is validated by this tag.

Let us understand, how to use validate tags with the help of illustrating examples.

1. ValidateLength

- The validate length tag is used for validating the length of the input string. This is one kind of common requirement in many applications. For example - *length of password must be between 6 to 8 characters.*
- For this tag there are two attributes used **minimum** and **maximum** for minimum and maximum length boundry.
- The syntax of using this tag is

```
<f:validateLength minimum=value maximum=value />
```

Example

Step 1 : Create an input form. The code is

Input.xhtml

```
<?xml version="1.0" encoding="UTF-8"?>
<!DOCTYPE html PUBLIC "-//W3C//DTD XHTML 1.0 Transitional//EN"
"http://www.w3.org/TR/xhtml1/DTD/xhtml1-transitional.dtd">
```

```
<html xmlns="http://www.w3.org/1999/xhtml"
  xmlns:h="http://java.sun.com/jsf/html"
  xmlns:f="http://java.sun.com/jsf/core">
  <h:head>
    <title>Converter Tag for Date/Time</title>
  </h:head>
  <h:body>
    <h:form>
      <h:inputText id="data" value="#{myBean.message}"
        label="Message" >
        <f:validateLength minimum="3" maximum="10" />
      </h:inputText>
      <h:commandButton value="submit" action="display"/>
      <h:message for="data" style="color:red" />
    </h:form>
  </h:body>
</html>
```

In above program the validateLength tag is used as for the **message** property

```
<f:validateLength minimum="3" maximum="10" />
```

The display of invalid input can be specified by following code

```
<h:message for="data" style="color:red" />
```

Step 2 : Create a Bean class containing the **message** property.

myBean.java

```
package com.mypackage;

import javax.faces.bean.ManagedBean;
import javax.faces.bean.SessionScoped;

@ManagedBean
@SessionScoped

public class myBean {
    private String message;

    public String getMessage() {
        return message;
    }

    public void setMessage(String message) {
        this.message = message;
    }
}
```

Step 3 : Now create and output page which will display the valid message.

display.xhtml

```
<?xml version="1.0" encoding="UTF-8"?>
<!DOCTYPE html PUBLIC "-//W3C//DTD XHTML 1.0 Transitional//EN"
"http://www.w3.org/TR/xhtml1/DTD/xhtml1-transitional.dtd">
<html xmlns="http://www.w3.org/1999/xhtml"
  xmlns:f="http://java.sun.com/jsf/core"
  xmlns:h="http://java.sun.com/jsf/html"
  xmlns:ui="http://java.sun.com/jsf/facelets">
  <h:body>
    <h4>The message is...</h4>
    <br />
    #{myBean.message}
  </h:body>
</html>
```

Step 4 : The output will be

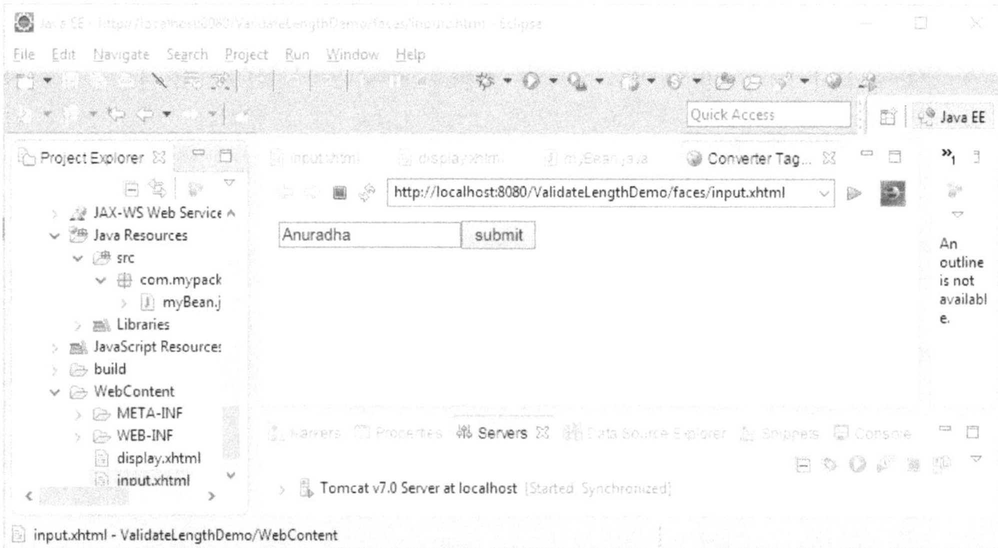

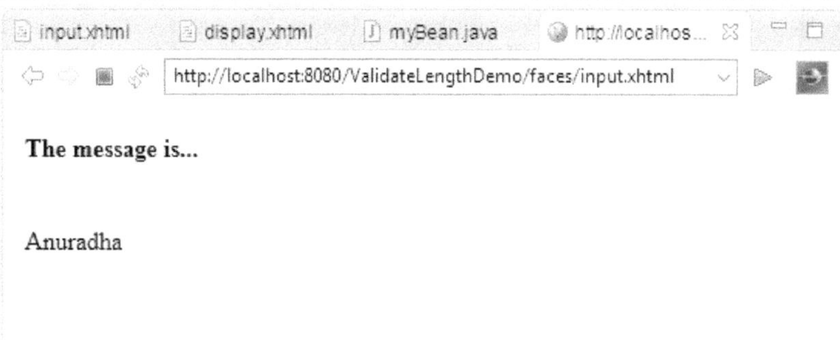

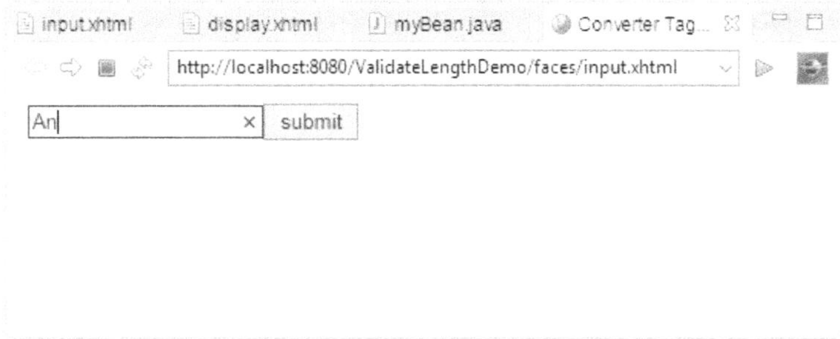

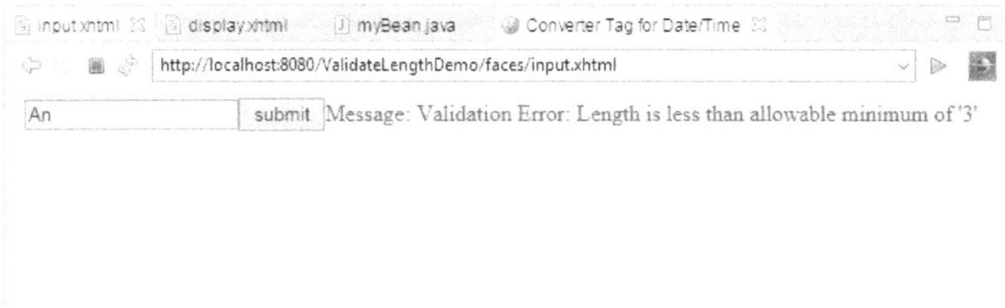

Similarly the input can be tested for maximum range by providing the message of more than 10 characters.

2. ValidateLongRange

- This tag is used for validating the long value in particular range.
- For this tag there are two attributes used **minimum** and **maximum** for minimum and maximum length boundry.
- The syntax of using this tag is

```
<f:validateLongRange minimum=value maximum=value />
```

The JSF application can be created just similar to the above created application for validateLength tag with appropriate changes.

3. ValidateDoubleRange

- This tag is used for validating the floating point value in particular range.
- For this tag there are two attributes used **minimum** and **maximum** for minimum and maximum length boundry.
- The syntax of using this tag is

```
<f:validateDoubleRange minimum=value maximum=value />
```

The JSF application can be created just similar to the above created application for validateLength tag with appropriate changes.

Review Question

1. *Explain how validationLength tag is used in JSF.*

5.13 JSF Event Handling

In JSF event handling can be done using **actionListener** attribute. The form element such as **commandbutton** can be associated with action listener method **processMyAction()** and when this button is clicked the action listener method is invoked.

The syntax of processMyAction method is

```
public void processMyAction(ActionEvent event) {

//action to be performed to process the event

}
```

Following is a simple event handling program in which implements handles the event using actionListener

Step 1 : Create and xhtml file on which command button is places. On clicking this button the action listener method is invoked.

test.xhtml

```
<?xml version="1.0" encoding="UTF-8"?>
<!DOCTYPE html PUBLIC "-//W3C//DTD XHTML 1.0 Transitional//EN"
"http://www.w3.org/TR/xhtml1/DTD/xhtml1-transitional.dtd">
<html xmlns="http://www.w3.org/1999/xhtml"
  xmlns:h="http://java.sun.com/jsf/html"
  xmlns:f="http://java.sun.com/jsf/core">
  <h:head>
    <title>EVENT DEMO</title>
  </h:head>
  <h:body>
  <f:view>
   <h:form>
   <h3>Click Me:</h3>
    <h:commandButton id="myid" value="#{myBean.status}"
    immediate="true" actionListener="#{myBean.processMyAction}" />
  </h:form>
  </f:view>
   </h:body>
</html>
```

Step 2 : Create a managed bean which will perform the desired action inside the methods

MyBean.java

```
package com.mypackage;

import javax.faces.event.ActionEvent;
import javax.faces.bean.ManagedBean;
import javax.faces.bean.SessionScoped;
```

```
@ManagedBean
@SessionScoped

public class MyBean {

    String status = "False";

    public String getStatus() {
     return status;
    }

    public void setStatus(String status) {
     this.status = status;
    }

    /* Action listener method */
    public void processMyAction(ActionEvent event) {

      if (status.equals("False"))
      {
       status = "True";
      }
      else
      {
       status = "False";
      }

    }
}
```

Step 3 : For obtaining the output, Right click on xhml file and run it on server.

The output can be verified by clicking the button on the form

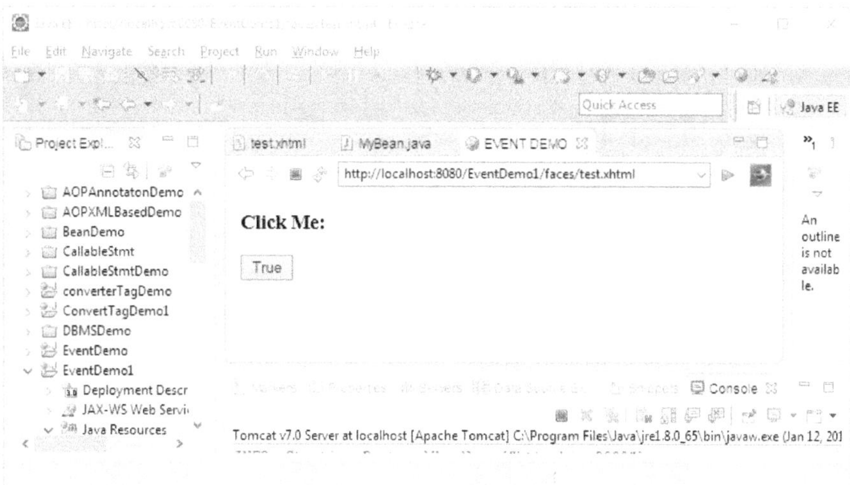

Click the command button and note that the value gets changed as follows.

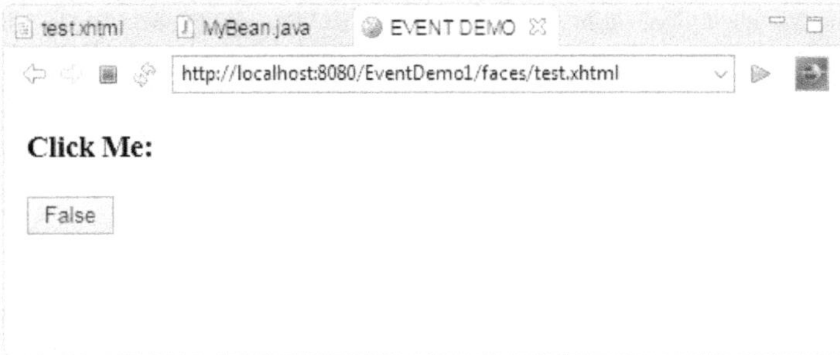

> **Review Question**
>
> 1. *Explain event handling technique used in JSF.*

5.14 Database Access

Establishing the connection with the backend database and accessing data from it is very common activity in any web application, especially at server side technology implementation.

JSF can establish connection with the database using JDBC driver class.

The database connection can be done by getting instance of **Connection** with the help of **DriverManager** class and **getConnection** method. Following is a typical code used for that purpose

```
    Connection connect = null;
//Establishing the connection with MySQL database
   String url = "jdbc:mysql://localhost:3306/DatabaseName";
   String username = UserName;
   String password = Passsword;

   try {
      Class.forName("com.mysql.jdbc.Driver");
      connect = DriverManager.getConnection(url, username, password);
   } catch (SQLException ex) { }
```

We can write a simple function for the above code and can invoke this function in our xhtml page.

Let us understand how to access the back-end database using JSF

Step 1 : Create a database and table in it. I have created **student_database** in MySQL and a table named **Student** in it. Inserted some data in this table. Following Screenshot shows the database.

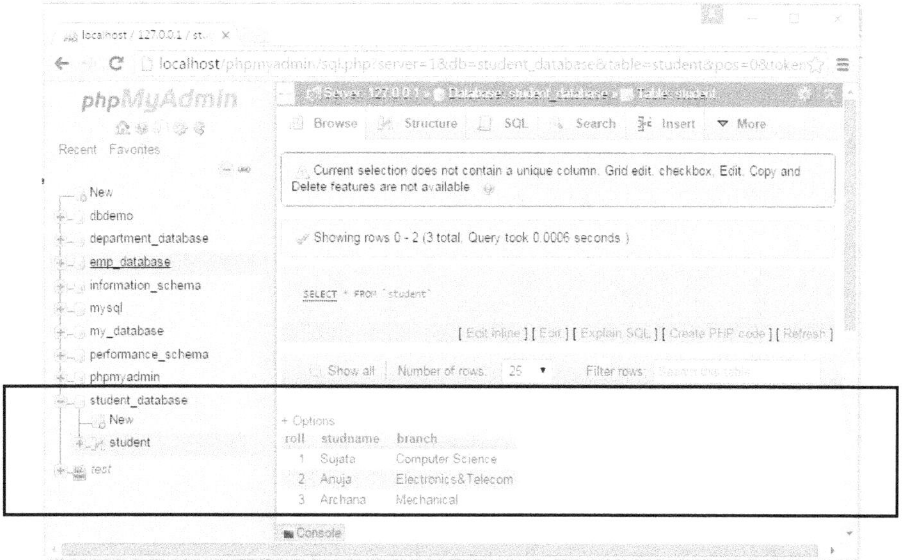

Step 2 : Open Eclipse. Create a Dynamic Web Project and specify the name to the project file. I have given the project name as **DatabaseAccessDemo**.

Make sure that Apache Tomcat and Java Server Faces configuration is made. (How?? We have already discussed these steps in earlier sections!!)

One more important thing : Add the database connector using Bulid-Path configuration. As I have using MySQL database I have a connector **mysql-connector-java.jar** file. Steps to add this connector are

Right click the Project name from Project Explorer window, click Build path. Select **Configure Build Path** and then click **Add External Jar files** button. Find the location of the **mysql-connector-java.jar** file in your computer, and select it. Following screen shot represents the required library files that must be present before running this application.

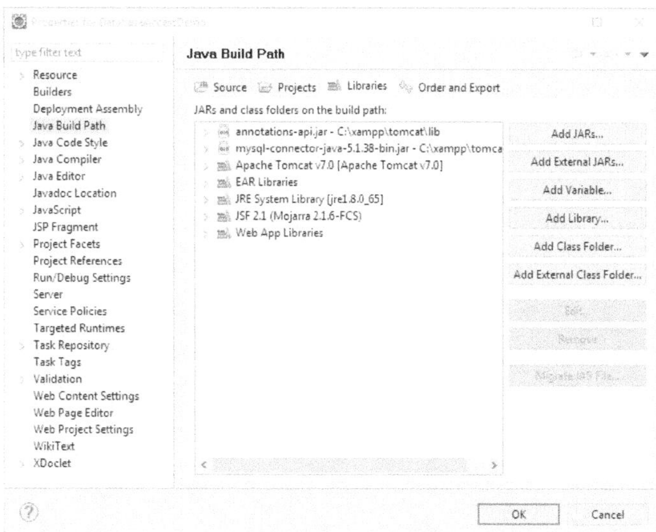

Create a simple package with suitable name. I have created a package named **com.mypackage** and inside it store Java class file for bean class. I have created a bean named **Student**. The code for this is

Student.java

```
package com.mypackage;

public class Student {
    private int roll;
    private String studname;
    private String branch;
    public Student(){}
    public int getRoll() {
        return roll;
    }
    public void setRoll(int roll) {
        this.roll = roll;
    }
    public String getStudname() {
        return studname;
    }
    public void setStudname(String studname) {
        this.studname = studname;
    }
    public String getBranch() {
        return branch;
    }
    public void setBranch(String branch) {
        this.branch = branch;
    }

}
```

Step 3 :

Now create one more bean class inside the package. This bean is for establishing the connection with the database and execution the query for retrieving the result. I have created a bean named **StudentBean**. The code for this is

StudentBean.java

```
package com.mypackage;

import java.sql.Connection;
import java.sql.DriverManager;
import java.sql.PreparedStatement;
import java.sql.ResultSet;
import java.sql.SQLException;
```

```
import java.util.ArrayList;
import java.util.List;
import javax.faces.bean.ManagedBean;
import javax.faces.bean.SessionScoped;

@ManagedBean
@SessionScoped

public class StudentBean {
    public List<Student> getStudents() throws ClassNotFoundException, SQLException
    {
      Connection connect = null;
 //Establishing the connection with MySQL database
     String url = "jdbc:mysql://localhost:3306/student_database";
     String username = "root";
     String password = "";

     try {
        Class.forName("com.mysql.jdbc.Driver");
        connect = DriverManager.getConnection(url, username, password);
    } catch (SQLException ex) { }
 //Creating ArrayList for storing student data
     List<Student> students = new ArrayList<Student>();
//Executing Query
     PreparedStatement pstmt = connect
          .prepareStatement("select * from Student");
     ResultSet rs = pstmt.executeQuery();
 //Getting result from database in rs object of Resultset
     while (rs.next()) {
        Student student = new Student();
        student.setRoll(rs.getInt("roll"));
        student.setStudname(rs.getString("studname"));
        student.setBranch(rs.getString("branch"));

//adding each record to students list
        students.add(student);

     }
     rs.close();
     pstmt.close();
     connect.close();
     return students;
  }
}
```

Firstly, using **rs.getXX** method we are getting the data from database. Secondly, using **student.setXX** method of the bean class **Student** the values are added to ArrayList **students** by **student.add** method

Step 3 : Create an xhtml page in which the JSF tags are used to establish the communication with these above created Bean program and display the result on the web page. I have created a file named **display.xhtml**. The code for it is

display.xhtml

```
<?xml version="1.0" encoding="UTF-8"?>
<!DOCTYPE html PUBLIC "-//W3C//DTD XHTML 1.0 Transitional//EN"
"http://www.w3.org/TR/xhtml1/DTD/xhtml1-transitional.dtd">
<html xmlns="http://www.w3.org/1999/xhtml"
  xmlns:f="http://java.sun.com/jsf/core"
  xmlns:h="http://java.sun.com/jsf/html">
<h:head>
  <title>DATABASE ACCESS DEMO</title>
</h:head>
<h:body>
  <h2>List of Students</h2>
  <h:dataTable value="#{studentBean.getStudents()}" var="stud" border="1">
    <h:column>
      <f:facet name="header">Roll No.</f:facet>
    #{stud.roll}
   </h:column>
    <h:column>
      <f:facet name="header">Student Name</f:facet>
    #{stud.studname}
   </h:column>
    <h:column>
      <f:facet name="header">Branch</f:facet>
     #{stud.branch}
   </h:column>
  </h:dataTable>
</h:body>
</html>
```

This method is present in **StudentBean** class for getting the data from database

This tag is used to retrieve the data from get methods of Student bean class

Note that in above xhtml file the **datatable** tag is used to display the data in tabular form.

Step 4 : Finally right click the xhtml file and click **Run As->Run on Server**. The output will be as follows -

Review Question

1. *Create a JSF application for accessing the database created by you.*

5.15 JSF Libraries : PrimeFaces

PrimeFaces is an Open source component library for Java Server Faces (JSF). PrimeFaces is developed and maintained by PrimeTek Informatics. PrimeFaces is a lightweight JSF component library with one JAR file that needs no configuration and does not contain any required external dependencies. The PrimeFaces library can be downloaded from http://primefaces.org/downloads.html

Features of PrimeFaces

1. It is **simple to use**. PrimeFaces is a lightweight library, all decisions made are based on keeping PrimeFaces as lightweight as possible. It is just one single jar with no dependencies and nothing to configure.
2. It has **rich set UI components**. It supports over 100 UI components so that rich user interface can be created with the help of PrimeFaces.
3. It provide support for **mobile UI components**.
4. It provide support for **client side validation**.
5. The PrimeFaces can be used in Spring-JSF application for User Interface.
6. It has got a **strong community support** that help in development of PrimeFaces by providing new ideas, bug reports and patches.

Review Question

1. *Write a short note on - PrimeFaces.*

❑❑❑

Notes

6 Hibernate 4.0

Syllabus

Overview of Hibernate, Hibernate Architecture, Hibernate Mapping Types, Hibernate O/R Mapping, Hibernate Annotation, Hibernate Query Language.

Contents

6.1 Overview of Hibernate

6.2 Hibernate Architecture **May-12, Summer-14, 16,**
.... **Winter-14,** ·············· Marks 7

6.3 Hibernate Mapping Types

6.4 Hibernate O/R Mapping **Summer-13, 15, 16,**
.... **Winter-13,** ·············· Marks 7

6.5 Hibernate Annotation

6.6 Hibernate Query Language (HQL) .... **Summer-13, 16,** ········· Marks 7

6.1 Overview of Hibernate

- Hibernate is an open source **object relational mapping tool** for the Java platform.
- Hibernate allows the Java developer to create **persistent classes** or **persistent data** without bothering about how to handle data.
- Hibernate query language is an extension to SQL.
- The **main task** of hibernate is **mapping of Java classes** to **database tables**. That means the Java data types are mapped to the SQL data types.
- Hibernate provides data query and retrieval facilities. This feature avoids wastage of development time in manual data handling in SQL and JDBC.
- The goal of hibernate is to **relieve the developer** from 95 % of common data persistence related **programming tasks**.
- The high performance , robust database application with Java can be easily built using the hibernate. For that purpose the developer has to do following things -
    - o Write the simple **P**lain **O**ld **J**ava **O**bject(POJO).
    - o Create an XML mapping file which describes the relationship between database and class attribute.
    - o Then call some hibernate API in order to store the persistent objects.
- There are **two alternatives for using hibernate** - Use of SQL for creating and retrieving the data in the database but this alternative is not as much attractive as hibernate. The second alternative is use of Enterprise Java Beans i.e. EJB. The EJB is really a good alternative for hibernate but it requires EJB container.

6.2 Hibernate Architecture

GTU : May-12, Summer-14, 16, Winter-14, Marks 7

Fig. 6.2.1 shows the simple three tier architecture of hibernate.

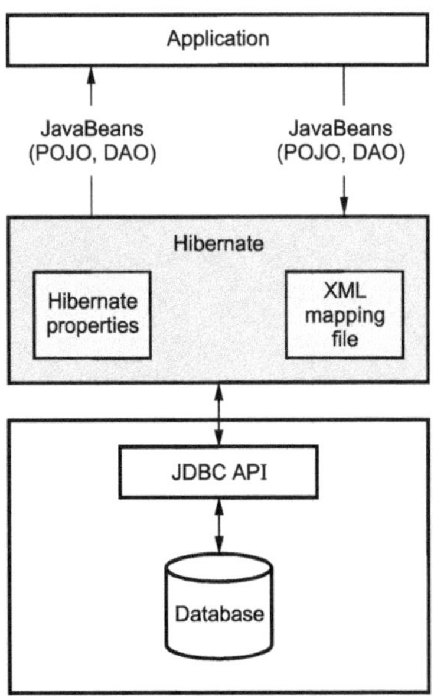

Fig. 6.2.1 Hibernate architecture

- The hibernate architecture is a three tier architecture in which an application is interfaced with the back end database using the hibernate as a middle layer.
- The most important thing in mapping the object to the database objects is to write the configuration file for hibernate. Hibernate is written in Java and is configured using two types of files named **hibernate.cfg.xml** and mapping description file having the extension **.hbm.**
- At the beginning the hibernate reads the XML configuration file for obtaining the database connection, string, password, database dialect and location of mapping files. Then hibernate searches for these files.
- The second type of configuration file that is mapping description file. This file helps hibernate to map data between specific Java class and database tables.
- There can be single **hibernate.cfg.xml** and multiple **.hbm** files for a simple mapping.
- Thus hibernate is useful for any Java application in which the data is moved from Java objects to database tables.

Hibernate caching architecture

The performance of Hibernate web application is improved using caching.

The cache actually stores the data already loaded from the database, so that the traffic between the application program and database will be reduced.

The cache architecture is divided into – i) First level cache and ii) Second level cache.

First level cache : This is a session cache. Through this cache all requests must pass.

Second Level Cache : This is an optional cache and first level cache will always be searched before locating an object into second level cache.

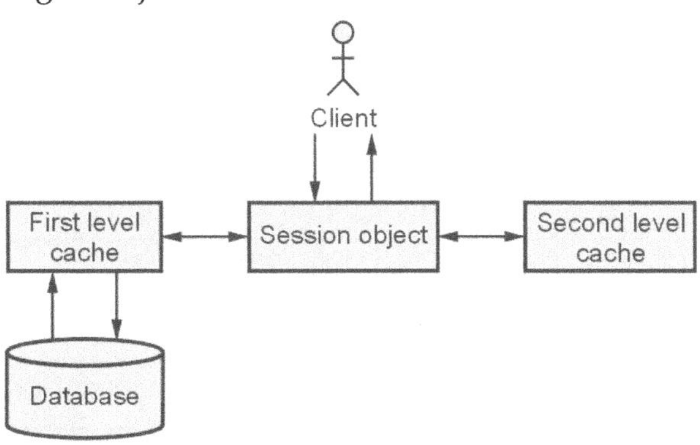

Review Questions

1. *Give the hibernate architecture and discuss each part in brief.*

   GTU : May-12, Summer-14, Winter-14, Marks 7

2. *Explain the Hibernate cache architecture.* **GTU : Summer-16, Marks 7**

6.3 Hibernate Mapping Types

- Hibernate deals with both the Java and JDBC representation of application data. While creating the Hibernate applications, it basically reads out the values from database and write them back.
- Basically Hibernate type is neither a Java type nor a SQL datatype; it provides a information about both.
- The **types** declared and used in the **mapping files** are not Java data types; they are not SQL database types either. These types are called Hibernate mapping types, which can translate from Java to SQL data types and vice versa.
- Following table represents the mapping type, Java type and corresponding SQL type.

Mapping type	Java type	ANSI SQL type
integer	int or java.lang.Integer	INTEGER
long	long or java.lang.Long	BIGINT
short	short or java.lang.Short	SMALLINT
float	float or java.lang.Float	FLOAT
double	double or java.lang.Double	DOUBLE
character	java.lang.String	CHAR(1)
string	java.lang.String	VARCHAR
byte	byte or java.lang.Byte	TINYINT
boolean	boolean or java.lang.Boolean	BIT
yes/no	boolean or java.lang.Boolean	CHAR(1) ('Y' or 'N')
true/false	boolean or java.lang.Boolean	CHAR(1) ('T' or 'F')
date	java.util.Date or java.sql.Date	DATE
time	java.util.Date or java.sql.Time	TIME
class	java.lang.Class	VARCHAR
Currency	java.util.Currency	VARCHAR

6.4 Hibernate O/R Mapping

GTU : Summer-13, 15, 16, Winter-13, Marks 7

Object/relational mappings (ORM) are usually defined in an **XML document**. The mapping language is Java-centric, meaning that mappings are constructed around persistent class declarations and not table declarations.

For example - Following is a sample mapping Document. It shows typical mapping that contains class mapping with table. That is the java class defined in **Student.java** is mapped with the table STUDENT with appropriate property name as corresponding column name.

This file has the extension **.hbm.xml**

Student.hbm.xml

```
<?xml version='1.0' encoding='UTF-8'?>
<!DOCTYPE hibernate-mapping PUBLIC
"-//Hibernate/Hibernate Mapping DTD 3.0//EN"
"http://hibernate.sourceforge.net/hibernate-mapping-3.0.dtd">
    <hibernate-mapping>
    <class name="com.mypackage.Student" table="STUDENT">
      <id name="roll">
       <generator class="assigned"></generator>
      </id>
       <property name="studname"></property>
      <property name="branch"></property>
    </class>
    </hibernate-mapping>
```

Explanation of Mapping Document

1. <hibernate-mapping> element :

The first or root element of hibernate mapping document is <hibernate-mapping> element. Between the **<hibernate-mapping>** tag class element(s) are present.

2. <class> element :

The <class> element maps the class object with corresponding entity in the database. It also tells what table in the database has to access and what column in that table it should use. Several classes can be mapped within <class>

3.<id> element :

The <id> element in unique identifier to identify an object. In fact <id> element map with the primary key of the table. Following is the attributes of <id> element

- **name** - Property name of the persistence model class
- **type** - The java data type used for that property
- **column** - Name of the column for that property of the persistence object

4.<generator> element :

Used to create primary key for new record, there are some commonly used generators type given below -

- **increment** - used to generate primary keys of type long, short or int that are unique only.
- **assigned** - is used when application code generates the primary key.
- **identity** - supports identity columns in DB2, MySQL, MS SQL Server, Sybase and HypersonicSQL. The returned identifier is of type long, short or int.
- **uuid** - Unique use ID of 128 bits generated from using algorithm and return type is String

5. <property> element :

Defines standard Java attributes and their mapping into database schema using **name** attribute.

Example 6.4.1 : *Implement the Hibernate using the O/R mapping.*

Solution : In this example we will create a database for storing the student information such as roll number, name and branch. The Hibernate application is created using following steps for inserting a data in the database.

Step 1 : Create the java project by **File Menu - New - project - java project** . Now specify the project name. I have named my project as **HibernateProg**.

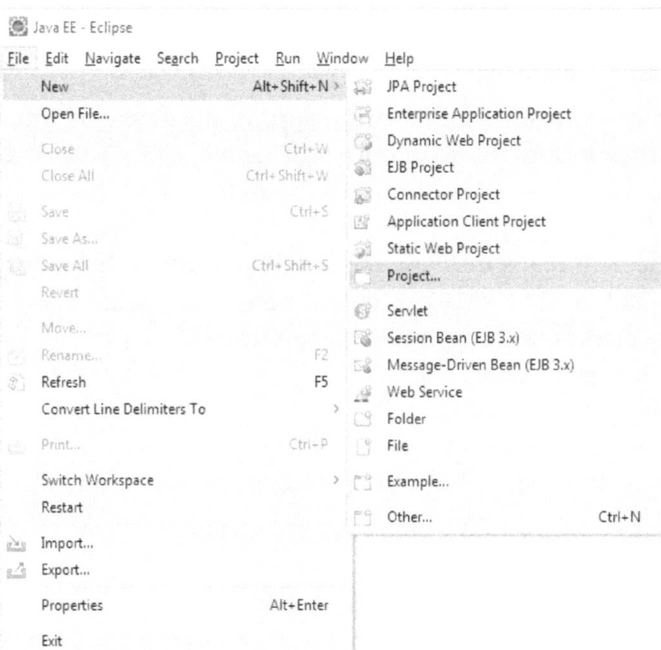

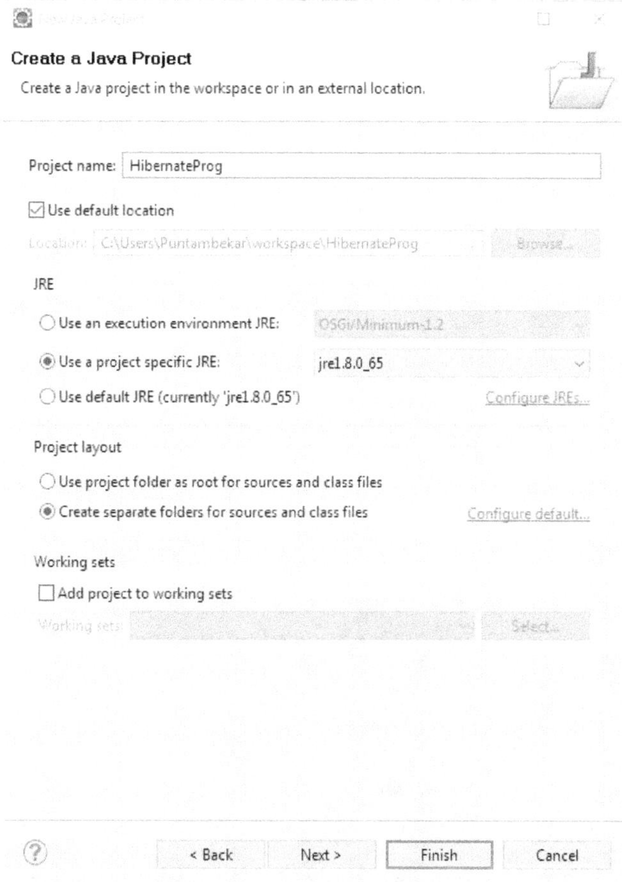

Click Next->Next and Finally click Finish.

Step 2 : Now add the required **hibernate jar files**. The required jar files must be downloaded from the net and must be stored in one folder.

To add the jar files **Right click on your project - Build path - Add external archives**. Now select all the jar files.

Add all these jar files in you project. Following screen shot illustrates it -

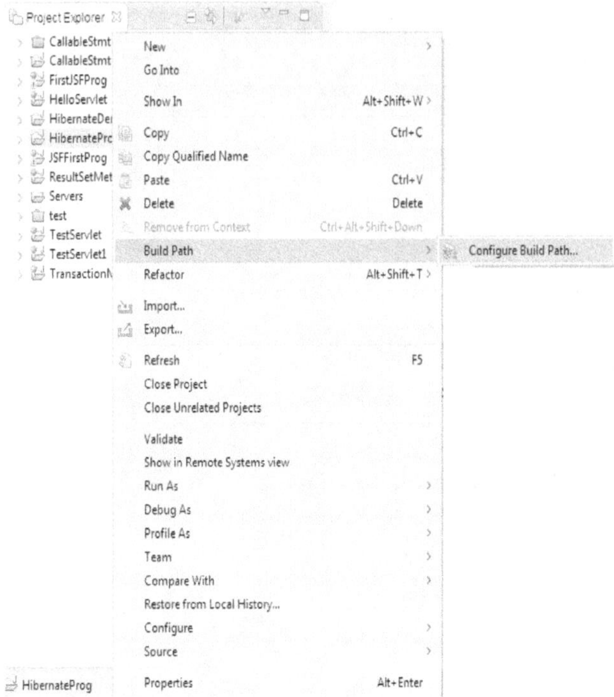

For connecting to the database created in MySQL you must have **mysql-connector-java.jar** file. This jar file must also be added using **Add External Jars**. You can identify it in above screenshot.

Step 3 : Now click on the Project **HibernateProg**. Select **src** and right click on it and create a package. Specify the suitable name to the package. In my case I have created a package named **com.mypackage**

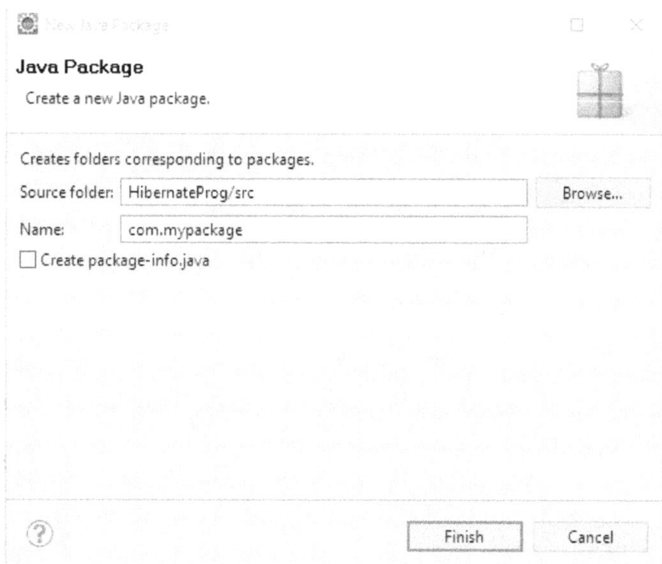

Click **Finish** and package will be created.

Step 4 : Create a persistent class in which getXX and setXX methods are defined. Remember, that you have to create this class under the package you have created. I have named this class as **Student**. Hence the file named **Student.java**

will get generated. Here is the screen shot for creating the persistent class under your package.

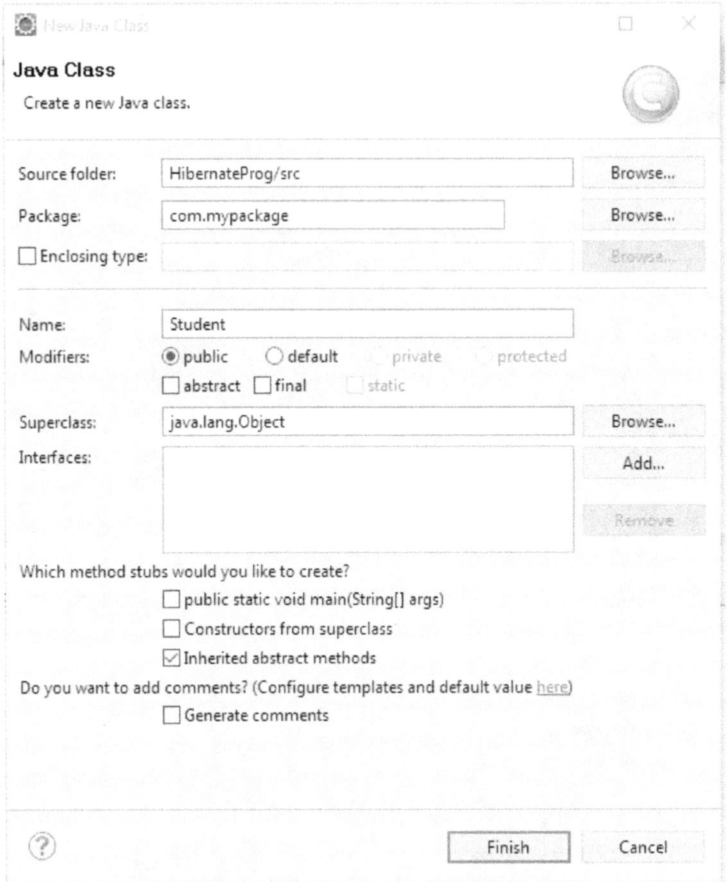

Just Click Finish. Then type the following code for **Student.java**

Student.java

```
package com.mypackage;
public class Student {
    private int roll;
    private String studname;
    private String branch;
    public Student(){} //empty Constructor
    public int getRoll() {
        return roll;
    }
    public void setRoll(int roll) {
        this.roll = roll;
    }
    public String getStudname() {
        return studname;
```

```
    }
    public void setStudname(String studname) {
        this.studname = studname;
    }
    public String getBranch() {
        return branch;
    }
    public void setBranch(String branch) {
        this.branch = branch;
    }
}
```

Step 5 : Create a mapping file for this persistent class. Just right click on **src** ->New -> other->file. Specify the filename as **student.hbm.xml.** Note that this file must be outside the package. Type following code for this mapping file as follows –

Student.hbm.xml

```
<?xml version='1.0' encoding='UTF-8'?>
<!DOCTYPE hibernate-mapping PUBLIC
"-//Hibernate/Hibernate Mapping DTD 3.0//EN"
"http://hibernate.sourceforge.net/hibernate-mapping-3.0.dtd">
    <hibernate-mapping>
    <class name="com.mypackage.Student" table="STUDENT">
     <id name="roll">
      <generator class="assigned"></generator>
     </id>
      <property name="studname"></property>
     <property name="branch"></property>
    </class>
    </hibernate-mapping>
```

Step 6 : Now create the configuration file.

This file contains information about the database such as connection url, driver class, database name, username, password. The **hbm2ddl.auto** property is used to **create table** in the database automatically when we specify the create attribute. But if we want to create a table explicitly, just make the attribute as update. For example

```
<property name="hbm2ddl.auto">update</property>
```

As I have created the database in MySQL, I have specified the driver for MySQL. Following screen shot illustrates, how I have created database in MySQL.(Although I have created database using phpMyAdmin , you can create it by typing the SQL queries on the MySQL prompt)

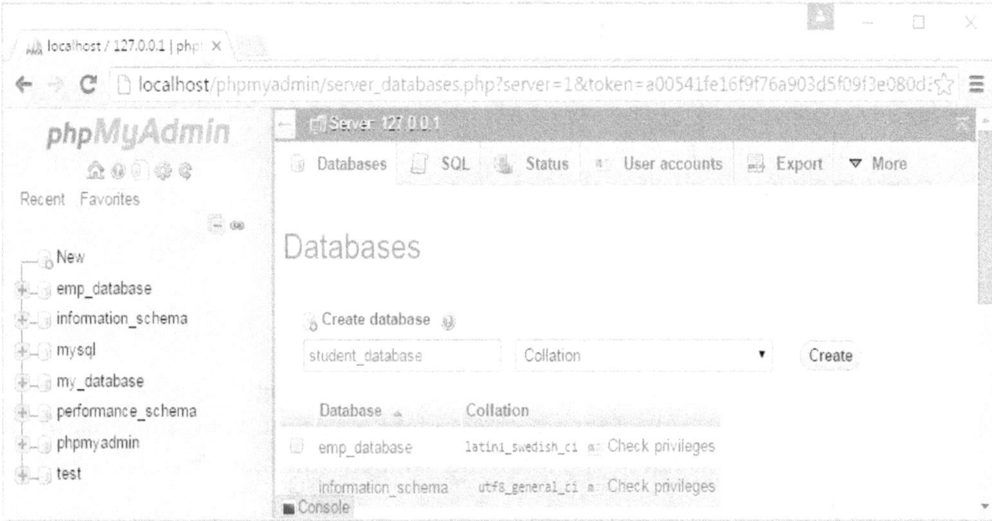

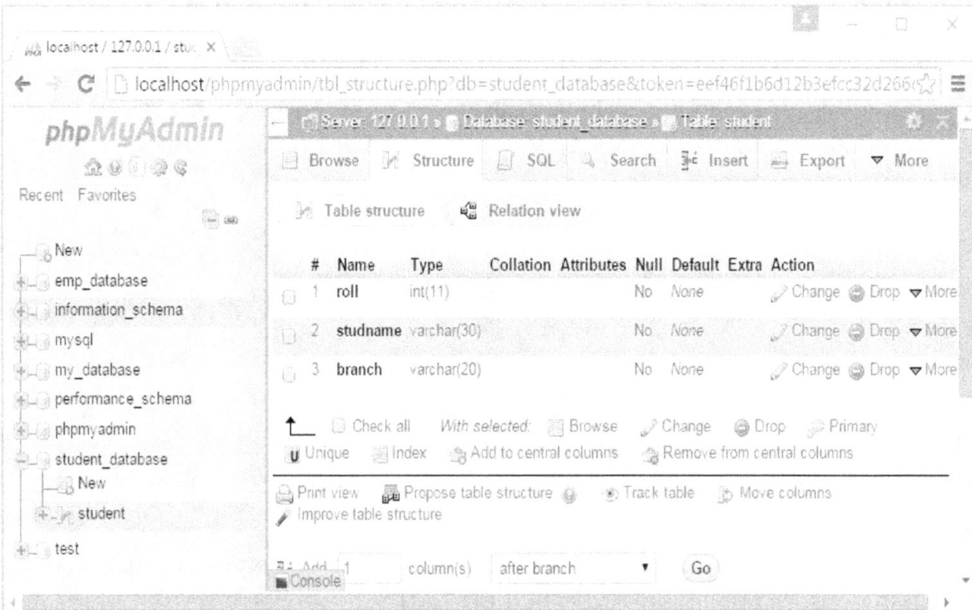

In order to create the configuration file right click on src - new - file. Now specify the configuration file name e.g. hibernate.cfg.xml. Type the following code in it.

hibernate.cfg.xml

```
<?xml version="1.0" encoding="utf-8"?>
<!DOCTYPE hibernate-configuration PUBLIC
"-//Hibernate/Hibernate Configuration DTD 3.0//EN"
"http://www.hibernate.sourceforge.net/hibernate-configuration-3.0.dtd">
 <hibernate-configuration>
<session-factory>
<property name="hibernate.connection.driver_class">com.mysql.jdbc.Driver</property>
```

```
<property name="hibernate.connection.url">jdbc:mysql://localhost:3306/student_database
</property>
<property name="hibernate.connection.username">root</property>
<property name="hibernate.connection.password"></property>
<property name="hibernate.dialect">org.hibernate.dialect.MySQLDialect</property>
<property name="show_sql">true</property>
<property name="format_sql">true</property>
<property name="hbm2ddl.auto">update</property>
<mapping resource="student.hbm.xml" />
</session-factory>
</hibernate-configuration>
```

Step 7 : Now create a Java class file for inserting data into the database. Again this class file must be within your package. I have named it as **InsertData.java.** Type following code in it.

InsertData.java

```
package com.mypackage;
import org.hibernate.Session;
import org.hibernate.SessionFactory;
import org.hibernate.Transaction;
import org.hibernate.cfg.Configuration;

public class InsertData {
    public static void main(String[] args)
    {
        Configuration cfg=new Configuration();
        cfg.configure("hibernate.cfg.xml");//populates the data of the configuration file

          //creating session factory object
          SessionFactory factory=cfg.buildSessionFactory();

          //creating session object
          Session session=factory.openSession();

          //creating transaction object
          Transaction t=session.beginTransaction();

          Student stud=new Student();
          stud.setRoll(1);
          stud.setStudname("Sujata");
          stud.setBranch("Computer Science");
          session.persist(stud);//persisting the object
```

```
        t.commit();//transaction is committed
        session.close();

        System.out.println("Inserted Data In Database!!!");

    }
}
```

Step 8 : Before running the code your directory structure must be like this

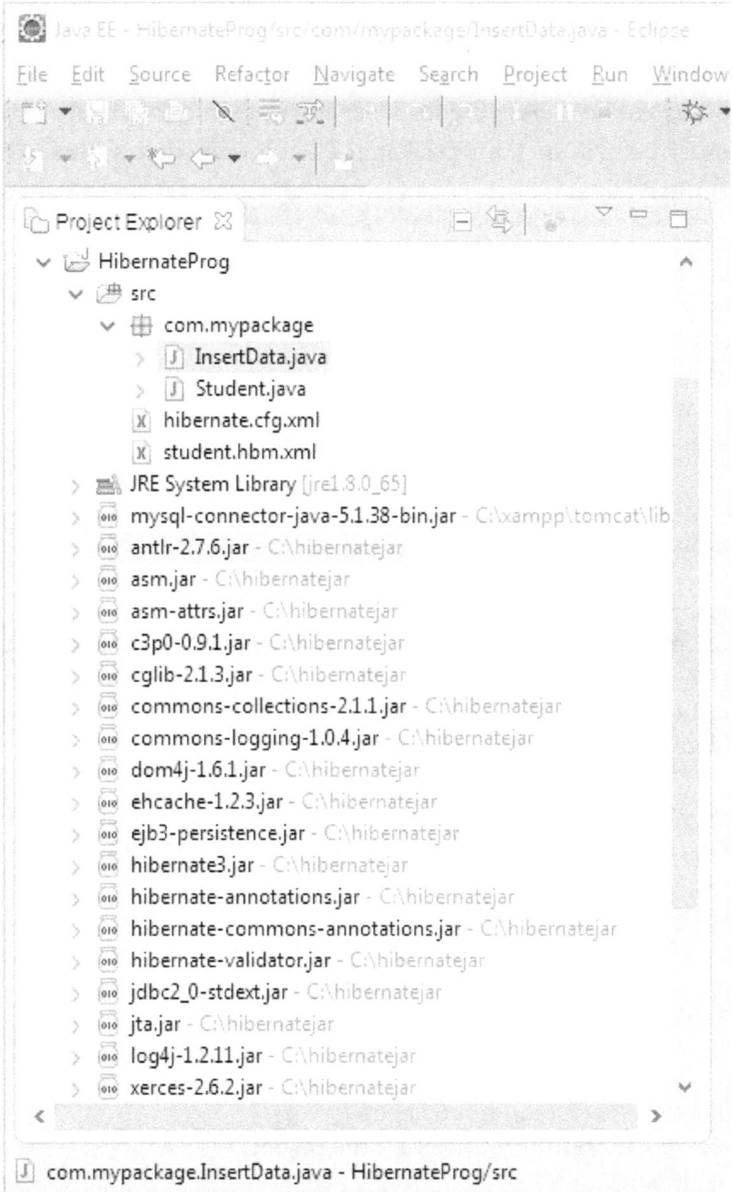

Step 9 : Now right click on **InserData.java** and click Run As->Java Application. The output will appear in the console window as follows -

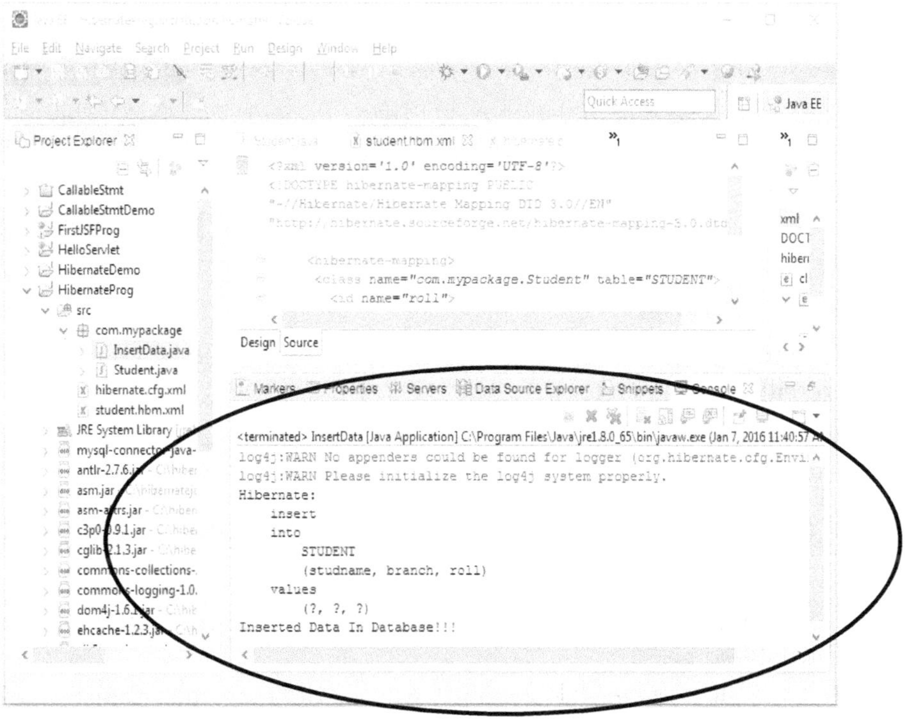

Step 10 : We can verify that the data is actually inserted in the table by opening the database. Following screenshot shows this.

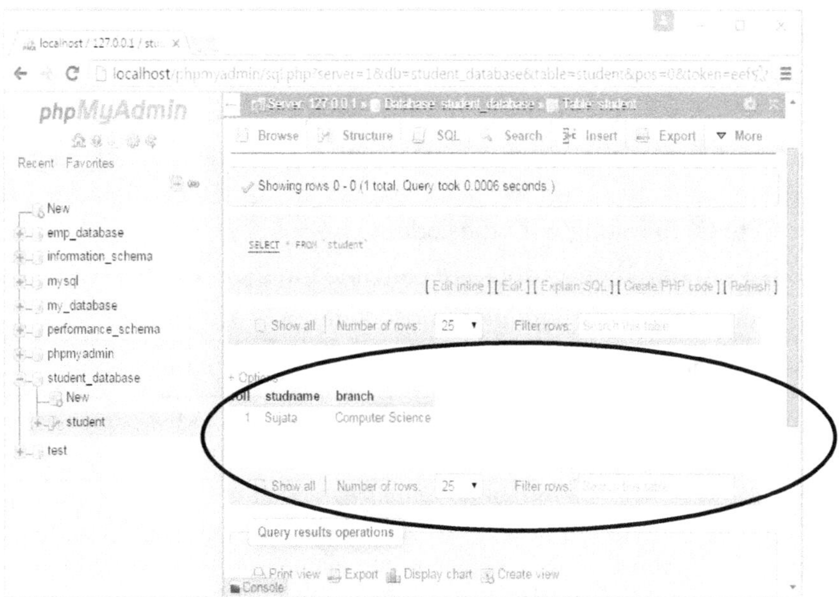

Review Questions

1. *Explain the OR mapping in Hibernate.* **GTU : Summer-13, Marks 7**
2. *Can you implement OR mapping in Hibernate. Give an example.* **GTU : Winter-13, Marks 7**
3. *Explain Hibernate Architecture and Object Relation Mapping in Hibernate with Java Code and required XML files.* **GTU : Summer-15, Marks 7**
4. *What is OR mapping ? Give an example of Hibernate XML mapping file.* **GTU : Summer-16, Marks 7**

6.5 Hibernate Annotation

- **Annotations** have been a very important part of Java. The annotations are represented by the prefix @.
- Annotation is Metadata. Metadata is data about data. So annotations are metadata for code.
- **Need for Annotation:** There are two reasons behind introduction of annotation -
  i) Prior to annotation (and even after) XML were extensively used for metadata. But for application developers, the XML maintenance was getting troublesome.
  ii) Annotation defines a standard way of defining metadata in code. Prior to annotations people also used their own ways to define metadata. Some examples are - using comments, transient keywords and so on. Each developer decided his own way to decide metadata, but annotation standardized things.
- Hibernate annotations is one of the method to define mappings without a use of XML file (i.e. mapping XML file).
- Instead of using mapping file (.hbm.xml) we use annotations.
- Hibernate Annotations is the powerful way to provide the metadata for the Object and Relational Table mapping. All the metadata is clubbed into the Plain Old Java Object (POJO) file along with the code.
- The EJB 3 standard annotations are contained in the **javax.persistence** package.
- Various annotations that are used most commonly are -

Annotation	Description
@Entity Annotation:	We use the @Entity annotation to the particular class which marks that class as an entity bean.
@Table Annotation:	The @Table annotation allows you to specify the details of the table that will be used to persist the entity in the database. The @Table annotation allows you to override the name of the table.

@Id Annotations:	Each entity bean will have a primary key, which you annotate on the class with the @Id annotation. The primary key can be a single field or a combination of multiple fields depending on your table structure.
@Column Annotation:	The @Column annotation is used to specify the details of the column to which a field or property will be mapped. Various attributes that can be used along with this annotation are - • **name** attribute permits the name of the column to be explicitly specified. • **length** attribute permits the size of the column used to map a value particularly for a String value. • **nullable** attribute permits the column to be marked NOT NULL when the schema is generated. • **unique** attribute permits the column to be marked as containing only unique values.

Example 6.5.1 : *Write an Hibernate application to implement Annotation.*

Solution : This example is similar to the example created in previous section. The only thing in this example is that we have used annotations and there by there is no need for **.hbm.xml file.**

Step 1 : Create the java project by **File Menu - New - project - java project** . Now specify the project name. I have named my project as **HiberAnnotations.**

Step 2 : Now add the required hibernate jar files. The required jar files must be downloaded from the net and must be stored in one folder. To add the jar files **Right click on your project - Build path - Add external Jars**. Now select all the jar files.

For connecting to the database created in MySQL you must have **mysql-connector-java.jar** file. This jar file must also be added using **Add External Jars**.

Step 3 : Now click on the Project **HibernateProg**. Select **src** and right click on it and create a package. Specify the suitable name to the package. In my case I have created a package named **com.mypackage**

Step 4 : Create a persistent class in which getXX and setXX methods are defined. Remember, that you have to create this class under the package you have created. I have named this class as **Department**. Hence the file named **Department.java** will get generated. Here is the screen shot for creating the persistent class under your package.

Note that in this class we are using **annotation.**

@Entity annotation marks this class as an entity.

@Table annotation specifies the table name . If you don't use @Table annotation, hibernate will use the class name as the table name by default.

@Id annotation marks the identifier for this entity.

Here is the persistent class file

Department.java

```
package com.mypackage;
import javax.persistence.Entity;
import javax.persistence.Id;
import javax.persistence.Table;
@Entity
@Table(name="department")
public class Department {
@Id
    private int id;
    private String deptname;
    public Department(){} //empty Constructor
    public int getId() {
        return id;
    }
    public void setId(int id) {
        this.id = id;
    }
    public String getDeptname() {
        return deptname;
    }
    public void setDeptname(String deptname) {
        this.deptname = deptname;
    }

}
```

Step 5 : Now create the configuration file for adding mapping of persistent class in configuration file.

This file contains information about the database such as connection url, driver class, database name, username, password.

In order to create the configuration file right click on **src - new - file.** Now specify the configuration file name e.g. hibernate.cfg.xml. Type the following code in it.

hibernate.cfg.xml

```
<?xml version="1.0" encoding="utf-8"?>
<!DOCTYPE hibernate-configuration PUBLIC
"-//Hibernate/Hibernate Configuration DTD 3.0//EN"
"http://www.hibernate.sourceforge.net/hibernate-configuration-3.0.dtd">

<hibernate-configuration>
<session-factory>
<property name="hibernate.connection.driver_class">com.mysql.jdbc.Driver</property>
```

```
<property
name="hibernate.connection.url">jdbc:mysql://localhost:3306/department_database
</property>
<property name="hibernate.connection.username">root</property>
<property name="hibernate.connection.password"> </property>
<property name="hibernate.dialect">org.hibernate.dialect.MySQLDialect</property>
<property name="hbm2ddl.auto">update</property>
<mapping class="com.mypackage.Department" />
</session-factory>
</hibernate-configuration>
```

Step 6 : Create a database in MySQL name it as department_database. Create a table named **Department** within it. This table will have two columns namely id(INT), deptname(VARCHR).

Step 7 : Now create a Java class file for inserting data into the database. Again this class file must be within your package. I have named it as **InsertData.java.** Type following code in it.

InsertData.java

```
package com.mypackage;
import org.hibernate.*;
import org.hibernate.cfg.*;
public class InsertData {
    public static void main(String[] args)
    {
        Session session=new
AnnotationConfiguration().configure().buildSessionFactory().openSession();
                //creating transaction object
        Transaction t=session.beginTransaction();
        Department dept1=new Department();
        dept1.setId(1001);
        dept1.setDeptname("Accounts");
        session.persist(dept1);//persisting the object
        t.commit();//transaction is committed
        session.close();
        System.out.println("Inserted Data In Database!!!");
    }
}
```

Step 8 : Before running the code your directory structure must be like this

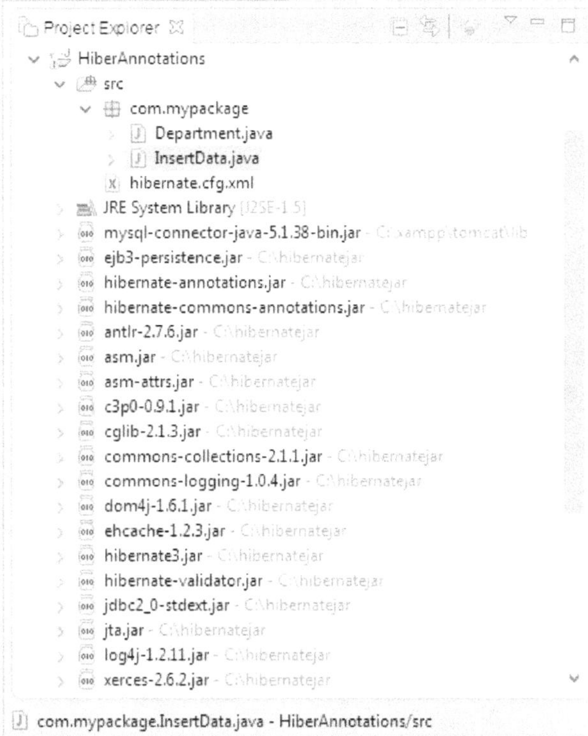

Step 9 : Now right click on **InserData.java** and click **Run As**->Java Application. The output will appear in the console window as follows -

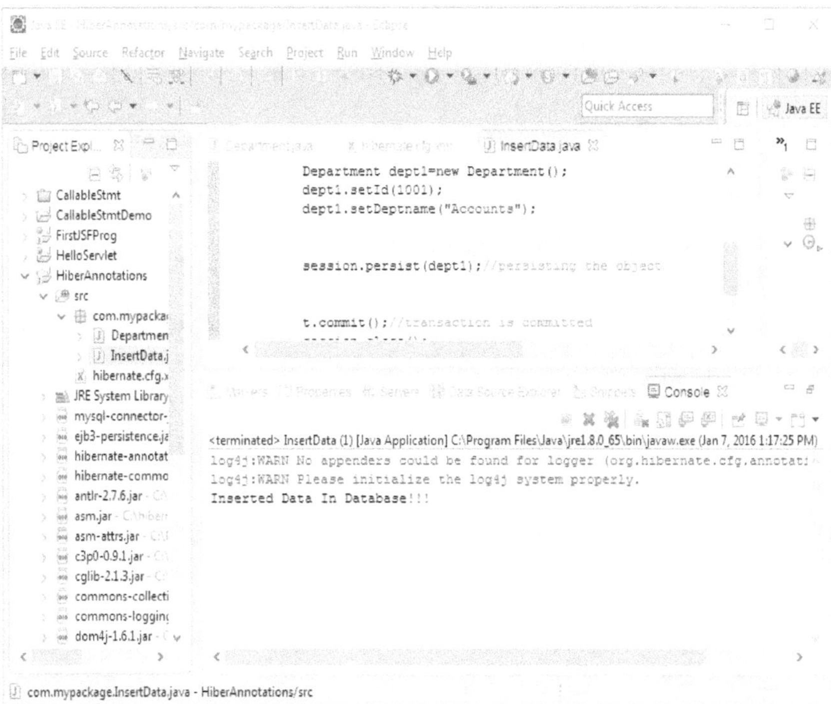

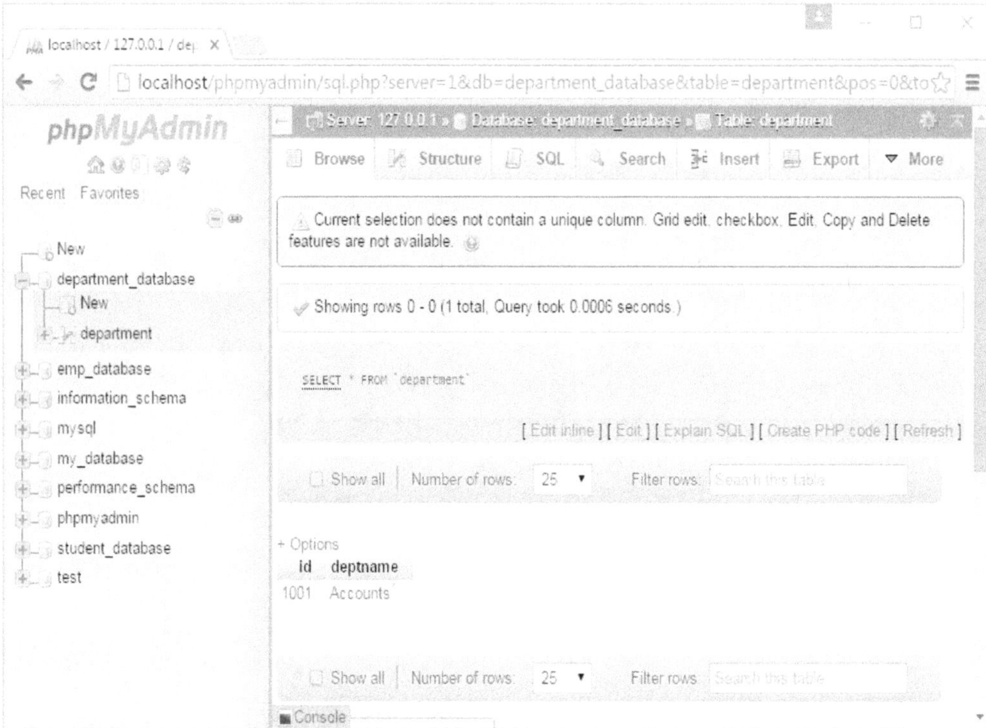

6.6 Hibernate Query Language (HQL)

GTU : Summer-13, 16, Marks 7

- Hibernate is supported by a very powerful query language which is just similar to SQL.
- The Hibernate Query Language is an object oriented query language.
- It works with persistent objects and its properties.
- HQL does not depend upon table of database. Instead of table name we use class name in HQL.
- The Hibernate Queries are translated into conventional SQL that in turn perform operations on database.
- These queries are case insensitive.

Difference between HQL and SQL

HQL stands for Hibernate Query Language and SQL stands for Structured Query Language. The syntax of HQL is similar to SQL. But the only difference between HQL and SQL is that HQL makes use of class name instead of table name and property name instead of column name. HQL is basically an object oriented query language. And HQL is database independent.

Advantages of HQL

1. The HQL can perform bulk of operations at a time on Hibernate.
2. HQL supports object oriented features such as inheritance, polymorphism, association and so on.
3. Instead of returning plain data HQL queries return the objects. These objects can be easily accessed, or programmed.
4. HQL is database independent. The same HQL can be executed on different databases whereas SQL is database dependent.

Here are some queries that are commonly used in HQL

1. FROM Clause

The FROM clause is used to load complete persistent object into the memory. For example

```
String myquery ="FROM Student";
Query q=session.createQuery(myquery);
List mylist=q.list();
```

2. AS Clause

The AS clause can be used to assign aliases to the classes. The AS clause is optional. That means you can specify AS keyword or without its specification we can represent the alias for the class name. For example

```
String myquery ="FROM Student AS s";
//It can be
// String myquery ="FROM Student s"
Query q=session.createQuery(myquery);
List mylist=q.list();
```

3. SELECT Clause

The SELECT clause provides more control than the FROM clause. Instead of loading complete object into the memory if we want to load few properties then we use SELECT clause. For example

```
String myquery ="SELECT s.rollnumber FROM Student s";
Query q=session.createQuery(myquery);
List mylist=q.list();
```

4. WHERE Clause

The WHERE clause is used to denote specific object. For example

```
String myquery ="FROM Student s WHERE s.rollnumber=1";
Query q=session.createQuery(myquery);
List mylist=q.list();
```

5. ORDER BY Clause

The ORDER BY clause is used to obtain the data in sorted order. The ASC is used to obtain the result in ascending order and DESC is used to obtain the result in descending order. For example

```
String myquery ="FROM Student s ORDER BY s.rollnumber DESC";
Query q=session.createQuery(myquery);
List mylist=q.list();
```

6. GROUP BY Clause

A query that returns aggregate values may be grouped by any property of a returned class. For example –

```
String myquery ="SELECT SUM(s.marks), s.name FROM Student s " +
 "GROUP BY s.name";
Query q=session.createQuery(myquery);
List mylist=q.list();
```

7. INSERT INTO Clause

The INSERT INTO clause is used to insert one object onto another object. For example

```
String myquery ="INSERT INTO Student (rollnumber, name,marks)"
Query q=session.createQuery(myquery);
int res=q.executeUpdate();
System.out.println("Row Inserted");
```

8. UPDATE Clause

The UPDATE clause is used to update one or more properties of the object. For example

```
String myquery ="UPDATE Student set name = :name " + "WHERE rollnumber =:roll";
Query q=session.createQuery(myquery);
q.setParameter("name",'AAA');
q.setParameter("roll",1);
int res=q.executeUpdate();
System.out.println("Row Updated");
```

9. DELETE Clause

The DELETE clause is used to delete one or more objects. For example –

```
String myquery ="DELETE FROM Student "+ "WHERE rollnumber =:roll";
Query q=session.createQuery(myquery);
q.setParameter("roll",1);
int res=q.executeUpdate();
System.out.println("Row Deleted");
```

10. Aggregate Methods

Just similar to SQL queries HQL also support for various aggregate methods such as sum, min, max and so on. These methods can be

min(Property name), max(Property name), sum(Property name), avg(Property name) and so on.

The name of these methods represent their purpose.

Review Questions

1. *What is HQL ? How does it differ from SQL ? Give its advantages.*

   GTU : Summer-13, Marks 7

2. *What is HQL ? How does it different from SQL? List its advantages.*

   GTU : Summer-16, Marks 7

❑❑❑

Notes

7 Java Web Frameworks : Spring MVC

Syllabus

Overview of Spring, Spring Architecture, bean life cycle, XML Configuration on Spring, Aspect – oriented Spring, Managing Database, Managing Transaction.

Contents

7.1 Overview of Spring . . . . **Summer-16,** · · · · · · · · · · · · · Marks 7

7.2 Spring Architecture

7.3 Creating First Application with Spring

7.4 The IoC Container

7.5 Bean Lifecycle

7.6 XML Configuration on Spring

7.7 Aspect-Oriented Spring

7.8 Managing Database

7.9 Managing Transaction

7.1 Overview of Spring

GTU : Summer-16, Marks 7

- The Spring framework is an **application framework for the Java Platform**. This is an Opensource framework which was initially designed by **Rod Johnson**. It was first released under Apache 2.0 in 2003
- The web applications are designed using the Java program and are run on the top of Java EE platform.
- Spring Framework 4.2.0 was released on 31 July 2015 and was immediately upgraded to the current latest version Spring Framework 4.2 which is released on 1st September 2015 which is compatible with Java 6,7 and 8.
- The next version of Spring Framework 4.3 is expected in March 2016.

Benefits of Spring Framework

1. It is a lightweight container framework. This framework enhances modularity and provides more readable code.
2. It provide loose coupling between different modules.
3. It supports declarative transaction, caching, validation and formatting and logging service.
4. It can be easily configured by XML Schema or annotation based style.
5. With a Dependency Injection approach, dependencies are explicit, and evident in constructor or JavaBean properties.
6. It does not require special deployment steps.
7. The spring framework is essentially a skeleton which provides solid ground work around which the application can be built.

7.1.1 Spring MVC Framework

The Spring Web model-view-controller (MVC) framework is designed around a **DispatcherServlet** that handles HTTP requests and responses, with configurable handler mappings, view resolution, locale, time zone and theme resolution as well as support for uploading files. The default handler is based on the @Controller and @RequestMapping annotations, offering a wide range of flexible handling methods.

This framework provides three important elements

Model : It is normally an application data containing POJO classes, i.e. Plain old Java Object Classes.

View : It is responsible for showing the result. This element generates the HTML output which can be displayed on client's machine.

Controller : This element is responsible for processing user requests.

Working

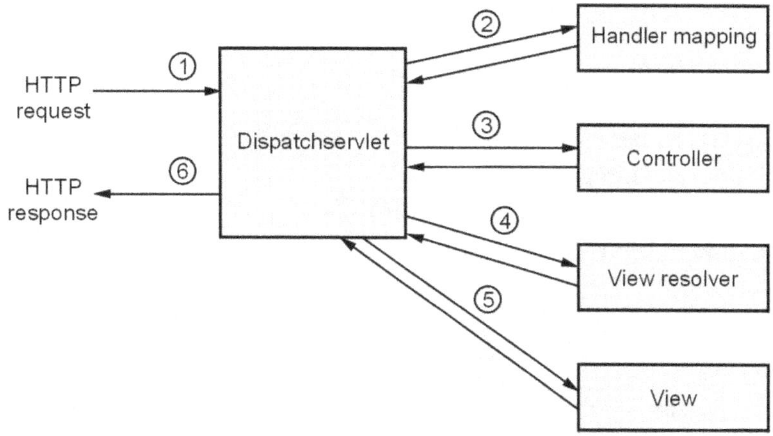

Fig. 7.1.1 MVC architecture

1. The DispatcherServlet receives the HTTP request
2. The DispatcherServlet consults HandlerMapping to call appropriate **Controller.**
3. The **Controller** takes the request and finds the appropriate service, sends GET/POST method for calling that service. This service on execution defines the business logic and returns the **view name** to DispatcherServlet.
4. Using **ViewResolver**, the DispatcherServlet will choose the appropriate **View**.
5. This **View** will then be returned to DispatchServlet to be displayed on the client's browser window.

Benefits of MVC Framework

Follwing are some advantages of having MVC framework

1. It provides clear separation of roles such as – controller, validator, model object, handler mapping, view resolver, view and so on.
2. It provides powerful and straightforward configuration of both framework and application classes as Java Beans.
3. It allows reusability of business code.
4. It also supports for customization, and application level validation.
5. It supports for simple yet powerful tag library.
6. It supports easy integration with any type of view.

Review Questions

1. *Explain benefits of Spring Framework.*
2. *Explain Spring MVC framework with suitable block diagram. Also explain the advantages of MVC architccture.*
3. *What is spring Web MVC framework? List its key features.* **GTU : Summer-16, Marks 7**

7.2 Spring Architecture

- There are around 20 modules in Spring Architecture.
- These modules are grouped into -
  - o Core Container
  - o Data Access-Integration
  - o Aspect Oriented Programming(AOP)
  - o Instrumentation
  - o Test

Let us discuss important modules of Spring Architecture

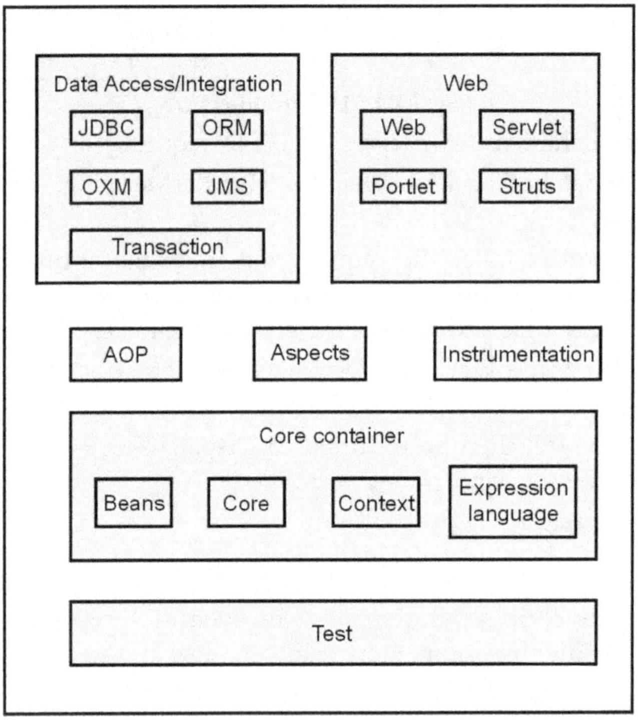

Fig. 7.2.1 Spring framework

Core Container

The important modules of core container are

1. **Core Module :** This is fundamental part of spring framework. This module consists of Dependency Injection features.
2. **Bean Module :** This module consists of BeanFactory class.
3. **Context Module :** This module is based on Core and Bean modules. The **ApplicationContext** interface is an important point in this module.
4. **Expression Language Module :** This module provide powerful expression language for manipulating an object graph at runtime.

Data Access/Integration

The important modules of Data Acccess/Integration layer are –

1. **JDBC :** When we use core JDBC programming then we have to write lot of code. The JDBC module of Spring framework removes this complexity by providing JDBC abstraction layer.
2. **ORM :** This module provide consistency to your code regardless of data access technologies. It provides code without worrying about catching exceptions specific to each persistence technology (ex: SQLException thrown by JDBC API).
3. **OXM :** It is used to converts object into XML format and vice versa. The Spring OXM provides a uniform API to access any of the OXM frameworks such as Castor, XStream, JiBX, Java API for XML and XmlBeans.
4. **Transaction :** The Transaction module supports programmatic and declarative transaction management for Plain Old Java Object (POJO) classes.

Web

It is consists of following modules

1. **Web :** This module provides the functionalities related to web. This module support the feature such as multipart file upload functionality.
2. **Web-Servlet :** This module contains the model view container based implementation for web application.
3. **Web-Struts :** This module provides the support for the integration of classic struts web tier within the spring application.
4. **Web-Portlet :** The Web-Portlet module provides the MVC implementation to be used in a portlet environment and mirrors the functionality of Web-Servlet module.

AOP

This module provide support for Aspect oriented programming implementation. You can introduce new functionalities into existing code without modifying it.

Aspects

Aspects module is a separate module which provides integration with AsepctJ.

Instrumentation

This module provides class instrumentation support and class loader implementations to be used in certain application servers.

Test

This module supports the testing of Spring components. It provides consistent loading of Spring **ApplicationContexts**.

Review Question

1. *Explain spring framework architecture with suitable block diagram.*

7.3 Creating First Application with Spring

Pre-requisite for executing Spring Applications

Following software must be installed and practiced before executing the various Spring programs in this chapter.

1. JDK for supporting Java application programs
2. Apache Web Server
3. Eclipse IDE
4. MySQL Database
5. Required Spring Jar files

Let us understand how to create the first Spring application with the help of an illustrating example -

Example 7.3.1 : *Give the stepwise implementation of simple Spring application program*

Solution :

Step 1 : Open Eclipse IDE. Go to **File** menu. Click **New->project->Java Project**. Mention the project name. I have given the project name as **SpringDemo**. Click **Finish**

Step 2 : Get and download the core jar files that are required for Spring from internet. Add these jar files to your Eclipse project using following steps

Right click on **Project->Build Path->Add External Jars**. Select the folder in which you have downloaded the jar core files for spring. Select all the Jar files and click **Open**.

Following Jar Files get added. Then Click **OK** button.

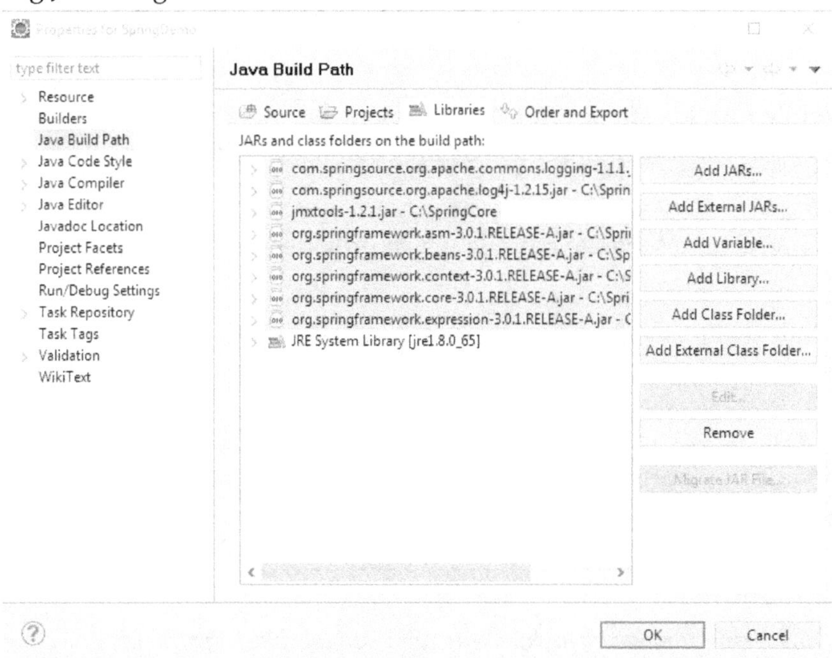

Step 3 : Now Right click on **src** and create a package. Name the package. I have given the name **com.mypackage**. Note that inside this package we are going to store two Java files. The first Java file will be our bean program and second Java file will be testing program that will invoke the method in bean program.

Java Bean is nothing but a simple Java class in which data properties and methods are stored. The method is by the set and get prefix, followed by properly with first letter of property in capital.

Let us create our first Java program i.e. the bean program. I have named it **Employee.java**

Employee.java

```
package com.mypackage;

public class Employee {
    private String empname;    // property name
    public String getEmpname() // get method with first letter capital for property
    {
        return empname; // This method returns property value
    }
    public void setEmpname(String empname) // set method
    {
        this.empname=empname; // This method sets property value
    }
    public void display()
    {
        System.out.println("Welcome "+empname);
    }
}
```

Note that in above program we have created a class named Employee. The property for this class is **empname**. Regular get and set methods for this property are written. Finally a method named **display** is defined in which the Welcome message is written. Remember that we are going to invoke this method from our second Java program which is written in step 5

Let us first define a xml file now.

Step 4 : Following is an xml document created outside the com.mypackage. For Creation of this file rightclick **src->New->Other->File.** Mention the filename with extension .xml. I have created the xml file named **empContext.xml**. The code for this is as below

empContext.xml

```
<?xml version="1.0" encoding="UTF-8"?>
  <beans
    xmlns="http://www.springframework.org/schema/beans"
```

```
    xmlns:xsi="http://www.w3.org/2001/XMLSchema-instance"
    xmlns:p="http://www.springframework.org/schema/p"
    xsi:schemaLocation="http://www.springframework.org/schema/beans
     http://www.springframework.org/schema/beans/spring-beans-3.0.xsd">

  <bean id="mybean" class="com.mypackage.Employee">
  <property name="empname" value="Sujata"></property>
  </bean>

  </beans>
```

This is a simple xml file. It performs two main tasks –(i) It gives the **id** to the bean program. I have mentioned the bean id as ***mybean***. (ii)The property value is set using the <property> tag.

Step 5 : Now it's the time to create our second Java program which is actually a test program that invokes the method defined in bean namely **display**. Note that this Java program must be created within the com.mypackage.

Welcome.java

```
package com.mypackage;
import org.springframework.beans.factory.BeanFactory;
import org.springframework.beans.factory.xml.XmlBeanFactory;
import org.springframework.core.io.ClassPathResource;
import org.springframework.core.io.Resource;
public class Welcome {
    public static void main(String args[])
    {
        Resource res=new ClassPathResource("empContext.xml");
        BeanFactory factory=new XmlBeanFactory(res);
        Employee emp=(Employee)factory.getBean("mybean");
        emp.display();
    }
}
```

The **Resource** object represents the information of **empContext.xml** file. The Resource is the interface and the **ClassPathResource** is the implementation class of the **Resource** interface.

The **BeanFactory** is required to return the bean. The **XmlBeanFactory** is the implementation class of the BeanFactory. There are various methods in the BeanFactory interface. Out of which one method is **getBean()**, which returns the object of the associated class.

Hence we are getting the object of Employee class using the getBean() method of **BeanFactory**.

Ensure the directory structure before running your application by following screenshot

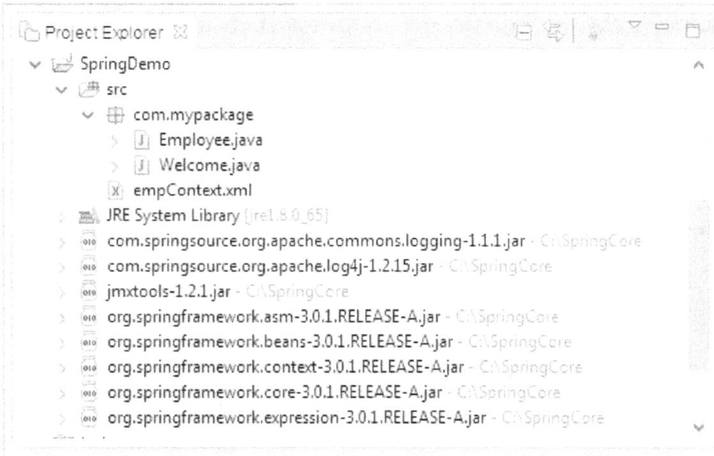

Step 6 : Right click on Welcome.java and Click on **Run As ->Java Application**. The output will be displayed on Console Window. Just refer following screenshot

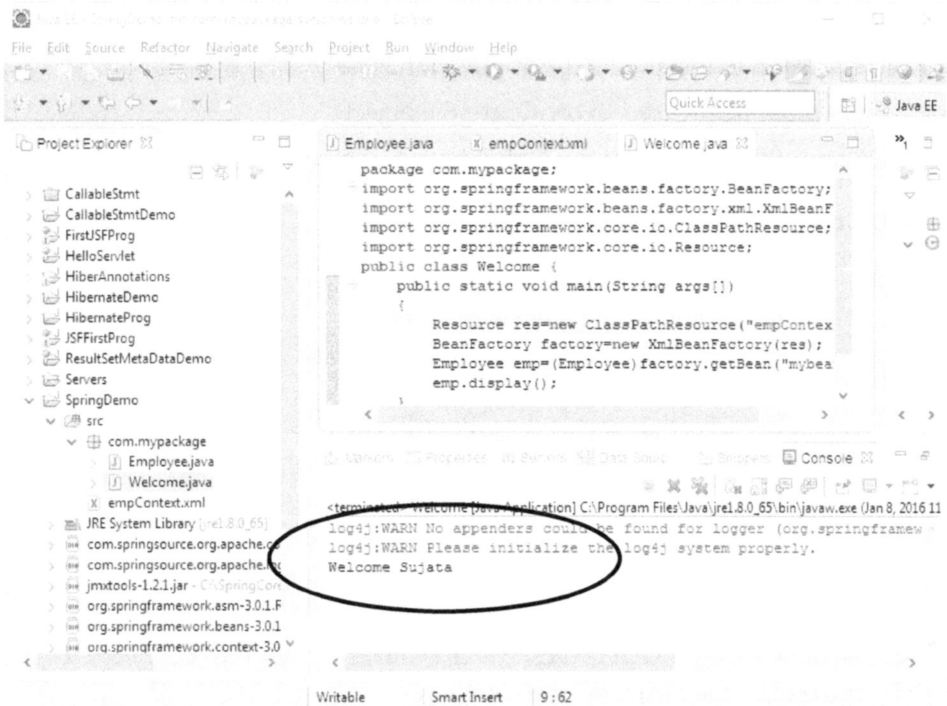

7.4 The IoC Container

- The core of spring framework is its **Inversion of Control(IoC) container**.
- The task of IoC container is to manage the Java objects from instantiation to destruction. These objects are basically called as Spring **Beans**. A Spring bean in the IoC container can typically be any POJO (plain old java object).

- The container gets its instructions about which are those objects to instantiate, configure, and assemble by reading configuration **metadata** provided. The configuration metadata can be represented either by XML, Java annotations, or Java code.
- The application POJO classes and configuration metadata are combined to have a fully configured and executable system or application ready for work.
- The Fig. 7.4.1 represents the role of IOC container in Spring framework.

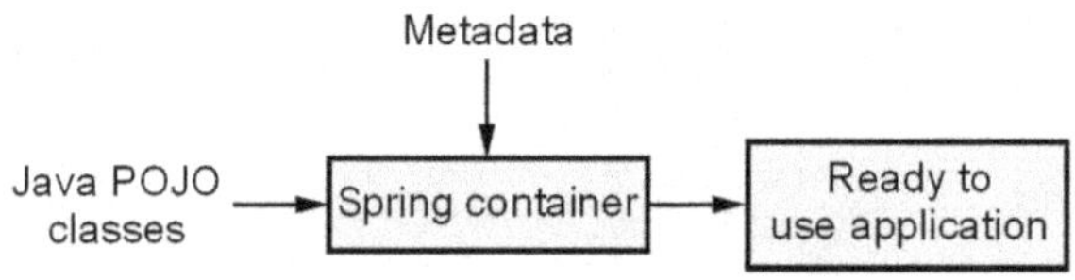

Fig. 7.4.1 Role of IoC container

Functions of IoC Container

The main tasks performed by IoC container are :

1. It is useful to instantiate the application class
2. The container is used to configure the object
3. It is useful to assemble the dependencies between the objects

Types of IoC Container

There are two types of IoC containers. They are :

1. BeanFactory 2. ApplicationContext

1. BeanFactory

The org.springframework.beans.factory.**BeanFactory** acts as IoC container. The **XmlBeanFactory** is implementation class for **BeanFactory** interface. For using the **BeanFactory** we need to get the instance of **XmlBeanFactory**. Following code is used for this purpose

```
Resource res=new ClassPathResource(name of context xml file);
        BeanFactory factory=new XmlBeanFactory(res);
```

The **XmlBeanFactory** class receives the **Resource** object so we need to pass the resource object to create the object of **BeanFactory.**

2. ApplicationContext

The org.springframework.context.**ApplicationContext** interfaces acts as the IoC container. The **ClassPathXmlApplicationContext** class is the implementation class of **ApplicationContext** interface.

The instance of **ClassPathXmlApplicationContext** class is required to create an instance of **ApplicationContext**. Following code is used for this purpose

```
ApplicationContext context = new ClassPathXmlApplicationContext(name of context xml file);
```

The *ApplicationContext* container includes all functionality of the *BeanFactory* container, so it is generally recommended over the *BeanFactory*. The **BeanFactory** can still be used for lightweight applications like mobile devices or applet based applications.

Review Question

1. *Write short note on IoC container.*

7.5 Bean Lifecycle

During the Bean Lifecycle there are two important phases- instantiation phase in which the initialization of bean is done and destruction or removal of bean in which cleanup is done.

We declare bean using <bean> along with the **init-method** and **destroy-method** parameters.

These methods can be defined as

```
public class BeanProgram {
...
...
    public void init() {
        // do some initialization work
    }
    public void destroy() {
        // do some cleanup work
    }
...
}
```

Following is a simple Spring application that illustrates the Bean life cycle.

Example 7.5.1 : *Implement the Spring Bean Lifecyle methods.*

Solution :

Step 1 : Open Eclipse IDE. Go to File menu. Click **New->project->Java Project**. Mention the project name. I have given the project name as **BeanDemo**. Click Finish

Step 2 : Get and download the core jar files that are required for Spring. Add these jar files to your Eclipse project using following steps

Right click on **Project->Build Path->Add External Jars**. Select the folder in which you have downloaded the jar core files for spring. Select all the Jar files and click **Open**.

Step 3 : Now Right click on **src** and create a package. Name the package. I have given the name **com.mypackage**. Note that inside this package we are going to store two Java files.

The first Java file will be our bean program and second Java file will be testing program that will invoke the method in bean program.

Let us create our first Java program i.e. the bean program. I have named it **BeanProgram.java**

BeanProgram.java

```
package com.mypackage;

public class BeanProgram {
    private String msg;
    public void setMsg(String msg) {
        this.msg=msg;
    }
    public void getMsg() {
        System.out.println("The message is: "+msg);
    }
    public void init(){
        System.out.println("Inside the init() method of Bean!!");
    }
    public void destroy() {
        System.out.println("Destroying Bean, Now!!");
    }
}
```

Let us first define an xml file now.

Step 4 : Following is an xml document created outside the com.mypackage. For Creation of this file rightclick **src->New->Other->File**. Mention the filename with extension .xml. I have created the xml file named **BeanContext.xml**. The code for this is as below

BeanContext.xml

```
<?xml version="1.0" encoding="UTF-8"?>

<beans xmlns="http://www.springframework.org/schema/beans"
  xmlns:xsi="http://www.w3.org/2001/XMLSchema-instance"
  xsi:schemaLocation="http://www.springframework.org/schema/beans
  http://www.springframework.org/schema/beans/spring-beans-3.0.xsd">

  <bean id="mybeanid"
    class="com.mypackage.BeanProgram"
    init-method="init" destroy-method="destroy">
    <property name="msg" value="Welcome, Introducing Bean Life Cycle"/>
  </bean>
</beans>
```

Step 5 : Now it's the time to create our second Java program which is actually a test program that invokes the method defined in bean methods. Note that this Java program must be created within the com.mypackage.

TestBean.java

```
package com.mypackage;
import org.springframework.context.support.AbstractApplicationContext;
import org.springframework.context.support.ClassPathXmlApplicationContext;
public class TestBean {
    public static void main(String[] args) {
        AbstractApplicationContext context=new
ClassPathXmlApplicationContext("BeanContext.xml");
        BeanProgram obj = (BeanProgram) context.getBean("mybeanid");
      obj.getMsg();
      context.registerShutdownHook();
    }
}
```

Note that we have used **ApplicationContext** IoC container to invoke the bean methods.

Step 6 : Right click **on TestBean.java** and Click on **Run As ->Java Application**. The output will be displayed on Console Window. Just refer following screenshot

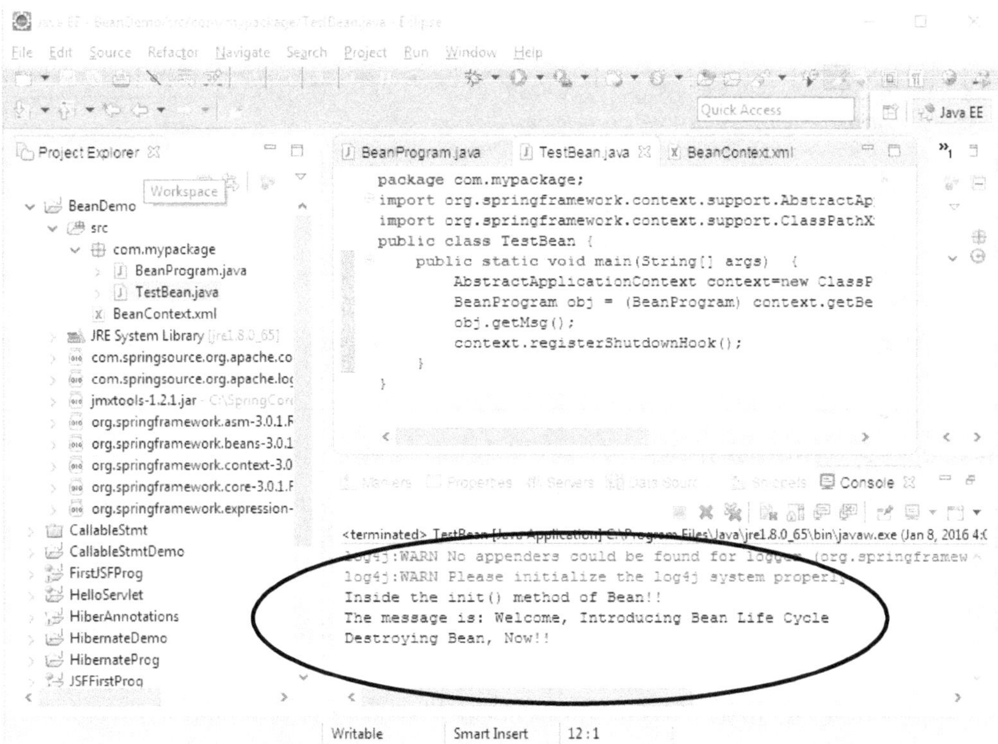

Review Question

1. *Explain Bean life cycle in Spring framework.*

7.6 XML Configuration on Spring

The Configuration file is an XML file in Spring. It binds the bean classes together.

When Spring application gets loaded into the memory, Framework makes use of the the XML configuration file to create all the beans defined and assign them a unique ID as defined in **<bean>** tag. You can use **<property>** tag to pass the values of different variables used at the time of object creation.

Here is an example of XML configuration file -

empContext.xml

```
<?xml version="1.0" encoding="UTF-8"?>
  <beans
    xmlns="http://www.springframework.org/schema/beans"
    xmlns:xsi="http://www.w3.org/2001/XMLSchema-instance"
    xmlns:p="http://www.springframework.org/schema/p"
    xsi:schemaLocation="http://www.springframework.org/schema/beans
     http://www.springframework.org/schema/beans/spring-beans-3.0.xsd">

  <bean id="mybean" class="com.mypackage.Employee">
  <property name="empname" value="Sujata"></property>
  </bean>

  </beans>
```

Bean ID is given

Bean Class Name

Value Assigned to Bean Property

Property of Bean

Review Question

1. *Explain XML configuration file in Spring framework with an example. What is the need for this file ?*

7.7 Aspect-Oriented Spring

Aspect Oriented Programming(AOP) is one of the important module in Spring Framework. This type of programming is another way of thinking about program structure.

Aspect oriented programming complements the object oriented programming. The key unit in OOP is **class** and in AOP is **aspect**.

Aspects enable the modularization of concerns such as transaction management that cut across multiple types and objects. The most prominent example of a crosscutting concern is **logging**. Logging is used mainly for debugging and troubleshooting issues mainly by tracing method calls and overall execution flow. It qualifies as a crosscutting concern because a logging strategy necessarily affects every logged part of the system. Logging thereby crosscuts all logged classes and methods.

Here are some important terminologies used in AOP. Let us get introduced with them

Terminologies	Purpose
Aspect	A module which has a set of APIs providing cross-cutting requirements. aspects are implemented using regular classes.
Join point	Join point is any point in your program such as method execution, exception handling, field access etc. Spring supports only method execution join point.
Advice	Advice represents an action taken by an aspect at a particular join point. There are different types of advices : • **Before Advice :** It executes before a join point. • **After Returning Advice :** It executes after a joint point completes normally. • **After Throwing Advice :** It executes if method exits by throwing an exception. • **After (finally) Advice :** It executes after a join point regardless of join point exit whether normally or exceptional return. • **Around Advice :** It executes before and after a join point.
Pointcut	It is an expression language of AOP that matches join points.
Introduction	It allows you to add new methods or attributes to existing classes.
Target object	This object is advised by one or more aspects. It is also known as proxied object in Spring
Weaving	Weaving is the process of linking aspects with other application types or objects to create an advised object. Weaving can be done at compile time, load time, or at runtime.

How to write Spring AOP ?

There are two ways of using Spring AOP –

i) Schema-based approach   ii) @AspectJ annotation style.

Let us discuss them in detail.

i) Schema Based Approach

Step 1 : XML Schema :

The most important file in this AOP implementation is its xml file. First of all we need to import the spring AOP schema as below

```
<?xml version="1.0" encoding="UTF-8"?>
<beans xmlns="http://www.springframework.org/schema/beans"
```

```
xmlns:xsi="http://www.w3.org/2001/XMLSchema-instance"
xmlns:aop="http://www.springframework.org/schema/aop"
xsi:schemaLocation="http://www.springframework.org/schema/beans
http://www.springframework.org/schema/beans/spring-beans-3.0.xsd
http://www.springframework.org/schema/aop
http://www.springframework.org/schema/aop/spring-aop-3.0.xsd ">
```

Step 2 : Declaration of Aspect

Then we need **to declare aspect**. The aspect can be declared using **<aop:aspect>** tag which is written within **<aop:config> </aop:config>**

```
<aop:config>
   <aop:aspect id="myaspectid" ref="mybean">
    ...
    ...

   </aop:aspect>
  </aop:config>

<bean id="mybean" class="..."/>
```

Step 3 : Pointcut Delaration

It is an expression language of AOP that matches join points. Join point is any point in your program such as method execution. The Join points are for the methods that are executed with different advices. These methods are determined using Pointcut. The pointcut will be executed with following syntax.

```
<aop:pointcut id=idname expression = execution(business Servicename)/>
```

For example- The code in XML file can be

```
<aop:config>
   <aop:aspect id="myaspect" ref="registration">
     <aop:pointcut id="pointCutID"
expression="execution(* com.mypackage.*.*(..))"/>
     ...
     ...
       ...

   </aop:aspect>
  </aop:config>
```

The *.* in above **execution** method represent execution of all the properties. We can restrict this execution to specific property.

Step 4 : Declaring Advices

Advice represents an action taken by an aspect at a particular join point.The advice can be declared inside **<aop:aspect>** tag.The syntax is

```
<aop:aspect>
        <aop:method1 name  ... />
        <aop:method2 name  ... />
        ...
</aop:aspect>
```

For example - Following boldfaced code represent the declaration of advices. The appropriate methods will be invokes and executed for each advice.

```
<aop:config>
   <aop:aspect id="myaspect" ref="registration">
     <aop:pointcut id="pointCutID"
expression="execution(* com.mypackage.*.*(..))"/>
     <aop:before pointcut-ref="pointCutID" method="beforeAdvice"/>
     <aop:after pointcut-ref="pointCutID" method="afterAdvice"/>
     <aop:after-returning pointcut-ref="pointCutID"  returning="ret"
method="afterReturningAdvice"/>
     <aop:after-throwing pointcut-ref="pointCutID"  throwing ="myexception"
method="AfterThrowingAdvice"/>
     </aop:aspect>
  </aop:config>
```

Let us now understand the above discussion by execution following example.

Example 7.7.1 : *Implement Aspect Oriented Programming in Spring using XML based Schema*

Solution :

Step 1 : Open Eclipse IDE. Go to **File** menu. Click **New->project->Java Project**. Mention the project name. I have given the project name as **AOPXMLBasedDemo**. Click **Finish**

Step 2 : Get and download the core jar files that are required for Spring. The two types of Jar files are required AOP and Core Jar files(Following Screenshot illustrates the names of these Jar files. You can get it downloaded from Internet). Add these jar files to your Eclipse project using following steps

Right click on **Project->Build Path->Add External Jars**. Select the folder in which you have downloaded the jar core files for spring. Select all the Jar files and click **Open**.

The most important jar files are

- aspectjrt.jar
- aspectjweaver.jar
- aspectj.jar
- aopalliance.jar

Following Jar Files get added. Then Click **OK** button.

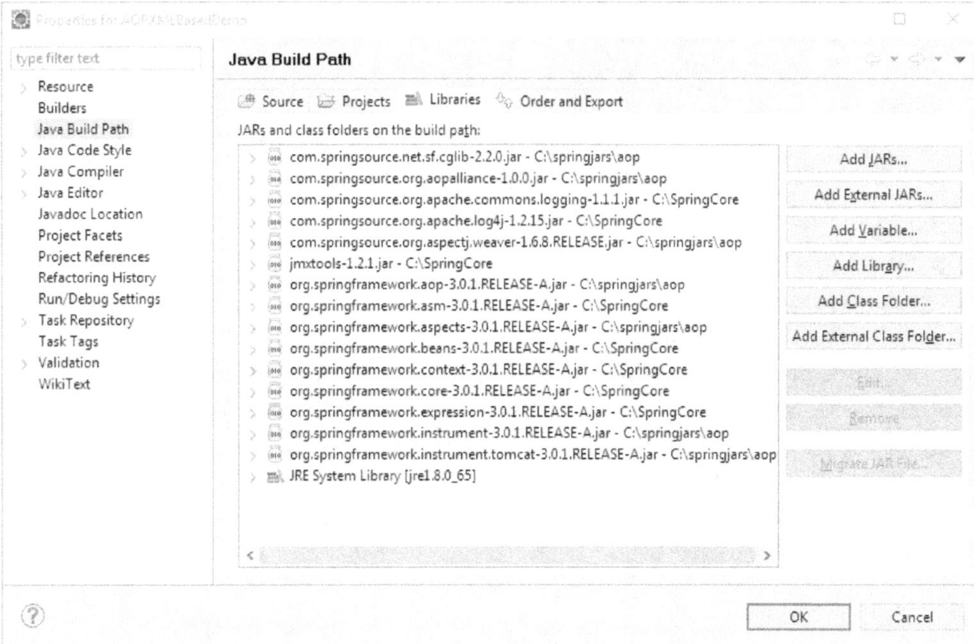

Step 3 : Now Right click on src and create a package. Name the package. I have given the name **com.mypackage**. Note that inside this package we are going to store the required Java files. The first Java file will be our bean program(Employee.java), the second Jar file will store the methods(Registration.java) that will be executed on AOP method invocation and third Java file will be testing program(TestApplication.java) that will invoke the method in bean program and AOP methods

Let us create our first Java program i.e. the bean program.

Employee.java

```
package com.mypackage;

public class Employee {
    private Integer empid;
    private String empname;
    public Integer getEmpid() {
        System.out.println("EmpID: "+empid);
        return empid;
    }
    public void setEmpid(Integer empid) {
        this.empid = empid;
    }
    public String getEmpname() {
        System.out.println("EmpName: "+empname);
        return empname;
```

```
    }
    public void setEmpname(String empname) {
        this.empname = empname;
    }
    public void printThrowException(){
        System.out.println("Exception raised");
        throw new IllegalArgumentException();
    }
}
```

Registration.java

```
package com.mypackage;

public class Registration {
    public void beforeAdvice()
    {

        System.out.println("Registering the Employee Profile...");
    }
    public void afterAdvice()
    {
        System.out.println("Registered the Employee Profile...");
    }
    public void afterReturningAdvice(Object ret)
    {
        System.out.println("Returning from Registration Process:\n Return Value =
"+ret.toString());

    }
    public void AfterThrowingAdvice(IllegalArgumentException myexception)
    {
        System.out.println("In AferMethod:Raised Exception!!!  "+myexception.toString());
    }
}
```

Step 4 : Following is an xml document created outside the com.mypackage. For Creation of this file rightclick **src->New->Other->File**. Mention the filename with extension .xml. I have created the xml file named **BeanContext.xml**. This is the file in which Schema based AOP is defined.

The code for this is as below

BeanContext.xml

```
<?xml version="1.0" encoding="UTF-8"?>
<beans xmlns="http://www.springframework.org/schema/beans"
  xmlns:xsi="http://www.w3.org/2001/XMLSchema-instance"
  xmlns:aop="http://www.springframework.org/schema/aop"
  xsi:schemaLocation="http://www.springframework.org/schema/beans
```

```
  http://www.springframework.org/schema/beans/spring-beans-3.0.xsd
  http://www.springframework.org/schema/aop
  http://www.springframework.org/schema/aop/spring-aop-3.0.xsd ">

  <aop:config>
    <aop:aspect id="myaspect" ref="registration">
      <aop:pointcut id="pointCutID"
expression="execution(* com.mypackage.*.*(..))"/>
      <aop:before pointcut-ref="pointCutID" method="beforeAdvice"/>
      <aop:after pointcut-ref="pointCutID" method="afterAdvice"/>
      <aop:after-returning pointcut-ref="pointCutID" returning="ret"
method="afterReturningAdvice"/>
      <aop:after-throwing pointcut-ref="pointCutID" throwing ="myexception"
method="AfterThrowingAdvice"/>

    </aop:aspect>
  </aop:config>

  <!-- Definition for employee bean -->
  <bean id="myempbean" class="com.mypackage.Employee">
    <property name="empid" value="1001" />
    <property name="empname" value="Shilpa"/>
  </bean>

  <!-- Definition for registration aspect -->
  <bean id="registration" class="com.mypackage.Registration"/>

</beans>
```

Step 5 : We will now create the testing program. I have named it as **TestApplication.java**. This file invokes the schema based XML file and access the bean program for its method invocation

TestApplication.java

```
package com.mypackage;
import org.springframework.context.ApplicationContext;
import org.springframework.context.support.ClassPathXmlApplicationContext;
public class TestApplication {
    public static void main(String[] args)
    {
        ApplicationContext context=new
ClassPathXmlApplicationContext("BeanContext.xml");
        Employee emp=(Employee)context.getBean("myempbean");
        emp.getEmpid();
        emp.getEmpname();
        try {
        emp.printThrowException();
```

```
        }catch(Exception e){}
    }

}
```

Step 6 : Right click on **TestApplication.java** and Click on **Run As ->Java Application**. The output will be displayed on Console Window. Just refer following screenshot

Output

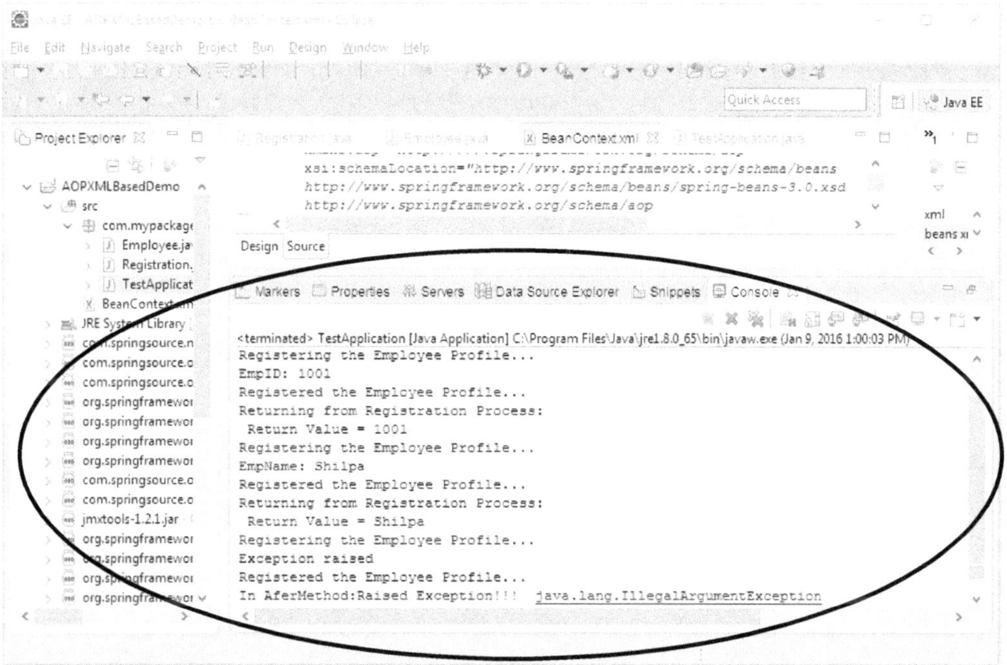

As we have mentioned *.*(..) in the execution method, we get the display of all the properties(Both empid as well as empname) for AOP methods(before, after, after-returning and after-throwingAdvice)

```
    <aop:aspect id="myaspect" ref="registration">
      <aop:pointcut id="pointCutID"
expression="execution(* com.mypackage.*.*(..))"/>
```

We can restrict this execution to one property i.e empname. For that purpose you have to simply make following changes in the BeanContext.xml file

BeanContext.xml

```
<?xml version="1.0" encoding="UTF-8"?>
<beans xmlns="http://www.springframework.org/schema/beans"
  xmlns:xsi="http://www.w3.org/2001/XMLSchema-instance"
  xmlns:aop="http://www.springframework.org/schema/aop"
  xsi:schemaLocation="http://www.springframework.org/schema/beans
  http://www.springframework.org/schema/beans/spring-beans-3.0.xsd
  http://www.springframework.org/schema/aop
  http://www.springframework.org/schema/aop/spring-aop-3.0.xsd ">
```

```
  <aop:config>
    <aop:aspect id="myaspect" ref="registration">

      <aop:pointcut id="pointCutID"
expression= "execution(* com.mypackage.Employee.getEmpname(..))"/>

      <aop:before pointcut-ref="pointCutID" method="beforeAdvice"/>
      <aop:after pointcut-ref="pointCutID" method="afterAdvice"/>
      <aop:after-returning pointcut-ref="pointCutID"  returning="ret"
method="afterReturningAdvice"/>
      <aop:after-throwing pointcut-ref="pointCutID"  throwing ="myexception"
method="AfterThrowingAdvice"/>

    </aop:aspect>
  </aop:config>

  <!-- Definition for employee bean -->
  <bean id="myempbean" class="com.mypackage.Employee">
    <property name="empid"  value="1001" />
    <property name="empname"  value="Shilpa"/>
  </bean>

  <!-- Definition for registration aspect -->
  <bean id="registration" class="com.mypackage.Registration"/>

</beans>
```

Now the output will be

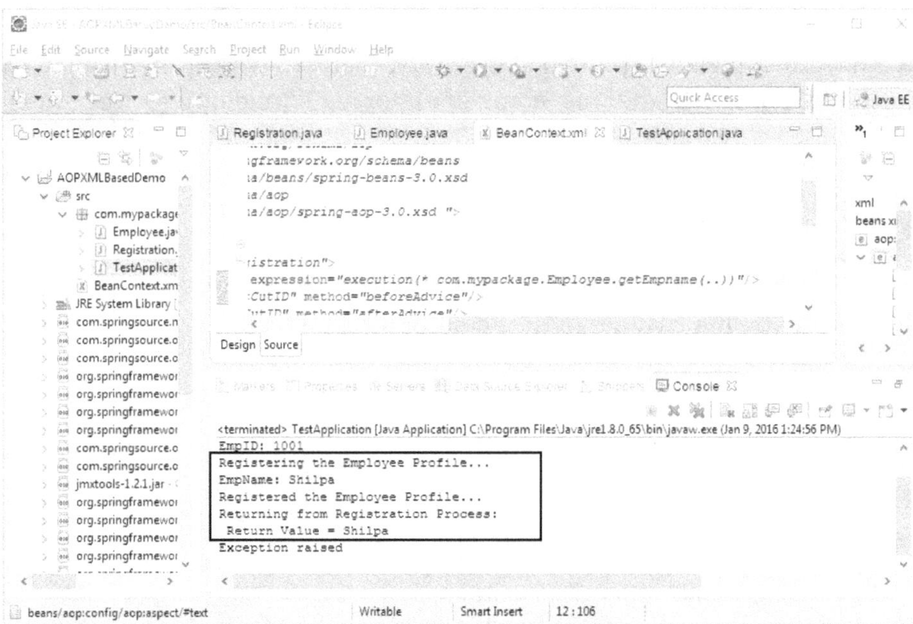

Note that The beforeAdvice, afterAdvice, afterReturnAdvice methods are invoked for **empname** property and not for **empid** as we have set the execution property to **Employee.getEmpname**. Thus we can point cut the aspect to certain property.

@AspectJ annotation style

Step 1 : Declaring aspectj-autoproxy

When the @AspectJ annotation is used the XML file gets simplified with simplest declaration as

```
<aop:aspectj-autoproxy/>
```

Step 2 : Declaration of Aspect

The aspect can be declared using the annotation @Aspect. For example

```
@Aspect
public class Registration {
...
...
}
```

This will be configured in the XML file as

```
<bean id="registration" class="com.mypackage.Registration"/>
```

Step 3 : Pointcut Delaration

The pointcut help to determine the join point methods. Using annotation @Pointcut the pointcut declaration can be done. For example

```
@Pointcut("execution(* com.mypackage.*.*(..))")
    private void myMethod(){}//pointcut name
```

Step 4 : Declaring Advices

Various advices using @Advicename for various advice methods can be defined. For example

```
@Before("myMethod()")
    public void beforeAdvice()
    {

        //method body
    }
    @After("myMethod()")
    public void afterAdvice()
    {
        //method body
    }
```

Let us now understand the above discussion by execution following example.

Example 7.7.2 : *Implement Aspect Oriented Programming in Spring using @AspectJ annotation style*

Solution :

Step 1 : Open Eclipse IDE. Go to **File** menu. Click **New->project->Java Project**. Mention the project name. I have given the project name as **AOPAnnotationDemo**. Click **Finish**

Step 2 : Get and download the core jar files that are required for Spring. The two types of Jar files are required AOP and Core Jar files. Add these jar files to your Eclipse project using following steps

Right click on **Project->Build Path->Add External Jars**. Select the folder in which you have downloaded the jar core files for spring. Select all the Jar files and click **Open.**

The most important jar files are

- aspectjrt.jar
- aspectjweaver.jar
- aspectj.jar
- aopalliance.jar

Then Click **OK** button.

Step 3 : Now Right click on **src** and create a package. Name the package. I have given the name **com.mypackage**. Note that inside this package we are going to store the required Java files. The first Java file will be our bean program(Employee.java), the second Jar file will store the methods(Registration.java) that contains the annotations, and third Java file will be testing program(TestApplication.java) that will invoke the method in bean program and AOP methods

Let us create our first Java program i.e. the bean program.

Employee.java

```
package com.mypackage;

public class Employee {
      private Integer empid;
      private String empname;
      public Integer getEmpid() {
            System.out.println("EmpID: "+empid);
            return empid;
      }
      public void setEmpid(Integer empid) {
            this.empid = empid;
      }
      public String getEmpname() {
```

```
        System.out.println("EmpName: "+empname);
        return empname;
    }
    public void setEmpname(String empname) {
        this.empname = empname;
    }
     public void printThrowException(){
          System.out.println("Exception raised");
        throw new IllegalArgumentException();
      }
}
```

Registration.java

```
package com.mypackage;
import org.aspectj.lang.annotation.After;
import org.aspectj.lang.annotation.AfterReturning;
import org.aspectj.lang.annotation.AfterThrowing;
import org.aspectj.lang.annotation.Aspect;
import org.aspectj.lang.annotation.Before;
import org.aspectj.lang.annotation.Pointcut;

@Aspect
public class Registration {
    @Pointcut("execution(* com.mypackage.*.*(..))")
    private void myMethod(){}//pointcut name
    @Before("myMethod()")
    public void beforeAdvice()
    {

        System.out.println("Registering the Employee Profile...");
    }
    @After("myMethod()")
    public void afterAdvice()
    {
        System.out.println("Registered the Employee Profile...");
    }
    @AfterReturning(pointcut="myMethod()", returning ="ret")
    public void afterReturningAdvice(Object ret)
    {
        System.out.println("Returning from Registration Process:\n Return Value =
"+ret.toString());

    }
    @AfterThrowing(pointcut="myMethod()", throwing ="myexception")
    public void AfterThrowingAdvice(IllegalArgumentException myexception)
    {
```

```
        System.out.println("In AfterMethod:Raised Exception!!! "+myexception.toString());
    }
}
```

Step 4 : Following is an xml document created outside the **com.mypackage**. For Creation of this file rightclick **src->New->Other->File**. Mention the filename with extension .xml. I have created the xml file named **BeanContext.xml**. This is the file in which Schema based AOP is defined.

The code for this is as below

BeanContext.xml

```
<?xml version="1.0" encoding="UTF-8"?>
<beans xmlns="http://www.springframework.org/schema/beans"
  xmlns:xsi="http://www.w3.org/2001/XMLSchema-instance"
  xmlns:aop="http://www.springframework.org/schema/aop"
  xsi:schemaLocation="http://www.springframework.org/schema/beans
  http://www.springframework.org/schema/beans/spring-beans-3.0.xsd
  http://www.springframework.org/schema/aop
  http://www.springframework.org/schema/aop/spring-aop-3.0.xsd ">

  <aop:aspectj-autoproxy/>

   <!-- Definition for employee bean -->
  <bean id="myempbean" class="com.mypackage.Employee">
    <property name="empid" value="1001" />
    <property name="empname" value="Shilpa"/>
  </bean>

  <!-- Definition for registration aspect -->
  <bean id="registration" class="com.mypackage.Registration"/>

</beans>
```

Step 5 : We will now create the testing program. I have named it as **TestApplication.java**. This file invokes the schema based XML file and access the bean program for its method invocation

TestApplication.java

```
package com.mypackage;

import org.springframework.context.ApplicationContext;
import org.springframework.context.support.ClassPathXmlApplicationContext;

public class TestApplication {
    public static void main(String[] args)
```

```
    {
        ApplicationContext context=new
ClassPathXmlApplicationContext("BeanContext.xml");
        Employee emp=(Employee)context.getBean("myempbean");
        emp.getEmpid();
        emp.getEmpname();
        try {
        emp.printThrowException();
        }catch(Exception e){}
    }

}
```

Step 6 : Right click on **TestApplication.java** and Click on **Run As ->Java Application**. The output will be displayed on Console Window. It will be

```
Registering the Employee Profile...
EmpID: 1001
Registered the Employee Profile...
Returning from Registration Process:
 Return Value = 1001
Registering the Employee Profile...
EmpName: Shilpa
Registered the Employee Profile...
Returning from Registration Process:
 Return Value = Shilpa
Registering the Employee Profile...
Exception raised
Registered the Employee Profile...
In AfterMethod:Raised Exception!!! java.lang.IllegalArgumentException
```

7.8 Managing Database

Spring framework provides convenient **JdbcTemplate** class for performing all Database related operation. This is the central framework class that manages all the database communication and exception handling.

JdbcTemplate requires a DataSource which is **javax.sql.DataSource** implementation

The JdbcTemplate class executes various types of SQL queries. It also handles the exceptions.

For using the The JdbcTemplate class it is necessary to configure the **DataSource** in a Spring Configurable file. The data-source is the one interacting with the JDBC driver to obtain the connection. Then DataSource bean is shared into the Data Access Object (DAO) classes and the JdbcTemplate is created in the setter for the DataSource.

The DAO i.e. Data Access Object is an object which is commonly used for interaction with the databases. The DAO is created in order to read from or write to databases. It provides consistent way to interact with the database.

Here is a procedure to set up the communication between JdbcTemplate class and backend database.

Step 1 :

Create a database using suitable DBMS package such as MySQL, ORACLE and so on. I have used MySql. Create a table inside this database.

Step 2 :

We need to supply a DataSource to the JdbcTemplate so it can configure itself to get database access. You can configure the DataSource in the XML file. Spring provides an inbuilt data-sources using **org.springframework.jdbc.datasource.DriverManagerDataSource**. It returns **a new connection every time the application requests a new connection**. The code for this can be written as

```
<bean id="ds" class="org.springframework.jdbc.datasource.DriverManagerDataSource">
```

Here is an XML file which is configured for establishing connection using datasource with MySQL database. Here the database which I have created is *department_database.*

```
<bean id="ds" class="org.springframework.jdbc.datasource.DriverManagerDataSource">

  <property name="driverClassName" value="com.mysql.jdbc.Driver"/>
  <property name="url" value="jdbc:mysql://localhost:3306/department_database"/>
  <property name="username" value="root"/>
  <property name="password" value=""/>
</bean>
```

Step 3 : The SQL queries can be executed using the JdbcTemplate methods. We can invoke the insert, delete, update methods for database tables using the object of JdbcTemplate class. For example

```
String query="insert into department values('"+d.getId()+"','"+d.getDeptname()+"')";
return jdbcTemplate.update(query);

String query="update department set deptname='"+d.getDeptname()+"' where
id='"+d.getId()+"' ";
return jdbcTemplate.update(query);

String query="delete from department where id='"+d.getId()+"' ";
return jdbcTemplate.update(query);
```

Typically a Java class for DAO is created in Spring and then above methods are written in it.

Let us understand how to manage database in Spring with some illustrating example

Example 7.8.1 : *Implement database connection using Spring framework*

Solution :

Step 1 : Create a Database. I have created a database named **department_database.** Inside this database create a table with suitable field names. I have created a table named **department** with two fields **id** and **deptname**.

Step 2 : Open Eclipse IDE. Go to **File** menu. Click **New->project->Java Project** Mention the project name. I have given the project name as DBMSDemo. Click **Finish**

Step 3 : Get and download the core jar files that are required for Spring. It also require the following jar files to be included –

- org.springframework.jdbc.jar
- org.springframework.transaction.jar
- Also include the mysql-connectior-java.jar file.

How to include these jar files ?

Right click on **Project->Build Path->Add External Jars**. Select the folder in which you have downloaded the jar core files for spring. Select all the Jar files and click **Open**. **Here is a Screenshot that shows the jar files added required for the project.**

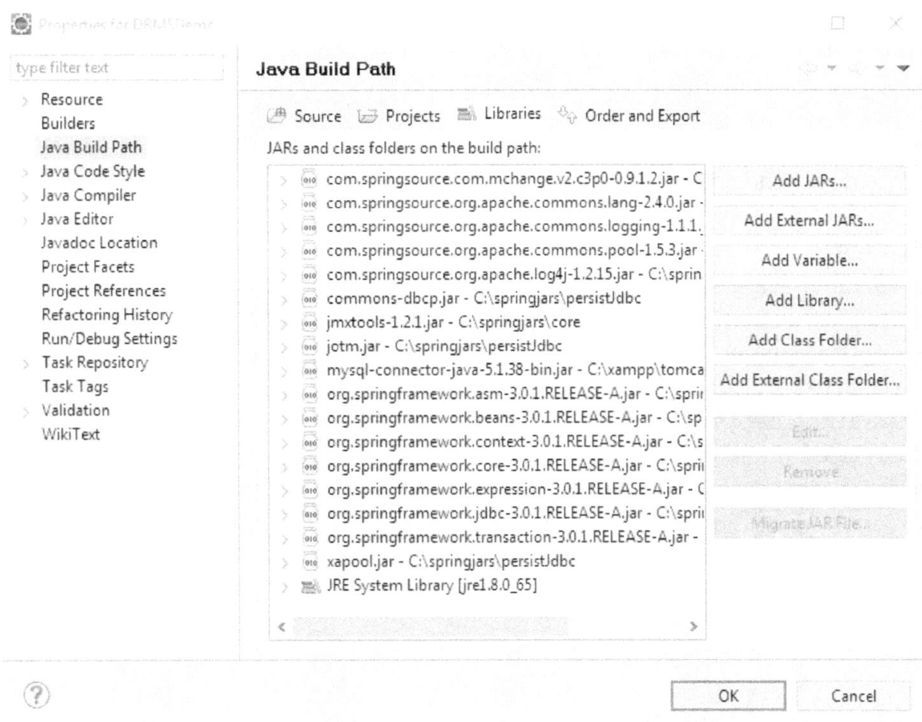

Step 4 : Now Right click on **src** and create a package. Name the package. I have given the name **com.mypackage**. Note that inside this package we are going to store the required Java files.

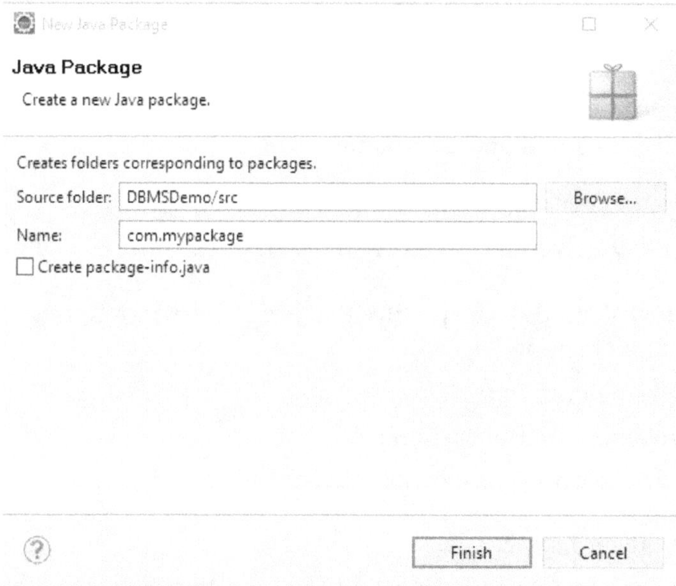

We will create a Java class file named **Department.java** which is actually a bean program. The getter and setter methods for the database fields are written within it.

The second type of Java class file, I have named it as **DepartmentDao.java.** This is a simple Java file in which the SQL queries are executed using the JdbcTemplate class object.

The third Java class file is for testing the application. This file we will discuss in Step 6. Let us write down the code for the first two Java files. Here is the code for them.

Department.java

```
package com.mypackage;

public class Department {
    private int id;
    private String deptname;
    public Department() {}
    public Department(int id, String deptname) {
        this.id = id;
        this.deptname = deptname;
    }
    public int getId() {
        return id;
    }
    public void setId(int id) {
```

```
        this.id = id;
    }
    public String getDeptname() {

        return deptname;
    }
    public void setDeptname(String deptname) {
        this.deptname = deptname;
    }
}
```

DepartmentDao.java

```
package com.mypackage;
import org.springframework.jdbc.core.JdbcTemplate;

public class DepartmentDao {
    private JdbcTemplate jdbcTemplate;
    public void setJdbcTemplate(JdbcTemplate jdbcTemplate) {
        this.jdbcTemplate = jdbcTemplate;

    }
    public int insertDepartment(Department d){

        String query="insert into department
values('"+d.getId()+"','"+d.getDeptname()+"')";
        return jdbcTemplate.update(query);
    }
    public int updateDepartment(Department d){

        String query="update department set deptname='"+d.getDeptname()+"' where
id='"+d.getId()+"' ";
        return jdbcTemplate.update(query);
    }
    public int deleteDepartment(Department d){

        String query="delete from department where id='"+d.getId()+"' ";
        return jdbcTemplate.update(query);
    }
}
```

Step 5 : We will now write down the configuration file in XML. It created outside the **com.mypackage**. For Creation of this file rightclick **src->New->Other->File**. Mention the filename with extension .xml. I have created the xml file named **BeanContext.xml**. This is the file in which data source is initialized. The connection with MySQL database is established.

The code for this is as below

BeanContext.xml

```
<?xml version="1.0" encoding="UTF-8"?>
<beans xmlns="http://www.springframework.org/schema/beans"
  xmlns:xsi="http://www.w3.org/2001/XMLSchema-instance"
  xsi:schemaLocation="http://www.springframework.org/schema/beans
  http://www.springframework.org/schema/beans/spring-beans-3.0.xsd ">

  <!-- Initialization for data source -->
  <bean id="ds"  class="org.springframework.jdbc.datasource.DriverManagerDataSource">
    <property name="driverClassName" value="com.mysql.jdbc.Driver"/>
    <property name="url" value="jdbc:mysql://localhost:3306/department_database"/>
    <property name="username" value="root"/>
    <property name="password" value=""/>
  </bean>
   <bean id="jdbcTemplate" class="org.springframework.jdbc.core.JdbcTemplate">
   <property name="dataSource" ref="ds"></property>
   </bean>
   <bean id="deptdao" class="com.mypackage.DepartmentDao">
   <property name="jdbcTemplate" ref="jdbcTemplate"></property>
   </bean>
</beans>
```

Step 6 : It is the time to create the testing file for the application. This is the file in which the queries are actually invoked by providing the values to them. Using the **ApplicationContext**, the configuration file is invoked and then using the **getBean** method for DAO Java class file(In this example it is DepartmentDao) the bean class is referred. The code for **insert query** is written in the following testing application Java file. Here is the code.

TestApplication.java

```
package com.mypackage;
import org.springframework.context.ApplicationContext;
import org.springframework.context.support.ClassPathXmlApplicationContext;

public class TestApplication {
        public static void main(String[] args) {
                ApplicationContext context=new
ClassPathXmlApplicationContext("BeanContext.xml");
                DepartmentDao dao= (DepartmentDao)context.getBean("deptdao");
                int status=dao.insertDepartment(new Department(1003,"Purchase"));
                if(status==1)
                    System.out.println("Record Inserted in database");
        }
    }
```

You can also perform the Update and Delete operations in the testing program

For updation of record

Following code can be written if we want to update record. Suppose we want to update record with id 1002 for Sales department name then the code will be

```
int status=dao.updateDepartment(new Department(1002,"Sales"));
```

For Deletion of particular record

Following code can be written if we want to delete a record. Suppose we want to delete a record with id 1002 then the code will be

```
Department d=new Department();
  d.setId(1002);
  int status=dao.deleteDepartment(d);
```

Step 7 : Before running the code, just make sure that you have created the above files appropriately. Following screen shot of Project Explorer shows it.

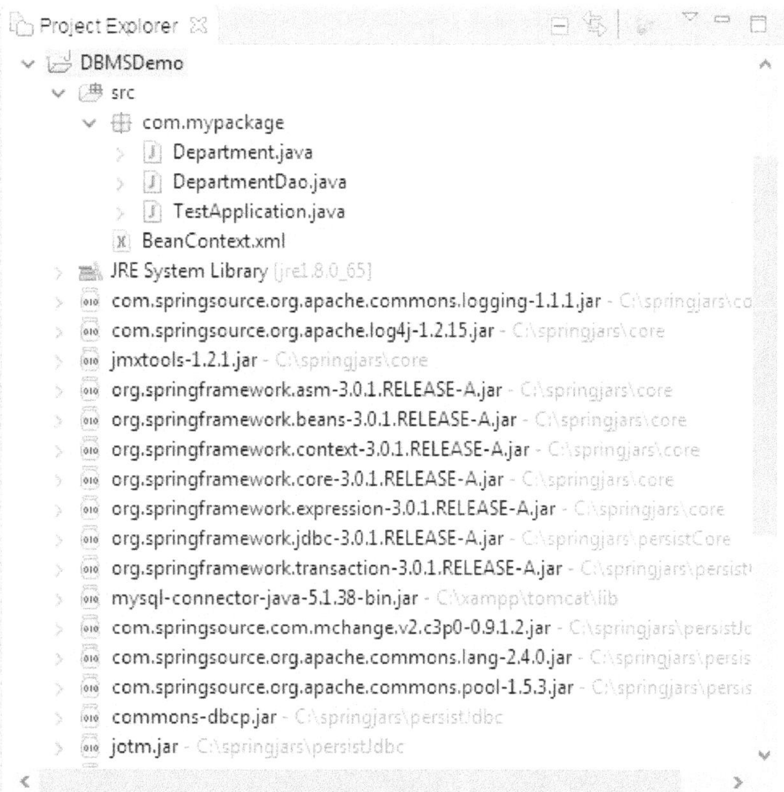

Step 8 : Right click on **TestApplication.java** and Click on **Run As ->Java Application**. The output will be displayed on Console Window. It will be

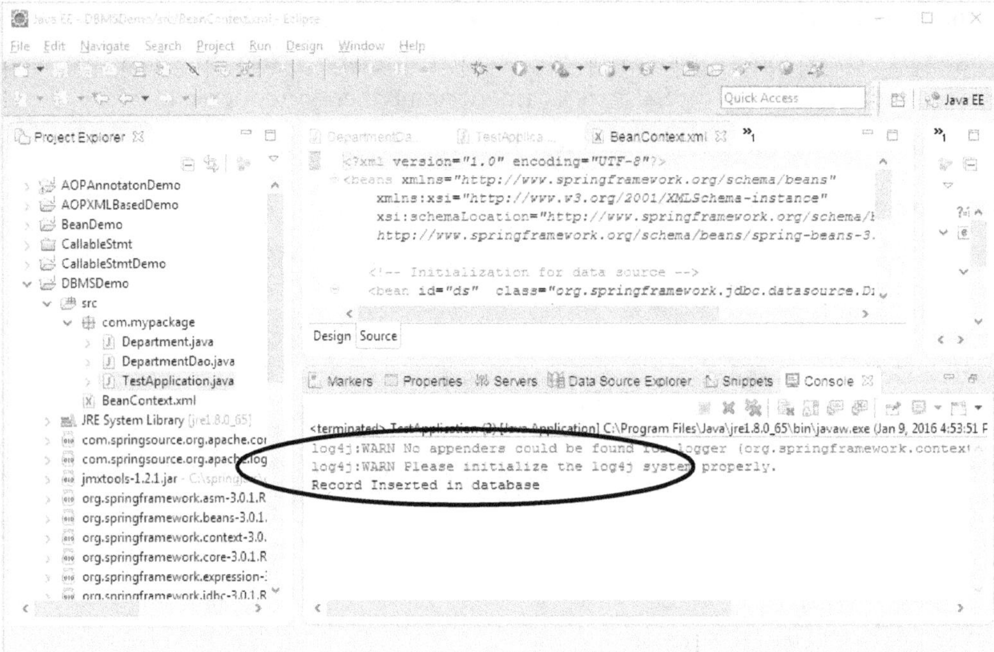

We can verify the insertion of record by opening the database table. Following is an evidence!!!

Review Question

1. *With the help of suitable example code explain how do you establish a connection with database in spring framework.*

7.9 Managing Transaction

- The transactions are set of actions that are treated as a single unit of work. Transaction management is an important activity in handling databases in order to maintain integrity and consistency. Spring framework provides a consistent abstraction for transaction management.
- A simple transaction is usually issued to the database system in a language like SQL in this form :
    - o Begin the transaction
    - o Execute several queries
    - o Commit the transaction (updates become visible if the transaction is successful)
- Spring supports both programmatic and declarative transaction management.
- Programmatic transaction management means, manage the transactions with the help of programs and declarative transaction management means the XML based or annotation based configurations are used to manage the transactions. In declarative transaction management the business code is separated from the transaction management.

Local and Global transactions in Spring

- Local transactions are resource-specific like JDBC connection. Local Transactions can work with multiple transactional resources.
- Global transactions help to work with multiple transactional resources like relational database and message queue. Global transactions are managed through JTA and JNDI.
- The important interface supported by Spring Transaction management is **PlatformTransactionManager**. Various methods supported by this interface are –

Sr. No.	Method	Description
1.	TransactionStatus getTransaction (TransactionDefinition definition)	This method returns a currently active transaction or create a new one, according to the specified propagation behavior.
2.	void commit(TransactionStatus status)	This method commits the given transaction.
3.	void rollback(TransactionStatus status)	This method performs a rollback of the given transaction.

- The **TransactionDefinition** is a core interface supported by the Spring for transaction management. This interface provides an abstraction for representing transaction properties that are required for customizing the transactions.

The TransactionDefinition object describes following five properties –

1. Isolation level
2. Transaction name
3. Transaction timeout
4. Read only
5. Propagation behavior

Various methods supported by this interface are –

Sr. No.	Method	Description
1.	int getIsolationLevel()	It returns the degree by which the transaction must be isolated from other transactions.
2.	String getName()	It returns the name of transaction.
3.	Int getTimeout()	This method returns the time in seconds in which the transaction must be complete.
4.	boolean isReadOnly	This returns true if the transaction is read only.
5.	int getPropagationBehavior()	This method returns the propagation behavior.

There are various methods for transaction management provided by Transaction interface. Here are those

Method	Description
boolean hasSavepoint()	This method returns true if this transaction internally contains a savepoint.
boolean isCompleted()	In order to check if transaction is completed, this method is used. That means it checkes, if transaction has been committed or rolled back.
boolean isNewTransaction()	This method returns true of there is a new transaction.
boolean isRollbackOnly()	This method returns whether the transaction has been marked as rollback-only.
void setRollbackOnly()	This method sets the transaction rollback-only.

Review Question

1. *Write short note on - transaction management.*

❑❑❑

Summer - 2016 **Advanced Java** Semester - VI (CE/CSE/IT)	**Gujarat Technological University** **Solved Paper**

Time : $2\frac{1}{2}$ Hours] **[Total Marks : 70**

Instructions :

1. *Attempt all questions.*
2. *Make suitable assumptions wherever necessary.*
3. *Figures to the right indicate full marks.*

Q.1 a) Answer the following questions : **[7]**

I) How does the JVM execute a servlet compared with a regular Java class ?

II) Consider a scenario in which 4 users are accessing a servlet instance. Among which one user called destroy() method. What happens to the rest 3 users ?

III) What is connection pooling ?

IV) Can one JSP or Servlet extend another Servlet or JSP? Justify your answer.

V) What happens if you add a main method to servlet ?

VI) What is phantom read in JDBC? which isolation level prevent it?

VII) Servlet is Java class. Then why there is no constructor in Servlet? Can we write the constructor in Servlet Justify your answer.

Ans. : I) A servlet is not invoked directly through a main method. In-fact, the class is loaded and run by a servlet container(Example **Tomcat**)

II) If 4 users are accessing the servlet instance and if one user called **destroy()** method then the thread which is calling **destroy** will be terminated and other threads will not be terminated.

III) Connection pooling is a feature in Java(used in JDBC) which allows multiple clients to make use cached set of shared and reusable objects which provide access to database.

IV) Yes one JSP or Servlet can extend another servlet or JSP. One servlet class can extend another servlet class using the keyword extends. While JSP can extend the another JSP or Servlet Class using the page directive support. For example - **<%@ Page extends "myPackage.Example" %>** where **myPackage** is name of the package and **Example** is the name of the class that has to be inherited.

V) There is no main method in Servlet because, the servlet executes according to life cycle methods in the servlet container. Even if we write main() method in servlet it is of no use, because the execution of servlet is based on life cycle methods.

VI) In JDBC, a phantom read occurs when, during the transaction, two identical queries are executed and the collection of rows returned by the second query differs from the first. There are some JDBC defined constants in which phantom read occurs. These constants are TRANSACTION_READ_UNCOMMITTED, TRANSACTION_READ_COMMITTED and TRANSACTION_REPEATABLE_READ.

The TRANSACTION_SERIALIZABLE is a constant which defines the serializable isoalation level and prevents the phantom read.

VIII) The servlet contains the **init()** method, which itself acts as a constructor. Yes syntactically we can write our own constructor in Servlet instead of using **init** method. If we write parameterized constructors then its is neccessary to write a zero-argument constructor but servlet containers still will only call your zero argument constructor and we canont have access to a **ServletConfig** or **ServletContex.**

b) *What is JDBC? List out all various types of JDBC driver. Explain Thick and Thin driver. Write code snippet for each type of JDBC connection. Comment on selection of driver.* **(Refer section 2.11)** **[7]**

Ans. : Thick and Thin Drivers : JDBC type 2 driver is called thick driver because this driver uses native API or partly Java driver to communicate to client's database. On the other hand, the JDBC driver type 4 is a thin driver because this driver is written in pure Java, its portable across all platform, which means you can use same JAR file to connect to MySQL even if your Java program is running on Windows, Linux or Solaris.

Type 1 : First of all we load database specific driver by calling Class.forName.

Syntax : Class.forName("sun.jdbc.odbc.jdbcOdbcDriver");

Then we will obtain the instance for the connectionusing getConnection method.

Syntax :

Connection con=DriverManager.getConnection(jdbc:odbc:<datasourcename>,"userid","password");

Type 4 : We load database specific driver by calling Class.forName.

Syntax : Class.forName("com.mysql.jdbc.Driver");

Then we will obtain the instance for the connectionusing getConnection method.

Syntax : Connection con=DriverManager.getConnection

(jdbc:mysql://localhost/databasename,root,password);

Q.2 a) *Show the use of PreparedStatement object to run precomplied SQL statement. Also write example of java snippet for Prepared Statement.* **[Refer section 2.9.1]** **[7]**

b) *Write a TCP or UDP client and server program to do the following :* **[7]**

client > java client localhost/IP Port <enter> **[Refer example 1.8.2]**

Enter text : Welcome to Gujarat Technological UNIVERSITY <enter>

Response from server: ytisrevinu LACIGOLONHEt TARAJUg TO EMOCLEw

client> exit.

OR

b) *Write a client - server program using TCP or UDP where the client sends 10 numbers and server responds with the numbers in sorted order.*
[Refer example 1.4.3] **[7]**

Q.3 a) *Explain the Hibernate cache architecture.* **[Refer section 6.2]** **[7]**

b) *Write small web application which takes marks of three subject and pass to servlet. Servlet forward to model class having method getClass() and getPercentage(). Display class and percentage in .jsp page.* **[Refer example 4.12.3]** **[7]**

OR

Q.3 a) *Differentiate the followings : Any (Three)* **[7]**

i) GenericServlet vs HttpServlet *ii) doGet() vs doPost()*

iii) Servlets vs CGI *iv) Session and Cookie* *v) JSP vs Servlet*

Ans. : **I) GenericServlet :** It is protocol independent. Generic Servlet only supports service() method.

HTTPServlet : It is protocol dependent and mainly suitable for HTTP protocol.
HttpServlet supports also doGet(), doPost(), doPut(), doDelete(), doHead(), doTrace(), doOptions()etc.

II) doGet() : In doGet method the parameters are appended to the URL and sent along with header information.

doPost() : In doPost, parameters are sent in separate line in the body

III) Servlet Vs CGI : Refer section 3.1

IV) Session and Cookie : Sessions are server-side files that contain user information, while Cookies are client-side files that contain user information.

V) JSP Vs Servlet : Refer section 4.2.1

b) *Write a student bean class with property student_name, enrollment_no, address and cpi. Write jsp page to set and display all property.* **[Refer example 4.15.5]** **[7]**

Q.4 a) *List and explain various stages of JSP life cycle. Briefly give the function of each phase.* **[Refer section 4.3]** **[7]**

b) *Write servlet displayed following information of client.* **[7]**

i) Client Browser *ii) Client IP address* *iii) Client Port No*

iv) Server Port No *v) Local Port No.*

vi) Method used by client for form submission

vii) Query String name and values **[Refer example 3.5.1]**

OR

Q.4 a) *List and Explain various stages of Servlet life cycle. Explain role of web container.* **[Refer section 3.4]** **[7]**

b) *Write line(s) of code in JSP for following.* **[7]**

i) Session read and write.

ii) URL rewriting sending and retrieving parameter(s)

iii) URL redirection

iv) Print "hello world" as output

v) Include the other JSP file statically

vi) Expression to display date as output

vii) Method of setting the JSP parameters to user in JSTL **[Refer example 4.16.1]**

Q.5 a) *Draw the JSF request processing life cycle and briefly give the function of each phase.* **[Refer section 5.5]** **[7]**

b) *What is HQL? How does it different from SQL? List its advantages.* **[Refer section 6.6]** **[7]**

OR

Q.5 a) *What is spring Web MVC framework? List its key features.* **[7]**

[Refer section 7.1.1]

b) *What is OR mapping? Give an example of Hibernate XML mapping file* **[Refer section 6.4]** **[7]**

❑❑❑

Winter - 2016 **Advanced Java** Semester - VI (CE/CSE/IT)	**Gujarat Technological University** **Solved Paper**

Time : $2\frac{1}{2}$ Hours] [Total Marks : 70

Instructions : *1. Attempt all questions.*
2. Make suitable assumptions wherever necessary.
3. Figures to the right indicate full marks.

Q.1 a) *What is JDBC ? Explain the types of JDBC drivers ? Write a code snippet for each type of JDBC connection.* **(Refer section 2.11)**

Code snippet for JDBC Types : **(Refer Q.1(b) of Summer - 2016)** [7]

b) *Explain JSF standard component in detail.* **(Refer section 5.9)** [7]

Q.2 a) *Explain the use of prepared statement with appropriate example.* **(Refer section 2.9.1)** [7]

b) *What is filter ? What is its use ? List different filter interfaces with their important methods.* **(Refer section 3.10)** [7]

OR

b) *Write a short note on JSF Facelets.* **(Refer section 5.10)** [7]

Q.3 a) *What is server socket ? Explain in detail with an example.* **(Refer section 1.7)** [7]

b) *Write a TCP client-server program to get the date and time details from server on the client request.* [7]

Ans. : Client.java

```
import java.net.*;
import java.io.*;
public class Client {
   public static void main(String[] args) throws UnknownHostException,IOException {
         //Step 1. Create a client socket to connect to Server
      Socket cs= new Socket("LocalHost",1234);//client communicating
            //with server using same port number
      System.out.println("Enter Date/Time");
      //Step 2.Receive Date Sent by Server
      BufferedReader fromserver=new BufferedReader(new
      InputStreamReader(cs.getInputStream()));
      System.out.println(fromserver.readLine());
```

```
        fromserver.close();
        cs.close();
    }
}
```

Server.java

```
import java.net.*;
import java.io.*;
import java.util.Date;
public class Server {
    public static void main(String[] args)throws IOException {
        System.out.println("Server Started...");
        //Step 1. Reserve a port number on the Server to offer this service
        ServerSocket ss= new ServerSocket(1234);
        //Step 2. Now create a Client Socket on Server for Bidirectonal Communication.
        //Socket is created only when client communicates with the server
        Socket cs=ss.accept();
        Date d=new Date();
        String str="Current Date & Time from Server is:"+d;
        //Step 3. Send String str to client via client socket
        PrintWriter toclient=new PrintWriter(cs.getOutputStream(),true);
        toclient.print(str);
        toclient.close();
        cs.close();
        ss.close();
    }
}
```

Output

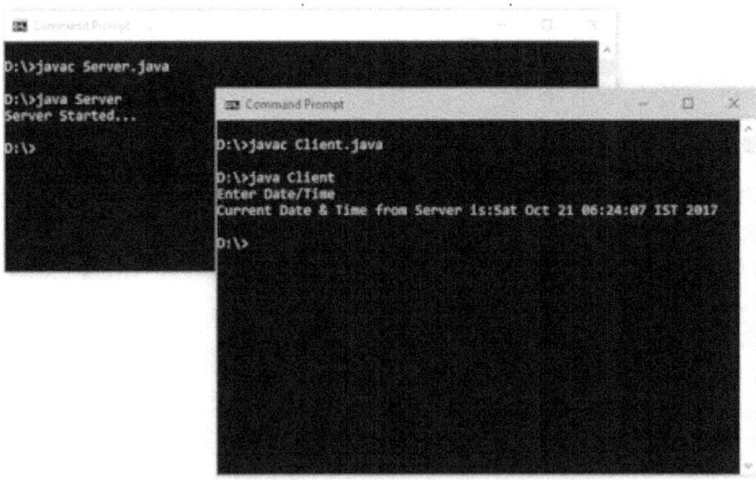

OR

Q.3 a) *What is datagram socket ? Explain in detail with example.* **(Refer section 1.5) [7]**

b) *Write a UDP client-server program in which the client sends any string and server responds with reserve string.* **[7]**

Ans. : Client Program

```
import java.io.*;
import java.net.*;
class UDPClient
{
 public static void main(String args[]) throws Exception
 {
   BufferedReader user_input=new BufferedReader(new InputStreamReader(System.in));
   //creating the client socket
   DatagramSocket client_socket=new DatagramSocket();
   //getting the IP address of host "aap"
   InetAddress IP_add=InetAddress.getByName("localhost");
   //creating the buffer for sending the data
   byte out_data[]=new byte[1024];
   //reading the input through keyboard
   String str=user_input.readLine();
   out_data=str.getBytes();
   //creating the datagram packet in which data is
   //encapsulated
  DatagramPacket Packet1=new
  DatagramPacket(out_data,out_data.length,IP_add,1234);
   //sending the packet to the server
   client_socket.send(Packet1);
   //closing the client's connection
   client_socket.close();
 }
}
```

Server Program

```
import java.io.*;
import java.net.*;
class UDPServer
{
 public static void main(String args[]) throws Exception
```

```
{
 //creating the socket for server
  DatagramSocket server_socket=new DatagramSocket(1234);
  //array which reserves the input data getting from
  //client
  byte in_data[]=new byte[1024];
  while(true)
  {
   //creating the datagram packet
   DatagramPacket Packet2=new DatagramPacket(in_data,in_data.length);
    //the data from the client is received in the packet
   server_socket.receive(Packet2);
   String str=new String(Packet2.getData());
   //printing the received data on the console of server
   String reverse="";
    int length = str.length();
    for ( int i = length - 1 ; i >= 0 ; i--)
       reverse = reverse + str.charAt(i);
     System.out.println("Reverse of entered string is: "+reverse);
  }
 }
 }
```

Q.4 a) *Explain JSP tag library with example.* **(Refer section 4.16)** [7]

b) *Explain request and response object in servlet.* **(Refer section 3.3)** [7]

OR

Q.4 a) *Compare JSP with servlet.* **(Refer section 4.2.1)** [7]

b) *Write a Java servlet to demonstrate the use of session management.* **(Refer section 3.11.2)** [7]

Q.5 a) *What is HQL ? How does it differ from SQL ? Give its advantages.* **(Refer section 6.6)** [7]

b) *Explain the action tags used to access the Java Beans from a JSP page with example.* [7]

Ans. : For using interacting with Java bean component, the JSP uses the <jsp:useBean> action tag. The declaration of this bean in JSP page is as specified below -

```
<jsp:useBean id = "beanName" class = "className"
```

scope = "page | request | session | application">

Here the id attribute specifies the name of the bean. Scope attribute specify where the bean is stored. The class attribute specify the fully qualified classname.

Example - Refer example 4.15.5.

OR

Q.5 a) *Draw and explain the architecture of Hibernate.* **(Refer section 6.2)** [7]

b) *Explain MVC architecture in detail with figure.* **(Refer section 7.1.1)** [7]

❑❑❑

Summer - 2017 **Advanced Java** Semester - VI (CE/CSE/IT)	**Gujarat Technological University** **Solved Paper**

Time : $2\frac{1}{2}$ Hours] **[Total Marks : 70**

Instructions : *1. Attempt all questions.*
2. Make suitable assumptions wherever necessary.
3. Figures to the right indicate full marks.

Q.1 Answer the following questions : [14]

1. *How to display IP address and host name for local machine.*

Ans. : The IP address and local host name for local machine can be displayed using the method **getLocalHost()**. This method belongs to **InetAddress** Class. For example, following code will display the IP address and local host name -

```
public static void main(String[] args)
{
  InetAddress address=InetAddress.getLocalHost();
  System.out.println("Local Host is: "+address);
}
```

2. *How can I determine whether a particular isolation level is supported by database or not ?*

Ans. : Setting the transaction isolation level for a connection allows a user to specify how severely the user's transaction should be isolated from other transactions.

First the instance of getMetaData is created and for this instance the boolean method **supportsTransactionIsolationLevel** is used to check whether particular isolation level is used or not.

3. *How to make ResultSet cursors held open when the method commit is called ?*

Ans. : The method ResultSet.next moves the cursor to the next row in the database. This method returns false if the cursor is positioned after the last row. This method repeatedly calls the ResultSet.next method with a while loop to iterate through all the data in the ResultSet.

4. *How to know information about columns in ResultSet object ?*

Ans. : When a getter method is called with a string and more than one column has the same alias or name as the string, the value of the first matching column is returned. These getter method getString(0),getInt(1), and so on.

5. *How to delete a session in servlet ?*

Ans. : Using the session timeout, the session can be deleted. There are two methods of session timeout -

1. Using the deployment descriptor, the session timeout period can be set, after the timeout the session does not last long. For example -

```
<session-config>
  <session-timeout>15</session-timeout>
</session-config>
```

2. Using the method **setMaxInactiveInterval()** the session timeout can be set manually. For example

```
HttpSession session=request.getSession();
session.setMaxInactiveInterval(15*60);
```

In above case, the session will be killed by the container if client doesn't make any request after 15 minutes.

6. *How to display the expiration date and last modified date for the following URL http://www.star.com/news/.*

Ans. : Using the getExpiration() and getLastModified() method the expiration and last modified dates can be obtained. The code snippet is as follows -

```
import java.net.HttpURLConnection;
import java.net.URL;
import java.util.Date;

public class Test{
 public static void main(String args[]) throws Exception {
  URL url = new URL("http://www.star.com/news/");
  HttpURLConnection httpCon = (HttpURLConnection) url.openConnection();

  long date1 = httpCon.getLastModified();
  if (date1 == 0)
   System.out.println("No last-modified information.");
  else
   System.out.println("Last-Modified: " + new Date(date1));
  long date2 = httpCon.getExpiration();
  if (date2 == 0)
   System.out.println("No expiration information.");
  else
   System.out.println("Expires: " + new Date(date2));
 }
}
```

7. *How to get the name of the HTTP method with which the request was made ?*

Ans. : Using the **getRequestMethod()** the name of the method of HTTP request is obtained. For example

```
import java.net.HttpURLConnection;
import java.net.URL;
import java.util.Date;

public class Test{
  public static void main(String args[]) throws Exception {
    URL url = new URL("http://www.google.com");
    HttpURLConnection httpCon = (HttpURLConnection) url.openConnection();
    System.out.println("Request method is " + httpCon.getRequestMethod());
  }
}
```

8. *How to get the fully qualified name of the client that sent the request in servlet ?*

Ans. : Using the method **String getRemoteHost()** the fully qualified name of the client that sent the request can be displayed in servlet.

9. *What is difference between include directive and jsp:include action tag ?*

Ans. : The difference is as follows -

1) Include directive includes the file at translation time - that is when the JSP gets converted into the equivalent servlet whereas the include action includes the file at runtime.

2) If the included file is changed but not the JSP which is including it then the changes will reflect only when we use include action tag. The changes will not reflect if you are using include directive as the JSP is not changed so it will not be translated for request processing and hence the changes will not reflect.

3) Syntax difference: Include directive: <%@ include file="file_name" %> whereas include action has like this <jsp:include page="file_name" />

4) When using include action tag we can also pass the parameters to the included page by using param action tag but in case of include directive it's not possible.

10. *How to declare in a JSP page that indicates whether or not the page in intended to be an error page of some other JSP page.*

Ans. : Using the page directive of JSP we can declare that particular page is error page or not. The attribute **isErrorPage="true"** is used for this purpose. For example

```
<%@ page isErrorPage="true" %>
```

Any JSP file declared with isErrorPage (and set to a value of true), is capable to receive exceptions from other JSP pages.

11. *How do we print "
 creates a new line in HTML" in JSP ?*

Ans. : We can use **c:out escapeXml** attribute to escape the HTML elements so that it get's shown as text in the browser, for this scenario we will write code like below.

```
<c:out value="<br> creates a new line in HTML" escapeXml="true"></c:out>
```

12. *How to send a page that auto-refreshes to a new page after a given time period to a user until their requests are being processed.*

Ans. : For the auto-refresh of the page, we need to use response header. The syntax is as follows -

```
response.setHeader("Refresh", "time; URL=url");
```

where **time** is specified in seconds and the **url** is replaced by the URL the page that has to be loaded eventually loaded. For example

```
response.setHeader("Refresh", "10; URL=http://localhost/test.html");
```

13. *What are different JSF converter tags ?*

Ans. : The converter tags are used in JSF when we want to convert the data into appropriate types being processed by the application. The different types of tags used are as follows -

1. Converter Number tag
2. Converter Date Time Tag
3. Converter Tag

14. *What are the advantages of Hibernate over JDBC ?*

Ans. : Following are the advantages of Hibernate over JDBC -

1. Hibernate is data base independent, same code will work for all data bases like ORACLE,MySQL ,SQLServer etc. In case of JDBC query must be data base specific.
2. Hibernate support two level of cache. First level and 2nd level. So you can store your data into Cache for better performance. In case of JDBC you need to implement your java cache .
3. As Hibernate is set of Objects , you don't need to learn SQL language.

   You can treat TABLE as a Object . In case of JDBC you need to learn SQL.
4. Development fast in case of Hibernate because you don't need to write queries.

Q.2 a) *Explain JDBC driver types in detail.* **(Refer section 2.11)** **[7]**

b) *Write a client server program using TCP where client sends a string and server checks whether that string is palindrome or not and responds with appropriate message.* **[7]**

Ans. : Step 1 :

```
/***************************************************************
      Client Program
***************************************************************/
import java.io.*;
import java.net.*;
class Client_Pal
{
public static void main(String args[]) throws Exception
{
  String Str=" ";
  String Str1;
  int flag;
  Socket s1=new Socket("127.0.0.1",5000);
  try
  {
  System.out.println("Enter Some string...");
  while(true)
  {
    BufferedReader input_user = new BufferedReader(new
InputStreamReader(System.in));
    DataOutputStream out_server=new DataOutputStream(s1.getOutputStream());
    BufferedReader in_server=new BufferedReader(new
InputStreamReader(s1.getInputStream()));
        Str=input_user.readLine();
      out_server.writeBytes(Str+"\n");
      Str1=in_server.readLine(); //obtaining the from server
      flag=Integer.parseInt(in_server.readLine()); //obtaining the from server
      if(flag==1)
      System.out.println(Str1+" is Palindrome");
   else
      System.out.println(Str1+" is not palindrome");
   s1.close();
  }//end of while
     }catch(Exception e){System.out.println(e.getMessage());}
 }
}
```

Step 2 :

```
/****************************************************************
      Server Program
****************************************************************/
import java.io.*;
import java.lang.*;
import java.net.*;
class Server_Pal
{
  public static void main(String args[]) throws Exception
  {
    ServerSocket s2=new ServerSocket(5000);
    String str="",rev="";
    int flag;
      System.out.println("\t\tServer started.....");
  while(true)
  {
    Socket s3=s2.accept();
    BufferedReader in_client=new BufferedReader(new
InputStreamReader(s3.getInputStream()));
    DataOutputStream out_client=new DataOutputStream(s3.getOutputStream());
    str=in_client.readLine();//getting data from client
    System.out.println("Receiving data...");
    int length = str.length();
    for ( int i = length - 1; i >= 0; i-- )
        rev = rev + str.charAt(i);
    if (str.equals(rev))
      flag=1;
    else
      flag=0;
     out_client.writeBytes(str+"\n");//sending string to client
    out_client.writeBytes(flag+"\n");//sending status of palindrome or not
    System.out.println("Data is sent...");
  }//end of while
 }//end of main
}//end of class
```

Output

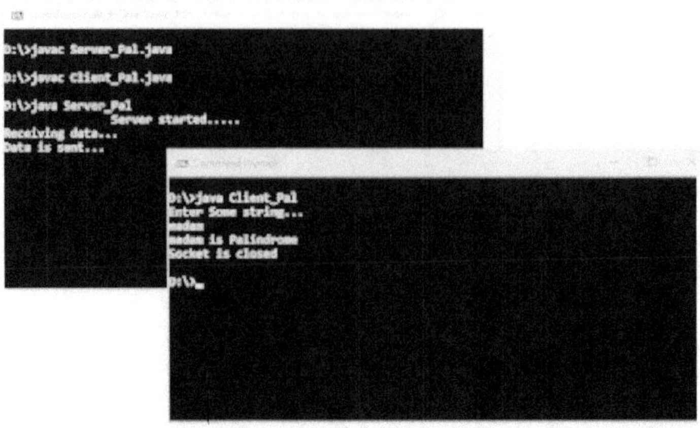

Fig. 1

OR

b) *Explain architecture of Hibernate.* **(Refer section 6.2)** **[7]**

Q.3 a) *Explain different stages of JSP page life cycle.* **(Refer section 4.3)** **[7]**

b) *Design a form to input details of an employee and submit the data to a servlet. Write code for servlet that will save the entered details as a new record in database table employee with fields (EmpId, EName, Email, Age).* **[7]**

Ans. : **Step 1 :** Create HTML form for inputting the employee details. The code for this is as follows -

```
<html>
<head>
<title> EMPLOYEE DATABASE</title>
</head>
<body>
<form method=GET action="http://localhost/examples/servlets/servlet/test">
ID: <input type='text' name='ID' value='' size=10/><br/><br/>
Name: <input type='text' name='Name' value='' size=30/><br/><br/>
Mail_ID: <input type='text' name='Mail' value='' size=20><br/><br/>
Age: <input type='text' name='Age' value='' size=3><br/><br/><br/>
<input type="Submit" value="Submit"/>
</form>
</body>
</html>
```

Step 2 : Create a servlet program which accept the employee details from above HTML form and insert it into the MySQL database. The same servlet then reads the database table and display it on the browser. The code for this servlet is as follows -

```
import java.io.*;
import java.util.*;
import javax.sql.*;
import javax.servlet.*;
import javax.servlet.http.*;
import java.sql.Connection;
import java.sql.DriverManager;
import java.sql.ResultSet;
import java.sql.SQLException;
import java.sql.PreparedStatement;

public class test extends HttpServlet
{
   public void doGet(HttpServletRequest request,HttpServletResponse response)
         throws IOException, ServletException
   {
      response.setContentType("text/html");
      PrintWriter out = response.getWriter();
  String str=request.getParameter("ID");
  int EmpId=Integer.parseInt(str);
  String EmpName=request.getParameter("Name");
  String Empmail=request.getParameter("Mail");
  str=request.getParameter("Age");
  int EmpAge=Integer.parseInt(str);
      out.println("<html>");
      out.println("<head><title>Employee Database</title></head>");
      out.println("<body>");

      // connecting to database
       Connection con = null;
       PreparedStatement ps=null;
       ResultSet rs=null;
      try
      {

         Class.forName("com.mysql.jdbc.Driver");
         con =DriverManager.getConnection
("jdbc:mysql://localhost:3306/my_database","root","");
```

```
        ps=con.prepareStatement("insert into employee_table(EmpId,EName,Email,Age)
values(?,?,?,?)");
     ps.setInt(1,EmpId);
     ps.setString(2,EmpName);
     ps.setString(3,Empmail);
     ps.setInt(4,EmpAge);
     ps.executeUpdate();
     String sql="select * from employee_table";
     ps=con.prepareStatement(sql);
        rs=ps.executeQuery();
        out.print("<table border=1>");

out.print("<tr><td>EmpId</td><td>EName</td><td>EmpMail</td><td>Age</td
></tr>");
        while(rs.next())
        {
           //Retrieve by column name
           int id  = rs.getInt("EmpId");
           String name = rs.getString("EName");
           String email = rs.getString("Email");
           int age = rs.getInt("Age");
           out.print("<tr><td>"+id+"</td><td>"+name+"</td>
<td>"+email+"</td><td>"+age);
           out.print("</td></tr>");
        }
        out.println("</table></body></html>");
      }catch (SQLException e)
      {
        throw new ServletException("Servlet Could not display records.", e);
      }
      catch (ClassNotFoundException e)
      {
        throw new ServletException("JDBC Driver not found.", e);
      }
      finally
      {
        try
        {
```

```
            if(rs != null)
            {
               rs.close();
               rs = null;
            }
            if(ps != null)
            {
               ps.close();
               ps = null;
            }
            if(con != null)
            {
               con.close();
               con = null;
            }
         }
         catch (SQLException e) {}
      }//end of finally
      out.close();
   }//end of service function
} //end of class
```

Output

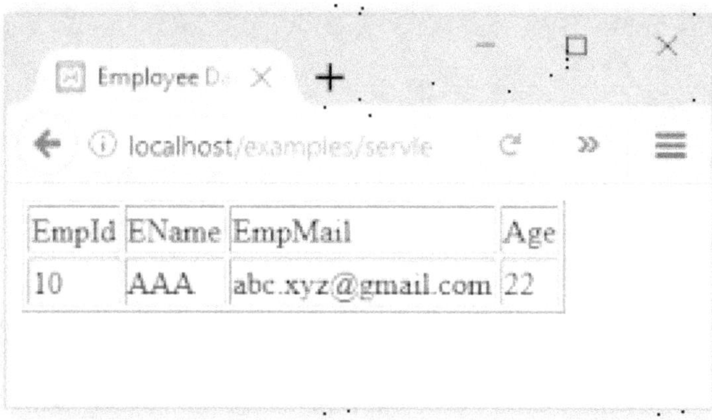

Fig. 2

OR

Q.3 a) *Explain role of prepared statement and callable statement with example.* **(Refer section 2.9)** **[7]**

b) *Explain architecture of spring MVC framework. Explain all modules in brief.* **(Refer section 7.1.1)** **[7]**

Q.4 a) *Explain use of <jsp:useBean> action tag with example.* **(Refer Q.5 (b) of Winter 2016)** **[3]**

b) *Write a JSP program using JSTL SQL taglib to display student details in tabular form by iterating through the database table student.* **[4]**

Ans. : We must create a Student database containing the fields roll, name and marks field. The JSP page containing the SQL taglib to display Student details in tabular form is written as follow -

```
<%@ taglib uri="http://java.sun.com/jsp/jstl/core" prefix="c" %>
<%@ taglib uri="http://java.sun.com/jsp/jstl/sql" prefix="sql"%>
<html>
<head>
<title>JSTL sql Tag Demo</title>
</head>
<body>

<sql:setDataSource var="DB" driver="com.mysql.jdbc.Driver"
url="jdbc:mysql://localhost/test"
 user="root"  password="mypassword"/>

<sql:query dataSource="${DB}" var="Rec">
SELECT * from Student;
```

```
</sql:query>
<center>
<h2>Student Database</h2>
<table border="1">
<tr>
<th>Roll_No</th>
<th>Name</th>
<th>Marks</th>
</tr>
<c:forEach var="row" items="${Rec.rows}">
<tr>
<td><c:out value="${row.roll}"/></td>
<td><c:out value="${row.name}"/></td>
<td><c:out value="${row.marks}"/></td>
</tr>
</c:forEach>
</table>
</center>

</body>
</html>
```

c) *What is O/R mapping ? How it is implement using Hibernate. Explain with example.* **(Refer section 6.4)** **[7]**

OR

Q.4 a) *Explain use of DatabaseMetaData with example.* **[3]**

Ans. : (1) The **java.sql.DatabaseMetaData** interface provides methods to get meta data of a database such as database product name, driver name, total number of tables and so on.

(2) The DatabaseMetaData object can be obtained using following statement

DatabaseMetaData databaseMetaData = connection.getMetaData();

Once we obtain this **DatabaseMetaData** instance, we can call methods on it to obtain the meta data about the database.

(3) Example -

```
import java.sql.Connection;
import java.sql.DatabaseMetaData;
import java.sql.DriverManager;

public class DatabaseMetaDataDemo
{
```

```
public static void main(String[] args) throws Exception
{
  Connection conn =get_mysql_Connection();
  DatabaseMetaData meta = conn.getMetaData();

  String productName = meta.getDatabaseProductName();
  String productVersion = meta.getDatabaseProductVersion();
  System.out.println("productName" + productName);
  System.out.println("productVersion" + productVersion);
  conn.close();
}
 public static Connection get_mysql_Connection() throws Exception
 {
  String driver = "org.gjt.mm.mysql.Driver";
  String url = "jdbc:mysql://localhost/my_database";
  String username = "root";
  String password = "";
  Class.forName(driver);
  Connection conn = DriverManager.getConnection(url, username, password);
  return conn;
 }
}
```

b) *Explain use of ServletConfig and ServletContext object with example.* **(Refer section 3.7)** **[4]**

c) *Explain JSTL core tags.* **(Refer section 4.16.1)** **[7]**

Q.5 a) *Write a servlet that redirect requests alternatively to JSP pages named odd and even.* **[3]**

Ans. : **Step 1 :** The html form which allows the user to input a number is as follows -

```
<html>
<head>
</head>
<body>
<form method="get" action="http://localhost/examples/servlets/servlet/OddEven">
 Enter number: <input type="text" name="t1"> <br>
 <input type="submit" value="SEND">
</form>
</body>
```

Step 2 : The servlet program that redirects the request alternatively between the JSP pages is as follows -

```
OddEven.java
import javax.servlet.*;
import javax.servlet.http.*;
import java.io.*;
public class OddEven extends HttpServlet
{
 public void service(HttpServletRequest req, HttpServletResponse res) throws
ServletException, IOException
 {
  res.setContentType("text/html");
  PrintWriter out = res.getWriter();

  String str = req.getParameter("t1");
  int num=Integer.parseInt(str);
  if(num%2==0)
  {
   res.sendRedirect("EvenPage.jsp");
  }
  else
  {
   res.sendRedirect("OddPage.jsp");
  }
  out.close();
 }
}
```

Step 3: The simple JSP pages are as follows

EvenPage.jsp

```
<html>
 <head>
 </head>
 <body>
 <%= new String("It is an Even number") %>
 </body>
</html>
```

OddPage.jsp

```
<html>
```

```
<head>
</head>
<body>
<%= new String("It is an Odd number") %>
</body>
</html>
```

b) *What is request dispatcher ? What is the difference between request dispatcher's forward() and include() method ?* **(Refer section 3.9)** **[4]**

c) *Explain JSF life cycle phases.* **(Refer section 5.5)** **[7]**

OR

Q.5 a) *What is dependency injection ?* **[3]**

Ans. : (1) The dependency injection is a technique whereby one object supplies the dependencies of another object. A dependency is an object that can be used.

(2) Dependency Injection is useful when it is required to pass the service to the client rather than allowing a client to build or find the service.

(3) Dependency injection allows a client the flexibility of being configurable.

(4) The Dependency Injection is a design pattern that removes the dependency of the programs. In such case we provide the information from the external source such as XML file. It makes our code loosely coupled and easier for testing. In such case we write the code as:

```
class Person {
Phone phone;

Person(Phone phone){
this.phone=phone;
}
public void setPhone(Phone phone){
this.phone=phone;
}
}
```

In such case, instance of Phone class is provided by external souce such as XML file either by constructor or setter method.

b) *What is spring IoC container ?* **(Refer section 7.4)** **[4]**

b) *Explain various session tracking mechanisms in servlet with example.* **(Refer section 3.11.2)** **[7]**

❑❑❑

SHORT QUESTIONS AND ANSWERS

Chapter 1 : Java Networking

Q.1 Which package contains the classes and interfaces required for Java networking ?

Ans. : java.net

Q.2 How many bits are there in single IP address ?

Ans. : 32 bit

Q.3 What is the full form of TCP/IP ?

Ans. : The full form is -Transfer Control Protocol /Internet Protocol

Q.4 What is the full form of DNS ?

Ans. : Domain Name Service

Q.5 The connection oriented protocol is TCP and connection less protocol is ___.

Ans. : UDP

Q.6 The URLConnection class can be used to read and write data to the specified resource referred by the URL ? (True/ False)

Ans. : True

Q.7 The java.net.InetAddress class represents an ?

a Socket	b IP Address

c Protocol	d MAC Address	**[Ans. : b]**

Q.8 What is the full form of URL ?

Ans. : The full form of URL is Uniform Resource Locator.

Q.9 Which of these exception is thrown by URL class's constructors ?

a URLNotFound	b MalformedURLException

c URLSourceNotFound	d URLNotFoundException	**[Ans. : b]**

Q.10 Which class is used to create servers that listen for either local client or remote client programs ?

Ans. : ServerSocket

Q.11 Which methods are commonly used in ServerSocket class ?

a public OutputStream getOutputStream()

b public Socket accept()

c public synchronized void close()

d None of the above **[Ans. : b]**

Q.12 Which constructor of DatagramSocket class is used to creates a datagram socket and binds it with the given Port Number ?

a DatagramSocket(int port)

b DatagramSocket(int port, InetAddress address)

c DatagramSocket()

d None of the above **[Ans. : b]**

Q.13 Name three important classes that help you to write Java programs that use datagrams to send and receive packets over the network.

Ans. : i) DatagramSocket ii) DatagramPacket and iii) MulticastSocket

Q.14 What is the purpose of the method InetAddress getByName(String hostname) ?

Ans. : The method InetAddress getByName(String hostname) returns the IP address when the hostname is given.

Q.15 How to display IP address and host name for local machine ?

Summer 2017, 1 Mark

Ans. : The IP address and local host name for local machine can be displayed using the method **getLocalHost()**. This method belongs to **InetAddress** Class. For example, following code will display the IP address and local host name -

```
public static void main(String[] args)
{
InetAddress address=InetAddress.getLocalHost();
System.out.println("Local Host is: "+address);
}
```

Chapter 2 : JDBC

Q.1 What is JDBC ?

Ans. : The JDBC stands for Java Database Connectivity. JDBC is a JAVA API which is used to connect and execute the query to database.

Q.2 Specify the purpose of java.sql package.

Ans. : The java.sql package -

i) Helps the client to store and retrieve the data to the databse.

ii) Helps to allow the client to update database.

Q.3 Which package contains the JDBC classes ?

a java.jdbc and javax.jdbc

b java.jdbc and java.jdbc.sql

c java.sql and javax.sql

d none of these **[Ans. : c]**

Q.4 List the four types of JDBC drivers.

Ans. : Type 1 : JDBC-ODBC Bridge

Type 2 : Native- API Driver

Type 3 : Network Protocol Driver

Type 4 : Native Protocol Driver

Q.5 Which type of driver provides JDBC access via one or more ODBC drivers ?

Ans. : Type 1

Q.6 Which kind of driver converts JDBC calls into calls on the client API for Oracle, Sybase, Informix, IBM DB2, or other DBMS ?

a JDBC-ODBC bridge plus ODBC driver

b Native-API partly-Java driver

c JDBC-Net pure Java driver

d Native-protocol pure Java driver **[Ans. : b]**

Q.7 Write simple SQL statement to display all the data in a table.

Ans. : SELECT * FROM table_name;

Q.8 Enlist the types of JDBC statements

Ans. : 1. PreparedStatement 2.CallableStatement

Q.9 What is the difference between Statement and PreparedStatement ?

Ans. : In case of **Statement** the query is compiled each time while in case of **PreparedStatement** query is compiled only once. Hence **PreparedStatement** is efficient than Statement.

Q.10 Can we execute stored procedures and functions ?

Ans. : Yes, using **Callable statement** interface we can execute stored procedures and functions.

Q.11 How can we store and retrieve the images from the database ?

Ans. : By using PreparedStatement Interface, we can store and retrieve image.

Q.12 The performance of the application will be faster if you use PreparedStatement interface because query is compiled only once. (True/False)

Ans. : True

Q.13 The JDBC API has always supported persistent storage of objects defined in the Java programming language through the methods getObject and setObject. (True/False)

Ans. : True

Q.14 Enlist the steps to connect to the database.

Ans. : Step 1 : Register the driver class

Step 2 : Creating connection

Step 3 : Creating statement

Step 4 : Executing queries

Step 5 : Closing Connection

Q.15 Write a statement for loading and registering JDBC ODBC driver.

Ans. : Class.forName("sun.jdbc.odbc.JdbcOdbcDriver");

Q.16 Write a statement for creating connection to database named My_Database

Ans. : Con=DriverManager.getConnection("jdbc:odbc:My_Database,user_name,password)

Q.17 What is the use of JDBC DriverManager Class ?

Ans. : The DriverManager Class manages the registered drivers.

Q.18 What does the JDBC ResultSet interface ?

Ans. : The ResultSet object represents a row of a table. It can be used to change the cursor pointer and get the information from the database.

Q.19 Explain Thick and Thin driver. Write code snippet for each type of JDBC connection. Comment on selection of driver. **Summer 2016, 3 Marks**

Ans. : **Thick and Thin Drivers :** JDBC type 2 driver is called thick driver because this driver uses native API or partly Java driver to communicate to client's database. On the other hand, the JDBC driver type 4 is a thin driver because this driver is written in pure Java, its portable across all platform, which means you can use same JAR file to connect to MySQL even if your Java program is running on Windows, Linux or Solaris.

Type 1 : First of all we load database specific driver by calling Class.forName.

Syntax : Class.forName("sun.jdbc.odbc.jdbcOdbcDriver");

Then we will obtain the instance for the connectionusing getConnection method.

Syntax : Connection con=

DriverManager.getConnection(jdbc:odbc:<datasourcename>,"userid","password");

Type 4 : We load database specific driver by calling Class.forName.

Syntax : Class.forName("com.mysql.jdbc.Driver");

Then we will obtain the instance for the connectionusing getConnection method.

Syntax : Connection con=

DriverManager.getConnection

(jdbc:mysql://localhost/databasename,root,password);

Q.20 What is connection pooling ? **Summer 2016, 1 Mark**

Ans. : Connection pooling is a feature in Java(used in JDBC) which allows multiple clients to make use cached set of shared and reusable objects which provide access to database.

Q.21 What is phantom read in JDBC ? Which isolation level prevent it ? **Summer 2016, 1 Mark**

Ans. : In JDBC, a phantom read occurs when, during the transaction, two identical queries are executed and the collection of rows returned by the second query differs from the first. There are some JDBC defined constants in which phantom read occurs. These constants are TRANSACTION_READ_UNCOMMITTED, TRANSACTION_READ_COMMITTED and TRANSACTION_REPEATABLE_READ.

The TRANSACTION_SERIALIZABLE is a constant which defines the serializable isoalation level and prevents the phantom read.

Q.22 How can I determine whether a particular isolation level is supported by database or not ? **Summer 2017, 1 Mark**

Ans. : Setting the transaction isolation level for a connection allows a user to specify how severely the user's transaction should be isolated from other transactions.

First the instance of getMetaData is created and for this instance the boolean method **supportsTransactionIsolationLevel** is used to check whether particular isolation level is used or not.

Q.23 How to make ResultSet cursors held open when the method commit is called ? **Summer 2017, 1 Mark**

Ans. : The method **ResultSet.next** moves the cursor to the next row in the database.This method returns false if the cursor is positioned after the last row. This method repeatedly calls the ResultSet.next method with a while loop to iterate through all the data in the ResultSet.

Q.24 How to know information about the columns in ResultSet object ? **Summer 2017, 1 Mark**

Ans. : When a getter method is called with a string and more than one column has the same alias or name as the string, the value of the first matching column is returned. These getter method getString(0),getInt(1), and so on.

Chapter 3 : Servlet API and Overview

Q.1 The Java ____ specification defines an application programming interface for communication between the Web server and the application program.

a Servlet
b Server
c Program
d none of these

[Ans. : a]

Q.2 Servlet runs each request in _____

a JVM
b JRE
c Servlet Container
d none of these

[Ans. : c]

Q.3 Name the class that provides the implementation for service() method.

Ans. : GenericServlet provide the implementation for the service() method.

Q.4 What is deployment descriptor ?

Ans. : Java web applications use a deployment descriptor file to determine how URLs map to servlets, which URLs require authentication, and other information. This file is named web.xml

Q.5 Deployment descriptor is used for initializing parameters (True/False).

Ans. : True

Q.6 Which method is called only once in servlet life cycle ?

Ans. : The **init()** method is called only once in servlet life cycle.

Q.7 Name the package that support the Generic Servlet class.

Ans. : javax.servlet

Q.8 Who is responsible to create the object of servlet ?

Ans. : The web container or servlet container is responsible to create the object of servlet.

Q.9 What is the difference between GenericServlet and HttpServlet ?

Ans. : The GenericServlet is protocol independent while HttpServlet is HTTP protocol Specific.

Q.10 What is the difference between ServletConfig and ServletContext ?

Ans. : The container creates object of ServletConfig for each servlet whereas object of ServletContext is created for each web application.

Q.11 What is the purpose of Request Dispatcher Interface ?

Ans. : The RequestDispatcher interface enables to call one servlet from inside other servlet. That means using RequestDispatcher we can dispatch the request to any source such as HTML, servlet, JSP, image and so on.

Q.12 What are different types of filter ?

Ans. : Various types of filter are - 1. Authentication filter 2. Encryption filter 3. Logging filter 4. Data compression filter.

Q.13 If the client has disabled cookie in the browser which session management mechanism could the web container employ ?

a Session management using URL rewriting

b Session management using Cookies

c Either Cookies or URL rewriting

d Cookies and URL rewriting must be used together **[Ans. : a]**

Q.14 Which statement is true for request.getSession(true) method ?

a if session already exist, it return the existing session else create a new session

b getSession(true) method always returns a new session

c getSession(true) method always returns a pre existing session

d None of these **[Ans. : b]**

Q.15 How does the JVM execute a servlet compared with a regular Java class ?
Summer 2016, 1 Mark

Ans. : A servlet is not invoked directly through a main method. In-fact, the class is loaded and run by a servlet container(Example Tomcat).

Q.16 What happens if you add a main method to servlet ? **Summer 2016, 1 Mark**

Ans. : There is no main method in Servlet because, the servlet executes according to life cycle methods in the servlet container. Even if we write main() method in servlet it is of no use, because the execution of servlet is based on life cycle methods.

Q.17 Consider a scenario in which 4 users are accessing a servlet instance. Among which one user called destroy() method. What happens to the rest 3 users ?
Summer 2016, 1 Mark

Ans. : If 4 users are accessing the servlet instance and if one user called destroy() method then the thread which is calling destroy will be terminated and other threads will not be terminated.

Q.18 Servlet is Java class. Then why there is no constructor in Servlet ? Can we write the constructor in Servlet Justify your answer. **Summer 2016, 1 Mark**

Ans. : The servlet contains the init() method, which itself acts as a constructor. Yes syntactically we can write our own constructor in Servlet instead of using init method. If we write parameterized constructors then it is neccessary to write a zero-argument constructor but servlet containers still will only call your zero argument constructor and we canont have access to a ServletConfig or ServletContex.

Q.19 Differentiate : GenericServlet vs HttpServlet. **Summer 2016, 2 Marks**

Ans. : GenericServlet : It is protocol independent. Generic Servlet only supports service() method.

HTTPServlet : It is protocol dependent and mainly suitable for HTTP protocol. HttpServlet supports also doGet(), doPost(), doPut(), doDelete(), doHead(), doTrace(), doOptions()etc.

Q.20 Differentiate : doGet() vs doPost(). **Summer 2016, 2 Marks**

Ans. : **doGet() :** In doGet method the parameters are appended to the URL and sent along with header information.

doPost() : In doPost, parameters are sent in separate line in the body

Q.21 How to delete a session in servlet ? **Summer 2017, 1 Mark**

Ans. : Using the session timeout, the session can be deleted. There are two methods of session timeout - 1. Using the deployment descriptor, the session timeout period can be set, after the timeout the session does not last long. For example -

```
<session-config>
        <session-timeout>15</session-timeout>
</session-config>
```

2. Using the method **setMaxInactiveInterval()** the session timeout can be set manually. For example

```
HttpSession session=request.getSession();
session.setMaxInactiveInterval(15*60);
```

In above case, the session will be killed by the container if client doesn't make any request after 15 minutes.

Q.22 How to display the expiration date and last modified date for the following URL http://www.star.com/news/ **Summer 2017, 1 Mark**

Ans. : Using the getExpiration() and getLastModified() method the expiration and last modified dates can be obtained. The code snippet is as follows -

```
import java.net.HttpURLConnection;
import java.net.URL;
import java.util.Date;

public class Test{
public static void main(String args[]) throws Exception {
URL url = new URL("http://www.star.com/news/");
HttpURLConnection httpCon = (HttpURLConnection) url.openConnection();
```

```
    long date1 = httpCon.getLastModified();
    if (date1 == 0)
      System.out.println("No last-modified information.");
    else
      System.out.println("Last-Modified: " + new Date(date1));
    long date2 = httpCon.getExpiration();
    if (date2 == 0)
      System.out.println("No expiration information.");
    else
      System.out.println("Expires: " + new Date(date2));
  }
}
```

Q.23 How to get the name of the HTTP method with which the request was made ?

Summer 2017, 1 Mark

Ans. : Using the **getRequestMethod()** the name of the method of HTTP request is obtained. For example

```
import java.net.HttpURLConnection;
import java.net.URL;
import java.util.Date;

public class Test{
 public static void main(String args[]) throws Exception {
  URL url = new URL("http://www.google.com");
  HttpURLConnection httpCon = (HttpURLConnection) url.openConnection();
  System.out.println("Request method is " + httpCon.getRequestMethod());
 }
}
```

Q.24 How to get the fully qualified name of the client that sent the request in servlet ?

Summer 2017, 1 Mark

Ans. : Using the method **String getRemoteHost()** the fully qualified name of the client that sent the request can be displayed in servlet.

Chapter 4 : Java Server Pages

Q.1 What is JSP ?

Ans. : JSP stands for Java Server Pages. It is used to create dynamic web page. The JSP page is internally converted into servlet.

Q.2 JSP is transformed into ___.

Ans. : Java Servlet

Q.3 In JSP action tag which tag is used for bean development?

Ans. : The jsp:useBean tag is used for bean development.

Q.4 JSPs eventually are compiled into Java servlets, you can do as much with JSPs as you can do with Java servlets. (True/False)

Ans. : True

Q.5 What is EL in JSP ?

Ans. : The EL stands for Expression Language in JSP. The accessibility of the object becomes simplified due to EL. Using param, requestScope, sessionScope, request, , session etc to access the object.

Q.6 Enlist various types tags provided by JSTL.

Ans. : The tags are -

i) Core tags ii) Sql tags

iii) Xml tags iv) Function tags

Q.7 Which programming language does JSP support ?

a JavaScript only b VB Script only

c Java Only d All of the above **[Ans. : c]**

Q.8 Which directive is used in JSP custom tag ?

Ans. : The JSP taglib directory

Q.9 The pageContext is an implicit object in JSP(True/False)

Ans. : True

Q.10 How to include static files in a JSP page ?

Ans. : The static file can be included in a JSP page using include directive.

Q.11 How to restrict page error display in JSP page ?

Ans. : The "ErrorPage" attribute is set to the name of the error page in JSP and then in error jsp page set isErrorpage="TRUE". Due to this errors can be stopped from getting displayed.

Q.12 What is JSP Scriptlet ?

Ans. : It a JSP tag that encloses Java code in JSP pages. Their syntax is <% %>. Code written in scriptlet executes every time the program is run.

Q.13 How can we pass information from one JSP page to another ?

Ans. : Using the tag <jsp:param> we can pass the information from one JSP page to another.

Q.14 Enlist various scopes that are used for scope values for <jsp:useBean> tag.

Ans. : 1. application 2. request 3. page 4. session

Q.15 How can we avoid scriptlet code in JSP ?

Ans. : Using JavaBeans or Custom tags can be used instead of scriptlet code.

Q.16 Can we define class inside JSP page ?

Ans. : Yes we can define class inside JSP page within <%! %>. But defining a class inside a JSP page is not a good practice.

Q.17 Can one JSP or Servlet extend another Servlet or JSP ? Justify your answer. **Summer 2016, 1 Mark**

Ans. : Yes one JSP or Servlet can extend another servlet or JSP. One servlet class can extend another servlet class using the keyword extends. While JSP can extend the another JSP or Servlet Class using the page directive support. For example <%@ Page extends "myPackage.Example" %> where myPackage is name of the package and Example is the name of the class that has to be inherited.

Q.18 Differentiate : Session and Cookie. **Summer 2016, 2 Marks**

Ans. : Session and Cookie : Sessions are server-side files that contain user information, while Cookies are client-side files that contain user information.

Q.19 What is difference between include directive and jsp:include action tag ? **Summer 2017, 1 Mark**

Ans. : The difference is as follows -

1) Include directive includes the file at translation time - that is when the JSP gets converted into the equivalent servlet whereas the include action includes the file at runtime.
2) If the included file is changed but not the JSP which is including it then the changes will reflect only when we use include action tag. The changes will not reflect if you are using include directive as the JSP is not changed so it will not be translated for request processing and hence the changes will not reflect.
3) Syntax difference : Include directive : <%@ include file="file_name" %> whereas include action has like this <jsp:include page="file_name" />
4) When using include action tag we can also pass the parameters to the included page by using param action tag but in case of include directive it's not possible.

Q.20 How to declare in a JSP page that indicates whether or not the page is intended to be error page of some other JSP page. **Summer 2017, 1 Mark**

Ans. : Using the page directive of JSP we can declare that particular page is error page or not. The attribute **isErrorPage="true"** is used for this purpose. For example

<%@ page isErrorPage="true" %>

Any JSP file declared with isErrorPage (and set to a value of true), is capable to receive exceptions from other JSP pages.

Q.21 How do we print "<br>" creates a new line in HTML in JSP ?

Summer 2017, 1 Mark

Ans. : We can use **c:out ...escapeXml** attribute to escape the HTML elements so that it is shown as text in the browser, for this scenario we will write code like below.

```
<c:out value="<br> creates a new line in HTML" escapeXml="true"></c:out>
```

Chapter 5 : Java Server Faces

Q.1 What is JSF ?

Ans. : The JSF stands for Java Server Faces. It is a web application framework used to develop the web application with rich user interface.

Q.2 Enlist what is required for developing JSF application ?

Ans. : i) JDK ii)JSF 1.2 iii) Tomcat or any standard application server iv)IDE such as Eclipse

Q.3 JSF architecture is based on ____ pattern.

Ans. : MVC or Model View Controller.

Q.4 What do you understand by rendering of page in JSF ?

Ans. : Every JSF page as described has various components made with the help of JSF library. JSF may contain h:form, h:inputText, h:commandButton, etc. Each of these are rendered (translated) to HTML output. This process is called encoding.

Q.5 What is the purpose of javax.faces.component.UIComponent ?

Ans. : A set of javax.faces.component.UIComponent classes for specifying the state and behavior of UI components.

Q.6 What is managed bean ?

Ans. : Managed bean is nothing but a simple Java class. This class is used to hold the form data. When the front end input form accepts the user data and when the user submits this form then the input data is actually stored in the managed bean. This managed bean can also contain some business logic.

Q.7 What is the use of JSF expression language ?

Ans. : JSF expression language allows the user to access the data dynamically from the Java Bean component.

The Expression language can be denoted using the following syntax -

#{expression}

Q.8 Enlist the type of expression language used in JSF ?

Ans. : 1) Property Expression 2) Method Expression

Q.9 Enlist any two JSF components.

Ans. :

h:form	HTML form
h:inputText	Single line text input con
h:inputTextArea	Multiline text input control

Q.10 What is the purpose of h:inputSecret component ?

Ans. : In JSF, the h:InputSecret component is used for password input control.

Q.11 What is JSF Facelet tag ?

Ans. : The JSF Facelet Tag is used to display the contents of the web page at header, footer or content section.

Q.12 What is JSF Converter tag used for ?

Ans. : During the web application, the data entered by the user need to be converted into their appropriate types. For that purpose the JSF converter tag is used.

Q.13 The <f:validateLength> tag is used to _____.

Ans. : validate the length of the string in JSF

Q.14 In JSF ___ can be done using actionListener attribute

Ans. : event handling.

Q.15 What is PrimeFaces ?

Ans. : **PrimeFaces** is an open source component library for Java Server Faces(JSF).

Q.16 How to send a page that auto-refreshes to a new page after a given time period to user until their requests are being processed. **Summer 2017, 1 Mark**

Ans. : For the auto-refresh of the page, we need to use response header. The syntax is as follows -

```
response.setHeader("Refresh", "time; URL=url");
```

where **time** is specified in seconds and the **url** is replaced by the URL the page that has to be loaded eventually loaded. For example

```
response.setHeader("Refresh", "10; URL=http://localhost/test.html");
```

Q.17 What are different JSF converter tags ? **Summer 2017, 1 Mark**

Ans. : The converter tags are used in JSF when we want to convert the data into appropriate types being processed by the application. The different types of tags used are as follows -

1. Converter Number tag
2. Converter Date Time Tag
3. Converter Tag

Chapter 6 : Hibernate 4.0

Q.1 What is Hibernate ?

Ans. : (i) Hibernate is an open source object relational mapping tool for Java platform. (ii) Hibernate allows the Java developer to create persistent classes or persistent data without bothering about how to handle data.

Q.2 What is the main goal of Hibernate ?

Ans. : The primary goal of Hibernate is to map the Java classes to database tables. That means the Java data types are mapped to the SQL data types.

Q.3 POJO stands for ____

Ans. : Plain Old Java Object.

Q.4 Hibernate is ____

a open source b Lightweight

c ORM d All of the above **[Ans. : d]**

Q.5 What is the full of ORM ?

a Object Rate Mapping b Object Relational Mapping

c Operating Related Mapping d Operating Rate Mapping **[Ans. : b]**

Q.6 Does Hibernate support Polymorphism ? (Yes/No)

Ans. : Yes

Q.7 Which of the following is not the mapping association used in Hibernate ?

a Many to Many b One to Many

c one to one **[Ans. : b]**

Q.8 Select the extension of SQL

a My SQL b HQL

c MS SQL **[Ans. : b]**

Q.9 What is the name of Hibernate XML configuration file ?

Ans. : hibernate.cfg.xml

Q.10 What is the extension of the mapping description file in Hibernate ?

Ans. : .hbm

Q.11 The full form of the term HQL is

a Hibernate Queue Language

b Hibernate Query Location

c Higherlevel Query Language

d Highspeed Query Language **[Ans. : b]**

Q.12 What is the difference between HQL and SQL.

Ans. : The HQL makes use of class name instead of table name and property name instead of column name.

Q.13 Hibernate framework simplifies the development of Java application to interact with the database(True/False)

Ans. : True

Q.14 How many Layers are available for Hibernate architecture ?

a 2 b 3

c 4 d 5 **[Ans. : b]**

Q.15 What is Hibernate annotation ?

Ans. : The Hibernate Annotations is the powerful way to provide the metadata for the Object and Relational Table mapping without using XML file.

Q.16 What are the advantages of Hibernate over JDBC ? Summer 2017, 1 Mark

Ans. : Following are the advantages of Hibernate over JDBC -

1. Hibernate is data base independent, same code will work for all data bases like ORACLE,MySQL ,SQLServer etc. In case of JDBC query must be data base specific.
2. Hibernate support two level of cache. First level and 2nd level. So you can store your data into Cache for better performance. In case of JDBC you need to implement your java cache .
3. As Hibernate is set of Objects , you don't need to learn SQL language.

   You can treat TABLE as a Object . In case of JDBC you need to learn SQL.
4. Development fast in case of Hibernate because you don't need to write queries.

Chapter 7 : Java Web Frameworks : Spring MVC

Q.1 Spring is ________

a a free framework b an open source framework

c a licensed framework d none of these **[Ans. : b]**

Q.2 The ____ handles the HTTP Request and Response in Spring

Ans. : DispatchServlet

Q.3 The full form of MVC is ______

Ans. : Model View Controller

Q.4 Controller in Spring is _______

a concrete class b abstract class

c an interface d final class **[Ans. : c]**

Q.5 Beans defined in spring are ______

a Abstract b Singleton

c Factory d None of these **[Ans. : b]**

Q.6 The concept of an endpoint in web service is much like that of a controller in web applications(True/False)

Ans. : True

Q.7 What is IoC in Spring Framework ?

Ans. : The IoC stands for Inversion of Control.

Q.8 What is the main task of IoC ?

Ans. : The task of IoC container is to manage the Java objects from instantiation to destruction. These objects are basically called as Spring Beans.

Q.9 What is Dependency Injection in Spring ?

Ans. : (i) In Spring frameowork, Dependency Injection (DI) design pattern is used to define the object dependencies between each other. (ii) It exits in two major types : a)Setter Injection b)Constructor Injection.

Q.10 Enlist the types of IoC container

Ans. : There are two types of IoC containers - 1. BeanFactory 2. ApplicationContext

Q.11 Name the class which is required to create an instance of Application Context.

Ans. : The ClassPathXmlApplicationContext class is the implementation class of ApplicationContext interface.

Q.12 ___ and ___ are the two methods supported by Bean Lifecycle.

Ans. : init-method and destroy-method

Q.13 What aspect oriented programming in Spring ?

Ans. : Aspect oriented programming complements the object oriented programming. The key unit in OOP is class and in AOP is aspect.

The aspect oriented programming is an enterprise level application programming which is used to add different cross cutting functionalities.

Q.14 What is the meaning of cross cutting functionalities ?

Ans. : cross-cutting functionalities means adding different types of services to the application at runtime automatically. For example - logging is a cross-cutting functionality.

Q.15 What is the use of aspect in AOP of spring ?

Ans. : (i) In AOP the unit of modularity is the aspect.

(ii) Aspects help to modularize cross-cutting concerns, which means cross-cutting concerns can be described by any functionality that affects multiple types and objects.

Q.16 What is join-points in aspect oriented programming ?

Ans. : (i) A Join Point is a point in the execution of the application where an aspect can be plugged in. (ii)This point could be a method being called, an exception being thrown, or even a field being modified.

Q.17 What is JdbcTemplate ?

Ans. : Spring framework provides convenient JdbcTemplate class for performing all Database related operation. This is the central framework class that manages all the database communication and exception handling.

Q.18 Name the three jar files that are required for MySql database connection using spring framework

Ans. : (i) org.springframework.jdbc.jar (ii) org.springframework.transaction.jar

(iii) mysql-connector-java.jar

❑❑❑

Notes

Winter - 2017 Advanced Java Semester - VI (CE/CSE/IT)	Gujarat Technological University Solved Paper

Time : $2\frac{1}{2}$ Hours] **[Total Marks : 70**

Instructions : 1. *Attempt all questions.*
2. *Make suitable assumptions wherever necessary.*
3. *Figures to the right indicate full marks.*

Q.1 a) *Discuss the application design with MVC architecture.* **(Refer section 4.5)** **[3]**

b) *Discuss the use of GET and POST with example.* **[4]**

Ans. :

GET	POST
Using GET request limited amount of information can be sent.	Using POST large amount of information can be sent.
GET request is not secured as information is visible in URL	This is a secured request.
This request is can be bookmarked.	This request can not be bookmarked.
This request is more efficient.	This request is less efficient.

c) *Write a program to insert student record to database using prepared statement.* **[7]**

Ans. :

```
import java.sql.*;
public class JDBCDemo5
{
 public static void main(String [ ] args)
 {
    Connection con = null;
    try
    {
  int rollnum=2;
       String name="Parth";
  Class.forName("sun.jdbc.odbc.JdbcOdbcDriver") ;
       con = DriverManager.getConnection("jdbc:odbc:My_database"," "," ");
```

```
    PreparedStatement ps=con.prepareStatement("INSERT INTO My_table
VALUES(?,?)");
  ps.setInt(1,rollnum);
  ps.setString(2,name);
  int result=ps.executeUpdate();
  if(result!=0)
    System.out.println("Values inserted in the table");
  else
    System.out.println("Values are not inserted in the table");
  String sql="SELECT * FROM My_table";
  ps=con.prepareStatement(sql);
  ResultSet rs=ps.executeQuery();
  System.out.println("Displaying the contents of the table...");
  while(rs.next())
  {
     int RollNo  = rs.getInt("Roll");
     String Name = rs.getString("StudName");
    //Display values
    System.out.print("Roll Number: " + RollNo);
    System.out.println(", Student Name: " + Name);
  }
  rs.close();
  ps.close();
      con.close();
   }
   catch (ClassNotFoundException e)
   {
    System.err.println("Exception: "+e.getMessage());
   }
   catch (SQLException e)
   {
    System.err.println("Exception: "+e.getMessage());
   }

  }
}
```

Q.2 a) *Discuss the difference between the Socket and ServerSocket class.* **[3]**

Ans. :

Sr. No.	Socket	ServerSocket
1	It is used at client side.	It is used on server side.
2	It is used for sending the request to the server.	It is used for listening the client.
3	This class encapsulates the behavior of the active side.	This class encapsulates the behavior of the passive side.

b) *Discuss callable statement with example.* **(Refer section 2.9.2)** **[4]**

c) *Write a client server program using UDP socket. Client send the list of N strings and server responds the concatenation of those strings.* **[7]**

Ans. : Client Program

```
import java.io.*;
import java.net.*;
class UDPClient
{
 public static void main(String args[]) throws Exception
 {
   BufferedReader user_input=new BufferedReader(new InputStream
Reader(System.in));
   //creating the client socket
   DatagramSocket client_socket=new DatagramSocket();
   //getting the IP address of host "aap"
   InetAddress IP_add=InetAddress.getByName("localhost");
   //creating the buffer for sending the data
   byte out_data[]=new byte[1024];
   String str="";
   //reading the input through keyboard
   for(int i=1;i<=3;i++)
   {
     System.out.println("Enter number(Put#at the end of each number)");
    str=str+user_input.readLine();
    }
    str=str+"\n";
   out_data=str.getBytes();
   //creating the datagram packet in which data is
   //encapsulated
```

```
    DatagramPacket Packet1=new DatagramPacket(out_data,out_data.length,
 IP_add,1234);
    //sending the packet to the server
    client_socket.send(Packet1);
    //closing the client's connection
    client_socket.close();
  }
 }
```

Server Program

```
import java.io.*;
import java.net.*;
import java.lang.*;
class UDPServer
{
   public static void main(String args[]) throws Exception
   {
      //creating the socket for server
      DatagramSocket server_socket=new DatagramSocket(1234);
      byte in_data[]=new byte[1024];
      String[] temp;
      int a[],i,sum;
      a=new int[10];
      sum=0;
      while(true)
      {
         //creating the datagram packet
         DatagramPacket Packet2=new DatagramPacket(in_data,in_data.length);
         //the data from the client is received in the packet
         server_socket.receive(Packet2);
         String str=new String(Packet2.getData());
         temp=str.split("#");
         try{
            //printing the Sum of received numbers on the console of server
            for (i = 0 ; i <temp.length ; i++)
               a[i]=Integer.parseInt(temp[i]); //creating array of integers from string
         }catch(NumberFormatException e){}
         for (i = 0 ; i <temp.length ; i++)
```

```
            sum=sum+a[i];//calculating sum of N numbers
         System.out.println("The Sum of elements is: "+sum);
      }
   }
}
```

OR

c) *Write a client-server program using UDP socket. Client send the list of N strings and server responds the concatenation of those strings.* **[7]**

Ans. : **Client Program**

```
import java.io.*;
import java.net.*;
class UDPClient
{
 public static void main(String args[]) throws Exception
 {
   BufferedReader user_input=new BufferedReader(new InputStreamReader
(System.in));
   //creating the client socket
   DatagramSocket client_socket=new DatagramSocket();
   //getting the IP address of host "aap"
   InetAddress IP_add=InetAddress.getByName("localhost");
   //creating the buffer for sending the data
   byte out_data[]=new byte[1024];
   String str="";
   //reading the input through keyboard
   for(int i=1;i<=3;i++)
   {
  System.out.println("Enter Name(Put#at the end of each number)");
    str=str+user_input.readLine();
    }
    str=str+"\n";
   out_data=str.getBytes();
   //creating the datagram packet in which data is
   //encapsulated
   DatagramPacket Packet1=new
   DatagramPacket(out_data,out_data.length,IP_add,1234);
   //sending the packet to the server
   client_socket.send(Packet1);
```

```
    //closing the client's connection
    client_socket.close();
  }
 }
```

Server Program

```
import java.io.*;
import java.net.*;
import java.lang.*;
class UDPServer
{
 public static void main(String args[]) throws Exception
 {
  //creating the socket for server
   DatagramSocket server_socket=new DatagramSocket(1234);
   byte in_data[]=new byte[1024];
   String[] temp;
   String new_str="";
   while(true)
   {
    //creating the datagram packet
    DatagramPacket Packet2=new DatagramPacket(in_data,in_data.length);
     //the data from the client is received in the packet
    server_socket.receive(Packet2);
    String str=new String(Packet2.getData());
    temp=str.split("#");
    //concatinnating the names
     for (int i = 0 ; i <temp.length ; i++)
        new_str=str+temp[i];//concatenation
     new_str=new_str+"\n";
    System.out.println("The Concatenated List of Names: "+new_str);
  }
 }
}
```

Q.3 a) *What is session ? List the different ways to manage the session.*
(Refer section 3.11.2) **[3]**

b) *Discuss the possible uses of the ServletContext and ServletConfig object.*
(Refer section 3.7) **[4]**

c) *Write a servlet RegistrationServlet to get the values from registration.html html page and display the contents. Write the web.xml file.* **[7]**

Ans. : **Step 1 :** Create an HTML document as follows –

registration.html

```
<html>
<head>
<body>
<div align="center">
  <br> <br>
  <form action="http://localhost/examples/servlets/servlet/RegistrationServlet"
 method="post">
     Enter First Name:
     <input type="text" value="" name="fname" size='5'>
     <br/><br/> Enter Surname:
     <input type="text" value="" name="sname" size='5'>
     <br/><br/> Enter Address:
     <input type="text" value="" name="address" size='30'>
     <br/><br/> Enter Phone:
     <input type="text" value="" name="phone" size='12'>
     <br/> <br/> <br/>

     <input  type="submit" value="Register">
  </form>
</div>
</body>
</html>
```

Step 2 : Now create a servlet program named **RegistrationServlet** which collects the data for registration entered by above HTML file and display it.

RegistrationServlet.java

```
import java.io.*;
import javax.servlet.*;
import javax.servlet.http.*;

public class RegistrationServlet extends HttpServlet
{
  protected void doPost(HttpServletRequest req, HttpServletResponse res) throws
  ServletException, IOException
```

```
{
    res.setContentType("text/html");
    PrintWriter out=res.getWriter();
    // get request parameters from HTML document created in Step 1
        String FirstName = req.getParameter("fname");
  String SurName = req.getParameter("sname");
  String Address = req.getParameter("address");
  String Phone = req.getParameter("phone");
  out.println("<h4>First Name:"+FirstName+"</h4>");
  out.println("<h4>Last Name:"+SurName+"</h4>");
  out.println("<h4>Address:"+Address+"</h4>");
  out.println("<h4>Phone:"+Phone+"</h4>");
  }
}
```

Step 3 : The web.xml file will be as follows –

web.xml

```
<?xml version="1.0" encoding="ISO-8859-1"?>
...
      <servlet-name>RegistrationServlet</servlet-name>
      <servlet-class>RegistrationServlet</servlet-class>
   </servlet>
   <servlet-mapping>
      <servlet-name>RegistrationServlet</servlet-name>
      <url-pattern>/servlets/servlet/RegistrationServlet</url-pattern>
   </servlet-mapping>
...
</web-app>
```

OR

Q.3 a) *What is filter ? List the applications of filter.* **(Refer section 3.10)** [3]

b) *Briefly explain the servlet life cycle.* **(Refer section 3.4)** [4]

c) *Write a Login servlet. Take input username and password from HTML file login.html and authenticate user. Write web.xml.* [7]

Ans. : Step 1 : Create HTML form for accepting user name and password

Input.html

```
<html>
<head>
</head>
```

```
<body>
<form action="http://localhost/examples/servlets/servlet/LoginServlet" method ="get">
User Name:<input type="text" name="uname"/>
<br/>
Password:<input type="password" name="pwd"/>
<input type="submit" value="Submit"/>
</form>
</body>
</html>
```

Step 2 : Create the servlet program to read user name and password and validate it.

LoginServlet.java

```
import java.io.*;
import javax.servlet.*;
import javax.servlet.http.*;
public class LoginServlet extends HttpServlet
{
  public void doGet(HttpServletRequest req,HttpServletResponse res) throws
ServletException,IOException
  {
    PrintWriter out=res.getWriter();
    res.setContentType("text/html");

    String username=req.getParameter("uname");
    String password=req.getParameter("pwd");
    if ((username=="Ankita")&&(password=="1234"))
        out.print("Welcome "+username);
    else
      out.println("Invalid username");
  }
}
```

Step 3 : The web.xml file is as follows –

web.xml

```
<?xml version="1.0" encoding="ISO-8859-1"?>
...
      <servlet-name>LoginServlet</servlet-name>
      <servlet-class>LoginServlet</servlet-class>
   </servlet>
```

```
    <servlet-mapping>
        <servlet-name>LoginServlet</servlet-name>
        <url-pattern>/servlets/servlet/LoginServlet</url-pattern>
    </servlet-mapping>
...
</web-app>
```

Q.4 a) *List JSP implicit objects and explain any two.* **(Refer section 4.11)** **[3]**

b) *Briefly explain JSP life cycle.* **(Refer section 4.3)** **[4]**

c) *Develop JSP page to display student information with subjects for particular semester from database.* **(Refer example 4.15.5)** **[7]**

OR

Q.4 a) *Compare JSP with servlet.* **(Refer section 4.2.1)** **[3]**

b) *List the JSTL core tags and explain any four with example.* **(Refer section 4.16.1)** **[4]**

c) *Write login.jsp page to get the login information from user and authenticate user with database with JSTL SQL tags.* **[7]**

Ans. :

Login.jsp

```
<%@ taglib uri="http://java.sun.com/jsp/jstl/core" prefix="c" %>
<%@ taglib uri="http://java.sun.com/jsp/jstl/sql" prefix="sql"%>
<%@ page import="java.io.*" %>
<html>
<head>
<title>JSTL sql Tag Demo</title>
</head>
<body>
<form method=post action="http://localhost/examples/jsp/login.jsp">
Enter User Name:
<input type="text" value="" name="uname"/>

Password:
<input type="password" value=" " name="pass"/>
<br/><br/><br/>
<input type="Submit" value="Submit"/>
</form>
<sql:setDataSource var="DB" driver="com.mysql.jdbc.Driver"
url="jdbc:mysql://localhost/dbdemo"
```

Creating form for allowing user to enter username and password

Connecting to database

```
    user="root"  password=""/>
<sql:query dataSource="${DB}" var="Rec">
SELECT * from Logins;          ← Login Table stores the user name and password.
</sql:query>
<center>
<c:set var="user" value
="${param.uname}" />           ← Setting values to variables for entered user name and password
<c:set var="pass" value
="${param.pass}" />
<c:forEach var="row" items
="${Rec.rows}">                ← Iterating through each record present in the table
<c:if test
="${row.name==user
&& row.pwd==pass}">            ← If a match is found for submitted username and password then authentication message will be displyed
<strong>
You are an authenticated
User!!!"</strong>
  </c:if>
</c:forEach>
</center>
</body>
</html>
```

Q.5 a) *List the JSF facelets tags and explain any two.* **(Refer section 5.10)** **[3]**

b) *What is hibernte ? List the advantages of hibernate over JDBC.* **(Refer section 6.1)** **[4]**

c) *Develop program to get all students data from database using hiernate. Write necessary xml files.* **(Refer section 6.4)** **[7]**

OR

Q.5 a) *List the JSF validation tags and explain any two.* **(Refer section 5.12)** **[3]**

b) *Briefly explain spring bean life cycle.* **(Refer section 7.5)** **[4]**

c) *Develop small application using spring MVC framework.* **(Refer section 7.3)** **[7]**

❑❑❑

Summer - 2018 **Advanced Java** Semester - VI (CE/CSE/IT)	**Gujarat Technological University** **Solved Paper**

Time : $2\frac{1}{2}$ Hours] **[Total Marks : 70**

Q.1 a) *What is hibernate ? What is main advantage of using hibernate than using SQL ?* **(Refer section 6.1)** **[3]**

b) *What is JSF tag library ? Explain any four html tag.* **(Refer sections 5.4 and 5.9)** **[4]**

c) *List the different types of JDBC drivers. Compar the various driver types for their advantages and disadvantages.* **(Refer section 2.11)** **[7]**

Q.2 a) *Compare the include and forward action tags in JSP.* **(Refer section 3.9)** **[3]**

b) *Explain the configuration of filter using deloyment descriptor.* **(Refer section 3.10)** **[4]**

c) *Write servlet program to create cookie. Also write code to display contents of cookie on page.* **(Refer section 3.11)** **[7]**

OR

c) *Answer following.* **[7]**

1. *Difference between socket and server socket.* **(Refer Q.2 (a) of Winter-2017)**

2. *What is object serializtion ? What is need of it ?*

Ans. : Object serialization is a mechanism of converting the state of object into a byte stream. And deserialization is a reverse mechanism in which the byte stream is used to recreate the actual java object in memory.

Need : 1) This mechanism is used to save the state of the object.

2) This mechanism is useful for helping the object to travel across the network.

Q.3 a) *What is dependency injection ?* **(Refer Q.5 (a) of Summer-2017)** **[3]**

b) *What is session object in JSP ? Show its use with proper example.* **(Refer section 4.14)** **[4]**

c) *Explain the action tags used to access the JavaBeans from a JSP page with example.* **(Refer section 4.10)** **[7]**

OR

Q.3 a) *Write a servlet the redirect requests alternatively to JSP pages named odd and even.* **(Refer Q.5 (a) of Summer-2017)** **[3]**

b) *What is request dispatcher ? What is the difference between request dispatcher's forward() and include() method ?* **(Refer section 3.9)** **[4]**

c) *Write JSP page to demonstrate shopping cart using session feature of JSP.* **[7]**

Ans. : Step 1 : Create an HTML login page. User can enter user name and password.

LoginPage.html

```
<html>
<body>
<form action="ShowCart.jsp" method="post">
User Name:<input type="text" name="username">
Password:<input type="text" name="password">
<input type="submit" name="LOGIN">
</form>
</body>
</html>
```

Step 2 : There will be a JSP page that will verify the user and then display all the items and Add to cart web page. For recognizing the user, the session tracking technique is used.

ShowCart.jsp

```
<%@ page import="java.sql.*" %>
<%
try{
  Class.forName("sun.jdbc.odbc.JdbcOdbcDriver");
  Connection con=DriverManager.getConnection
                    ("jdbc:odbc:ItemsDB","root","password123");
  Statement stmt=con.createStatement();
  String name=String.valueOf(session.getAttribute("username"));//Recognising User
                                                              //using Session
  ResultSet rs;
  rs=stmt.executeQuery("select * from Items");
%>
<html>
<head>
<title>ONLINE SHOPPING</title>
```

```
</head>
<body>
  Welcome <%=name %>
  <%
    while(rs.next())
    {
  %>
  <table border=1>
  <tr>
  <td>Name :</td><td><%=rs.getString("Itemname") %></td>
  <td>Price :</td><td><%=rs.getString("price") %></td>
  <td>Status :</td>
  <td>
    <%
  if(rs.getString("quantity").equals("0"))
  {
    out.println("<font color=red>Not Available</font>");
  }
  else
  {
  %>
  <font color=green>Available</font>
  </td>
  <form action="Addtocart" name="formsubmit" method=post>
  <td><input type="hidden" name="id" value=<%=rs.getString("id") %></td>
  <td><input type="hidden" name="qty" value=<%=rs.getString("quantity")
%></td>
<td><input type="hidden" name="price" value=<%=rs.getString("price") %></td>
      <td>Quantity
        <select name="selq">
         <option value=1>1</option>
         <option value=2>2</option>
         <option value=3>3</option>
         <option value=4>4</option>
         <option value=5>5</option>
         <option value=6>6</option>
         <option value=7>7</option>
         <option value=8>8</option>
```

```
        <option value=9>9</option>
        <option value=10>10</option>
  </td>
      <td></select><br><input type=submit value="ADD TO CART"></td>
      </form>
      <%
       }
      %>
  </tr>
  <%
  }
  %>
   </table>
</body>
</html>
<%
}catch(Exception e){ out.println(e);}
%>
```

Q.4 a) *Explain use of action tag with example.* **(Refer section 4.10)** **[3]**

b) *What is web.xml ? Explain it with code.* **(Refer section 3.6)** **[4]**

c) *Write a client server program using TCP where client sends a string and server checks whether that string is palindrome or not and responds with appropriate message.* **(Refer Q.2 (b) of Summer-2017)** **[7]**

OR

Q.4 a) *Explain architecture of spring MVC framework.* **(Refer section 7.1.1)** **[3]**

b) *What are the different methods to call java code from JSP page ? Explain them.* **(Refer section 4.9)** **[4]**

c) *Write a java servlet to print BE semester 7 marksheet of entered entrollment number by user using JDBC.* **[7]**

Ans. : Step 1 : Create a database in MySQL and store records of various students along with the subject names and marks.

Step 2 : Create an HTML page to accept the roll number. The code for HTML document is

Input.html

```
<html>
<body>
<form action="http://localhost/examples/servlets/servlet/MarkSheet" method="post">
```

```
Enter your Rollno:<input type="text" name="roll"/><br/>
<input type="submit" value="Submit"/>
</form>
</body>
</html>
```

Step 3 : Create a servlet program, to accept the roll number submitted by user using above HTML page. This servlet will display the marksheet of the student whose roll number is entered by the user. The code is

MarkSheet.java

```
import java.io.*;
import java.sql.*;
import javax.servlet.ServletException;
import javax.servlet.http.*;

public class MarkSheet extends HttpServlet {
  public void doPost(HttpServletRequest request, HttpServletResponse response)
  throws ServletException, IOException {
    response.setContentType("text/html");
    PrintWriter out = response.getWriter();
    String rollno=request.getParameter("roll");
    int roll=Integer.valueOf(rollno);

    try{
      Class.forName("com.mysql.jdbc.Driver");
      Connection
con=DriverManager.getConnection("jdbc:mysql://localhost/student","root","");
      PreparedStatement ps=con.prepareStatement("select * from SeventhSem where
RollNo=?");
      ps.setInt(1,roll);
      out.print("<table width=50% border=1>");
      out.print("<caption><h2>BE Sem VII Computer Engineering
</h2></caption>");
      ResultSet rs=ps.executeQuery();

      /* Printing column names */
      ResultSetMetaData rsmd=rs.getMetaData();
      int total=rsmd.getColumnCount();
      out.print("<tr>");
```

```
        for(int i=1;i<=total;i++)
        {
          out.print("<th>"+rsmd.getColumnName(i)+"</th>");
        }
        out.print("</tr>");
        /* Printing result */
        while(rs.next())
        {
          out.print("<tr><td>"+rs.getInt(1)+"</td><td>"
          +rs.getString(2)+"</td><td>"+rs.getString(3)
          +"</td><td>"+rs.getString(4)+"</td><td>"+rs.getDouble(5)
          +"</td><td>"+rs.getString(6)+"</td><td>"+rs.getDouble(7)
          +"</td><td>"+rs.getString(8)+"</td><td>"+rs.getDouble(9)
          +"</td><td>"+rs.getString(10)+"</td><td>"+rs.getDouble(11)
          +"</td><td>"+rs.getString(12)+"</td><td>"+rs.getDouble(13)
          +"</td></tr>");
        out.print("</table>");
        double total_marks=0,percentage;
        total_marks=rs.getDouble(5)+rs.getDouble(7)+rs.getDouble(9)+rs.getDouble(11)
        +rs.getDouble(13);
          out.print("<tr><td>Total marks out of 500 = "+total_marks+"</td></tr>");
        percentage=total_marks/5;
        out.print("<br/><tr><td>Marks in Percentage = "+percentage+"</td></tr>");
        }
      }catch (Exception e2) {e2.printStackTrace();}
      finally{out.close();}
    }
}
```

Output

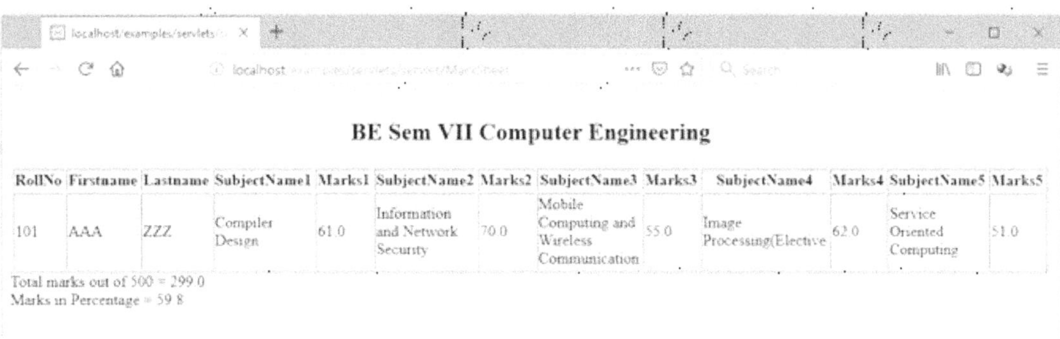

BE Sem VII Computer Engineering

RollNo	Firstname	Lastname	SubjectName1	Marks1	SubjectName2	Marks2	SubjectName3	Marks3	SubjectName4	Marks4	SubjectName5	Marks5
101	AAA	ZZZ	Compiler Design	61.0	Information and Network Security	70.0	Mobile Computing and Wireless Communication	55.0	Image Processing(Elective	62.0	Service Oriented Computing	51.0

Total marks out of 500 = 299.0
Marks in Percentage = 59.8

Q.5 a) *Explain various session tracking mechanisms in servlet with example.* **(Refer section 3.11.2)** **[3]**

b) *Explain JSF life cycle phases.* **(Refer section 5.5)** **[4]**

c) *Design a form to input details of an employee and submit the data to a servlet. Write code for servlet that will save the entered details as a new record in database table employee with fields (EmpId, EName, Email, Age).* **(Refer Q.3 (b) (OR Part) of Summer-2017)** **[7]**

OR

Q.5 a) *Explain use of DatabaseMetaData with example.* **(Refer section 2.13)** **[3]**

b) *Explain use of ServletConfig and ServletContext object with example.* **(Refer section 3.7)** **[4]**

c) *Write a java bean named "student" having roll no and name having getter and setter methods. Write a JSP page to set the roll number and name for a student object and then print them by reading from object.* **(Refer example 4.15.5)** **[7]**

❑❑❑

Winter - 2018
Advanced Java
Semester - VI (CE/CSE/IT)

Gujarat Technological University
Solved Paper

Time : $2\frac{1}{2}$ Hours] [Total Marks : 70

Q.1 a) *What is difference between include directive and jsp:include action tag ?* **(Refer Q.19 (short ans) of chapter-4)** **[3]**

b) *Draw and explain hibernate architecture.* **(Refer section 6.2)** **[4]**

c) *List different types of JDBC drivers and explain any two of them.* **(Refer section 2.11)** **[7]**

Q.2 a) *Write a java program to find an IP address of the machine on which the program runs.* **(Refer example 1.8.1)** **[3]**

b) *Explain difference between ServletConfig and ServletContext object.* **(Refer section 3.7)** **[4]**

c) *Write a client-server application using TCP sockets where clinet can send message and server respond with the reverse of them.* **(Refer example 1.8.2)** **[7]**

OR

c) *Write a servlet that takes two numbers as an input and display all the prime numbers between them. Also write web.xml description for the servlet.* **[7]**

Ans. : Step 1 : We will create an HTML Page for accepting two numbers as input. The code for HTML document is as follows –

Input.html

```
<html>
<head>
<body>
<div align="center">
  <br> <br>
  <form action="http://localhost/examples/servlets/servlet/PrimeNumbersRange"
 method="post">
    Enter First Number:
    <input type="text" value="" name="Number1" size='5'>
    <br/><br/> Enter Second Number:
    <input type="text" value="" name="Number2" size='5'>
    <br/> <br/> <br/>
```

```
    <input  type="submit" value="Submit">
  </form>
</div>
</body>
</html>
```

Step 2 : Create a servlet that accepts these two numbers and displays the prime numbers between these two numbers. The code is as follows –

PrimeNumbersRange.java

```
import java.io.*;
import javax.servlet.*;
import javax.servlet.http.*;

public class PrimeNumbersRange extends HttpServlet
{
  protected void doPost(HttpServletRequest req, HttpServletResponse res) throws
 ServletException, IOException
  {

      int flag=0,i,j;
      res.setContentType("text/html");
    PrintWriter out=res.getWriter();
    int a = Integer.parseInt(req.getParameter("Number1"));
    int b = Integer.parseInt(req.getParameter("Number2"));
      out.println("<h4>The prime numbers in between the entered limits are
    :</h4>");
    for(i = a; i <= b; i++)
    {
       for( j = 2; j < i; j++)
       {
          if(i % j == 0)
          {
             flag = 0;
             break;
          }
          else
          {
             flag = 1;
          }
```

```
            }
            if(flag == 1)
            {
               out.print(" "+i);
            }
   }
    }
}
```

Q.3 a) *Explain ResultSetMetaData with suitable program.* **(Refer section 2.13)** [3]

b) *List the JSTL core tags and explain any two with example.* **(Refer section 4.16.1)** [4]

c) *What is CallableStatement ? Show that how to use it to call a stored procedure running at database layer.* **(Refer section 2.9)** [7]

OR

Q.3 a) *Explain DataBaseMetaData with example.* **(Refer Q.4 (a) (OR) of Summer-2017)** [3]

b) *Explain any two page directive in JSP with example.* **(Refer section 4.8)** [4]

c) *Explain the use of the PreparedStatement object of the JDBC with an appropriate example.* **(Refer section 2.9.1)** [7]

Q.4 a) *List advantages of JSP over servlet.* **(Refer section 4.2.1)** [3]

b) *What is servlet ? Explain servlet life cycle.* **(Refer sections 3.1 and 3.4)** [4]

c) *What is MVC acrhitecture ? Explain spring architecture with neat sketch.* **(Refer section 7.1.1)** [7]

OR

Q.4 a) *Differentiate between GenericServlet and HttpServlet.* **(Refer Q.3 (a) (OR) of Summer-2016)** [3]

b) *Explain JSP life cycle phases.* **(Refer section 4.3)** [4]

c) *What is ORM ? Explain object/relational mappings in hibernate.* **(Refer section 6.4)** [7]

Q.5 a) *What is filter ? List the applications of filter.* **(Refer section 3.10)** [3]

b) *What is dependency injection ?* **(Refer Q.5 (a) (OR) of Summer-2017)** [4]

c) *Draw the JSF request processing life cycle and briefly give the function of each phase.* **(Refer section 5.5)** [7]

OR

Q.5 a) *List the JSF facelets tags and explain any two.* **(Refer section 5.10)** **[3]**

b) *Briefly explain spring bean life cycle.* **(Refer section 7.5)** **[4]**

c) *List the JSF validation tags and explain any two.* **(Refer section 5.12)** **[7]**

❑❑❑

Summer - 2019
Advanced Java
Semester - VI (CE/CSE/IT)
(2160707)

Gujarat Technological University
Solved Paper

Time : $2\frac{1}{2}$ Hours] **[Total Marks : 70**

Q.1 a) *Mention advantages of J2EE.* **[3]**

Ans. : 1. It is open-source technology, due to which the open source libraries are easily available for developers.

2. It provides some key functionalities to support cross-platform portabilities.
3. Enterprise level applications can be easily deployed in server side.
4. The J2EE technology itself is maintained according to W3C standard and hence can be adopted globally.

b) *Write a Web application using servlet to find the sum of all the digits of an input integer.* **[4]**

Ans. :

Step 1 : We will create an HTML document for accepting a number from user whose digit sum need to be obtained.

digit_sum_input.html

```
<html>
<body>
<form action="http://localhost:8089/examples/servlets/servlet/DigitSum"
method="post">
Enter some number:<input type="text" name="user_num"/><br/>
<input type="submit" value="Submit"/>
</form>
</body>
</html>
```

Step 2 : Now create a servlet program that reads the number entered by the user in step 1, calculates the sum of digits and display the sum. The servlet code is as follows -

DigitSum.java

```
import javax.servlet.*;
import javax.servlet.http.*;
import java.io.*;
```

```
public class DigitSum extends HttpServlet
{
  public void service(HttpServletRequest req, HttpServletResponse res) throws
ServletException, IOException
  {
    res.setContentType("text/html");
    PrintWriter out = res.getWriter();

    String str = req.getParameter("user_num");
    int num=Integer.parseInt(str);
    out.print("<h3> The sum of "+num+" is ");
    int sum=0;
    while(num!=0)
    {
      sum=sum+num%10;
      num=num/10;
    }
    out.print(" "+sum+"</h3>");
    out.close();
  }
}
```

Output

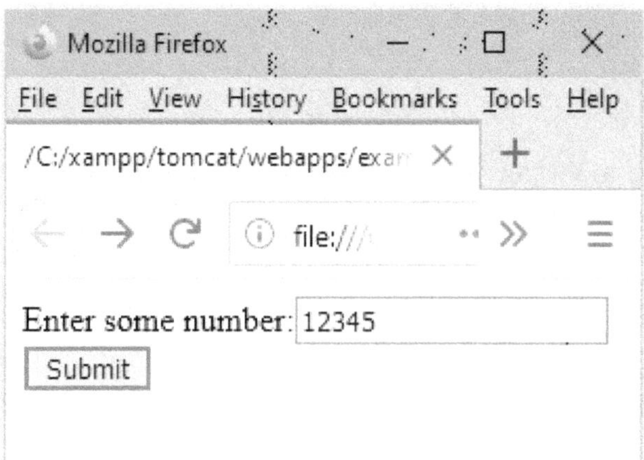

c) *Describe the servlet life cycle with life cycle methods.* **(Refer section 3.4)** **[7]**

Q.2 a) *What do you mean by MVC architecture ? Explain its role in modern applications with its advantages.* **(Refer section 4.5)** **[3]**

b) *Write a web application using servlet to find whether entered number is prime or not.* **[4]**

Ans. :

Step 1 : We will create an HTML document for accepting a number from user for testing whether the number is prime or not.

```
<html>
<body>
<form action="http://localhost:8089/examples/servlets/servlet/IsPrime" method="post">

Enter some number:<input type="text" name="user_num"/><br/>
<input type="submit" value="Submit"/>
</form>
</body>
</html>
```

Step 2 : Now create a servlet program that reads the number entered by the user in step 1, finds if the sum of digits and display the sum. The servlet code is as follows -

```
import javax.servlet.*;
import javax.servlet.http.*;
import java.io.*;

public class IsPrime extends HttpServlet
```

```
{
  public void service(HttpServletRequest req, HttpServletResponse res) throws
ServletException, IOException
  {
    res.setContentType("text/html");
    PrintWriter out = res.getWriter();
    String str = req.getParameter("user_num");
    int n=Integer.parseInt(str);
    int i,m=0,flag=0;
     m=n/2;
    if(n==0||n==1)
    {
      out.print(n+" is not prime number");
    }
    else
    {
      for(i=2;i<=m;i++)
      {
        if(n%i==0)
        {
          out.print(n+" is not prime number");
          flag=1;
          break;
        }
      }
      if(flag==0)
      {
        out.print(n+" is prime number");
      }//end of else
      out.close();
    }
  }
}
```

Output

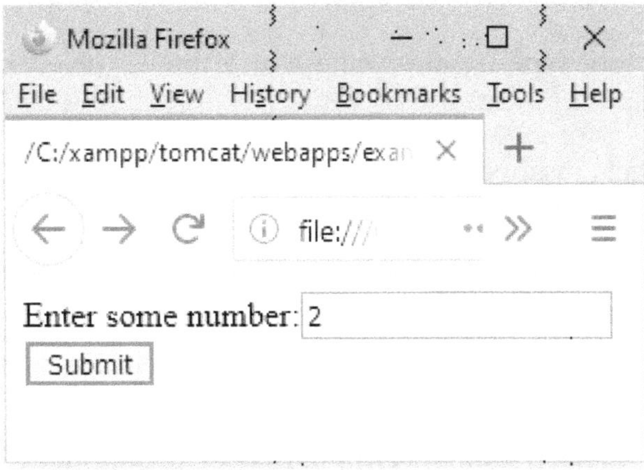

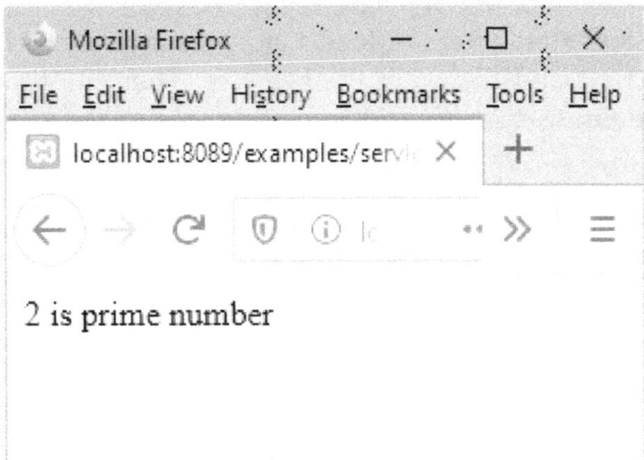

c) *Explain JSF application life cycle with diagram.* **(Refer section 5.5)** **[7]**

OR

c) *Explain Hibernate architecture and object relation mapping in hibernate with Java code and required XML files.* **(Refer section 6.4)** **[7]**

Q.3 a) *Explain functionality of cookie.* **(Refer section 3.11.5)** **[3]**

b) *What is session ? Explain session management using HTTP session.* **(Refer section 3.11.1)** **[4]**

c) *Write a client-server program using TCP sockets to echo the message send by the client.* **(Refer section 1.4.1)** **[7]**

OR

Q.3 a) *Discuss concept of JDBC.* **(Refer section 2.1)** **[3]**

b) *Explain JSP object scope : i) Page ii) Request iii) Sessions iv) Application with example.* **[4]**

Ans. : There are four types scopes using which the JSP object can be used.

1. Page scope :

- The bean object gets disappeared as soon as the current page gets discarded.
- The **default scope** for a bean in JSP page is a page scope.

2. Request scope :

- The bean object remains in existence as long as the request object is present.
- The **request scope** is used for all the objects that are using the same request.

3. Session scope :

- A session can be defined as a **specific period of a time** the user spends browsing the site.
- For instance - if you start Firefox Mozilla browser and starts browsing the net for some amount of time and then quit the browser. Then the time spend by the user from starting to quitting a site is said to be **one session.**
- From the same browsers (preferably a single user); if the request is made for the object then **session scope** is used.

4. Application scope :

- During application scope the JSP object will get stored to **ServletContext.** Hence particular JSP object is available to all the servlets in the same web application.

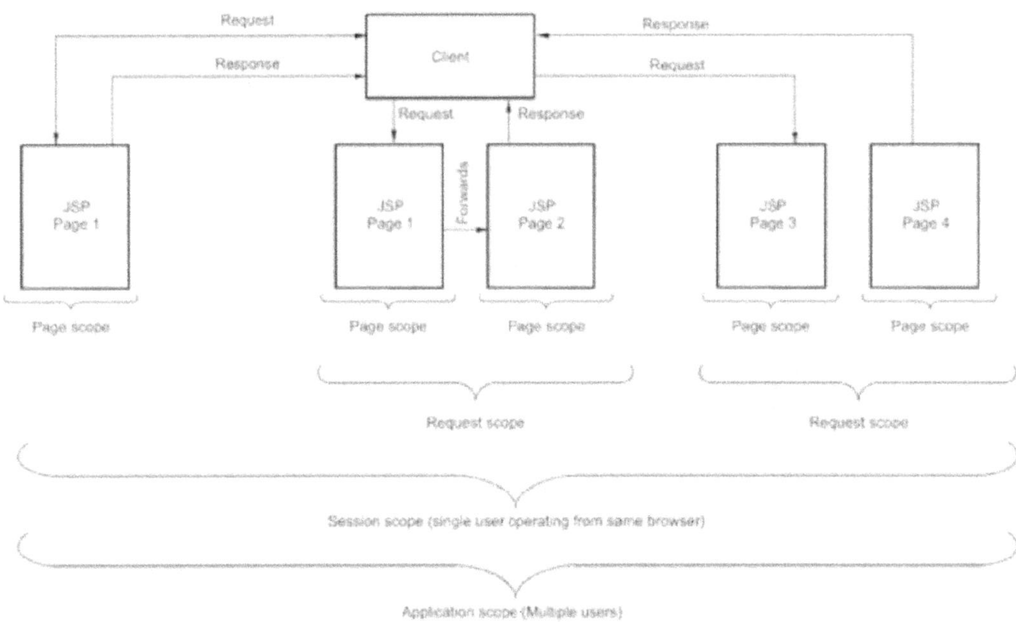

Fig. 1 Representation of various scopes

- Application scope is the **broadest scope** provided by JSP and it should be used only when it is necessary.
- The objects in the **application scope** are accessible to **all the users of the application.**

c) *Write a client-server java programs using TCP sockets to get server date on client machine.* **(Refer Q.3 (b) of Winter-2016)** [7]

Q.4 a) *Explain the following classes with their use. i. URL connection class ii. Datagram Socket iii) Datagram Packet class* **(Refer section 1.6)** [3]

b) *Write a JSP page which use available java bean. Discuss functionality of used java beans.* **(Refer example 4.15.5)** [4]

c) *Develop a jsp code which reads the student detail from web page and stores it in database.* **(Refer section 4.15)** [7]

OR

Q.4 a) *Explain JSP i) Page ii) include iii) taglib directive with attribute, description.* **(Refer section 4.8)** [3]

b) *Discuss JSP exception handling.* **(Refer section 4.19)** [4]

c) *Write a servlet code to demonstrate prepare statement and callable statement to retrieve and store employee data.* **(Refer section 4.15.1)** [7]

Q.5 a) *Discuss Hibernate Query Language.* **(Refer section 6.6)** [3]

b) *Discuss Java Bean life cycle with one example.* **(Refer section 7.5)** [4]

c) *Draw and explain spring framework architecture.* **(Refer section 7.1.1)** [7]

OR

Q.5 a) *Discuss JSF convertor tag.* **(Refer section 5.11)** [3]

b) *Explain following tags in JSTL with example ; i) Core ii) XML* **(Refer sections 4.16.1 and 4.20)** [4]

c) *Write a java servlet to print BE semester marksheet of entered enrollment number and sem no by student using JDBC.* **(Refer Q.4 (c) OR part of Summer-2018)** [7]

❑❑❑

Notes

www.ingramcontent.com/pod-product-compliance
Lightning Source LLC
Chambersburg PA
CBHW080208170726
48282CB00030B/1044
* 9 7 8 9 3 3 3 2 2 3 8 5 0 *